Stand Up & Sock it to them Sisters

Funny, Feisty Females.

by
Gwenno Dafydd

Parthian

T0167996

Parthian, Cardigan SA43 1ED
www.parthianbooks.com
First published in 2016
© Gwenno Dafydd 2016
All Rights Reserved
ISBN 9781910901557
Cover design by Marc Jennings
Typeset by Elaine Sharples
Printed and bound by Printed in EU by Pulsio SARL
Published with the financial support of the Welsh Books Council
British Library Cataloguing in Publication Data
A cataloguing record for this book is available from the British Library.

CONTENTS

CHAPTER 3: APPRENTICESHIP OF A CLOWN

In which I find out how they honed their funny bone!

- How did you learn to be funny?
- Family
- University Courses
- Improvisation
- Competitions
- 'Taking the Mike' – What made you get up on stage the first time?
- Harnessing the demons – Who or what made you think you could do it?

CHAPTER 4: LAYING THE FOUNDATIONS

In which I find out about Role Models, Battling with Bears & Alter Egos

- Role Models
- Pioneers
- Before the break – Life before stand-up
- The mechanics of juggling – Who does your washing?
- Bitch Goddess – You're not like that in real life, are you?

CHAPTER 5: WELCOME TO THE PIRANHA POOL! – WORKING LIFE ACHIEVEMENTS

In which I find out what life is like for a FSUC

- A leap in the dark – How to deal with venues and audiences.
- Hysterical – Am I funny or am I not?
- Power is the ultimate aphrodisiac – and what of humour?
- Old wives tales – Where do you get your material?
- 'Impropriety is the soul of wit' – back to dainty or dirty
- 'Don't knock me, I can do it better' – Self-deprecation.

- Fishwives and street hawkers –Just 'cos I'm a woman don't mean I can't swear.
- Fifteen minutes of fame – Television.

CHAPTER 6: STAND-UP AND BE COUNTED – BARRIERS AND DIFFICULTIES OVERCOME

In which I get my chisel out to chip away at the glass ceiling
- Sticks and stones – Dealing with drunks and hecklers.
- An iron hand in a velvet glove – Safety.
- The buck stops here – Practicalities and realities.
- Green-eyed monsters – Subversive tactics.
- 'The woman that deliberates is lost' – Self-Confidence.
- 'Curioser and curioser!' cried Alice – Why do they do it?

CHAPTER 7: 'TIPS FOR THE TOP'

In which I share with you the reader the advice I was given
'Stand Up & Sock it to them Sister' – Female stand-up comics and other successful in the comedy industry reveal the tricks of their trade and give great advice to ANY woman wanting to make a success of her working life.

INTRODUCTION

When I was growing up I used to love comedy but could never find out an awful lot about funny women, there just weren't any specific books about them. I loved to make people laugh and liked nothing better than to have a laugh and mess about but by the time I was a teenager in the seventies and had started to really question my place in society – it seemed to be men who were creating the funny on the telly and women were the ones being made fun of by the men. Very curious!

As I grew older and started working as a professional performer, there didn't seem to be many funny roles for women (which was a big shame as I felt I'd be great at them) to apply for and when I did get those funny roles (see the Appendix for photos) I felt I had to wait an awful long time before the next opportunity arose. Now why was this and why was I constantly being told that women weren't funny? I was funny. I made people laugh and I had loads of female friends who were also funny, so what was all that nonsense about?

When I got to my mid-thirties in the mid-nineties, my itinerant life as a professional performer did not fit in with being the mother of a brand new baby, although it didn't deter me from making four programmes for S4C travelling 3,000 miles in six weeks around the continent on a motor bike!!!!! (Thanks to my Mam and Dad and 'Papa' for looking after the babe!) and I went to Cardiff University to do a Master's Degree in Women's Studies. For my thesis I chose to do a study about women working in a non-traditional working environment and, as I still had lots of unanswered questions and I wanted to link into one of my passions, I decided to study female stand-up comics and find out more about their lives.

The initial study consisted of five comics including three very well-known comics at the time, Jo Brand, Jenny Éclair and Donna McPhail, as well as young black comic Lorraine Benloss and Welsh comic Wendy Kane. It was very well received, I wanted to find out more, and this led me to continue to research the topic until I arrived in 2016 having spoken to and picked the brains of well over eighty people. An awful lot has happened to women's participation in the comedy scene from when I began my master's degree back in 1996, to when I finally put my pen down late 2016 when I amalgamated all my research into this comprehensive and definitive study of women's stand-up comedy – 'Stand Up & Sock it to them Sisters! Funny, Feisty Females'. In this book you will find out what these exciting developments are, how we can all learn so much from FSUCs (Female Stand Up Comics) and how we can integrate those feisty elements to make our own lives as empowering as possible, whether we are male or female. I learnt a heck of a lot and so could you!!

One of the most important things I found when researching, was how important other (female) Comic Role Models were to present FSUCs and also how invisible large chunks of women's history had become. This is largely because publishing costs lots of money, and is not necessarily about reflecting a true account of events – it can be someone's specific perspective of it and it is often about making money. Historically, publishing houses were usually run by men and they would be the ones making choices and decisions about what their customers wanted, what would and wouldn't sell. This lost history, or 'her' story belongs rightfully to us as women, we can learn so much from those who came before us (if we only knew about them!) and with the advent of self-publishing and ebooks, we are no longer as dictated to by male whims and decisions as we were previously.

This book will do several things, the first one being to totally blow right out of the water the **BIG MYTH** that women are not funny. Secondly it will capture and reinvigorate for future generations, some of the phenomenally strong, determined and funky, feisty, funny females who have for the most part been lost from women's history. These amazing women have historically given birth to the direct lineage of their fiery twenty first century offspring and it will be an honour to, thirdly, introduce you to the funny women surfing solidly on what I consider to be the emerging excitement of a new fourth wave of feminism.

And finally, if you can make it in the stand-up comedy world, one of the most emotionally challenging and misogynist environments to work in, then the barriers you will encounter in any other environments such as politics, banking, law or education etc. will seem comparatively easy. One of the findings that I had from my research, was that the glass ceiling can be shattered by the same tools no matter what the profession.

Throughout the book you will hear about various aspects of their lives: how they were brought up, their education, where they were able to flex their comedy muscles, who helped them, either practically or by inspiring them, what sort of environments they work in, including a patriarchal society with unspoken and invisible rules defined by men, and see how they have blasted their way through their own glass ceilings to make a success. I will also be backing up what they say by referring to other people's research to really strengthen my case and putting in my own pennyworth.

The final chapter is called, 'Tips for the Top – How to make it in a funny man and any man's world'. 'Tips for the Top' will certainly give you some very useful advice directly from some incredible women and some very supportive men, not only those who are FSUCs, but also those who are involved in other aspects of comedy, in films, animation, comedy promoters and even some funny female politicians who have also found a space in society to verbalise their experience as FSUCs have done. I hope you will find this book both interesting and entertaining. There are a few jokes in places but to actually see my Interviewees in action and laugh your pants off – check out their websites, go and see them perform, check out Google, check out youtube and come to the same conclusion as I have, that women can be hilariously funny so let's just accept that and move on!

It has taken me nearly twenty years to engage with all these women and men and all the advice they have given me has all come from them directly either through face to face interviews, phone to phone, Skype or email or Facebook messaging.

As this book has been growing progressively over the last twenty years all the interviews are just snapshots of a time when I spoke to a particular person. Their professional and personal circumstances may have changed dramatically since that time, so do bear this in mind. People marry, divorce, split-up, change partners, go to live in another country, have children etc. etc. All you need to bear in mind is that when I spoke to that person this is what they told me. I have tapes of their conversations and a note book full to the brim of things they told me and a lot of those things will never ever be disclosed!!

I have seen an awful lot of these female comics live and none of them have 'bombed' or 'died' whilst I have been in the audience. I am not making any judgements on any of their work, just presenting them to you so that you can make your own decisions. I feel highly privileged to have been able to connect with them all on a personal level and for them to trust me enough that I will not misrepresent them in any negative way. I have honoured that promise and thank them from the bottom of my heart.

They form a vast variety of individuals at various points in their careers, from Britain, America, Canada, Australia, New Zealand, Japan, India, Greece and South Africa. Some are at the top of their game such as Joan Rivers (RIP – she was alive when I met her!)

and Amy Schumer and others taking the mike for their first few years such as Holly Burn and Fern Brady. I have interviewed some utterly AMAZING FSUCs. They include:

- The world's oldest FSUC
- The world's youngest FSUC
- The world's first Muslim FSUC
- The first Black British FSUC
- The first Indian FSUC
- The first Greek FSUC
- The first British Asian FSUC
- The first Northern Irish FSUC
- Two pioneering Latina FSUCs
- An original British Alternative FSUC
- Two sets of New York based Mother and daughter FSUCs
- FSUCs who like to mask their talent
- FSUCs who bare their souls to the world
- One FSUC who reveals her nether regions on stage
- One FSUC who is very demure and dresses entirely in black.
- FSUCs who have children and those who don't
- FSUCs who have disabilities and those who don't
- Lesbian FSUCs
- Heterosexual FSUCs
- A Transexual FSUC
- A ventriloquist FSUC
- A pioneering Comedy Commissioner who was a FSUC
- FSUCs who work as M.C.'s
- Some very politically active FSUCs
- A FSUC who used to be an SMP politician
- Two funny politicians who aren't FSUCs
- FSUCs who have made an impact on our televisions

- Those who run Comedy & Improvisation Clubs
- One funny Oscar nominated animator
- One funny Hollywood director

I have tried to access and have as wide a variety as possible of every type of female comic voice that is trying to be heard and this book is an opportunity for you to benefit from all the amazing advice they have given me personally. And just a few words to those of you of a nervous disposition, there may be some naughty words and rude bits intermingled. You have been warned!

And finally to round off my Introduction, some support from two men who have spent some considerable time researching and writing about male comics themselves.

Firstly a message I received from William Cook Guardian Comedy Critic and author of 'Ha Bloody Ha – Comedians Talking' and 'The Comedy Store – The Club that changed British Comedy'. (At some point before 2003, when I only had twenty five Interviewees)

William Cook – Guardian Comedy Critic and Author of books about Comedy

"It sounds like a fascinating subject for a book especially with your background as an actress and your passion for comedy. You've got a very good list of interviewees and when your book is published, I'd be delighted to see a copy."

And this message from Dr. Oliver Double (again when I had about twenty five Interviewees and not the total eighty four interviewees) who lectures on stand-up comedy at the University of Kent and has published several books on the subject, such as 'Britain had Talent – a History of Variety Theatre' and 'Getting the Joke'.

Dr. Oliver Double – Author of numerous Comedy books
"A book celebrating the excellent female comedians this country has produced will make an important contribution to the comedy industry, by encouraging more women to take up the mike. I'm impressed Gwenno that you've got to all those people to be honest. Yes very. Very impressed. I'd be envious of that fat roster of interviewees. Very, very, much so."

I am incredibly grateful to all those who participated and gave so generously of their time, so without further ado let's 'Stand up & Sock it to them Sisters!

Gwenno Dafydd & sister Siwan, circa 1962.
Guess which one was the naughty girl?

CHAPTER 1

SUFFRAJESTS

In which I discover the female comedy family tree

THE MAN? "DONT YOU WISH YOU WERE A MAN
MRS. SPANKHURST"?
THE SUFFRAGETTE: YES, DONT YOU WISH YOU WERE"?

SUFFRAJESTS

An Historical overview

Contrary to that most popular myth that women are not funny, which for ease of purpose, from now on I will call **THE BIG MYTH**, *they have actually always been funny but few in a public sphere. As I have already suggested, the present day female stand-up's are direct descendants of bawdy but brilliant artistes who performed in the 'Music Halls' which had become popular by the end of the nineteenth century, women like Jenny Hill and Marie Lloyd, who were both extremely successful. In this chapter I am going to find out as much as I can about those women so we have a solid base of knowledge to place our present day comics in context and also to shine a light on some fabulous feisty Role Models who have for the most part been hidden from history, so let's bring them out from behind the proscenium arch. Let's bring them credit where credit is due and put them once and for all in the limelight. A direct link from present to the past is Dr. Naomi Paxton, who I interviewed about her alter ego, comic Ada Campe.*

Naomi Paxton – aka Ada Campe

"I recently completed my Ph.D. on the Actresses Franchise League and edited the Methuen Drama – 'Book of Suffrage Plays'. 'The Actresses' Franchise League were a group of performers who came together in 1908 to support the suffrage movement through theatre, performance and education. They were fantastically prolific, creative and ambitious – and wanted to change the way women participated in the business of theatre for the future. Previously thought of as a small and one-issue organisation that ceased after the First World War, I've discovered that they were large, diverse and embedded in the networks of the mainstream theatre in the first half of the twentieth century, had

strong international influence and remained active until the late 1950s, developing a portfolio of projects that were designed to support and improve the lives of women both in and out of the theatre industry. Their work shows that there are strong shoulders to stand on for present day female performers, writers and producers – a tradition of women writing and performing comedy and political theatre and a network of feminist women and men unafraid to be open about their politics and passions."

However, before women started to organise themselves in any way politically or culturally at the beginning of the century before last, I want to look at the Pioneers, the very first professional singer, the very first professional dancer, those women who defined new directions, the stars and those who were popular in their time. Then I will look at the very defined form of entertainment I previously mentioned, Music Hall, which brought professional performance to the masses and where women started empowering themselves in a very specific way, both economically and creatively. I am going to look at how they were able to succeed in this medium, the sort of work they did, what sort of environments they worked in, how their audiences were made up and how they dealt with those audiences, I will also be asking the same questions to my present day Female Stand Up Comics (FSUCs) and Interviewees to see what has changed, if anything? I will then look at how the forms developed through mechanical developments such as radio, television and cinema and how stars from one medium entered another and into our consciousness. It is one long golden thread of talent, persistence and feisty funny females from the pioneers of performance, the Music Hall to the 'Alternative' Comedy Scene in the late seventies and early eighties, (at which point The BBC's 'Good Old Days' was still being shown on our television screens and I was still belting out some of those songs with the English Comedy Club in Brussels) which has then led to the present batch of female comics, some of whom are heavily politicised and leading the vanguard of what I perceive to be the powerful new fourth wave of feminism and others who are just happy to be 'aving a laugh.

The BBC's 'Good Old Days' was the longest running TV variety show in the UK, which ended its 30-year run in 1983, the year when I returned from Belgium where I had been living, working and learning my craft of performance for five years. All the cast and performers reproduced songs and acts that had been made popular in the British Music Halls and all the audience dressed up in period costume. The host for the entire thirty year run was Leonard Sachs and every show ended with the audience singing 'Down at the Old Bull and Bush'.

I'd like at this point to thank the world's foremost authority on Music Hall and someone who also appeared on 'The Good Old Days', Roy Hudd, for his generosity in lending me the photographs that appear in this chapter which came from his own private collection. So without further ado, let's go and join them in them 'Good Ole Days' way back in time.

The 'Music Halls' started off as pubs, drinking dens for men with a little colourful entertainment thrown in to encourage them to stay and spend their hard won money on booze, not so different from the lap and pole dancing clubs of today. The 'Music Halls' regulars were mostly men, and like present day lap-dancing clubs, they had a reputation as being a bit on the seedy side and no place for a 'lady'. The few women who were there were prostitutes who were there trying to earn a few bob in the world's so called 'oldest profession' (It's nice to see prostitution elevated to the level of doctors and lawyers!) rather than on a girls night out. Roy Hudd in his 1976 book 'Music Hall' mentions the Wilton's Music Hall, which as well as selling food and numerous types of beer also boasted a private entrance to the brothel next door.

At the same time, you could actually say this joke 'Why did the woman cross the road? Cross the road! Who the hell let her out of the kitchen in the first place!!' and it would have been true in Victorian times when women had very little power or control over their own lives and were answerable either to their fathers or their husbands. This present government seems intent on returning women to the comfort of the kitchen, with women suffering far more than men in this long-standing recession. Pregnancy was called either 'lying in' or if you were a polite urban Victorian you would be an 'invalid'. Whichever way you looked at it and whatever terms were used, pregnancy and childbirth were the most dangerous times in a nineteenth century woman's life. Not a very jolly time for women in general with women dying in childbirth with not a whiff of gas and air to be found. Children popped out at the rate of one a year with no disposable nappies or ready-made pizzas to give Mum a chance for some 'quality time' with the kids. Queen Victoria had nine children so there was no respite from childbirth even for the rich and famous, although apparently she was quite fond of marihuana – in particular for her period pains.

Before the Music Halls came into being, at the beginning of the nineteenth century, all the different strands of society used to gather together in the large 'Assembly Rooms' of coffee houses and taverns. Here was a chance for both men and women to meet, drink, make merry and sing the popular ditties of the day. These clubs were called 'Catch and Glee Clubs'. Singers in search of a 'busman's holiday' also frequented them after their performances from the Theatres Royal. 'Glee Clubs' are still very much in vogue in the States with many universities having one in their music departments. There are also 'Glee' Comedy Clubs. These clubs eventually went in two specific ways. The wealthier and more discerning men gradually moved to the new concept of 'Song and Supper Rooms' in the 1830's leaving the taverns to the men and women of the working classes. As a result the 'Catch and Glee Clubs' were considered to be a little vulgar. Only men went to the 'Song and Supper Rooms' and as the name suggests these provided songs and suppers to the early hours of the morning. The proceedings were run by the host who acted as Chairman and who invited his patrons to do a 'turn' to entertain those present. Many of those who did perform became some of the first professional entertainers as a result of these experiences.

The first and probably the most well – known of these was 'Evans's at Covent Garden. Evans, (A Welsh name if there ever was one!) the proprietor, who had been a successful comic actor at the Theatre Royal, Covent Garden, converted the first floor of the hotel into a 'Song and Supper Room'. It became incredibly popular serving 1,200 diners in one evening. The shows were considered so shocking that genteel 'ladies' were, if they were very lucky, only allowed to watch them from a screened off area behind the safety of a railed balcony. In this environment it is probably true to say that if women were hardly allowed to take a peep at the entertainment, there was very little likelihood that they were able to be performers. However 'ladies' and 'women' didn't necessarily belong to the same sex. Even at that time there were two types of women, the Madonnas and the Magdalenes! The taverns at the same time were also developing and becoming popular with the working classes. There were numerous taverns around London, which had a music license. They were not as organised as the 'Song and Supper' rooms but sprang out of 'Bar Parlour Concerts', 'Sing Songs' and 'Harmonic meetings' which gave singers, again all male, an opportunity to display their vocal chords.

The first professional female singer 1860 – Miss Caulfield

It is interesting to note that the very first professional female singer, a Miss Caulfield, did not make an appearance until 1860 at the Evans's Song and Supper Rooms' at Covent Garden. (I wonder if she was related in some way to Jo Caulfield, one of my Interviewees, a present day FSUC and comedy consultant to Graham Norton?) She was indeed a pioneer and very unusual for her time. You would think that she would have a few paragraphs detailing her contribution in the books devoted to the history of the Music Halls, but she remains for the most part enigmatic and invisible. At the beginning of the 1850's 'The Canterbury Arms', a glorified pub offering men food, drink, fun and skittles, had a hall built specifically to accommodate entertainment and is generally regarded as the first real Music Hall. It was successful for the next sixty years. 'The Canterbury Hall' was opened in Lambeth, London in 1852 by Charles Morton and became an immediate success. Under the lights of an enormous gas-lit chandelier, 1,500 people would eat, drink and have a ball. The audience had to pay a small charge for the entertainment provided and this marked the change from previous ad-hoc arrangements for the taverns and supper rooms. As a result of paying an entrance fee, the entertainment also became a little more organised, varied and professional, and we see over the following years, women arriving on stage either as singers or dancers. The success of the 'Canterbury Hall' led to rapid growth in the Music Halls and by 1868 there were two hundred Music Halls in London and another three hundred across the country.

A few weeks after the 'Canterbury Hall' was opened, the Alhambra in Leicester Square opened as competition. It became in time a model for the 'Folies Bergere' in Paris. It was also, along with the Metropolitan and Collins, one of the last three genuine Music Halls in London. Their popularity declined after World War I and the Alhambra was demolished to make way for the Odeon on Leicester Square. It was demolished in 1936 and a cinema built in its place. But in its heyday, between 1880 and

1910 the Alhambra became one of hundreds of Music Halls built throughout the country, many more than the 'straight' theatres constructed at the same time. The Alhambra allowed middle class women to be present in the audience as early as the 1860's but generally the audiences drawn to them would be working class and the lower middle class. The first few 'Music Halls', because they had started off as public houses, were still seen as very rough and ready and the females in the audience as of 'morally dubious character'. Prostitutes found willing clients at the Music Halls but they found willing clients wherever they carried out their 'profession'.

Wives had been present in the audience since the time of the Canterbury Hall and some consideration was given to trying to make the Music Halls more 'respectable', cleaning up the artistes material and controlling the riotous behaviour of the audience so that wives would feel more comfortable in this environment. Money was poured into the developing industry of the Music Halls. The 'London Pavilion' in 1895 with all its luscious splendour and glory made the Music Hall more acceptable to the middle classes. From the time of the 'Glee Clubs' and 'Song and Supper Rooms' at the beginning of the 19th Century a lot had changed for women. From not even being permitted in the audience, they had progressed from Miss Caulfield's first professional engagement at Covent Garden to dancing on the stage and being able to appreciate this from the comfort of a seat rather than from behind a screen! The Music Halls had acquired a new respectability that appealed to all members of the family.

A journalist who visited a Music Hall in Bradford in 1887 estimated that about a quarter of the audience consisted of husbands and wives, those being presumably young wives who had not had any young children to stop them gallivanting and gadding about. When these young women became mothers for the first time, very little changed. Even textile workers were able to afford to pay for another woman to look after their child, with some money left over to pay for some fun and relaxation. With the second child and more, this was not always possible due to the high cost, even then, of childcare and the women took their 'rightful place' by the hearth and mangle with not even 'Eastenders' to keep them entertained, until their children grew up and they could return to their leisure activities. Because of this, the Music Halls became mostly the haunts of bachelors, playboys, fathers and sons. This environment was noisy, boozy and boisterous and was a difficult venue for any performer, let alone a woman to play, especially as the performers had to project their voices above the din of dinner plates and raucous beer swilling, with no P.A. systems or fancy radio mikes to fall back on. Charles Morton, who set up the Canterbury Hall, obviously had a very clear insight into what made a man's mind tick. He decided that the easiest way to get them to prolong their visits and empty their pockets was to have pretty women in various stages of disarray flaunting their long partly clad legs.

The first female Music Hall dancer – Lydia Thompson (1838 – 1908)

One of the first dancers mentioned in 'A hard act to follow' – A Music Hall Review by Peter Leslie is 'Lydia Thompson and her Imported English Blondes'. Lydia Thomsen was a child pantomime star who later found success on the London stage by dancing a parody of the extraordinary Spanish dancer Perea Nina. She had also toured throughout Europe performing in musical comedies. There is very little mention of her career in Britain and this may be because she was considered a little scandalous, but it seems she was tremendously successful in the Baltic where her popularity was such that her portrait was given equal importance with that of the Czar's, one either side of the stove in every kitchen in Riga! Lydia became a huge success in the States in 1869 when, for the first time ever in show business history, her 'girls' appeared in skin coloured tights in a show called 'Ixion' which shocked and astounded the New York audiences. As the first women to perform 'tights plays' Lydia's 'Imported English Blondes' appeared on stage exhibiting their bodies just because they were nice to look at. 'Tights plays' were considered very risqué and probably the work of the devil himself but nevertheless Lydia and her long legged troupe wowed them all over the States for over twenty years.

At the same time as Lydia was titillating the American public, the Music Halls were starting to have a very definite form. Because of the Lord Chamberlain's censorship of plays for the 'legitimate' stage, Music Halls were not allowed to present any act that had more than one person speaking, otherwise it would be considered as a play. Sketches were not allowed and neither were double acts, monologues, ballets and songs. So this was in fact extremely important as it allowed individuals and their acts to filter through, many of whom were women. These rules meant that certain types of acts were bound to develop and by the end of the nineteenth century, the most popular ones were the comics who usually presented songs in character or with some easy patter with the audience to link the songs. The content of the songs had varied over the years depending on what the audiences found acceptable and the civilising effect of wives on their husbands in the audience. These songs had started to become a little cheekier and very often tongue in cheek. The biggest taboo at the time was sexuality. Any word relating to sex was not to be used in public and as it was difficult to talk openly about sex the next best thing was to refer to it in a hidden way, to 'protect the ladies'. David A. Gershaw in his online blog 'A line on life – The skirts of Queen Victoria' says:

"*Nicer*" words were devised for any word that might hint of sexuality. Breasts became "*bosom*", and legs became "*limbs*". Why are legs sexual? First, trees have limbs. Where two limbs come together, there is *no* organ. This is not the case where legs come together. In fact, Queen Victoria even covered "*limbs*" of tables, pianos and beds. You still can sometimes see pianos or beds with "*skirts*".

This suppression of sexuality undoubtedly gave birth to the 'double entendres' that comics like Frankie Howerd, "Titter ye not!", Kenneth Williams, Larry Grayson, Julian Clary, Graham Norton, Alan Carr, Sarah Millican and countless others have made their own.

Although the comic songs and singers were the most popular acts, the Music Hall had a huge variety of types of entertainment, including acrobats, dancers, straight singers specialising in sentimental crooning and patriotic fervour, conjurers and jugglers. The audiences themselves had to have some stamina, they could be entertained for up to three or four hours at a time by as many as thirty acts, a bit like 'Britain's Got Talent' nowadays. Although many of the singers performed monologues or funny stories about the audience's lives and linked their songs with a little dialogue with the audience, telling a string of unrelated jokes was a style that had not yet been invented. And in the same way that sex was an unspoken subject, the Music Hall songs gave their singers an opportunity to comment and poke fun at issues affecting people's lives and for which they had no other outlet. Most ordinary men in society were not particularly powerful. Even in 1912, one third of all adult males did not have the vote, those who were live-in servants, and the poorest paid working-men.

It was even worse for women, none of them had the vote and they had no one to talk publicly about any issues that might be relevant to their lives. However, in 1903 the Women's Social and Political Union was founded by Emmeline Pankhurst and her daughters Christabel and Sylvia, which in time became the 'Suffragette' Movement. They wanted women to have the right to vote. There is an insightful postcard from 1912 reproduced in Diane Atkinson's 'Funny Girls – Cartooning for Equality', which shows:

'What a woman may be, and yet not have the vote:
Mayor, Nurse, Mother, Doctor or Teacher, Factory Hand.

What a man may have been, and yet not LOSE the vote:
Convict, Lunatic, Proprietor of White Slaves, Unfit for Service,
Drunkard."

Next time you get invited to put your cross in the box, don't forget that less than a hundred years ago – women's opinions were generally considered worse and of less consequence than the opinions of lunatics, drunks and convicts!

Because so many halls had sprung up all over the country, all needing instant 'professional performers' there was the potential, if one was prepared to work hard, not only to make a decent wage in comparison to factory work, but the freedom to travel throughout Britain and in some cases even further afield. In Lancashire 'gaffers' from the local mines used to go to the Music Halls early on in the week, to report on the quality of the acts so that they could be recommended or not to their fellow workers. The audiences at Music Halls throughout the country didn't change from week to week as people tended to stay in their 'square mile' and so it was the acts that circulated. This was also the case in London where a 'circuit' of sorts was being developed. Some artists were booked to appear at several halls in one evening, which, with travel in London even worse than these days, must have been an exhausting feat! However, some working-class women did benefit from the Music Halls in that it was one of the few ways that they could claw their way out of the factories and on to the road to independence and even fame and fortune. Britain had even more distinct class segregations at that time than now. Surprisingly, the vast majority of women who made a success in the halls were mostly from the working classes. Marrying out of your class and improving your lot happened as rarely as winning the Lottery these days.

Jenny Hill (1850 – 1896)
The first female Music Hall 'Star'

However, one real exception was Jenny Hill. She well and truly did win life's Lottery. Born in 1850, she worked in an artificial flower factory where legend has it she sang for a few coppers to encourage the workers to be productive, a bit like the guys who read the papers aloud to fat, fleshy, flatulent and fiftyish guys (sorry to disappoint you lads, but it's not dusky maidens) rolling cigars in Havana!

The owner of the factory was a certain Bob Botting who also owned the Marylebone Music Hall, where she developed her talents. She then spent seven years working her apprenticeship as a comic singer and dancer in a pub in Bradford. Those applicants to the 'X Factor' and 'Britain's Got Talent' take note – seven years of hard graft and no overnight success. At the same time that Miss Caulfield was taking her first tentative steps out on to the boards of Evans's Song and Supper Rooms in Covent Garden in 1860, Jenny Hill was perfecting her craft as a child performer. She became known as 'The Vital Spark' not only because of her dramatic character impersonations but also because of her phenomenally energetic performances. She was exhausting both on stage and off and changed agents, admirers and residencies whenever the fancy took her. She dominated twenty years of performance but because she did not survive into the age of recordings, did not achieve the same sort of recognition that we may have given to better-known performers such as Marie Lloyd or Vesta Tilley.

Female performers in the Music Halls were initially very few and far between and as such were able to demand healthy fees due to their rarity. Jenny made and spent a great deal of money, and amongst other things, bought a farm at Streatham, a pair of ponies and a four wheeled trap and the Rainbow Music Hall in Southampton in 1884, which was highly unusual at that time, as women were never in a position to buy property independently of a man. In fact women were not ordinarily 'allowed' to take the reigns of power in any place in society. The only way a woman could manage, let alone buy, a Music Hall was if she were the widow of a manager who had died in service. The licensing authorities allowed this to happen as long as the widow had the necessary expertise, such as with Anne, the widow of John Collins, who ran the John Collins Music Hall in Islington for three years after his death. Jane Mackay, another one of the women I interviewed for 'Sock it' and her Twenty First Century management of comedy clubs in Scotland until her retirement in 2005 could never have happened at this time. Although the authorities may have accepted female managers, the public had other ideas. Adelaide Stoll, wife of John Stoll, who died in 1880, ran the Parthenon in Liverpool, but had to pretend to receive messages and directions from a male manager, by way of her son 14 year old Oswald, in order to gain credibility with agents and visitors. Oswald's early experiences stood him in great stead, as he later became a Music Hall magnate and was instrumental in presenting the Royal Variety Performance (originally Royal Command Performance). He was a philanthropist and was knighted by King George V in 1919.

Jenny Hill married an acrobat called John Woodley, whose stage name was Jean Pasta in 1866 at the age of 16 and bore him a daughter, Lettie, who also took to the boards when she was 13 under the name of Peggy Pryde. The marriage broke down, as it must have been quite difficult for Pasta to see his wife becoming so successful whilst he was literally tying himself in knots. From her London debut in the 1860s at the Dr. Johnson Concert Rooms, Bolt Court, Fleet Street, where she received three shillings a night and refreshments, Jenny went on to be the most successful female Music Hall performer of her time. She was a particularly good self-publicist through the medium of her 'card' advertisements, which normally appeared as a reminder to her public of her activities, at the head of the first column of the back page of the *Era* from 1876 until her death in 1896. A present day similarity would be Madonna or Lady Gaga, who are both incredibly successful at re-inventing themselves, creating publicity and capturing the zeitgeist. Nowadays this potential is available to all of use, even those with no marketing experience at all, with Twitter, LinkedIn and Facebook enabling us all to be our own marketing gurus. Although I have to mention here that someone contacted me on LinkedIn a few months ago and said she was getting rather fed up of seeing my postings about everything I was doing – grrrrrrrr I thought that that was what it was for!! – to grow businesses and relationships. They're not going to grow unless people know what you are doing and you may well annoy people in the process, which I obviously did!!! (by the way, she was in a well-paid secure job, so what was she doing seeing my posts in work time!!!!) Jenny's cards are positive and bubbling with self-confidence such as the one on the ninth of June 1878: 'Jenny Hill commands a greater salary by £10 than any single lady *Artiste* ever received in the Music Halls' and on the third of March 1882: '£294 taken at the doors. Biggest benefit by £40 this season'. Certainly a bit of an improvement on the three shillings and a half a shandy she got every night at Doc. Johnson's. One of the cards also mentions the pace at which she worked: '336 turns in 108 nights. No rest. No disappointments' (Thirteenth of August 1887). No wonder she died at the relatively early age of forty-six, from exhaustion probably. This lady knew how to work, and work she did, sometimes working four halls a night, wearing out both body and soul. In some of her northern tours she would often sing over 70 songs a week. A modern day equivalent would probably be the late great Amy Winehouse.

She was also a particularly determined, witty and prolific speechmaker, which would even be unusual these days but at that time was extremely unusual. At the beginning of the twenty first century, the BBC Wales in Cardiff, who at that time were very aware that women were reticent to speak publicly, established a Diversity Database. It was set up especially to encourage women and ethnic minorities to have a more public voice. It has taken over ten years for this message to get through to London (that's why we need an electric train connection so that London can find out about the great things happening in Wales!!) Jenny Hill would have been in great demand as an all-round broadcaster, had she lived in this century. A report of her 1879 London season benefit at the South London Palace says, 'Miss Hall is one of the few ladies who can make a speech ….to her oratory comes naturally.' The 'cards' and speeches were in themselves very challenging as her managers and agents often used to try and gag her by writing clauses into her contracts forbidding her from talking directly to the audiences but rebellious Jenny didn't listen and often sacked agents if she felt that they were cramping her style. She was independent, very much her own woman, determined and feisty. She was more popular with the women in the audience than the men, probably because she publicly verbalised their experiences in a way that no one else was doing.

She travelled extensively and was one of the earliest English artistes to cross the Atlantic and appeared at Tony Pastor's Music Hall in New York. On her last tour in 1894 she performed in Johannesburg and found to her dismay that the audience was 'so peculiar – nothing but men'. (Exactly the same experience of another of my 'Sock it' Interviewees, JoJo Smith in South Africa nearly a century later!). Her biggest fans were mostly the working class wives and mothers who were able to relate to the songs she sang about women in circumstances similar to theirs. It must have given the audience a big buzz to see this tiny, attractive, wiry and energetic woman talking and singing about things relative to their lives that no one else did. Of course, as a female of independent means she did not have to worry about offending any man in her life, which was not the case with the vast majority of her audience. It was still to be another thirty years and more before the first female M.P. was elected to the House of Commons in 1919. They would not have dared poke fun at the breadwinner in their lives in case he refused them money for food or beat them to a pulp, again a situation that many women nowadays can also attest to. A horrendous **1 in 4 women** will be a victim of domestic violence in their lives and although only a minority of incidents of domestic violence are reported to the police, the police still receive one call about domestic violence for every minute in the UK, according to figures released in 2015 by Women's Aid.

Jenny's performances on stage were quite captivating, concentrating mostly on character songs about the serving girls and female street-sellers that her audience could relate to. Her face was immensely mobile and could be pulled into any variety of grotesque shapes to accentuate the characters she would be portraying. Although she was a very attractive woman, she didn't care, the object of the game was to make her audience laugh. She thoroughly rejected the notion that femininity and good looks were central to being accepted by society. The sort of songs that she sang were also very challenging such as 'I'm determined no longer to stand it' and 'Woe is the mother who owns eleven' a tribute to those women who did not have the daily pill to control the size of their families, and 'I've been a good woman to you' in which an 'outspoken wife' complains:

'I've been a good woman to you
And the neighbours all know that it's true
You go to the pub
And you blue the kids' grub
But I've been a good woman to you'.

Apart from an occasional mention in the press, many of these songs were lost to history, as the ones that were written down would be the ones that could be sold as piano partitions for 'nice' middle class women to sing in company on a Sunday afternoon with all the family gathered around the aspidistra. Of course 'nice' middle class women would not want to sing about the poverty, domestic violence and other depressing social problems that Jenny shone a light on and these songs disappeared in time. The Music

Hall songs about women that remained for posterity in print, were mostly the ones sung by men. This was the time when, as I mentioned previously, publishing with many other seats of power were controlled by men. These songs were particularly scathing, vitriolic and downright nasty towards women, and often sung by men in drag such as Harry Randall, who with his grotesque harridans would make today's pantomime dames look like wilting wallflowers in comparison. So although sexist jokes hadn't been invented at that time, putting down women and demonising them had. Sex, innuendo and smut were becoming more and more acceptable in the acts and Jenny was there with the best of them.

She was able to get her audience on her side not only in her songs but also in the quick-fire improvised patter that she scattered her audience with. She was a real character who challenged conventions and rebelled against the constricting censorship of the Lord Chancellor but the audience loved her for it. She was openly bawdy and in the early part of her career a part of her act was the acrobatic dancing she had learnt and developed with her husband, Jean Pasta. She was very physical and quite the exhibitionist, things that women at that time just weren't. Part of her act consisted of jumping from a kitchen table into a half filled bathtub, and she frequently used to finish her act by dancing about and playing the hornpipes. Her daughter, Peggy Pryde was just like her mother, quite a character, and she was charged with indecency in her act. The offending article was a song, which spoke about a voyeuristic servant girl laughing at the sexual gymnastics of her newly married employers. The prosecution found that she had pushed the boundaries of taboo subjects a little too far.

Other female performers at that time
Bessie Bellwood (1856 – 1896)
First Female Singer of Cockney Songs

Bessie Bellwood was another rags to riches story who as a child was a 'rabbit puller' or 'skin dresser' and skinned rabbits in Bermondsey before venturing on to the stage. She was born Elisabeth Ann Katherine Mahoney in 1857 daughter of two Irish immigrants from County Cork, Ireland. She was related to 'Father Prout', a renowned literary and poetic priest and often liked to discuss books and poetry. A devout Catholic, she started her career at the 'Star' in Bermondsey, singing Irish ballads and became the first female singer of cockney songs. She was the wildest dare-devil of them all and particularly adept at handling a rowdy audience. She once held a five-minute slanging-match with a fifteen stone coal heaver who had dared to interrupt her act. He left the theatre with his ego totally deflated and demoralised. Another story about her tells of the time when, very soon after a meeting with Cardinal Manning to discuss a Catholic charity, she was arrested in the Tottenham Court Road for attacking a cabman who she thought had insulted her lover at the time. Not a woman to tangle with. She was a particularly good-looking woman and one of the first true 'characters' produced by the halls. Like many of the female singers, she died young in 1896, the physical and psychological demands of exhausting performance wearing her out at an early age. She was thirty-nine, finally devoured by the demon drink and debt.

Bessie Bonehill (1855-1902) – One of the very first Male Impersonators

Bessie Bonehill started performing with her two sisters as a clog dancer and became very rich and famous not only in Britain but also in the States where, at the height of her success, she owned a 600 acre estate on Long Island, New York. She was one of the very first male impersonators, paving the way for later success for Vesta Tilley.

The next generation of performers benefited from these pioneers preparing the way and included women like Kate Carney – 'The Coster Queen' and the well-known Marie Lloyd. Jenny Hill was an original 'coster' girl and they sang mostly about drinking and getting drunk in songs such as 'Every pub we saw, we went inside of it' and 'Four ale Sal'. The songs were very bawdy, risqué and witty and told about the consequences of too much of the devils brew.

Kate Carney (1869 – 1950) –
"The Coster Queen"

Kate Carney was born into a family who performed in the Music Halls and married a fellow comic performer, George Barclay. Her first stage appearance was at the Albert Music Hall in Canning Town. She dressed in the 'coster' dress of 'pearly', which in time became the uniform for the cockney pearly kings and queens. She was quite flamboyant and loved to wear hats trimmed with enormous ostrich feathers. She performed opposite the great 'costers' of the day, who included the famous Albert Chevalier (1861-1923) (No relation to Maurice!). In Albert's autobiography 'Before I forget', he comments on the difference between legitimate theatre and Music Hall. It is interesting to see that his comments are as valid now as they were then, but now it could even be a tipsy woman!

"What makes it interesting to produce effects artistically and legitimately in a Music Hall is that you are never quite certain of your audience. One tipsy man in the gallery is sufficient to upset all your calculations."

Kate Carney did not die young but went on performing to the grand old age of 80, by which time she had accrued her own company of step-dancers (where the footwork is the most important part of the dance – similar to Michael Flatley and the

Lord of the Dance and tap-dancing) and cakewalkers and after World War I, a mouth organ band. She performed in a Royal Command Performance at the London Palladium in 1935 in a 'Cavalcade of Variety'. The very first Royal Command Performance in 1912 had given 'the Victorian Music Hall' its Royal seal of approval. It had finally been accepted as 'respectable', and was at its peak of popularity. It also began its downfall, as in this year the Lord Chamberlain changed the laws allowing food and drink to be consumed in the halls and brought them more in line with the theatres. Bars were still allowed outside the halls but this, as well as the fact that printed programmes had replaced the gavel-banging Chairman, robbed the halls and their audiences of their previous intimacy and close relationships with the performers.

Marie Lloyd (1870 – 1922) – 'The Queen of the Saucy Song'

The honour of performing at the very first Royal Command Performance in 1912 was not given to that other great Music Hall artiste, Marie Lloyd, 'The Queen of the Saucy Song' as she was considered too vulgar. However, Marie gave the establishment a resounding 'V' for Victory in her own inimitable way by staging her own show at the London Pavilion with printed strips stuck on the posters saying 'Every Performance by Marie Lloyd is a Command Performance' and 'By Order of the British Public'. Even though her material was considered too risqué for King George V, Marie Lloyd had been tremendously popular since the 1880's. Critic and caricaturist Sir Henry Maximilian Beerbohm, (1872-1956), considered Marie Lloyd, Queen Victoria and Florence Nightingale to be the three most memorable women of his times.

Marie Lloyd was born Matilda Alice Victoria Wood in 1870 and came from a family of performers. Her four sisters: Daisy Wood, Rosie Lloyd, Alice Lloyd and Grace Lloyd all followed in her footsteps with varying degrees of success. Alice achieved great success in America in Vaudeville. Although Marie's mastery of innuendo confused and baffled American audiences who did not take to her. British comedy has never travelled particularly well across the Atlantic. Even to this day, few British comics have enjoyed huge Stateside success. They just don't understand why we can't be direct and call a spade a spade rather than a 'metallic gardening implement'. She made her stage debut at the age of 15 in 1885 at 'The Eagle Music Hall' under the name of Bella Delmare. She changed her name to Marie Lloyd and within two years was earning £100 a week. (Today's equivalent would be nearly thirty times as much.) Her fortune of £100,000 had been made by the time she was forty – an incredible and highly unusual achievement for any Cockney at that time, let alone a woman. Her popularity with the public was based on the saucy songs and the cheeky knowing wink, which added a fruitier meaning to the words she sang (So that's where Anne Robinson pinched the wink!). Two of her most famous songs were 'Don't Dilly Dally' and 'A little of what you fancy does you good'. Even though she was only 5ft 2 inches tall, her stage presence was confident and assertive, highly energetic and celebratory. She had two chief stage personas, as described in Colin MacInnes's History of Pop – song, from 1840-1920, 'Sweet Saturday Night', one of which was very sweet and childlike in the early part of her career;

She wore, according to Marie Kendall 'a white lace dress with pink and blue ribbons and her golden hair right down there, natural … and her big blue eyes and her tiny baby's cap of lace. And she came with a hoop, and looked like a toy doll.' Later, as she grew older, she became much grander in the same sort of style.

Ella Retford tells us, 'she wore a fabulous gown that was slashed up to the waist and showed pink tights…. with a wonderful diamond garter. And she had the smallest little hat over one eye – the one she used to wink. And don't forget the stick. A long, long cane, all studded with diamonds'. Ella Retford speaks of the 'the way she handled her beads… and rubbed them across her teeth with that saucy look and that wonderful smile'. Marie's charisma and sexuality were closely linked and heavily underplayed with innuendo. One of her famous ad-libs concerned an umbrella that she flapped and waved in front of her until it opened – 'Thank God! I haven't had it up for months!' which resulted in screams of laughter from the audience. She didn't offend them, but rather 'tickled their fancy'.

She had an enormous heart and sense of social responsibility. In an interview in 'The Sketch' 25th December 1895 it was reported that she was paying nightly for one hundred and fifty beds for the homeless and destitute of 'darker' London. The demands of performance wore her out both in public and private, and she often performed when in a great deal of physical pain. The eternal 'trooper' she accepted an invitation by Sir Oswald Stoll to perform at the Edmonton Empire when she was seriously ill. Whilst singing 'One of the ruins Cromwell knocked about', and staggering on the stage in character as a drunken woman, she fell and died three days later. Such was her popularity in 1922, that her coffin was followed by 10,000 people and twelve cars full of flowers. The taps in the bars around Leicester Square were draped in black crepe to honour the magic of Marie. She left a daughter, also called Marie, at least two husbands and numerous suitors to mourn not only her death but also the death of an era, that of Music Hall.

They were the first now here's some of the rest

The first female pioneers of the Music Halls allowed women the first real opportunity not only to develop their skills at entertaining and making an audience laugh, but also for many women to earn a far better living than they would have in any other way. They were numerous and included a vast array of talent such as some of the more familiar names noted in Raymond Mander and Joe Mitchenson's book 'British Music Hall'. When I first started doing my research for 'Sock it' way back in the mid 1990s there was no such thing as Google or Wikipedia, just dusty old libraries where you had to get permission to take a look at books and it all took a very long time to find out anything about everything. It is SO easy these days to access any knowledge and once you have a name it is so easy to do further research on that person and their life, so without further ado let me present some other seriously funny females that you can find out more about if you Google them, most have Wikipedia pages so many thanks to those who have gathered that research.

Name: Annie Adams
Lived: 1843 – 1905
Personal life: A husband called Harry Whiting (aka comic singer Harry Wall) and a son also called (very originally!) Harry.
Professional Life: Performed at Weston's Music Hall, Turnham's Music Hall and The London Pavilion.
Remembered for: The song 'When the band played on' by G.W. Hunt.

Interesting facts: It was said that her voice was so strong that glasses trembled across tables when she sang. A huge mountain of a woman, she had a personality to match her bulk. She set off on a musical tour of America in 1871.

Name: Ada Lundberg – Born Margaret Ada Clegg Everard.
Lived: 1850 – 1899
Personal life: A son called Edward Everard
Professional life: The Marlebone, The Middlesex, The Royal Albert, Canning Hall and the Britannia in Hoxton.
Remembered for: Singing 'Tooralladie', 'Cowardly, Cowardly Custard' and being one of the 'Queens of low comedy' and an outstanding Music Hall 'comedienne'.
Interesting facts: She was a native of Bristol who ran away to the circus at the age of eleven. 'Miss Ada Lundberg is a thorough-going character-vocalist, who, in her delineation of the pleasure-loving ladies in the lower walks, shows great earnestness and an enjoyable amount of humour.' (The Entr'acte, London, Monday, 7 August 1886, p.12a/b)

Name: Nelly Power
Lived: 1854 – 1887
Personal life: No family noted
Professional life: She started working in the Music Halls at the age of eight and worked extensively in Music Hall, Pantomime, Vaudeville and Burlesque.
Remembered for: Being the original singer of 'The boy I love is up in the gallery', which was written for her by songwriter and composer George Ware
Interesting facts: She was one of the earliest male impersonators. She rarely wore the full male regalia as later impersonators did, but added a hat and cane to her basic stage kit of tights and spangles. When she died, her funeral attracted three to four

thousand spectators at Abney Park Cemetery and a further great crowd at the start of the procession from her home.

Name: Marie Loftus. She was born in Glasgow of Irish parents, reputedly in Stockwell Street, close to the site of the Scotia Music Hall, where she danced as a young girl.

Lived: 1857-1940

Personal life: Loftus married fellow-entertainer Ben Brown and their daughter, Cecelia (1876-1943) was born in Glasgow and, as Cissie Loftus, became famous as a Music Hall performer and mimic as well as a "serious" actress

Professional life: She first appeared at Brown's Royal Music Hall in Dunlop Street in 1874, and in London at the Oxford in 1877. As "The Sarah Bernhardt of the Music Halls", she rose to become a leading national star, touring abroad to the USA and South Africa and by the late 1890s commanding £100 a week, a huge sum for the time.

Remembered for: Marie Loftus was considered to be the first true female variety star: i.e. the first woman to top Music Hall bills nationwide.

Interesting fact: In Glasgow her local background made her enormously popular. While appearing at the Britannia, Trongate, in 1894 she left an order with a local bootmaker for 150 pairs of strong boots to be distributed by the priest among the poorest children of the parish. A famously buxom pantomime principal boy, she appeared at the Theatre Royal Glasgow as Robinson Crusoe in 1889 and 1900, and as Sindbad the Sailor in 1895.

Name: Matilda Alice Powles, adopted at the age of 11, the stage name Vesta Tilley.

Lived: 1864 – 1952

Personal life: Husband – Walter de Frece

Professional life: She was a star in both Britain and the United States for over thirty years.

Remembered for: Being probably the most famous male impersonator of her era

Interesting facts: Her father, known as Harry Ball, was a comedy actor, songwriter, and music hall chairman; with his encouragement, Tilley first appeared on stage at the age of three and a half. At the age of six she did her first role in male clothing, billed as "The Pocket Sims Reeves", a reference to the then-famous opera singer.

Name: Nellie Wallace – one of the first female 'Dames'.

Lived: 1870 – 1948

Personal Life: None recorded, she worked until she died at the age of 78.

Professional life: British Music Hall star, actress, comedienne, dancer and songwriter who became one of the most famous and best loved Music Hall performers.

Remembered for: She became known as "The Essence of Eccentricity". She dressed in ultra-tight skirts (so tight in fact, that she would lie down on the stage and shuffle back and forth on her back to pick up whatever she had contrived to drop), her hat sported a lone daisy, feather or a fish bone and once even a lit candle (supposedly, so she could see where she was going and where she had been.

Interesting facts: Not a naturally pretty woman, a reviewer noted her 'grotesque get-up', which started the audience laughing the moment she appeared on stage; her cleverness, vivacity and facial expressions were second to none. Her main character was a frustrated spinster singing ribald songs

Name: Vesta Victoria
Lived: 1873 – 1951
Personal life: William Herbert Henry Terry 1912–1926 (divorced) one daughter. Frederick Wallace McAvoy;1897 (divorced) one daughter.
Professional life: Although born in Leeds, Yorkshire, Vesta adopted a Cockney persona on stage. She began her career as a small child appearing with her father.
Remembered for: Singing 'Daddy wouldn't buy me a bow-wow'
Interesting facts: Vesta's comic laments delivered in deadpan style were as popular in the United States as in her homeland and she toured and recorded in America in 1907, where she was one of the most highly paid vaudeville stars. Between appearances, she lived on a houseboat, moored near Hampton Court.

Name: Florrie Forde. Born in Fitzroy, near Melbourne, Australia.
Lived: 1875 – 1940
Personal life: On 2 January 1893 in Sydney, she married Walter Emanuel Bew, a 31-year-old police constable. On 22 November 1905 at the register office, Paddington, London, as Flora Augusta Flanagan, spinster, she married Laurence Barnett (d.1934), an art dealer.
Professional life: In 1897, she made her first appearances in London at three music halls – the South London Palace, the Pavilion and the Oxford – all in the course of one evening!
Remembered for: Famous songs such as; 'She's a Lassie from Lancashire', 'Goodbyee', 'It's a long way to Tipperary', and 'Pack up your troubles in your old kit bag', 'Down at the Old Bull and Bush' (Songs which I sang in Brussels with the English Comedy Club of Brussels Music Hall Concerts!).
Interesting facts: At the age of sixteen she ran away from home to appear on the Sydney Music Hall stage then came to London at the age of 21. She became an immediate star, making the first

of her many sound recordings in 1903 and making 700 individual recordings by 1936. One of the greatest stars of the early 20th Century Music Hall.

Name: Cissie Loftus – a brilliant mimic and daughter of Music Hall star Marie Loftus and performer Ben Brown.

Lived: 1876 – 1943

Personal life: When she was seventeen, she eloped with Justin Huntley McCarthy. The groom was twice as old as the bride. The marriage failed, and the couple divorced. In 1908, she married Alonzo Higbee Waterman, an American doctor. By 1914, both her marriage and health were in a perilous state, and an acrimonious divorce ensued in 1920. Her health and the premature birth of their son, Peter, had made her increasingly dependent on alcohol and painkillers.

Professional life: She was a Scottish actress, singer, mimic, vaudevillian and Music Hall performer in the late 19th and early 20th centuries, who performed extensively in both Britain and America.

Remembered for: Loftus became an international favourite in Vaudeville along with Vesta Tilley and Harry Lauder.

Interesting facts: In November 1922, she was arrested for possession of morphine and atropine. Her fellow actress, Eva Moore bailed her for a surety of £100, and she was put on probation for twelve months at the Great Marlborough Street Magistrates Court. In 1923, she left Great Britain for good, and sailed to New York City to return to Broadway and pursue a career in Hollywood.

Name: Sophie Tucker

Lived: 1887 – 1966 (Born in the Ukraine. Died in New York.)

Personal life: Sophie Tucker was married three times, each marriage lasting no longer than five years. Her first marriage was to Louis Tuck, a local beer cart driver, with whom she eloped in 1903. The marriage produced Tucker's only child, a son named Albert. In 1906 the couple separated and Tucker left Albert with her sister, supporting them with money from her singing jobs in New York. They were legally divorced in May 1913.Tucker's second and third marriages were to Frank Westphal (1917–1920), her accompanist, and Al Lackey (1928–1934), her manager. Both ended in divorce and produced no children.

Professional life: Her career encompassed the genres of Music Halls, vaudeville, variety and television. She appeared with the Ziegfeld Follies at the age of 22 and on the Ed Sullivan Show on October 3, 1965. The color broadcast was her last television appearance, where she performed "Give My Regards To Broadway", "Louise" and her signature "Some Of These Days".

Remembered for: She was called 'The last of the Red Hot Mamas', as her hearty sexual appetite was a frequent subject of her songs, unusual for female performers of the day after the decline of vaudeville (Lydia Nicole, present day L.A. comic has also performed in a Latino troupe called the Red Hot Spicy Mamitas)

Interesting facts: Tucker was born Sonya Kalish (Russian Соня Калиш) to a Jewish family en route to America from Tulchyn, Vinnytsia Region, Russian Empire. The family appropriated the last name Abuza, settled in Hartford, Connecticut, and opened a restaurant. At a young age she sang in the restaurant for money.

Name: Ida Barr.
Lived: 1884 – 1967
Personal life: Husband – Singer Gus Harries. Left him for success in America. No children.
Professional life: She was Britain's red-headed premier singer of rag time melodies
Remembered for: She made 'Oh You Beautiful Doll', a song she

brought back with her from one of her trips to America, very popular.

Interesting facts: She was born Maud Barlow. On making her Music Hall Debut in 1897 she adopted the name of Maude Laverne and then eleven years later, Ida Barr. She was nearly six foot tall.

Name: Gertie Gitana
Lived: 1889 – 1957
Personal life: Husband – Actor and singer Don Ross.
Professional life: Gitana is Spanish for (female) 'Gipsy' and she was a member of Tomlinson's 'Royal Gipsy Children' at the age of four. On account of her petite form and supposed gipsy origins, she was sometimes billed as 'The Staffordshire Cinderella'. She made her professional debut in 1896 at the age of seven on the stage of The Tivoli in Barrow on Furnes and worked very successfully until 1950.
Remembered for: Her most famous song was 'Nellie Dean'
Interesting facts: During the 1914 – 1918 war she was the Forces' sweetheart and often entertained the war wounded in hospitals. In her prime she was reputed to have earned in excess of £100 per week and her name was always sufficient to ensure a full house. In cockney rhyming slang Gertie Gitana means a banana.

The list is not an extensive one and these are just the ones that have been carefully noted by historians, there must have been many others lost to the passage of time. All tremendous role models, these women performed in difficult environments, which were loud, noisy and sometimes laced with violence, in places that were not always safe or suitable for women, still no change there either – society has always been a dangerous place for women and the dangers are different between the sexes. They shunned the popular opinions of the time, which saw performance as an unsuitable life for 'nice' girls, (more of that word later) a thought still shared by some nice respectable Muslim families including two of my Interviewees, Shazia Mirza, and pioneering Indian comic Aditi Mittal, whose parents would have much preferred had they studied to be doctors. These pioneers showed great determination in achieving success in work that, less than a hundred years previously they would not even have been permitted to see, let alone take part in. Through their songs and patter with the audience they spoke about the experiences other women had in their lives and had the gumption to be outspoken enough to silence their critics. They sowed the seeds for comic potential for future generations of women who saw their performances as giving them the permission to be funny in their own lives. Irene Handl, the prolific character actress, who I loved as a child, used to go every Friday to the Met in the Edgeware Road. "The comedians used to go three times. I think they had a cab waiting for them, and then they went from one to the other. Marie Lloyd did, I remember". How much of Marie's magic rubbed off on to her it is hard to say, but the fact that there were feisty females on stage may have showed Irene that it was at least possible to be female and funny.

By the time of Marie's death in 1922 the Music Halls were also drawing their last breaths. By the time the First World War had broken out in 1914, a new form of entertainment called 'Revue' was making its mark. The War actually gave some women opportunities that they had never previously had, in 1915 women were actively recruited for 'men's jobs' in the Armament Factories because of their absence at the Front. Revue was a mixture of Music Hall and spectacular musical comedies, with artists appearing throughout the different scenes instead of in or as just one act. The plots were often a little on the shaky side as was the scenery and the flimsy costumes were often more resilient than the songs themselves. 'Revue' competed with 'Variety', which was, in essence, good all round family entertainment and the Music Hall performers were assimilated into these two mediums. However, other pressures had also come to threaten the existence of the Music Halls.

'The Empire' showed the first 'cinematograph' in 1896 and presented a 'bioscope' of news and events as a 'turn' at the end of an evening's performance. These became immensely popular and soon spread to other halls. However, this was vision with no sound. Another invention that was proving to be very popular by 1896 was Edison's 'phonograph'. The artistes themselves were recording their songs on wax cylinders. These could be bought for home use if one could afford them or you could go to converted shops to listen to these 'records' by way of a hand-operated machine. This somehow miraculously transformed the grooves in the surface of the black disc into the voice of their favourite singer through a pair of stethoscope like earpieces. What would they have made of present day C.D.'s, DVD's, mp3's and itunes I wonder? These two curious novelties the cinematograph and the phonograph would eventually combine to become the cinema, which would in time close hundreds of Music Halls throughout Britain.

New opportunities to perform

These new inventions also brought about the creation of radio and also, in time, film and television. Those who were successful in Variety and Music Hall found new opportunities with the BBC who, until the late 1930s, found all the talent for their radio programmes there. Another woman who has had little recognition for creating a style, much copied, was Florence Desmond. Impersonating famous characters was not new but what Florence Desmond did was to get those characters to interact with each other at once. The characters she created for a BBC broadcast in films. The 'Carry On' films became an instant British tradition with their saucy goings on. Women's roles in them were mostly either the terrifying 'Matron' type or the cheeky 'floozy' personified by the ultimate 'Carry On' girl, Barbara Windsor. Barbara Windsor won her first role in 'The Belles of St. Trinians, (Comic and Interviewee Kate Smurthwaite's favourite film) then appeared in 'Carry On Spying', 'Carry On Doctor' which led to her legendary moment as a sixteen year old bra-flying schoolgirl in 'Carry On Camping'. Born Barbara Ann Deeks in 1937 she was the daughter of a dressmaker and a bus driver. A very bright child, her mother spent a fortune on elocution lessons for her daughter, an ironic touch considering her iconic role for several years as common as muck Peggy in the ever-popular BBC soap *Eastenders*. She started her career as a singer and comic in West end night-clubs. Having to deal with heckling audiences gave her the confidence to embark on a very colourful career and life which included nine 'Carry On' films and dalliances with renowned members of London's Gangland. In 1970 she landed the role of Music Hall legend Marie Lloyd in the musical-biopic 'Sing A Little Song'.

June Whitfield – The Comic's Tart

June Whitfield is another comic actress still very popular with present day audiences. Another 'Carry On' veteran, she appeared with Leslie Phillip's girlfriend in *Carry On Nurse*, she was the

1932, called 'The Hollywood Party' were very popular at that time and included such well known movie stars as Greta Garbo, Gracie Fields and Marlene Dietrich.

Florence Desmond (1905 – 1993) – The first person to create interacting impersonated characters

Variety perpetuated the tradition established in the Music Halls of lambasting and humiliating women, with its grotesque stereotypes of harridans and sexually desperate old maids. It made domestic violence a humorous topic in much the same way that the Punch and Judy shows did, and warned women of the dangers of climbing out of society's straightjackets of behaviour "permitted" to the 'gentler' sex. What is curious though is that the very establishment that tried to correct women's behaviour was also giving them opportunities to become comics. This would be similar to all those present day trashy magazines (I won't mention names unless I get sued – but the guilty ones know who they are!!!) that put down and humiliate women when they become successful by telling them they are too old, too fat or too ugly in a way which men are never described. Some, though not many of them, became popular on radio. The stars were mostly men like Harry Tate, Max Miller, Billy Bennett and Will Hay, who performed a refined and toned-down version of their stage shows.

One woman who found success on the radio was Mabel

Constanduros with 'The Bugginses'. Radio led to work in the new world of opportunities in the cinema and she appeared in 'Caravan' in 1946 with future smoothy radio D.J. Pete Murray or Peter Murray as he was then known. Pete Murray was quite prolific as a D.J. when I was a teenager, but I didn't realise that he had already been around for numerous years by then. Mabel Constanduros also appeared in the comedy film 'Easy Money' with a very young Petula Clark in 1948. I also have a tenuous link with Petula Clark, having recorded her famous single 'Downtown' in Belgium in the early eighties. It got into the Belgian charts no less, and was often played as wallpaper music in very large supermarkets so you could say it was a success of sorts! I also sang it on a Belgian television programme appearing alongside Kim Wilde. If I'd known at the time she was going to become such a 'Gardening Guru', I'd have asked her for tips on how to put together a good compost rather than how to conquer the British charts! It is also now my party piece at karaoke clubs. However, bad records aside, comedy on the radio consisted entirely of 'acts' running in the same way as a Music Hall bill, with a new line up every week. There were no situation comedies or sketch-shows as we know them now.

The very first ground-breaking radio 'situation-comedy' show was 'Band Waggon' which was first broadcast on 5th January 1938. It starred Arthur Askey and Richard Murdoch and became a series of regular hour-long programmes. It gained popularity with the introduction of the regular theme of Askey and Murdoch living in a flat in Broadcasting House. This led in time to the radio comedy series 'It's that man again', or ITMA as it became known. During the war it was recorded in Bangor north Wales (where my Mother grew up, and she recently told me that she had met one of the stars, Tommy Handley, at that time) where we see the character 'Mrs. Mopp' and to the concept of radio comedy series. Hattie Jacques(1924-1980) was also to find success in ITMA as

Sophie Tuckshop, the greedy schoolgirl. Jacques trained as hairdresser and worked during the war initially as a nurse and th as an arc-welder. She became famous in the Music Halls, wh fed performers into radio, television and cinema. Jacques bec the terrifying Matron of so many 'Carry On' films, appearin a total of fourteen. She married John Le Mesurier who found later in life in 'Dad's Army'. Radio gave new opportuni performers such as, Jon Pertwee, Robert Beatty, Carole Ca Watson, Benny Hill, Patricia Hayes, Benny Lee and comic talent of Harry Secombe, in a series of sketch 'Listen my children' which ran successfully for ten week This format of sketches with a satirical edge became a h and led to a new series but with a change of nam Division-Some Vulgar Fractions'. The original cast re with the addition of Margaret Lindsay, Bruce Belf who were later to make a huge impression on the in Britain, Peter Sellers and Michael Bentine. The Pat Dixon and the scriptwriters Frank Muir and with additional material by Paul Dehn. Out of th in Jimmy Grafton's pub, legend has it, came t with Spike Milligan, Peter Sellers, Harry Seco Bentine, which was to influence and have an i comics and the comedic audience in Britain f the twentieth century. I can vaguely rememb shrill 'He's fallen in the water!' coming out o radio.

Radio, cinema and television gave new performers who had worked their appre Halls, Revue and Variety giving them a than treading the boards. Joan Sims, (1 character actress, made her debut on sta Theatre in 'Intimacy at Eight' and v serving female member of the 'Carry

June W
present
briefly a

Jun

frigid wife Evelyn Blunt in *Carry On Abroad*, the women's lib protestor Councillor Prodworthy in *Carry On Girls* and in full circle, Leslie Phillips' wife as the Queen of Spain in the *Carry On Columbus*. Roy Hudd calls her 'The Comic's Tart' because 'she has served them all' and she had been the object or 'butt' of more male humour than probably any other actress. She has worked with Ted Ray, Eric Morecambe, Arthur Askey, Bob Monkhouse, Peter Sellers, Sid James, Tommy Cooper, Spike Milligan, Tony Hancock – the list goes on! (It's curious that Roy Hudd links sex and comedy and in fact her subservient position within that comedy). She has even 'served' Roy Hudd himself in 'The News Huddlines' radio's longest running comedy show and from 'Eth' of the 'Glums' in radio's 'Take it from here' (1953 – 1960) then progressed to television series such as 'Beggar my Neighbour' (1966), 'Happy Ever After' (1974 –79) 'Terry and June' (1979-87) to 'Ab Fab' (1992 –96, 2001, 2003, Christmas Special 2011 & 2012, Olympic Special 2012, Film 2016), she seems never to have been off our screens and in 2015 played Granny Wallon in a BBC One adaptation of Laurie Lee's classic novel *Cider with Rosie* and in her nineties seems to still have a thirst for performance unquenched by her advancing years. Lacking the self-confidence to take herself seriously as an actress, she developed a kind of aversion to heavy serious roles so concentrated on comedy which came naturally to her. She figured that since the audience was going to laugh at her anyway, she might as well appear in things that were intended to be funny.

Another great comic character actress who made an appearance in 'Carry on Constable' was Irene Handl, (1902 – 1987) who as we saw previously, was influenced greatly by the unique Marie Lloyd, who she saw perform on a regular basis. She did not start acting until she was forty years old. Forty is not particularly old by today's standards but my impression of the characters she portrayed was that she was always 'old'. She was able to carve out a very successful career for herself and was frequently cast as a charlady or maid and brought her own brand of eccentricity to the mother, cook and landlady roles that she portrayed. She appeared in 'The Belles of St. Trinians' 1954 with Barbara Windsor. This was intriguingly about rebellious girls in a single-sex school, which as you continue to read, played an important role in the lives of many of my Interviewees.

Beryl Reid (Born June 17th 1920 – 13th October 1996) also made an appearance in this film, before leading on to further acclaim in 'The Killing of Sister George' in 1968. She served her apprenticeship in Variety, and started out in 1936 as an impressionist with the North Regional Follies in Bridlington, which gave her the opportunity to develop her talents as a stand-up comic who did not necessarily have to hide behind greasepaint and costume to make the audience laugh. One of her most popular characters was Marlene, who had a very thick Brumie twang, the first time the Birmingham accent was used in a comic fashion. In 1977 she was appearing in Edward Albee's 'Counting the Ways' at the National Theatre. At one point all the actors had to improvise out of character, for five minutes – a very frightening experience but one that held no terrors for Beryl Reid who was able to draw on her experience doing stand-up to overcome this difficulty.

Joyce Grenfell (1910 – 1979) – The First FSUC

'St Trinians' also gave Joyce Grenfell 'The Queen of Comic Monologues' an opportunity to show off her comic talents in the character of Ruba Gates. Born Joyce Phipps in 1910, her mother was Nora Longhorne, the sister of Nancy Astor, the first woman to enter the House of Commons in 1919. A year previously some women, but not all, were given the vote. Nancy Astor was herself quite a witty woman and was attributed with these classic quotes by Michelle Lovric in 'Women's Wicked Wit'. 'I married beneath me, all women do'. And 'In passing, also, I would like to say that the first time Adam had a chance, he laid the blame on a woman'. Joyce Grenfell was regarded as the first FSUC and was famous for her unique monologues, so much so, that in a series of stamps commissioned by the Royal Mail in 1998 to commemorate five of Britain's greatest comedians, Joyce was the only woman to appear along with Eric Morecambe, Tommy Cooper, Les Dawson and Peter Cook. Joyce was a former journalist and radio critic and made her mark with her first solo show 'Joyce Grenfell requests the pleasure'. She toured the world with her very special brand of comedy based as it was on a 'Women's Institute Member'. Her biggest fan ever, apart from Victoria Wood, is Kate Smurthwaite who is quickly becoming recognised as an impressive political pundit. When Victoria Wood was six, her family went to see Joyce Grenfell at the theatre. Seeing a woman on the stage on her own, that zest for nuance; those things stayed with Victoria always. 'Joyce Grenfell could cut people down to size, but from a moral point of view, not just to be horrible'. After the show, the older Wood sisters went backstage but Joyce Grenfell made a point of going outside the theatre to find the youngest. 'Hello Vicky,' she said. 'Like a fairy godmother coming to bestow the magic gift of the monologue'. Meera Syal, who starred in the pioneering Asian comedy 'Goodness Gracious Me', was also strongly influenced by Joyce Grenfell.

From Hattie Jacques, who still had a foothold in the Music Halls days, to June Whitfield in the very popular twenty first century series of 'Absolutely Fabulous', the links connecting funny women overlap through the medium of radio, television and film and weave back and fro through revue and variety. Those women who made a mark in radio, television and cinema deserve a book in their own right. There is only enough space here to look at how serving the apprenticeship of live performance led to their success in the intimacy of our own homes or on the big screen. There are other funny women that can only briefly be named but whose contributions should not be underestimated such as Mollie Sugden and her phenomenal success in the cult classic 'Are you being served', which also introduced the comic talents of the late Wendy Richard as a perky underwear sales assistant. Unfortunately, we no longer had an opportunity to see her comic talents as she was for the latter part of her career stuck in a rut as the miserable and world weary Pauline in Eastenders. That's what happens when you go from selling to washing undies!

Other women who have made me laugh throughout the years have been Dora Bryan, Wendy Craig in Carla Lane's 'Butterflies', Sheila Hancock (in the 60's classic 'The Rag Trade'), Prunela Scales, Maureen Lipman, Penelope Keith in both 'The Good Life' and 'To the Manor born', the totally original Patricia Routledge as 'Hyacinth Bucket, the legendary Marti Caine, Pam Ferris and on to Caroline Aherne, Sue Johnston and Lis Smith in 'The Royle Family' and the present day glut of funny women such as Sarah Millican, Ronni Ancona, Nina Conti, Catherine Tate, Miranda Hart, Tamsin Greig, Lucy Porter, Meera Syal, Shappi Khorsandi, Susan Calman, Bridget Christie et al.

And how could we talk about funny women without including Janet Brown, one of the very first female impersonators, whose faultlessly daring impersonations of Margaret Thatcher, nearly amounted to treason! She was not the first female impersonator. That honour, as previously mentioned, belonged to Cissie Loftus who premiered her impersonations of both male and female Music Hall stars and Florence Desmond, with her interacting characters in 'The Hollywood Party' in 1932. The 'interacting characters' became much copied by later comics but it was a women who came up with the idea initially. Only a few years later, the late great Janet Brown who was born in 1924, was setting out on her career in theatre and radio.

Rumour has it that she was the only woman present in the back room of Jimmy Grafton's pub when the 'Goons' came together for the first time, but as far as history is concerned, she doesn't get a mention. Her popularity did not wane over the years and she was seen as Rhona Cameron's mother in 'Rhona' (2000) Rhona Cameron had a great deal of media coverage because of her feisty views on the first 'I'm a celebrity, get me out of here'. She is a Scottish FSUC who was quite prolific and considered one of the best on the circuit at one time and she appeared in 'Rhona' with Mel Giedroyc, one half of the comedy duo Mel and Sue. Cambridge educated Sue Perkins and Mel Giedrock have had a lot of success on our screens in various capacities in recent years, and who seems to have become incredibly passionate about cakes (that hot bed of radical feminism!!) of late.

But before we can start looking at the careers of FSUCs of the twenty first century such as Rhona Cameron, there is a chapter of comic history, which more than anything, has changed the way women exist within comedy and that is the 'Alternative Comedy' scene, which was starting to bubble away in the background at the same time as television was giving three minutes of potential stardom for new 'hopefuls'.

Marti Caine (1945-95) Sheffield born and bred winner of 'New Faces' started doing stand-up comedy in 1964 around the Northern clubs. Her apprenticeship of seventeen years, again look and learn all you X Factor Wannabees, paid off eventually with her own series and also to 'poacher turned gamekeeper' as presenter of 'New Faces'. The working-men's clubs were perhaps the direct descendants of the Music Halls, full of boozy, belligerent, testosterone charged 'he men' (such as Bernard Manning) a difficult place for anyone to perform. For an attractive woman being funny in clubs, where she would often be the only woman present, it must have been a scary proposition. She broke that holy of holy taboos 'women's plumbing' and was the first to mention 'sanitary towels' on stage, something that was considered incredibly shocking at that time. 'New Faces' gave her an opportunity to develop her talents.

Other performers who came to prominence as a result of this programme, between the years of 1973 and 1978, were Lenny Henry, Jim Davidson and Victoria Wood. Victoria Wood was described on a *South Bank Show* as Britain's first FSUC, obviously they hadn't heard of Joyce Grenfell! Although she does do 'stand-up', I see Victoria Wood more as an all-round entertainer in the old 'Variety' mould, but her contribution to the history of female comics should never ever be underestimated. She has been a Role Model to aspiring female comics more than any other woman I would imagine, and I would have loved to meet and interview her. However, she is notoriously reclusive and private and although I did try really very, very hard to garner an interview it was not to be.

'Alternative' to what?

The 'Alternative' comics of the early 1980s established a different form of comedy, and rejected the easy techniques of racist or sexist jokes on which so many mainstream television and club comics relied. Women started making the jokes rather than being on the receiving end of the jokes as had happened so often in the past. One of the reasons the alternative circuit in Britain developed was because of an explosion of 'stand-up' comedy in the United States, accompanying the expansion of the cable televisions during the 1980s. 'Stand-up' comedy was cheap to produce and helped feed cable television's enormous appetite for programming, a bit like that great bastion of masculinity, Dave on our televisions nowadays. One of my American Interviewees, Betsy Salkind, was part of this revolution and said that all the 'politics' was taken out of the comedy at that time so that it would appeal to a wide audience, so it must have been pretty bland work. Budd and Silverman had opened the New York Improvisation Centre in

1963. Mitzi Shore opened the Los Angeles Comedy Store on Sunset Boulevard in 1972 and as a result both places began to create 'stars', who then fed into the cable television network. The list of those who have performed at the Comedy Story Sunset is totally epic. It is the bedrock of America comedy, and I have been very fortunate to speak to several female comics who have performed there on a regular basis. This is where I met resident pianist and M.C. Jeff Scott on a visit to L.A. in 2004 and we have kept in touch ever since. He introduced me to the fabulous Tanyalee Davis.

Don Ward (who I met when I was alongside him and others on a panel of people talking about women in comedy at the end of the nineties on the Esther Rantzen programme) and Peter Rosengard, who had visited Mitzi Shore's Los Angeles club, the Original Comedy Store, established 'The Comedy Store' in London in 1979. Don did say at one point that I could launch the book there but changed his mind when he heard I'd actually written it!! Initially there was no great difference in the sort of jokes told and many of the performers belonged to the old 'sexist, racist' school of the working-men's clubs. However, there were many other changes happening in the performance world that coincided with the opening of the London Comedy Store. Some of the left wing 'Fringe' theatre groups which had developed in the sixties and seventies such as '7.84', 'CAST' and 'Belts and Braces' had their grants cut by a severe funding crisis in the Arts Council. These had used the techniques from variety and 'stand-up' in a very political way.

Change is often brought about by adversity – the old 'sink or swim' solution and many of the performers from the now defunct companies, who had no venues to perform in, saw an opportunity to have a direct political influence on a new audience who were being drawn to the Comedy Store. We may very well see the next few years having a similar effect as present day Arts Council grants lurch from financial crisis to financial crisis, although new environments such as Twitter and Facebook are becoming powerful platforms for vast political activity. (Change.org, sumofus.org, and the radical People's Assembly are all using the web to campaign for change). Barack Obama was probably the first politician to spot the potential of web-based forums and Marmite Man and comic Russel Brand (You either love him or hate him!!) has around twelve million Twitter followers so let's not underestimate the power of persuasion that this can create. However, back in 1979, the year Margaret Thatcher became Britain's first woman Prime Minister and the year I went to live in Belgium, the instantaneous magic of the world-wide-web which connects people on a global level in a matter of split seconds, had not yet entered the collective consciousness.

I remember the excitement of going to 'Maison Blanche' (The White House) in Brussels where women were talking about 'Feminism'. Germaine Greer's book *The Female Eunuch*, had been published less than ten years previously and she came into my life and became a huge influence on my thinking. Little did I know at that time that I was going to spend the evening in her company half a lifetime away. There were anti-nuclear marches, pro-abortion rallies (The Abortion Bill had only been made law twelve years previously in 1967) and an excitement in the air that things were going to change for the better for women. The sexual liberation of women had begun in 1963 with the pill being available on the NHS. Women could have it all! (Or so it seemed at the time – we now know better!) The civil rights movement of the sixties which included this new wave of feminism which had begun with the Suffragettes, Martin Luther King, Black Power demonstrations, all led to a situation where sexist and racist humour was no longer politically correct or tolerated. Both the London Comedy Store and the Comic Strip, another London club, saw an opportunity to develop a new exciting form of comedy and were keen to show that they weren't being sexist – by giving women an opportunity to perform. Women started to explore new work possibilities and change their expectations and limitations like no other time in history.

Present day FSUCs are a result of all the changes brought about by the women I have spoken about in this chapter. Some of the women that I have interviewed have performed at the London Comedy Store, a venue that gave rise to the present day network of well over a 120 comedy clubs on the circuit in London alone.

The London Comedy Store was the starting point for French and Saunders and also gave valuable opportunities to women such as my Interviewees Helen Lederer and Hattie Hayridge. This apprenticeship eventually led to the very successful television career that French and Saunders have enjoyed. They are often quoted as positive Role Models for women, and in fact I feel that they and the late Victoria Wood were the Holy Trinity of British female comedy, but the foxy ferret couldn't persuade them either to grant me an interview, even though I pleaded and offered to ply them with Cadwalader's wonderful ice-cream when they came to Cardiff to do a gig a few years ago.

Many of the 'Comic Strip' producers were women and they put French and Saunders in a very fortunate position as they were willing for them not just to write and perform but to help direct and edit, to discuss lighting and to become knowledgeable about many technical aspects which would prove invaluable to them in their knowledge of television. French and Saunders created their highly successful series 'Girls on Top' simply because there were no major parts for women in 'The Young Ones'. Their very successful partnership continued to evolve and develop into their own brand of humour in the highly successful series 'French and Saunders', which led on to their own personal television projects such as 'Absolutely Fabulous' and 'The Vicar of Dibley', all still rolled out regularly at Christmas. I was very aware of the achievements of women like Victoria Wood and French and Saunders when I started doing comic roles. They were an inspiration and tremendous Role Models. But for all the advancements women have had in their lives, it's still a man's world and women need strong, powerful and inspirational female Role Models who can inspire us with their stories of how they overcame the challenges in their lives.

It is interesting to note that many of the women and men who appear on our televisions nowadays on panel shows and in the lucrative world of voice-overs worked their apprenticeships in front of heckling, jeering audiences in live venues. It seems that if you can cope with 'Foul-mouthed from Fishguard', 'Drunkard from Derby' and 'Legless from Lancashire' you are more than capable of dealing with a nice man behind a camera, a P.A. who doesn't swear at you and a 'Green Room' full of those dainty little 'dim sum' things from Marks and Spencer's. Nevertheless, men still outnumber women heavily in television comedies, and most definitely so in comedy panel shows.

There used to be very few women in key managerial positions in television. In 1994, around the time when I started my initial research which has led to this book, research carried out by the 50/50 Campaign reported that all prime time commissioning editors of the BBC and the ITV Network Centre were men. There has been a dramatic improvement since that time with the post of first 'Controller of Comedy ITV Network' having being held by Sioned Wiliam appointed June 1999, a Welsh woman, who became the BBC Radio 4 and Radio 4 Extra 'Commissioning Editor for Comedy' in 2015 and another of my Interviewees.

By 2004, only ten years later, women were starting to make their presence felt in powerful positions that determined the images, the programmes and the content of those programmes: Danielle Lux, Formerly Channel 4 Head of Entertainment (Director of Celador Productions) and Jane Lush, BBC Controller of Entertainment Commissioning and Caroline Raphael, Commissioning Editor of Drama and Comedy at Radio 4, as well as Claudia Rosencrantz, ITV's Controller of Entertainment.

Other powerful women in television at the beginning of the twenty first century have included Lorraine Heggessey and Jane Root, Controllers of BBC1 and BBC2 respectively. At one time, no comedy show (or any other programme for that matter) could be commissioned without their consent.

Ten years later, it seems we still have a long way to go, but at least powerful women are being acknowledged and benchmarked. In 1987 in a book called 'The Joke's on us' by Morwenna Banks and Amanda Swift, both Jenny Lecoat and Sheila Hancock said that the situation for women in comedy would not improve until there were more women in positions of authority who would fight for other women's right to prove that they could do the job and do it well. With Sioned Wiliam leading the way by having the very first panel show entirely populated by women ('The Unbelievable Truth' September the 14th 2015 !!!!!!) and others finally in a position only dreamt of nearly thirty years ago, when Banks & Swift's book was published in 1987, the next few years may prove to be very exciting indeed for female comics.

However, television and live performance are two very different mediums in which to perform. Television is more contrived, rehearsed and controlled. Audiences are generally well behaved, sober and vetted beforehand. Live performance, on the other hand, is not as controlled, and as such is far more spontaneous, subject to change, fluid and, at times, physically dangerous.

All the women that I have interviewed for 'Stand Up & Sock it to them Sisters! Funny, Feisty Females', have thrown caution to the winds and taken on board all the men and women who might cross their paths and upset all their calculations.

In the Appendix I have noted a gallop of significant events that have created women's comic history as well as the legislation that has really impacted greatly on women's lives enabling us to have lives with a great deal more choice and variety than the Suffrajests had. In this chapter we have rediscovered women's comic history and made nonsense of those claims that women aren't funny – you have the evidence in front of your eyes and I, like a modern Miss Marple, have revealed some of the attributes that women have had to develop in what was considered men's territory. And we have seen the sort of woman who embarked on this path – gutsy, scary, determined, talented women undeterred by criticism and opposition. Was it the same sort of woman who would want to embark on such a dangerous trajectory in the twenty first century? Was there a blueprint or an identikit model for an aspiring FSUC? There must be something special, odd or unusual about them for them to want to succeed in this medium. Mrs. Worthington was told not to put her daughters on the stage as it was incredibly unstable – the future that was, not the stage!

This was what I found out next and I am delighted to be able to share my new knowledge that I unearthed with you. 'Stand Up & Sock it to them Sisters! Funny, Feisty Females' is chock a block full of women you may have heard of and others who you will most certainly not have but will want to know more about, all brilliant Role Models who have achieved success in what has been considered in the past very much a man's world. Find out how all these fabulously determined and genuinely funny women overcame all the challenges they encountered in this macho world, which according to many men, women don't belong in.

I hope you have enjoyed reading about some of these seriously funny women whose history has become mostly invisible. I wanted to collate them to make some meaningful discoveries about women's histories which have for the most part faded into time and which have been conveniently forgotten when men assert that women aren't funny. But let me now introduce you to my present day FSUCs. They form a vast variety of individuals at various points in their careers, from Britain, America, Canada, Australia, New Zealand, Japan, India, Greece and South Africa. Some are or were at the top of their game such as Joan Rivers (RIP) and Amy Schumer and others taking the mike for their first few years in the comedy profession such as Holly Burn and Fern Brady. I have interviewed some utterly AMAZING FSUCs. My opinion is, if you can make it as a female comic you can make it in any profession, so if you want to be inspired, if you want to find some new Role Models who you can pattern your life upon, carry on reading!

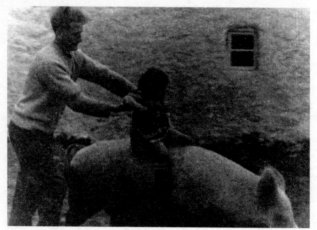

Daddy's girl and sow jockey, circa 1960

CHAPTER 2

MRS. WORTHINGTON'S
DAUGHTERS

In which I hunt for the blueprint of a female comic

Here comes trouble! –
Were you like that as a kid?

My first years as a child were spent in Anglesey North Wales, the second daughter in a family of four. I was a tomboy and loved riding my Dad's sows (as I wasn't allowed to have a horse!) and climbing trees. I adored farming with my Dad, potching about on the moor which surrounded the little smallholding where we lived and being naughty. My big issue as a kid was wandering off in County Shows and other events looking for adventures and my parents would be frantic because I was nowhere to be found and they would often have to respond to megaphone messages asking for them to come and pick me up. I was very sociable as far as I can remember and couldn't speak any word of English until I was about seven. We moved to Pembrokeshire, West Wales as a family for my Dad's new job as a Farm Manager for Kraft, when I was about that age and quickly had to learn to speak English and also adopt a new Welsh dialect. As I had a musical ear and had been performing in singing competitions since I was about four, I had no problem in mimicking the locals. I'm a right polly parrot. My Mother was a teacher and a lot of focus was put on the importance of education. Shortly after we arrived in Pembrokeshire my Dad was made redundant from his new job, last in, first out and since that time he did contract milking and some small scale farming of sheep and cattle. My Mother eventually returned to teaching and became the Head Teacher of a small Primary School. Growing up in West Wales, I was a bit of a 'horsey woman', as my Mother called them and my playground was the rocks and cliffs around me – we lived about a mile from the sea and I am convinced that my rugged environment made me pretty fearless in all of the circumstances where I have found myself in my life.

In this Chapter, I wanted to find out how the environments where my Interviewees had grown up had formed them so I looked at their backgrounds; were they stable or traumatic, what class did they feel they belonged to, their schooling, what sort of affinity did they have with masculine and feminine energies, were they tomboys or Daddy's girls and how did they get on in school? Did they rebel against societal structures placed upon them as young women, where we label babies from the moment they are born with the colours of oppression – pink for girls – blue for boys so that even from the first weeks of their life, expectations of their potential and life direction are being made in the blink of an eye? Were they channelled into stereotypical straightjackets of future careers or was there some element of choice present? What differences were present when people grew up in different circumstances?

You will notice that from now on a lot of these women are talking about themselves, and saying 'I', something a lot of women are generally not really comfortable in doing. I think it's a great idea myself and women should get into it more often. It is empowering as it draws attention to us and our egos, so therefore, the more we do it the better we will feel about ourselves, something which I'm all for! As my Interviewees came from all sorts of places world-wide, their stories were quite a bit more exotic than mine was, growing up in Fishguard, West Wales as I did.

Spring Day

"My real name is and was Spring Day and I moved a lot as a kid. I'm originally from a city called Graine Valley which is a suburb of Kansas City, America, but I live in Bunkyoky, Tokyo, Japan. My class had 100 people in it and we learnt Japanese. I had a twin sister who died at birth – this has informed my comedy a lot. The only thing we did together as a family was to laugh a lot (at Roseanne) and I was funny to get attention from my parents. My entire family squints a lot but we have no Japanese blood at all – I come from a long line of squinty people. Japan was as far away from my family as I could get. I have cerebral palsy, which leaves me with very little control of my right side – it destroyed my violin career! My talents were few. I have a slightly drunk look but I'm very good at hiding it. I sometimes address it in my comedy. Oddly enough, the drunker the audience is the more the audience pick up on it. Comedy protected me. My family pushed me into independence. I don't do drink. My parents were hippies and did a lot of drugs (too many to talk about) They destroyed my father's confidence. I made friends through being funny because of moving about and having a disability. The hell of dealing with unpleasant kids who are merciless – it prepares you for life."

Adrienne Truscott

"I moved around a lot as a kid because my Mum came from England and my Dad's from the States and I lived in England but moved back because my Mum had become too Americanised, and lived in lots of places around the States."

Shazia Mirza

"I was born in Birmingham at the Queen Elizabeth Hospital on 3rd October 1975. My parents are from Pakistan and I am Asian but I would say I was British/Asian. My mother is a teacher and my father is a businessman. Not a very good one. Well he owned loads of cash-and-carries. Then he went bankrupt. And now he still works in setting up Asian businesses as he's obviously such a tremendous role model! I remember sitting round with the family at Eid (The birth of the Holy Prophet Muhammad) the aunties and uncles asking the children what they wanted to be when they grew up and all the kids saying they wanted to be doctors. They were only six or seven, but they were really well trained. I said I wanted to be an actress. Afterwards, my mother told me I was on no account to show them up again. My father was a Saddam Hussein-type figure. He told me 'The only way you're going to get a decent husband is if you're in a decent profession yourself'. So I became a stand-up comedian! My Mother trained as a teacher in Pakistan but she didn't teach until after she'd had us children. I was second in the family and I've got three brothers and one sister. So there's five of us altogether. I had a beard when I was a kid. I know this is funny but it's also true. Obviously being an Asian girl, my dad was very hairy and I had loads of hair as a child. Like when I was thirteen, I had a beard, a moustache, and sideburns. I was just really hairy, I had really hairy arms and I wasn't very attractive. I used to get taunted; I used to get called 'the hairy monster', and 'the werewolf' and stuff like that. Also occasionally, because I was brought up in a very white area, I got racist comments occasionally but not that often."

Tanyalee Davis

"I am a Canadian citizen living in the United States, but I work all over the world. I am a Caucasian little person (3ft 6inches tall) with an Ukrainian, Scottish, Welsh, Irish heritage. My father was an airline pilot for Air Canada and my mother was a teacher. I have one sister who is 5 years younger than me. My parents got divorced shortly after my sister was born. I had never heard the term midget before until I started school. I would come home crying thinking that the other kids were swearing at me. I endured teasing and bullying throughout my school years but I figured those taunts and or comebacks from taunts would come in handy when I was older and I drew on them when I first started writing my comedy."

JoJo Smith

"I was born in 1961 in Ziebruken, Germany. My Dad was in the Canadian Air force, although he's British. I lived in Canada until the age of nine. I used to love writing when I was a kid and used to make my own fashion magazine."

Donna McPhail

"I was born in Bangor, North Wales in 1962, when my father was based in RAF Valley, Anglesey with sea rescue and mountain rescue helicopters. I had quite a transient childhood, every two years there was a different posting, mostly in East Anglia because that's where the RAF bases were. I have an older brother. My mother became a businesswoman in the 70s. She worked away during the week and came back at the weekends. She was quite ambitious and driven and good at it."

Jo Caulfield

"I was born in 1963 in St. Asaph, North Wales. My Mum and Dad were from Ireland and my father was a teacher in the Forces. He was stationed in Wales when I was born. My older brother and sister were both born in Northern Ireland. I was the Welsh one in the family. My Mum was also a teacher – English and French."

Jenny Éclair

"I was born in 1960 in Kuala Lumpur, Malaysia on a British army base but no one spoke anything but English. My father was a Major in the British army. My mother never did a day's work in her life – the idle bitch! I'd say I was Northern Middle Class, which is quite different to Southern Middle Class – it's a little bit more straight-laced, it's not sort of Bohemian. I'm now lapsed middle-class I suppose, I'm a bit downwardly mobile. I had an exceptionally happy childhood, all Enid Blyton, Arthur Ransom and Swallows and Amazons. We didn't have television in Germany so I didn't see any telly until I was about 8 or 9 and so we did a lot of puppet shows. We had a lot of creative time. We had a big cellar and we'd do shows down the cellar, me and my sister and we'd have a laugh. My parents never pressurised me to go into an academic direction. I've got a brother and a sister who were both barristers. I think my mother thought that if she interfered any more, I would end up in the gutter with needles sticking out of my arm. I'm the second child. I think it was harder for my sister. I got away with a lot more. I had a lot of charm. My sister's cleverer than me but I had a lot more native cunning."

Jojo Sutherland

"My father was Major Douglas Sutherland and I grew up in a castle in Scotland. I was the youngest of seven and I was a complete show off and was never shocked by anything. I had four older brothers."

Nina Wadia

"I was born in Bombay, India. My Mum used to be an accountant, with British Airways, and my Dad used to be an Air Steward for Air India, and then when we went to Hong Kong he became a hotel manager. We moved to Hong Kong when I was eleven, so my teenage years were growing up in Hong Kong, then I moved to England when I was nineteen. We travelled an awful lot. That was probably the best experience that I had, our summer holidays were always in a different country, and that made me very, very cosmopolitan at a very young age."

Sindhu Vee

"I grew up mostly in India (except from age 5-10 when our family was in the Philippines where my Father (a Senior Civil Servant) was posted). My parents are both professionals and I have an elder sister who lives in the US. I had a stammer until I was twenty two and people used to make fun of me because of it."

Aditi Mittal

"My Mum died when I was very young. My mother's sister was one of the very first Production Managers in India. My Dad is hilarious and we have a tradition of cracking jokes at Grandma. My father is very paternalistic and hates me drinking after my act."

Julia Morris

"I was born in 1968 in Sydney Australia. I'm Australian middle class. My father manages a race club for racing horses. Mum used to be a medical secretary now she's chief of home care maintenance she reckons, that's housewife to you and me. I have a brother who's eighteen months older than me."

Kitty Flanagan

"My father, John Flanagan is an Australian author, best known for the 'Ranger's Apprentice' novel series. My Mother was a stay at home Mum. My sister is Penny Flanagan and she's a singer/songwriter/musician and novelist, and she appears in my shows and writes and performs original music. I also have a brother, who is a chef and runs a coffee shop in the snowfields of Japan. I'm the eldest in my family but I was always the youngest and very much the smallest in my class."

Michele A'Court

"Levin, North Island New Zealand, where I was born and grew up was and is your typical small (pop. 18,000) town – voted

"NZ's Most Boring Town" a couple of years ago. Boys played rugby, girls got pregnant at 14. Let's say it wasn't a town that celebrated people who were a bit different. I'm Pakeha (which means non-Maori NZer) We're vague about which class we belong to in NZ (all our ancestors came here to build a "class-less" society) but in England I guess my family would be firmly middle-class. My parents owned a clothing manufacturing business while I was growing up, employing a lot of local women. Politically, they're conservative, but have a strong social conscience. I joined a communist party when I was a teenager and I'm still a pinko-leftie. I have a brother who is 2 years older. We've always been very close. I just didn't fit in when was a kid– didn't play sport, loved theatre, debating… all the geeky things. I was younger and much smaller than all the kids in my class. You could either do netball or drama – not both, and it wasn't a difficult choice for me to make. It was kind of me and the asthmatic boys in the debating team. My mother was a professional actor before she had kids, and did oodles of amateur theatre when I was growing up, so my own stage career started when I was about 6, with drama and dance."

June Whitfield

"My mother was a very keen amateur actress but she wasn't allowed to do it so it was always made very easy for me, I went to dancing lessons and did competitions and all those things and then I went to Drama School. When I started out my career I didn't particularly intend to go into comedy, but right from the time I was a child and went to dancing school I was always given the comedy roles and I think I sort of grew into it."

Mandy Knight

"I was born in Lewisham, London in 1969. I'm English. My father was a train driver who died when I was five. My Mother abandoned me when I was six, she couldn't cope. I had five sets of foster families, the last of which I went to when I was about fifteen. I regard my last set of foster parents as my parents. My adoptive father dropped dead on my first day of filming on Jo Brand's series. He worked in a three – piece-suite factory and my mother used to say 'If you wanted to go into upholstery there wouldn't be a problem'. I have one real brother, who I don't see and a half sister who has the same mother but a different father. Therefore in a way I am both the youngest and the oldest."

Hattie Hayridge aka Holly Red Dwarf

"I was born in Greater London. I'd say I was from a white British working class background. My Father was an agricultural labourer, my Mother a pub cleaner. I was an only child. I was very short sighted so I was never very good at sports. I was teased because of that rather than heavily bullied".

Maureen Younger

"My family is Scottish but I grew up in London and have an international background. I have done lots of different jobs".

Lorraine Benloss

"I was born in Forest Gate, East London in 1972. I call myself Black British and Afro Caribbean. Both my parents were born in Jamaica, they came to Britain in search of streets of gold, they were cheated, as were so many people. I remember my Dad telling me that some guy came up to him and wanted to touch him to see if his skin would come off, then they were going to come over to try to get his skin off with bleach. I was aware of racism when I grew up but I never actually had it really bad – I remember one kid calling me 'black jack' but that's all really. My father worked with British Rail, my mother was a cleaner in the caring profession. I'm the third of four children, three girls and a boy. I was quite fat in Primary School and I got bullied a lot. I suppose I started messing about in class to combat the bullying.

Angie Le Mar

"I was born in October '65, in Lewisham, London. I'm working class and Black/British. My father ran his own electrical company and my mother did the accounts. I have four older brothers. I went to a mixed sex Primary School where there was a wonderful teacher, Mr Wood, he believed in me and he let me join the drama group when I was really too young, that's all I lived for, Drama Club. I was diagnosed as having dyslexia after I left school, but I didn't know it at the time. I used to crack jokes to get chucked out of the classroom just in case I had to read, which was my biggest worry. I knew I was funny because that would always get me out of trouble. When I found out that I was dyslexic, I just thought 'Oh no, it's labelled 'disability' – I am unable to do something that everybody else can do', and I never told anyone

Josie Taylor

"I'm Welsh, I come from Cardiff originally. My Mum has had three husbands so I've got several half brothers and sisters. My Mum is an award winning film and television editor and my Dad is well known in Wales as a television and radio presenter, producer and performer. Both of my parents have exposed me to the landscape of 'entertainment' through their work… so they're both to blame for my current passion for theatre/performance/ comedy. I had dyslexia when I was growing up but it was never a problem, if anything, the fact that I am, probably explains why I've always been attracted to 'practical' classes and have ended up working in the sphere of Drama. I think it also colours the way in which I approach the creative process in that my brain works a bit differently!!"

Nadia Kamil

"I was born in Swansea to a Welsh mother and an Iraqi father. When my mother died, I was 6yrs old, and my father panicked and took us to live in the Middle East. So I'd describe my background as Wales meets Middle East with very questionable parenting decisions. I describe myself as being blessed with a talent for phlegmy languages."

Bethan Roberts

"I'm from a working class Welsh background. I was awkward as a kid and had a face to be a comedian. I was always the joker in the group but was never one of the 'populars'. I have one older sister who went to Oxford. There's three years difference. I always performed and started dancing at the age of six in Bridgend."

Helen Lederer

"I was born in Llandovery, Wales, in the late fifties. My father was Czechoslovakian, my mother was from the Isle of White. He came over as a boy because of the war, they met after the war in some club for graduates. They were both quite bohemian. My father was a civil engineer and he worked with Harold Wilson. My Dad was a Jew, we were different, he was a non-believer and I had a Czechoslovakian Grandmother. I have a sister. I had asthma so when I was between ten and twelve I had these cortisone injections that made me even more sort of moon faced. I was short and my memory is that I was very fat at that time. The Jew thing wasn't an issue in that it was more to do with being foreign, having a foreign background. When I was ten I just wanted to perform. I wrote a play at school and it was great, but I wasn't encouraged to go to Drama School and I just lost confidence."

Sara Sugarman

"Growing up in North Wales as a Jew I definitely felt like an outsider looking in, but I feel that that was a blessing and a lot of people who end up in the entertainment business feel like an outsider for one reason or another."

Wendy Kane

"I was born at the end of 1959 and I'm annoyed because I wasn't a child of the sixties! I was very insecure as a child. My mother was a single parent, which was a big deal in the early sixties, and had three jobs. She was determined to be both mother and father to me. We lived in a council estate area in Swansea. My roots are very much working class, there was great poverty but also a good community spirit."

Joanna Quinn – Oscar Nominated Cartoonist

"I was born in Birmingham. England on February 1962 and grew up in London, although I've lived in Wales since the eighties. *(I call her an Irish Cockney Brum!)* My career in art began at the age of 4 when I was a runner up in a Kelloggs cornflakes colouring in competition and won a kite. By the age of 6 I had covered every inch of my bedroom with drawings. In fact, I wanted to draw so much that I momentarily dreamed of going to prison because I liked the idea of being left alone to draw. I was an obsessive drawer. My Dad was Irish and a great story-teller."

Brenda Gilhooly aka Gayle Tuesday

"I was born in 1963 in Epsom, Surrey. My parents were both Irish from Sligo. I grew up in England but all my relatives were Irish. There are lots of Irish, Catholics and Jewish people in comedy. When you see the world at a slight angle as an outsider you see things in a more quirky way, it's a good place to observe things – you have a slightly more distant perspective than the average person. Having a family that's not the nationality of the country you're living in probably makes you see things differently. I was brought up as a Catholic. My parents were both psychiatric nurses, and definitely working class. I went to state schools. I'm the youngest of three, I have a sister who is ten years older and a brother who's three and a half years older. I was quite popular at school. Until I was sixteen I went to a mixed school."

Jo Enright

"I was born in Aston in Birmingham and we moved a few miles up the road to Erdington when I was six years old and that's where I spent the whole of my childhood. My father did factory and bar work. I went to a mixed Junior and Infants school and a mixed Comprehensive school, both Catholic, both in Birmingham. We would generally go to Ireland for a couple of weeks most years as that's where both my parents came from originally."

Nuala McKeever

"I was born in 1964 in Belfast. I'm Irish and middle class. My father was a retail chemist, my mother a supply teacher. I'm the youngest of seven. I have two sisters and four brothers. I grew up in West Belfast, during the troubles. The closest I came to the troubles was when I was seven years old. I was with my mother in a restaurant. It was blown up shortly afterwards. The café was called the Abercorn, it was infamous, many people were killed. It was packed on a Saturday. I am a 'Child of the Troubles' – that is, I didn't know anything but violence. I'm not Republican, more middle class. We lived in a totally Nationalist area.

Rhona Cameron

"I'm an only child. I was brought up in Musselburugh, on the East Coast of Scotland, outside of Edinburgh, a fishing town. I entertained the family, I put on little shows that I would write.

I'd make up plays when I was about ten years old for the kids and I was always writing poems and songs. I was a bit of a show off. It was just natural for me to entertain people".

Jane Mackay – Owner of 'The Stand Comedy Club', Edinburgh, Glasgow

"I was born in 1957, Inverness. I'm Scottish (7/8th Mackay) Since I am from the remotest fastnesses of the Scottish Highlands my class origins would most properly be described as peasant. My father was a policeman, latterly sergeant at early retirement, then a crofter and light-house-keeper, so we moved round Sutherland (the mainland's most northerly county) where I was brought up. My mother worked from time to time as a hotel cook and did dressmaking from home. Latterly, she also worked the croft. I have two younger brothers. In small communities your father being the policeman set you apart, you lived in the police house – with an office and cell as an extension – and with the district nurse on the other side. I went to four primary schools because my father moved and, at times, my mother was very ill."

Nina Conti

"I was born in London in 1975. I'm half Scottish/half Italian but I grew up in London. I'm an only child. My father's an actor (Tom Conti) and my Mum was an actor as well until she had me and then she was a full-time mother, but now she is a writer. I always grew up with creativity around me. I was quite precocious up to the age of about eight. I wanted to sing in assembles and we were always putting on shows in the back garden for friends of my parents. But then suddenly I became really shy and I still am in a way and I am not really sure what changed. Maybe it was changing schools. I remember singing once when I was a kid and being mocked. It really hurt and embarrassed me; I don't really sing any more now."

Rosie Kane – Scottish FSUC & Former Member of the Scottish Parliament

"I'm Scottish, have four brothers and I'm the only girl. My pram had a fire engine and a tomahawk in it. I used to play footy and climbed trees a lot as a kid. I had a great relationship with my Dad. The tree climbing came in handy when I was a motorway protestor. There was always lots of humour in our house, I always competed with my brothers to be the funniest and I always won. We were always very silly."

Jo Brand

"I'm the middle child with a brother either side of me. I'm English, and I was born in 1957. My father used to be an engineer. My Mum went to train as a social worker at the age of 32, when I was thirteen. She was bored and frustrated being a housewife. Although my mother had quite strong feminist views, somehow I always ended up being the one who got the tea ready, so I suppose I was the most resentful of the three of us. I suppose my childhood was quite idyllic because we moved out of London from the age of about five and from then until the age of fourteen we lived in little country villages. The best time for me was when we lived in a house virtually in the middle of nowhere. My Dad had a big field with a pond in it and loads of woods around it which was ideal for kids, we used to jump in the pond and at one point a woman put three donkeys in the field, so we had one each and we used to do donkey rodeos with them. My mother loved reading *Little Women*, the character of Jo was one that she admired immensely, she was courageous and independent. Jo cut off her hair and sold it to a hairdresser to make wigs. She kept the money and sent it to help with the war effort. I was named after her. I would say that I'm probably middle class, my Mum and Dad, their first house was in South London with an outside toilet and no money, but by the time I got to the age of twelve they had a nice house and a good income and two cars. So within the space of ten years they had become middle class. So I would never say I was working class."

Oddly enough, I was also influenced by that story of Jo in Little Women, *although not in such an altruistic way as her. I'd had about six inches of long brown hair cut off. It was neatly tied with a red ribbon. I remember going to all the local hairdressers in Fishguard and Goodwick (the nearest towns) when I was about eleven years old and asking them if they wanted to buy my hair to make wigs. My motive was not to help the war effort but more likely some dosh to help buy some Christmas presents!!!! I was quite entrepreneurial at a very young age!*

Holly Burn aka Kirst Kay
"I'm the only child of a Mother who used to be a lawyer and who is now a businesswoman and a father who is a property developer."

Maria Kempinska – Owner of Jongleurs Comedy Chain
"My parents were Polish immigrants. My mother was a mathematician and my father was a barrister in Poland but when we came here we lived in a council house and there were six of us in one room. I've got nothing to lose apart from my chains. I'm an outsider and I just got on with it."

Thenjiwe Tay Moseley
"I'm from Durban in South Africa. I went to school during apartheid. I grew up in a township Kwamashu, which was one of the most violent townships. Between 1976 and the early 90s there was a lot of violence and the house was burnt down. I was born out of wedlock – my parents were very, very young. I was brought up by my maternal Grandmother and Grandfather, who was very funny. I grew up laughing at everything even the violence."

Lydia Nicole

"I come from New York, my mother was from Saint Thomas in the Caribbean and she was a prostitute and my father came from Puerto Rico and he was a pimp, the same as Richard Prior's parents. As a kid, I didn't know any different, that was normal there. I was raised by a pack of comedians, I grew up in Harlem, New York, I'm Latino and I had lots of siblings, I had five brothers and four sisters and I grew up amongst junkies and drug-dealers, I'd talk to everyone. My brothers taught me how to fight and I modelled myself more on males when I was growing up, they were independent, they had voices, girls didn't and I wanted my voice to be heard and be seen. I was always competing with the boys. I wanted to be visible. I always had a big mouth as a kid and was very opinionated, had to have my say and was very inquisitive."

Cynthia Levin

"I grew up in Chicago and had a very bad childhood. I was neglected as a child. There were three girls in my family. My whole way of survival was by being funny and if it weren't for comedy I'd be dead by now. I was very, very, good at finding the funny in all the awfulness. I started doing stand-up in 1989. Stand-up saved my life. When I opened my mouth – I felt I'd found my soul."

Lynn Ruth Miller

"I was born in Toledo, Ohio and was very unloved as a child. I'm from an upper-middle class family and never knew what poverty was growing up, although now I live at half the poverty level of $14,000 but I'm really happy. I had no idea when I was growing up that stand-up could be a career choice."

Joan Rivers

"I was born Joan Alexandra Molinsky, June 8, 1933 in Brooklyn, New York I had a good relationship with my father and I was the youngest of two sisters."

Rhonda Hansome

"I grew up in Brooklyn, New York and used to make up characters and silly songs. I wanted to have recognition from my father, who was not in my life from an early age. He was mostly invisible. My mother was a seamstress and had aspirations for the stage. I trained as an actress, had a degree in performing arts and studied with a negro ensemble."

Nancy Witter

"I grew up in an affluent area of New York (Garden City) I was the sixth kid out of seven. My mom died at age 49 of cancer when I was 15. She left behind 7 kids. Bill O 'Connor (my step mother Phyllis' husband) also died of cancer at age 51 leaving 9 kids so when Mrs. O'Connor came into my Dad's life, I became one of sixteen kids. Comedy came easy for me because I was always trying to get attention, and it was hard to stand out when there were so many of us."

Susie Felber

"I was born in 1971 on Long Island, NY. I'm an US citizen. Jewish. Father originally from Germany, mother from NYC. Class? I got no class. I have two older brothers and a supportive Dad. I was bullied and teased. For my odd clothes, for my freaky curly hair, for not caring what people thought, for enjoying the company of boys more than girls. The middle brother is also a comedy writer/performer. My eldest brother now runs an arts festival he started in Hell's Kitchen, NYC. My father was an orphan of the Holocaust who left Germany for France and came to this country on a philanthropist ship for children. He worked his way through medical school doing menial jobs and eventually became a haematologist. Mom had a few jobs but after she had three children, she went back to writing, selling opinion pieces to newspapers. Then became a published novelist. She's called Edith Layton and she wrote numerous books. I had an Uncle who wrote for Sid Ceaser but he didn't help me in any way. My Aunt played a role in the 'Honeymooners' so I come from a very creative background."

Cathy Ladman

"I grew up and went to school in New York I'm the youngest of three daughters. I was very independent and quite street smart. I made a decision at the age of thirteen that I was going to be a stand-up comic. I had the lead role in 'Once upon a mattress'.

Betsy Salkind

"I'm American, have three brothers and they were my play mates. I was a scrawny looking kid. My whole family was very clever and sarcastic. I learnt to swear from my mother."

Lynn Marie Hulsman

"I'm American and I'm the youngest of five, I have four older brothers."

Dana Goldberg

"I was born on April 12th in Albuquerque, New Mexico, USA. I was raised by a wild pack of Jews. I'm the baby of the family. My older brother is gay, older sister is straight. My brother and I talk a lot about it, as long as she acts gay in public we don't have a problem with it. It's not her fault, she was born that way. My kindergarten teacher told my mother I was the funniest five year old she had ever met. I don't know who my competition was, but

I'll accept the title graciously. When I was a child and people asked me what I wanted to be when I grow up my answer was always "a stand-up" comedian. I was a tomboy growing up and I was definitely teased. I went on the university to get my degree in Physical Education. I'm a lesbian, it's the law!!."

Katerina Vrana

"I grew up in Athens, Greece. My father is now retired, but he worked in film production and had a distribution company, Mum was and still is in antiques. I have a close relationship with both my parents. I have two brothers and I'm the eldest. My younger brother is 17 and he is the source of a lot of my new material."

Such a huge variety of stories with some similarities and patterns. There are a lot of transient childhoods, the Forces seems to appear quite often, perhaps they should put that in their adverts, 'Join the Army – see the world and learn to become a stand-up comic!' (certainly beats killing and maiming innocent civilians!) Moving about a bit whether it was with the Forces like Jo Caulfield, Donna McPhail and JoJo Sutherland or because your Daddy was a flight attendant, like Nina Wadia, actor like Nina Conti, hippy like Spring Day or contract milker seemed to give the funny bone a bit of a growth spurt and enabled lots of my Interviewees to make friends quickly in new environments.

Landing in a new environment and having to make new friends and break into their already established cliques can be a scary enough prospect for an adult let alone a child. For these girls they realised that comedy had a power which enabled them to integrate quickly into otherwise difficult environments.

Most of these seem to be from working class or middle class backgrounds. There are very few comics who ever come from the upper classes. Comedy seems to need to be able to challenge or overcome something, and what have the rich got to overcome other than horrendous death duties, terminal stupidity, goofy teeth, receding chins and serious inbreeding issues! I do feel by now that we need to have a new way of describing our backgrounds as 'working class' is a bizarre concept – most of us work if we can find work, as is the concept of the colour of a collar. I would suggest we define ourselves as privileged, not privileged or under privileged and highly privileged as those who would previously have been defined as 'middle-class' will often have to have some help from Family Credit for them to be able to survive these days (until the Conservatives get rid of it any minute now!!!) Women from a 'working-class' background tend to have a lot more barriers to overcome than 'middle-class' women to make a success of their lives. Poverty is probably the biggest barrier for anyone, be they male or female, but comedy is extremely accessible for those from impoverished backgrounds, be that Harlem or a council house in Swansea.

There seems to be a lot of 'youngest or only children' who become comics for some strange reason, maybe because they are indulged by their parents and allowed to get away with behaviour that their older siblings were not. Parents tend to be stricter with older children and more relaxed by the time the youngest turns up. Or it could be that they found by being funny they were able to offer something their other siblings couldn't – something guaranteed to give positive feedback rather than having the screaming abdabs in the aisles of Tesco which probably would have resulted in some not so positive feedback like a clip around the ear hole and no sweeties till Friday! Victoria Wood was also a youngest child. Joan Rivers was the youngest of two sisters.

Being 'other' or 'different' whether that is by being Jewish, Asian, Irish or Black/British, second generation settlers, or being of a different religion allowed some of these women to have a very different 'take' or perspective and viewpoint on the world, their experiences are entirely different to the cultural 'norm' that the vast majority of British people encounter. Things which if examined from an outside perspective may be very funny. The things that make us different are many, but ethnicity, nationality, religion, sexuality and culture are some of the liquorice allsorts that make up the rich sweetie bag of life in Britain.

Both Angie le Mar and Josie Taylor must have felt very isolated by their dyslexia but they were actually in very good company. There are countless individuals who have overcome this condition to make a huge contribution in so many different fields. Performers like Eddie Izzard, Fred Astaire, River Pheonix, Harrison Ford, Tom Cruise, Robin Williams and Susan Hampshire. Artists such as Leonardo da Vinci and Pablo Picasso and photographers like David Bailey and Ansel Adams. Ann Bancroft didn't let it get in her way as she trekked her way across the Arctic. It never stopped Richard Branson from establishing Virgin Enterprises and making his millions. That Grande Dame of the Murder Mystery, Agatha Christie had dyslexia as did Hans Christian Andersen. It also seems to have been more or less a pre – requisite to being a great political leader as Winston Churchill, Thomas Jefferson, John F. Kennedy, Nelson Rockerfeller, Woodrow Wilson and George Washington all had symptoms of dyslexia or related learning problems. And, according to a report conducted by Tulip Financial Research, (Gill Daily Mail, 06/10/03) here comes the best news of all for those with dyslexia, self-made millionaires are four times more likely to suffer from dyslexia than the rest of the population.

Another aspect of this comedy power was as a defence mechanism. Quite a few were insulted, humiliated, taunted or bullied about being 'different', or 'other', whether that was; having a moustache and a beard like Shazia Mirzah, being tall and gangly like Ronni Ancona and Sindhu Vee, being a 'midget' like Tanyalee Davis or short like Michele A'Court and Kitty Flanagan, being short sighted like Hattie Hayridge, being fat like Lorraine Benloss and Helen Lederer, having dyslexia like Angie le Mar and Josie Taylor, having a physical disability like Spring Day and Liz Carr. a Canadian accent like Jo Jo Smith, or being fostered like Mandy Knight or adopted like Rhona Cameron.

I was taunted in school for having prominent ears and a flat chest (the words 'Dumbo' and 'pancake' still fill me with dread, and they were the kindest words hurled in my direction!) In the same way an oyster needs sand to grow a pearl, this seems to have given some an 'edge', a defence mechanism to cope with which gave them the positive feedback of laughter. Far better to learn to deflect some negative comments with a joke than to end up in a morgue as so many innocent victims have done – unable to cope with the taunts and vitriol hurled in their direction.

In that respect, the power of comedy can literally save someone life. With the recent growth of on-line bullying which has prompted many young people to kill themselves, perhaps comedy should be taught to girls in the same way that they encourage self – defence classes to be taught. Kids can be awfully cruel. Who ever said 'Sticks and stones may break my bones but words will never harm me' was talking through their belly-button. There's nothing more dangerous than a well-aimed caustic comment to puncture and totally deflate one's self-confidence. Humour is a very portable weapon enjoyed by both sexes and doesn't show up on airport x-ray machines (not like vibrators – try explaining that to a Customs and Excise Officer when there's a huge queue lining up behind you!)

Many of these comics just realised at an early age that performing was in their blood, an instinctive feeling that here was something magical that they could tap into at will and which generated happiness. Perhaps having a successful performer in the family, as did Nina Conti, Kitti Flanagan, Annie Witter, Ashley Storrie and Josie Taylor etc. was an inspiration to follow in their footsteps.

Some had great Role Model Mothers who either worked as teachers, as mine did, that good old 'stand-by' rather than 'stand-up' profession for women or as a social worker, an accountant, in business or as a writer. Perhaps inspired by the fact their mothers managed to achieve a role outside of the home, like comics Annie Witter and Ashley Storrie who followed in their Mothers comic footsteps, or even rejecting their mother's decision to stay at home, like Jenny Éclair, they decided that the world was their oyster and that they would tread a different path.

However, their relationships with the men in their formative lives may have been even more influential than that with the female relationships. I used to have really fabulous constructive discussions with my father about every subject under the sun and loved helping him out dehorning cattle, delousing sheep, stacking bales, washing out churns and clearing up slurry – yep that's how I grew up folks. Wasn't I the lucky one! Talk about a rich childhood!

Male influence: But my heart belongs to Daddy?
Brenda Gilhooly

"I was very close to my father. My Dad never treated me particularly in a girly way. He really treated me as a person. He valued my opinions and we had an equal exchange of opinions. My Mum was very calm. My Dad was quite a character, and quite opinionated, he used to shout at the telly at people he didn't like, he had a real sort of Irish temper and I've got that and we used to disagree and argue about things all the time. But I used to give as good as I got."

Angie le Mar

"My Father has always been there for me and that has given me great confidence. It's been a very direct love from a male figure, and my four brothers, supporting me".

Cathy Ladman

"My Dad was a very funny guy with a very dry sense of humour. I was really close to him but he was quite an angry person."

Hattie Hayridge aka Holly Red Dwarf

"I had a close relationship with my father. He'd take me up the football. I used to have dolls and train sets and cars. So I had a mixture of being treated like a boy and a girl."

Sarah Sugarman

"I was very lucky, I had a very kind nurturing father but it made me a tomboy, because the female when I was growing up in the seventies, the women had to clean the table, do the dishes, clean the house and be there to support the men who brought in the money. So I became a tomboy."

Donna McPhail

"My Mum worked away during the week in the seventies so I was alone with my father and brother."

Tanyalee Davis

"I remember my father making up "Henry the Chicken" stories where he always gets chased by Colonel Saunders. His stories always made me laugh. I always loved to laugh but I wasn't really a class joker … until University."

Josie Taylor

"My Dad had his own t.v. and radio shows when I was growing up. He's immensely talented and has written songs and a musical. He used to encourage me to perform and also used to do recordings of me singing songs including some of his."

Nina Conti

"I travelled around a lot because of my father's work as an actor I had a lot of holidays abroad when I was young which I loved. I used to go and visit him because he'd sometimes spend long times abroad, about three or four months at a time, so my Mum would take me out and we'd hang around the film set and I'd play cards with the make-up lady. I met David Bowie and I became completely infatuated with him, I suppose I was about seven or something. When I was still thinking about being an actress, my Dad didn't put me off. He was just encouraging. Although he probably secretly was frightened because it's such an unreliable profession. He swallowed that, I think he was frightened to damage my confidence."

He would have known that not only was the acting profession a highly precarious one with a very high percentage of actors not working in their chosen profession at any time but one in which there was far less work available for women. (Skillset Census 2001)

Twelve years on, the most recent SkillSet Census (2013) shows very little improvement in career possibilities for women in the creative industries where the invisibility of good roles becomes quite obvious once you hit your early to mid-thirties, with most work for women still in the 'traditional' creative areas. And it's even worse for women from Black and Minority Ethnic backgrounds.

"As in previous years, representation of women is highest in certain occupations: in particular make-up and hairdressing (81%) and costume and wardrobe (73%). Women also make up over half (56%) of the legal workforce, distribution, sales and marketing (55%), business management (52%) and broadcast management (51%) but less than half in every other occupational group."

Nina Conti, and several of the above women I spoke to, was very fortunate in having a father who had such faith in them. All their fathers valued them very much as individuals and treated them in a similar way to that which a boy would have been treated. However, some had very difficult or absent relationships with their fathers.

Jenny Éclair

"My father was away an awful lot of the time in Arabia from the time I was two to four. I remember seeing this man in a train station and making lots of 'Oh it's so great to see you Dad' noises and thinking 'Who the fuck's this', I didn't have a clue who he was."

Lorraine Benloss

"My father's a very quiet man, very much into himself, very secretive, he's almost pretty much invisible. My Dad didn't really feature much in my life really."

Wendy Kane

"I never knew my father. He left when I was 5 years old. My mother gave me this in built fear, 'If you see this man, run away and scream'. He wasn't a violent person at all, he was just an alcoholic really. He spent a lot of time in prison for petty crime. I look like my father. I thought for years that he didn't care. He died when I was seventeen. I can't get those years back."

Rhona Cameron

"My Dad died when I was fourteen. I was devastated."

Mandy Knight

"Who says lightning doesn't strike twice. My real father died when I was five. My adoptive father dropped dead on the first day of filming on Jo Brand's series when I was in my twenties."

Jo Brand

"I wasn't very sympathetic to my father who was emotionally fairly distant to me when he and my Mother were splitting up. (Well whose Dad wasn't?) They weren't very well suited and we were lucky it happened later rather than sooner so at least we were able to have a happy childhood."

Likewise, not having a father who was very present in your life gives you an opportunity to define yourself as you see fit or even allow the masculine side of the female psyche to develop.

I was very lucky that my Dad allowed me to tag along with him on his farming duties up until the age of about thirteen or so but then he seemed to disappear from my life as he started working longer and longer hours. However, by that time, I already loved the outdoor life and being independent. Being a tomboy was a thoroughly liberating experience for me. Whilst my sister was indoors making clothes for her dollies and learning to cook with my mother, I was out climbing trees, racing my bike, building dams in the river, trekking up the mountain and imagining I was 'Bodicea the Warrior Queen', breaking in and riding my horse bare backed – it seemed a darn sight more rewarding than making cup-cakes and frilly doll's knickers. Tomboys have a much more varied and interesting, mostly outdoor in the elements experience than that generally encouraged for girls, and you are more in touch with your physicality which in itself develops confidence. Was embracing ones physicality anything to do with comedy?

Mucking about with the boys

Sara Sugarman

"I was naturally good at football and sports and school captain in so many things and they stopped me from being in the football team and had to do girls sports and the girls thing was so awful and I'm so glad now to see that football is now much more co-ed, well it is in America."

Julia Morris

"I was a little bit of a tomboy until about ten when somebody said to me 'When are you going to grow some boobs?', and I was so distressed that I went home to Mum and had a good cry and never really went back to 'the corner of death' which is where we used to ride our bikes."

Susie Felber

"Was I a tomboy? Yes. One who enjoyed dresses and pink, but yes."

We start out in this country segregated from birth by the colours blue and pink which not only is a marker for our gender but also to a great extent how we are viewed not only by ourselves but also by society. This 'colour identification' doesn't happen at all on the continent – it would be interesting to see whether this has an effect on how babies and toddlers are perceived by a society which doesn't have an immediate 'marker' as to expected behaviour. By the time we reach school we have already been categorised into expectations of 'boy' and 'girl' behaviours which not only affect what we do but how we do it and the language that we use to carry out those activities are also vastly different, something I will look at in greater detail later on.

Stereotyping is a way of controlling behaviour and it starts as soon as babies are colour coded at birth and continues into the life, sport and job choices that we make. There's an expression, I think it may have been Confucius (but don't quote me – it could have been my Granny or Miss Thomas down the shop or I might have read it in a book!) 'Give me a child until he is seven and I will make of him a man!' meaning that who we are and what we will become is actually more or less worked out before we have even lost our front two teeth. (No mention of 'she' or 'woman' either, just to make us girls feel really wanted eh?)

The books that you can buy for girls these days aren't as bad as they used to be, e.g. 'Pirate Girl' by Cornelia Funke, but saying that, there was always 'Girls at Mallory Towers' (Enid Blyton) and 'Swallows and Amazons'(Arthur Ransome) where the girls were, for the most part, pretty assertive and just as mischievous as the boys. But cast your minds back to the 'John and Jane' books and what did we have? John would be underneath a bonnet up to his earlobes in grease and oil and Jane would be standing daintily, hands behind her back observing him. I could never ever relate to that model at all – why wasn't she getting stuck in and getting her hands dirty? Those 'girly pressures', though maybe not as bad as they used to be, are still ever present. You just have to look at any toy magazines (apart from 'The 'Early

*Learning Centre – God bless them!') and there they are, the girls
playing with their Tiny Tears and Barbie dolls and the boys with their
fearsome destructive implements and they're all gendered.*

Jo Brand

"I was devoted to my elder brother Billy. I wasn't allowed to have
a Sindy doll or a Jackie magazine so I was able to escape all those
'girly' pressures. I had to watch football with my brothers,
although I was a traditional little girl."

Nuala McKeever

"I would say it's the male part of me that wants to do stand up,
the boy, the tomboy. I had 4 brothers. My 2 sisters were away by
the time I was growing up, they were like 12 years older than me.
So I was mostly brought up with four brothers and me.

Angie Le Mar

"Having four older brothers was great. They were very protective;
but they treated me as one of them. I always felt that I was a
tomboy anyway; when they said 'we', I always felt a part of the
'we'. If there were any rocks in the area or any gang fights or
anything I wasn't about to run home, I was in there with them.
We were always very close and we still are. With four older
brothers – men have never ever intimidated me. Never."

*Being valued obviously had a great effect on Angie Le Mar's self-
confidence and self-worth. Western civilisation has moved on quite
dramatically over the last fifty years or so in women's pursuit of
equality but in other cultures world-wide, women are still very much
second class citizens, and therefore not as valued. For example, in
India since the availability of scanning in pregnancy, girls were
routinely aborted. In China, which up until the end of October 2015,
had a one child per family policy, boys have been more valued than*

girls and new-born baby girls were often left on mountain-side's to die or dumped in orphanages. Women in Saudi Arabia, regardless of age, are required to have a male guardian and for the most part are not permitted to drive a car.

We have traditionally taught girls subservient habits and boys to exercise dominance. However a lot of Westernised women have become more assertive and have been rejecting this position of inferiority in recent times. Some Westernised men are turning towards Asian women and mail-order brides in order to find women who are not challenging or who have their own minds, although that is one huge stereotype which Bombay born Nina Wadia does not adhere to.

Nina Wadia

"I was a big tomboy, in fact if I hadn't gone into acting I would have gone into sport because that's the other thing that I do well. I've played women's football, cricket, netball, you name it."

If I wasn't out and about playing I would be running cross-country, doing athletics, organising the various clubs I was captain of, playing hockey or doing rugby training with the boys, the only girl in the school who was allowed to do so, although they didn't consider me to be much competition as I was a 'girl'. The only way at that time you could combine sport and work as a girl was as a P.E. teacher which is what I initially went to train for. Women, even nowadays, have far fewer opportunities to make a living from doing sport than men. Even those who have achieved great things in sport have had to work a darn sight harder than men to chase their dreams. Paula Radcliffe's marathon running is a good example. When she set a new world women's record in the London Marathon April 2003 at 2 hours 15 minutes and 25 seconds, shattering the previous record she 'was fast enough to have won the men's Olympic gold medal in every games until 1984 – and to have qualified for the Great Britain men's Olympic Marathon Team for 2004'. (White, Guardian 20/05/03) She still holds the honour of having run the three fastest times EVER by a woman. She has now retired from running but with even the above fabulous credentials she will never make as much money from sport as a man delivering the same times as she does. And in other sports, the situation is similar, for example, Tiger Woods earns three times as much as Maria Sharapova who I bet a pound to a penny that Paula Radcliffe was also a tomboy!

Although Joan Rivers told me she was not at all a tomboy she did however, have a great relationship with her father. Many of these women had worked out one way or another, whether that was through a close relationship with their fathers or brothers or the freedom to express themselves without the possible suppression of a father figure, that the Y chromosome had more fun than the X. Maybe by virtue of spending more time with males, these girls had started to become more attuned to their language of wit. Women as we will later see, tend to communicate through the language of truth, men through the language of wit, meaning guys will exchange jokes and banter, girls will talk about the things that matter to them.

Although girls were often relegated into second place in many areas of society, girls were found to be far quicker off the mark in learning to speak than boys in research carried out at London's Institute of Psychiatry. (Rawstorne. Daily Mail 17/07/00)

It's a scientific fact that baby girls start talking earlier than baby boys. That's because the first thing girls play with is dolls, which encourages communication. The first thing most boys play with is themselves!

Another reason why girls talk earlier than boys is breast-feeding. Boys would rather breast feed than talk because they know they won't be getting that close again for fifteen years!

According to medical experts, women have bigger vocabularies than men because of this thing called the splenium, which is a path between the right and the left halves of the brain. They found it bigger in women (Jordan and Seaburn 1995). The splenium is why women can always see both sides of a problem and men can only see one side – theirs!

Although girls learn to develop a command for language quicker than boys, the way they use it is very different. Girls 'lack authority and seriousness, they lack conviction and confidence' and are 'tentative, hesitant, even trivial' according to Robin Lackoff's 1975 research. This was also something Deborah Tannen found in her 1990 best-selling book on the way men and women communicated. 'You just don't understand'. Men tend to use 'I', women tend to use 'we'. (Remember what I said at the beginning of this Chapter! Let's do it.) Men tend to tell while women tend to 'suggest'. Men tend to talk in public, while women tend to talk in private. So even in the way the female sex uses language we are timid and unadventurous compared to males. So in effect we are not able to communicate fully as we don't have full access to all the powerful aspects of language.

My Interviewee, Jane Duffus kept saying 'we' when she was talking about her comedy club, 'What the frock' and when I asked her who the 'we' were she said 'Oh no, there's only me, it's just that I feel uncomfortable using 'I' when I'm talking about my successes, it feels arrogant and self-important', something that most men have no problem at all with!!!!

Intriguingly, here's another one of society's myths linked in to devaluing the way that women talk, in much the way that they call our talk 'gossip'. (Kendall, Daily Mail 21/06/01) Men can gossip as much as women, although they have another word for it – they call it 'intrigue', another way of saying it is, 'he's in an important meeting'. (It's always 'important' isn't it) They like to make out that that's all we do is talk, and belittle it by calling it 'tittle tattle', 'prattling' and 'yacking'.

And whilst we are talking about talking, 'Why is it that The Oxford Dictionary of Quotations bulges with quotations by men… .when women (as men are the first to point out) do all the talking?'

Peg Bracken (American author) in Women's Wicked Wit by Michelle Lovric.

However a 2013 study by the University of Maryland School of Medicine, has concluded that there may be an enzyme in the brain which prompts women to speak on average, 20,000 words a day whilst men on the other hand only manage 7,000 so it's interesting that men tend to talk more in seminars as this would suggest that men are far more confident than women in putting forward and sharing their opinions.

Professor Petra Boynton, a psychologist at University College, London in her research on the nature of conversation found that men had just four subjects when talking to other men: jokes, sport, work and women. Women's conversation on the other hand, embraced more than forty subjects, ranging from health to house prices, politics to pregnancy and childcare to clothes. Professor Boynton said 'What is particularly interesting is that contrary to their own opinions of women, men are the ones resorting to small talk'. (Markham. Daily Mail 18/10/01)

I noticed this phenomena recently at a meeting of a mixed sex group that met quite regularly and knew each other quite well. Some new male members joined and the first few minutes were spent by the existing male members swapping jokes with the new male members. Curious eh? What did I say about their language of communication?

Now you put six women who don't know each other in a sauna, and by the end of half an hour, they'll have discussed the dimensions of the piles they gave birth to, how to stop their old man snoring, and how to make a pound of sausages go a long way! You put six men who don't know each other into a sauna, and by the end of half an hour they'll still be discussing the offside law in football!

I never learnt the offside rule firstly because I couldn't give a damn about it and secondly, rugby was the game played where I grew up in West Wales where I had most of my junior and secondary education. This is where I am now going to look for evidence as to what makes a woman passionate about comedy.

Education
Sioned Wiliam – BBC Radio 4's Commissioner for Comedy

"I'm the product of a Welsh Medium Education, which is now flourishing in Wales but which at the time I went to school, was very much in the minority. The Welsh Medium Schools are very closely linked with the Welsh League of Youth 'Urdd Gobaith Cymru' which holds an annual 'Eisteddfod' throughout Wales. The 'Eisteddfod' is Europe's largest youth festival and more than 40,000 children and young people compete annually in singing, dancing, recitation, instrumental, creative writing and arts competitions. The Eisteddfod has nurtured the talents of people like Bryn Terfel, Ioan Gruffydd, Rhys Ifans, Lisa Palfrey, Cerys Mathews, Connie Fisher, Mathew Rhys and Daniel Evans and most of the Super Furry Animals. At my Junior School we had a wonderful headmistress called Rachel Williams who made us perform, I was always performing, singing or reciting."

Josie Taylor

"I went to a Welsh medium Primary School in Cardiff until the age of eleven and the many opportunities to perform there for the 'Urdd Eisteddfod' probably propelled me into performing."

Blod Jones

"While I was in primary school I often performed in the Eisteddfod. My experiences with the Eisteddfod has given me a lot of confidence in standing in front of people and talking to them."

The 'Urdd Eisteddfod' and chapel were also the places where I served my apprenticeship on the stage. Chapel was the first place I sang in a big competition at the age of five and the weekly verse recitation in front of all assembled made sure you had a regular audience even if the verse was always the same week in week out. I remember I had a particular affection for 'I am the good shepherd' (farming again!)

Nina Wadia

"I went to a school in Mahim, India called, 'The Bombay Scottish Orphanage High School! B-S-O-H-S. We had Hindi classes and Gujurati classes, but it was an English school, and we were taught in English and then when I went to Hong Kong I went to a school called 'The Ireland School', which was one of the top schools in Hong Kong, and also 'The English Foundation School."

Lorraine Benloss

"Because I had been bullied because I was fat in Primary School I made a conscious decision when I went to Secondary School I was going to reinvent myself, I'd become a new me. So when I started Secondary School I wasn't this shy person any longer, I was more like this outspoken girl who had a bit of a sense of humour, could say dirty things and who didn't care. I literally woke up one morning and all of a sudden I had this awful filthy sense of humour."

Nadia Kamil

"I went to a private school for a short period of time, but it mostly made me appreciate the state school system as a place where you could get away with being much less well behaved."

Shazia Mirza

"The junior school I went to was mixed. What happened was I went to Harborne Junior School in Harborne in Birmingham, which was a mixed, mainly white, infants and junior school. When I got to the juniors, I got caught stealing cakes and biscuits out of the Headmaster's office because I didn't have enough money to buy cakes and sweets at break. Anyway my Dad found out and he wasn't very pleased so he moved me to a Roman Catholic school, even though I was a Muslim, which was also mixed, so me and my two brothers went there and we were the only Asians in the whole school."

Rhona Cameron

"Where I grew up you either went to the Protestant school or the Catholic school, and I went to the Protestant. It is one of my biggest regrets that I wasted my time at school and never went to art-college. Instead I spent several years drinking and doing menial jobs before following a lover to Australia in 1989."

Nina Conti

"Apart from my first year of school when I was five, when I spent a few months in New York because of my father's work as an actor and I was home-schooled by my Mum, I went to a mixed sex secondary school, which was quite free-spirited, and you called your teachers by their first names."

Jenny Éclair

"I had quite a transient childhood. I went to a progressive army school in Berlin, which was kind of funky in some respects, it was all quite arty. I always had an incredibly low threshold of boredom and that would make me do things at school that caused trouble, you know, loud-mouthed showy-offy kind of things."

Donna McPhail

"I went to ten different schools. It had a negative effect on me in retrospect and I'm quite resentful. I was always being dumped into a new school, always a new person, never being able to make a best friend."

Susie Felber

"I went to a Co-ed public school in New York. A very "good" school. A large portion of the kids were wealthy. It was a good school because the parents who moved there were hell bent on success for their kids. My Junior-high and High-school bully became a real estate tycoon – we're talking jumbo skyscrapers in

Manhattan — and then it all went south… he recently got out of prison for defrauding people out of millions. Ah, I love karma."

We have a few themes appearing here again: bullying, transient lifestyles, difference, the Welsh talent X Factory – The Eisteddfod (which means the 'sitty down place'!) and the way that for some of these children they found the magic potion of comedy to create a fabulously protective shield around their fragile egos. Some became the class clown – one of the best places to show comedic promise. I used to do anything to get a laugh but at the same time I was also the Class Councillor and various Team Captains so my own seeds of political and public activity were already being sown. What about my Interviewees?

Class Clowns and Jokers?
Victoria Jordy Cook
"I went to a very northern working class school in Whitley Bay. I tried to be the class clown but in a class full of Geordies you'd be hard pushed to find one that's not funny. Growing up in the North East I was surrounded by people who laughed a lot and constantly ribbed each other. There's no sense of humour like a Geordie one, though the Irish come pretty close."

Fern Brady
"I wouldn't describe myself as the class clown but I do vividly remember my Biology teacher telling me I should go into comedy and he'd be my manager. I was very studious at school but at the same time I used to do a lot of things to my teachers to try and take the piss out of them and almost heckle them. I'd always do it with a straight face though and most people at school thought I was a weirdo rather than funny. I found myself funny."

Blod Jones
"I would like to think that I was one of the class clowns. I remember spending a LOT of time trying to make my classmates laugh."

JoJo Smith
"By about the age of 12, I certainly started to become the class clown, probably as a defence mechanism against bullying."

Brenda Gilhooly aka Gayle Tuesday
"There were quite a few jokers in my class and I was one of them. Well you don't think whether or not you're funny when you're a child but by the time I got to University, probably, I think I must have known that that's how I was perceived and then I suppose I then began to see myself that way."

Nina Conti
"I was the class joker among a close set of friends. But I wasn't sort of eccentric in front of everybody, more with a smaller group."

Jo Caulfield
"I used to be the class joker, especially when I went to a new school, although I was also at the same time very shy."

Julia Morris
"I was very much the class joker because I loved making people laugh."

Shazia Mirza
"I read one of my school reports recently. When I was 11 one teacher put, in my report, 'Shazia enjoys being the class clown… but this distracts from her work and also distracts other people in the classroom'. And I remember being a Muslim girl, at home

with my Mum and Dad, never allowed to go anywhere, never allowed to do anything, not allowed to have hobbies, not allowed to talk to boys, I wanted to go to dancing lessons but I wasn't allowed that, my life was just like a prison, so really if I didn't laugh about it really I would have cried. So I think that going to school was a real outlet for me to be myself. And I think, without knowing it, when I look back, I was myself – that was me, making everybody laugh."

Wendy Kane

"I started clowning around in class, I would never sit down and work. I wanted to be liked and popular but I also wanted to be 'The Rebel'. I could never see myself doing office work from nine to five. I started to sing with a band at the age of 14. Bonny Tyler used to sing with the same band and we're still good pals even now. I started doing comedy sketches even then, but it was mostly visual comedy."

These, and many others that I interviewed, used to 'mess about' in class', which I also used to do a lot becoming 'comic junkies' and class clowns at an early age,. As a supply teacher for fifteen years of children from three to eighteen years of age, and present Entrepreneurship Role Model on behalf of the Welsh Assembly Government working in Post 11 and Further Education, I have noticed that this is allowed to grow quite naturally with boys but which I never saw encouraged in girls, who have to learn to conform, be sensible, 'Mama's little helpers' and keep quiet much sooner than boys.

'Laddish' behaviour in the classroom in the 14 to 16 year age group is often tolerated or encouraged by teachers and other adults according to Dr. Becky Francis at the University of Greenwich. In her 2000 research, Teachers, both male and female, often supported and encouraged 'roguish' behaviour of male class clowns when their behaviour was not challenging or offensive. 'Thereby contributing to

the increased status of 'laddish' boys. Boisterous, jovial and bantering behaviour seemed to be accepted more readily in boys than in girls. Boys in class are loud and make jokes', according to the research, published in a book 'Boys, girls and achievement: addressing the classroom issues.'

'Humour, defiance, strength, bravery, competition and brutality are generally seen as being male traits, so boys expression of 'laddism' and teachers response to them simply reflect attitudes in wider society' says Dr. Francis. In contrast, bantering by girls with a male teacher can be constructed as flirtatious and, generally, girls do not usually actively call attention to themselves in class. So there we have some proof, boys are encouraged to be funny even in adolescence, whereas girls are not (except perhaps in all-girls schools which I will look at later in greater depth)

Women are rarely allowed to be seen as 'rebellious', that is the preserve of men, (usually those with dark glasses, fast cars and short lives) but one of the most rebellious women ever is the American comic Roseanne Barr. She doesn't give two hoots about society's expectation of her to be of a specific size, shape, weight and refuses to be objectified or funnelled into permissible behaviour. She talks about whatever she wants, laughs at whatever she wants, has loosened her liberty bodices in no uncertain terms and is not dictated to by any of society's gender straightjackets. In my estimation, she was the original 'Loose Woman' I am really glad to see Roseanne becoming much more active politically – We women get things done and she will be a 'Rebel with a cause'.

Rebel, Rebel

© Joanna Quinn

Sara Sugarman – Film Director

"I used to be called mad because I won't conform to a status quo, but I'm not mad, I just have a different form of logic. It's easy to call a woman mad but they don't call men mad. I consider myself to be a 100 per cent Rebel Woman. When I was young I was baffled by misogyny and I would just rebel against it. I just can't conform to someone trying to oppress me. It is an unusual characteristic but I saw my Mother, an utterly brilliant and artistic woman suffer terribly with depression from a repressed energy of conforming to what was expected of womanhood and unfortunately for me it made me go towards the paternal side and take on more masculine characteristics in order to survive what a woman's role was supposed to be."

Fern Brady

"I wrote 'Radges' (BBC Comedy Feeds 2015 – Radges) about my own experience in a Scottish Pupil Referral Unit. There were mainly girls there and only three boys. I was their leader, so I wasn't deliberately trying to make the characters any specific way, that was just how they were and how I am. I don't understand the thing about not being politically correct – I was in a mental unit so I'm going to write how I experienced that. What was frustrating about the process was people involved who wanted it **not** to be in a mental unit, who didn't want to offend anyone. Well, I'm mental so surely it's wrong for middle-class men to be telling me what I can and can't say about my experience? Another annoying thing was the director and producer telling me how my lesbian characters should be in it. For me – a bisexual with a lesbian best friend, to have two heterosexual men telling me how homosexuals should be depicted was one of the most infuriating things to happen to me. It makes me inordinately happy now to see the response 'Radges' is getting from other mentally ill and gay people.

Naomi Paxton aka Ada Campe
"I don't really think of myself as a rebel but if there's anything rebellious about me then it's circumstantial – I only ever wanted to be a performer and have worked in theatre my whole life; I'm happily gay and embrace the difference within that community and I'm not quiet about my feminist views."

Nadia Kamil
"I'd like to describe myself as a Rebel. It sounds cool! I am definitely rebelling against our society which is so heavily structured with brutal inequalities across race, gender, sexuality and class lines."

Rosie Kane – Scottish FSUC & Previous Member of the Scottish Parliament
"When I became a member of the Scottish Parliament I refused to take the queen's oath and said 'My oath is to the people', which was probably pretty gutsy. It was all over the papers the next day. I refused to play by the rules as an M.P. and was jailed several times because of the Faslane Peace Camp Protests."

Cynthia Levin
"I was and am a rebel."

Lynn Ruth Miller

"I just can't seem to conform at all – I'm a real rebel woman. This is the only thing I have really stuck at."

I am myself a 'Rebel Woman of Renown' with more than my share of 'I couldn't give a F***ness.' I am, by this point in my life, completely unemployable. I hate being told what to do and how to behave by anyone. I plough my own farrow (here we go again, that old chestnut – farming – it's all my Dad's fault)! Many of these girls had broken free of the stereotypical assumptions that girls have thrown on them by society like a straightjacket almost from birth, and became REBELS!

A lot of them rebelled against the expectation that they were going to be 'nice' girls, that is quiet, accepting not breaking the 'rules', not playing the joker, refined, restrained and generally limited in their activities. They saw 'nice pretty girls' as quiet with no personality – but all of these were rebels! These were the sprouting seeds of what Kathleen Rowe in 1995 called 'Unruly Women'.

'Through her body, her speech and her laughter, especially in the public sphere, she causes a disruptive spectacle of herself…. A source of potential power…. Prototype of woman as subject' …

…rather than object and totally opposite to all those 'nice pretty girls' who did very little to cause havoc in the playground'.

Wow that sounds just like me, and it sounds like a veritable package of power – not what we generally imagine when we think of the socially accepted norm of docile dollies. One of the strangest findings of my research was how so very many of these women had gone to all-girls schools, something I knew nothing about, apart from the fabulous 'Saint Trinians' film which I loved, Enid Blyton's Twins at Saint Clares' and 'Mallory Towers' which I read avidly as a teenager until I moved on to my lifetime love of murder mystery novels with female protagonists, starting off with Agatha Christie and moving on to Sue Grafton and Sarah Paretski et al. What was so special about all-girls schools? Why did so many of these women who had gone there reject the 'docile dollies' straightjacket and end up in stand-up comedy?

Overdosing on oestrogen – Girls Schools
Maria Kempinska

"I went to an all-girls school and I was a rebel and the class clown – someone has to be the male energy. I started running shows in school."

Jane Mackay – Owner of 'The Stand Comedy Club', Edinburgh, Glasgow

"I went to a girls hostel from the age of eleven but, because I was brought up on the East coast all my friends were still at home and I didn't know anyone. Girls tended to hang with the people from their native township and it could be vicious at times. Consider it; these are peasants from the far-flung areas of the Scottish mainland. They are taken away from home when they are eleven, which is quite young. They have nothing, and a lot of them were very much not academic as well. And they gather together in their wee possies from whatever village they're from you know, Linlochbervie or Lochinver or whatever. And because they are all insecure and whatever else, they can be quite horrible to others. It's just usual, it's just worse because you are living there."

It's a shame that Jane Mackay didn't have a copy of Rosalind Wiseman's brilliant 2002 book "Queen Bees and Wanabbes" to help her at that time to 'survive cliques, gossip, boyfriends and other realities of adolescence'. The cult film 'Mean Girls', starring Lindsay Lohan, is based on this book which talks about the viciousness of young teenage girls. I personally think they are emotionally vicious to each other because they are very fearful of all the changes happening to them emotionally and physically and all creatures, when they become scared, prepare to attack. Girls also don't generally release all that pent-

up energy (which fear can create giving us the choice of 'fight or flight') through sport like boys so it's got to go somewhere. I rarely got involved in the 'Queen Bee' dynamic, their posturing and scrabbling for hierarchical positions were beyond my comprehension. I would have been, what is called in the book, a 'Floater' – happy to go from group to group, content and confident in my own physical power as an athlete and joining in with the boys for rugby circuit training,

Nina Wadia

"For one year when I lived in Hong Kong, my mother was ill. I was fifteen years old, and I had to come to England for that one year to be with her, and I went to Notting Hill and Ealing High Girls School, and that was such a surreal experience for me because I'd never been to a school that was just all female and I hated it, absolutely hated it. I mean, the school itself was excellent and the friends I made were good, but I just did not like the fact that there were no boys in my class to irritate!"

Sindhu Vee

"I went to Loreto Convent Lucknow, Woodstock School Mussoorie, Sardar Patel Vidyalaya, New Delhi. I didn't move schools because I kept getting expelled....my parents just moved a lot! The convent was an all-girls school and I went there from the age of eleven to thirteen. It was incredibly formative. I had been an outsider on so many levels, coming from a very small town mentality in my formative years, having a terrible stutter, my Mother a stay at home Mom just like all the others in the village, even though I had a sister there was six year difference so it was like being an only child and my father a senior civil servant. I woke up to a world where girls could do everything!!! I became fierce, was very good at sports and became the class storyteller. It made me somebody rather than a nobody. Then when I went to American schools I was one of the guys."

Helen Lederer

"I went to an all-girls school. I think I always enjoyed being in a state of hysteria, basically, because I'm quite a hysterical person and with the asthma I was always told to not get over excited which is a red flag to a bull to me because getting over excited was the most appealing state to be in. I can remember laughing about things hysterically. I was very happy to be in that laughter zone. If I was funny it was because I had a sense of anxiety from quite early on as well. I used humour for myself. I found it reassuring to be amusing about things."

Shazia Mirza

"I went to an all-girls secondary school until the sixth form. When I was at school I always loved making people laugh, which might have been a reaction to being considered 'the hairy monster' and the taunts that I had to endure. I think having a beard and a moustache when you are twelve, is a bit of a challenge!.."

Julia Morris

"I went to a private all girls' school for all a full thirteen years of my schooling and I spent most of my time being funny. I really maintain that you get a different level of confidence to go out into society when you go to an all-girls school."

Kitty Flanagan

"I went to a Catholic girls high school in Australia, although most schools in Australia are single sex schools anyway. I was a class clown cross goody two shoes hybrid so I never went too far, I was always too concerned about getting into trouble."

Angie Le Mar

"I went to an all-girls Secondary School for three years. I just got ruder and ruder and more disruptive and more problematic, because of my dyslexia I think, which was just covered up. I then went to a mixed school but I was just as disruptive there."

Lorraine Benloss

"I went to a local mixed Infants and Junior School and then went to an all-girls secondary school."

Jenny Éclair

"When my Dad came out of the army I did my 'Eleven Plus' and got a place at the Girls Grammar School at Lytham St. Anne's, where I spent most of my youth. I think all girls schools are a hoot though 'cause it's like a coven of witches and you develop that bitchy side, which has helped me with my stand-up by giving me just a little bit of defence. That school shaped me. It was very strict and dull. I'd get very bored and had to make my own entertainment. I was always the loudmouth at the back of the class, always in detention – usually given by my sister who was head girl and a real cow."

Jo Caulfield

"I went to an all-girls secondary boarding school and although I hated it, I think it's good for girls because you don't have boys in the class who are loud and make jokes. It was a Catholic School with nuns. Even at the time you think these nuns are off their heads. When we were nine, on Sunday afternoons we were allowed to wear our own clothes. I remember we had prayers after lunch and this nun stood up, and some girls were very young, five or six as well and this nun told us that we should be more like the Virgin Mary and said that we all looked like sluts! *(Here we go again!!)* We were all a bit curious about this word so we looked it up in the dictionary because we didn't know what it meant, and it said 'Unkempt woman' – which is a bit of a harsh description for a five year old! Some of the nuns were quite violent and one of the punishments when I was nine or ten, was that we had to be put in a cellar without the lights on. It was an old hydro or spa as it would be called today, very Gothic, in Derbyshire. I was really scared that I was going to have a visitation by the Virgin Mary and we'd pray that she wouldn't come then when we were in the dark in the cellar, but in the light of day. And our ambition was to become a saint!"

Mine was to become Emma Peel – well it takes all sorts!!

Jojo Sutherland
"I went to an all-girls school from 14 years onwards. I wanted to be a Catholic – I loved all the dressing up."

Rhonda Hansome
"I went to an all-girls Catholic school in New York from kindergarten to secondary school."

Maureen Younger
"I went to an all-girls school with lots of black girls. I had no white girlfriends at all until I was eighteen. I was a real outsider as are many comics."

Nuala McKeever
"I went to a local Primary school, St. Theresa's, which had both boys and girls but they were educated separately and then on to a Catholic Dominican Grammar School, again both boys and girls but educated separately, so I suppose you could say I went to an all-girls school."

Joan Rivers
"I went to Connecticut College for Women, New London, Connecticut"

Rigby Jones

"I went to an all-girls school for a year as a 14 year old. I loved it as the girls just focussed on learning and were not distracted by the boys."

Holly Burn aka Kirst Kay

"I went to an all-girls school where my default setting was 'funny'."

Aditi Mittal

"I went to an all-girls school and was always the class clown. The class clown would be taking the responsibility of the male in the class."

The following Interviewees also went to an all-girls school for some or all of their secondary schooling: Wendy Kane, Dr. Jane Davidson, Brenda Gilhooly, Jane Duffus, Naomi Paxton and Mandy Knight.

Fern Brady

"I went to school in a CAMHS Tier 4 day mental unit. There were mainly girls there and only three boys. I was their leader. Before that I was at a mixed state Catholic school."

According to the Hinsliff 2003 Edinburgh Study of Youth Transitions and Crime reported in the Guardian, 'Teenage boys have a tendency towards violent and aggressive behaviour which may be part of being male'. Girls on the other hand, either turn it verbally onto each other or internalise it into self-hatred, which has by now grown to epidemic proportions in the western world with female eating disorders and self-harm no longer being exceptional behaviour.

Kate Smurthwaite

"All the kids in the village were girls and I was always the leader. I was a big tomboy. My Dad worked away a lot and he was quite a monster in a way. I loved mucking about in school."

Rhona Cameron

"If I had a daughter I would send her to a single sex school. I feel that individual growth is stunted by the dominance of men and boys in the classroom, but I went to the local shit comprehensive school. Going to a girls-school where I was from was unheard of, too posh. I'm not from a posh family."

Of all they comics I interviewed, well over half of them had at one time in their lives, gone to an all-girls school. It may have given them an opportunity to sharpen their verbal claws and develop their bitchy side as suggested by Jenny Éclair. Girls are generally not encouraged to be as physical as boys with their constant football, football, although Angie Le Mar actually fought physically with her brothers, female fights have traditionally been more about hair pulling and scratching than packing the punches à la Muhammad Ali and that's why she is never intimidated by men!

Girls have little physical outlets to channel that physical energy, anger and frustration that comes from being a pimply hormonal teenager so rather than release that angst on a football carefully crafted by skilled child labourers for a pittance in Indonesia or Vietnam or by giving the boy you disagree with a good thumping, their vitriol becomes verbal and very vicious.

But is this because we have an expectation or a tolerance towards this sort of behaviour in boys? Do we "allow it" more often in boys than in girls? And do we encourage girls to suppress that anger and turn it inwards causing untold damage in the shape of depression rather than outwards? It is interesting to note that in Fern Brady's school which was a Scottish referral unit, most of the pupils were female.

Another aspect of all girl's schools that is important is the total physical separation from boys. This has several interesting outcomes. The first one I think is the amount of time and energy little girls and in their turn larger girls spend just thinking about, preening themselves for and trying to attract the attention of boys. When the objects of their affections are no longer present, all of a sudden a huge amount of time and energy is released which can be used to focus on other more rewarding things such as in Julia Morris' case, finding new ways of making her mates laugh.

Although I'm not advocating single sex schools at all, mixed sex schools don't seem to benefit anybody if you look at the performance tables. Girls have already been outperforming boys dramatically both at GCSE and A level for several years. Way back in 1998 at GCSE level the results reported by Halpin in the Daily Mail (just so you don't think I just read the Guardian!) began to be astonishing, with a whopping eight of the best results in State Schools going to Girls Schools, one to a boys school and one to a mixed school.

The Independent Schools Council produce an annual list in the Guardian of the top ten Independent Schools results at A level. In 2003, of the ten, five were all-girls schools, four were boys schools and only one was mixed. By the next year, five were all boys schools and five which were all girls schools. By 2011 the figure had increased to six out of the top ten were all-girls schools, only three were boys schools and the top school (Sevenoaks) was mixed.

Girls have been outperforming boys for many years and a great deal of resources have been poured into trying to re-dress the balance and as a result there has been some improvement in this area but nevertheless, girls are still outperforming boys at quite a substantial level. In a list of the top fifteen state schools of 2011, 8 of them were single sex female, four were mixed and only three were boys schools. The top school was an all-girls school. Although, by 2012, the boys seemed to have had a bit of a shock and outperformed the girls by this time. An American 2013 report shows that girls are also still outperforming boys dramatically Stateside.

The evidence that all-girls schools produce highly successful women is very impressive once you start to open your eyes, do your research, check Wikepedia and other reliable sources!

- *Joan Rivers – Connecticut College for Women, New London, Connecticut.*
- *Victoria Wood – Bury Grammar School for Girls*
- *Helen Fielding – Author of Bridget Jones' Diary – Wakefield Girls Grammar School*
- *Meera Syal – Walsall Girls Secondary.*
- *Davina McCall – Godolphin and Latymer School, London*
- *Anne Robinson – Farnborough Hill Girls School in Hampshire.*
- *Dido – The City of London School for Girls.*
- *Caroline Ahearne – Boarded at an all-girls arts school in Hertfordshire.*
- *Diane Abbott – First black woman M.P. in 1987 – Harrow County School for Girls.*

Margaret Thatcher and Indira Gandhi were both the products of single sex colleges, graduating from Cambridge. Most schools in Australia are single sex and they recently had their very first female Prime Minister, Julia Gillard, who I was very fortunate to meet in the Welsh Assembly in May 2015.

*According to Anne Lonsdale, President of New Hall, Cambridge (The Mail on Sunday 20/09/98) 'Women can seriously under-achieve in a mixed college. On a trip to America I met a dazzling array of statistics on the success of women from single sex colleges. More than 50 per cent of women from colleges I visited go on to gain PhD's. A large number are in the Fortune 500, the list of top earners, and an impressive number have become Senators and Congresswomen. The reason for their successes is quite clear – they do not learn to **defer to men**." So all-girls schools seem to be a breeding ground for not only female stand-up comics but also for successful women in general.*

Considering I know very few women in my immediate circles who went to all-girls schools, I was really astounded as to how many of my Interviewees had gone to single sex schools. I believe that the reason for this is that it allows women to develop confidence in their speaking skills, especially in public, because they don't have boys constantly interrupting them. Several academic studies I've looked at conclude that men not only tend to manipulate the course of conversations when they're in mixed sex groups, but also interrupt constantly, so all-girls schools allowed girls to develop their linguistic skills."

Does educating boys and girls separately have any effect on how girls develop? You would think that there was some element that was positive, considering that so very many of these girls who went on to perform in a very 'masculine' world went to all girls schools.

The present Director at Inspire, University of Wales, Trinity Saint David's and previous Minister for Education in the Welsh Assembly Government, Dr. Jane Davidson, who herself went to an all-girls school has this to say:

Dr. Jane Davidson – Former Cabinet Minister, Welsh Assembly Government

"I don't believe that girls become more confident if they are educated apart from boys. Some girls will become more confident, but some much less confident. The most important element educationally is to move away from a culture that criticises and belittles pupils and focuses instead on raising confidence and standards of both sexes."

However, it seems quite obvious that my Interviewees are the ones who became confident in single-sex school. A 2013 article from the Huffington Post, says that many women in America are choosing to go to all girls colleges, because 'They intuitively know they must first get to know themselves in an environment where women are the focus – one without the typical co-ed distractions. Not only that, the lecturers seem only to be too aware of the fact that men speak the majority of the time in seminars!

Put that together with the information about men manipulating not only the time to talk publicly in a mixed sex group and changing the topics talked about to suit them, it's amazing that women ever get a chance to express themselves at all, even though women apparently are supposed to do very little other than that according to some sources!

And just so that you can see I'm not biased and that I'm looking at the total picture, separating boys from girls also seems to have a beneficial effect on the boys too, lessening the 'peacock effect' of boys preening themselves and showing off, behaviour that they think impresses the girls, (Hinds, The Independent 26/11/98) so that the boys can focus on their work rather than on their feathers! However, very little research seems to have been done since then and over the last few years as to whether boys-only classes would raise academic standards for boys.

Academics at Homerton College, Cambridge found that all boy classes 'improve results' (Harris, Daily Mail 31/03/03) The study, commissioned by Ministers, was conducted to discover new ways to prevent boys being outperformed academically by girl in secondary education. Men are also being seriously outperformed by women in Further Education and have been for the last decade or so. What did my Interviewees study after leaving school which enabled them to be drawn into the world of comedy? Were there any opportunities there to encourage and develop women's 'comedy muscle'?

Further Education
Kate Smurthwaite

"I went to Oxford to study Maths (80 students – 20 were female) I used to hang out with geeks and I.T. guys. I was never part of the Oxford Review although I did go and watch them a lot."

Sindhu Vee

"I went to Hindu College, Delhi University and finally spent a year at Delhi School of Economics before going to Oxford University on the Radhakrishnan Scholarship where I read

Politics, Philosophy and Economics (PPE) there were four scholarships for the whole of India so I worked phenomenally hard to get that scholarship. I rowed and played basketball for uni which is the one place my height, I'm five foot ten inches tall which is insanely tall for an Indian woman, gave me some advantage and literally, quite an unique perspective. From Oxford I went to McGill University, Canada and then University of Chicago to do a PhD in Political Philosophy. But I got fed up of studying for years on end and hearing everyone say how being a professor in the USA was an impossible goal because 'There's a quota on H1 visas and green cards for Indians.' I quit my PhD and did a MA in Public Policy at the University of Chicago."

Nadia Kamil

"I went to Cambridge for my BA which is where I started doing comedy (with the Cambridge Footlights). I started doing stand-up because I had ideas I wanted to present to an audience directly, not through sketches or characters."

Sioned Wiliam – BBC Radio 4's Commissioner for Comedy

"I went to Aberystwyth University and did a degree in Drama and to Jesus College in Oxford and I went there to do a doctorate on Sean O'Casey – The Irish playwright. Whilst I was there I joined the Oxford Review, which is the equivalent of the Cambridge Footlights, and performed a lot of comedy. I was very lucky to meet people like Patrick Marber who's now a very well-known playwright – he wrote much of the Alan Partridge series with Steve Coogan ('Knowing me knowing you' and 'Paul and Pauline Calf's video diary') and Armando Iannucci, who's one of the great producers of comedy, 'The Day Today' and again 'The Alan Partridge Show' and a whole host of other things. They were there at the same time as me and I performed with them and I was just so lucky, it happened to be a bit of a golden era for comedy. I had no plans. I knew that going to Oxford would help me get into comedy, which is a disgraceful truth but I think it's true. I got into the BBC in 1988 because I'd been in the Oxford Review. I think it's unquestioning that it helped me enormously."

Monty Python's Flying Circus and all the comedy spawned in its wake was a fantastic fusion of phenomenal Oxford/ Cambridge (Oxbridge) talent in the late fifties, early sixties. Eric Idle, Terry Jones and Michael Palin were at Oxford and featured in the University Reviews. John Cleese and Graham Chapman met at Cambridge where they played in Footlights. For Sioned Wiliam, all it took was to choose the right University (Oxford or Cambridge) as a starting point for a career in comedy (As if getting to Oxford or Cambridge was as easy as getting a train ticket there!) Sioned you chose wisely!!

'Footlights' is undoubtedly one of the most powerful places for comedy development in the world and some surprising people have found and flexed their comedy muscles there, people like Germaine Greer, both Mel and Sue (Mel Giedroyk and Sue Perkins) Sandi Toksvig, Emma Thompson, Hugh Laurie, Sir David Frost, Stephen Fry ..... the list goes on and on. I once met Griff Rhys Jones (an ex-Foolighter) in his kitchen, whilst I was rifling through his fridge for a cheese sandwich, after I'd sung in a concert to raise money for his charity on his farm which is two hundred meters from where my parents live, but that's another story!

Afterwards, all of them began working in television and radio, writing and performing in a vast variety of popular shows such as 'Do not adjust your set', 'The Complete and Utter History of Britain', 'The Frost Report' and 'At last the 1948 Show'. These programmes also gave opportunities to people like future 'Goodies' Tim Brooke Taylor and Bill Oddie, the incorrigible and multi-talented David Jason, Ronnie Barker and Ronnie Corbett and David Frost. (Morgan, The Observer Magazine 03/10/99)

Monty Python was a great opportunity for men to dress up as women, which they did very often with their naughty boy sketches pretending to be Mummy. It seems even at that time, comedy was an all-male event. When we consider comedy, our first thought may be of the village idiot or with buffoonery but it's interesting to note that many of these women have been educated to the highest level possible.

Lynn Ruth Miller

"I have two Master's Degrees with honors, one in Creative Arts for Children at the University of Toledo, and the other, a Master of Arts degree in Communications from Stanford University. I have also done post-graduate work at Indiana University, Harvard, Oxford, Stanford and San Francisco State."

Maureen Younger

"I did a B.A. in German and Russian and then a Masters at the Royal Academy of Music and Drama in Glasgow. I hated University and never planned anything after the age of 22."

Tanyalee Davis

"I went on to University of Winnipeg, 1989 – 1993 where I felt my life began. My social circle flourished and I really came out of my shell."

Ronni Ancona

"I did a foundation course in Art and Design in York and then I went to the University of Kent, Canterbury where I studied Theatre and Drama for a year. I did my actual degree in St. Martins, Central St Martins as it was then called, which was a big art school. I did a degree in design, but while I was there I did a lot of performance and a lot of comedy."

Michele A'Court

"I trained as a journalist at Wellington Polytechnic, New Zealand and then spent 4 years at university doing a degree in English Lit and Drama, and worked on the student newspaper. People who knew me then are surprised to find that I work as a comedian now – apparently I was a deeply serious Communist making speeches at student meetings and going on protests. Though I did write one or two amusing things in the student paper."

Jane Duffus – Director Bristol Based Women's Comedy Club

"I have a background as a journalist for the last fifteen years and am now writing in a freelance capacity. I've always supported the arts and have written a lot about comedy."

Jane Mackay – Owner of 'The Stand Comedy Club', Edinburgh, Glasgow

"When I left school I worked in Dounreay for a while and was the only woman in the fast reactor maintenance section. I was the first person in my family to go to University (Stirling 1975-79 Honours English) I went to Stirling, rather than Edinburgh to do law for which I had the grades because, by then, I had a child. I then did a postgraduate diploma in Journalism Studies at University College, Cardiff (1979-80)."

Nina Wadia

"I went straight to Drama School from school, which was very upsetting for my mother, because I actually wanted to study Law, but I changed my mind at the last minute and thought, no, I want to try acting. So my Mum made me sign a piece of paper which said that if in five years I was not a jobbing actor, I would go back and study Law. She was very good, because I said to her no, no, no. I'll be a successful actress in five years time. She goes, 'Trust me, write down jobbing!' So she was being kind!"

Becoming a professional actor within five years was quite a bit of pressure on Nina Wadia as the unemployment rate amongst actors is extremely high. The Huffington Post in 2012 talks about the 90% unemployment rate for American actors. I imagine British statistics are very similar. I can't remember the last time I had an acting role for sure! Probably when I was about thirty five years old!

According to Charlotte O'Sullivan (Guardian, 01/04/01) 35 also seems to be a crucial age, not for beginning a career but for the end of a career as a Hollywood leading lady. The only way to avoid being dumped on Tinseltown's glamorous girlies refuse cart is to set up your own production companies like Jodie Foster and Sandra Bullock or to turn to the Independent Companies such as Andie Macdowell in 'The Sad Fuckers Club' aka 'A Certain Age' or Glenn Close in Rose Troche's 'The Safety of Objects'.

However, Rome was not built in a day and it takes a long time to change a culture, especially one that is so driven by machismo box office hits. 2011 was the year when US funny women finally led the way as 'Bridesmaids' hit the big screen. 'Bridesmaids', the US comedy and 'fem-friendship' movie was seen as a cultural landmark, as women got the killer lines and men appeared in only peripheral and supportive roles. 'Bridesmaids' was also being called a landmark moment for women in comedy. The Huffington Post called it a "cultural phenomenon" and it grossed more than $288 worldwide. Unfortunately this seems to have been a bit of a blip and the success has not spilled over to any other part of Hollywood production. There has been great excitement about Amy Schumer's 2015 'Trainwreck' and we can only wait and see how that does in the long term in the box-office. It seems the acting lives of female protagonists are short and sweet so the sooner the better you get stuck in there otherwise you may miss the boat. Someone should have *warned Helen Lederer before she wasted those twelve months making dough of a different kind.*

Helen Lederer

"After school I had a gap year. I worked on an adventure playground and sold bread and worked in a bakery, did loads of funny things and did a Social Science degree. There was a bit of pressure from my Mum to get a job but I wasn't too bothered. I was a Social Worker for a short period of time in Camden in London and did an M.A. part time. I joined a theatre group that met three times a week and then went to the Central School of Speech and Drama for a Post Graduate year where I did what I always dreamt of doing and never dared do, which was perform and write. That's really all I ever wanted to do."

Thenjiwe Tay Moseley

"I went to study Drama in university only because the queue to sign up was much shorter than for any other subject. I went to be an au-pair in America for two years. I came to England on a working holiday visa and studied law. I was so bored. I went to see two stand-up comedy shows and thought I could do better."

Lynn Marie Hulsman

"I have a degree in Acting and started improvising in 1995 then stand-up two years later."

Brenda Gilhooly aka Gayle Tuesday

"I went to university at Swansea to study Speech and Drama. I knew I was going to be a comedian. The reason I knew I was going to be a comedian was because I really wanted to be an actress and at Swansea one of the dissertations I did was 'Sexual Politics in the Theatre'. And it was so depressing how literally, and it is true when you watch films, the girls are girlfriends, they're not in the lead. And you might get Paul Newman and he's sixty but his girlfriend will be thirty and the men tend to have longer careers. The girls keep changing and it's because they stay at one age. And I was nineteen at the time and I was reading about if you're a character actress you'll get work when you're about thirty five and I thought I'm not going to wait that long to get work."

Nina Conti

"I studied Theatre Studies at 'A Level'. I was still thinking I was going to be an actress. But I decided after doing a 'Theatre Studies A Level' that I never wanted to study another bit of drama in my life. I didn't want anybody telling me to be a tree or all that nonsense that goes on in drama school. And so I thought I'd much rather do some serious learning so I went to the University of East Anglia and ended up studying Philosophy. And all the mostly male, wild-haired pipe-smoking and eccentric professors seemed so witty and they had such an objective take on life that everything was rendered absurd and I just loved that – it really inspired me."

Nina Wadia

"My first year at drama school was a great experience and was at a place called Actisize, in Richmond, then I had my second year of training at a place called 'The London Theatre School in Wandsworth, and when I finished, that was when I started auditioning and got my first job at my favourite theatre in the whole of London, which is the Theatre Royal, Stratford East. And that's how I got my break."

Holly Burn aka Kirst Kay

"I did a degree in English Drama in Kings College London and then Mountview. I wanted to do straight theatre but after years of getting nowhere workwise, I decided why rail against it. Girls in their twenties were ten a penny so it was very difficult."

Jenny Éclair

"I went to Manchester Polytechnic School of Theatre, which was a Drama School and an old Theatre. John Thompson and Steve Coogan both went there as well."

Mandy Knight

"I went to Southend Technical College to study hairdressing and then to the Webber Douglas in London to do a three-year performance course for a Drama Diploma. After leaving Webber Douglas I was a waitress. There's always that joke at Drama School that you study acting, dance and silver service."

Bethan Roberts

"I went to the Italia Conti Stage School for three years on a Musical Theatre Course and had a bit of a shock which knocked my confidence. I couldn't sing and I was terrified there. I did do a lot of dancing as promo and in bars. I then trained as a pastry chef as a back-up in the Westminster Kingsway College. It was like being with Gordon Ramsey every day."

Julia Morris

"I went to study for two years at an acting school called the Ensemble, in Sydney. Going to the acting course, I knew I wanted to be an actor, I knew I wanted to be in show business. I'd been in lots of amateur productions throughout my schooling and youth and always been involved in Youth Theatre and it just seemed like a logical step then because I liked it so much."

Shazia Mirza

"I went to Manchester University where I did a degree in Biochemistry which I hated. My parents wanted me to be a doctor, because there just aren't enough Asian doctors in Britain! I wanted to be an actress. I thought I was very funny; I wanted to make people laugh. And I knew I wanted to come to London; I wanted to be on the stage. The only way I could get to London was to do a Post-Grad or something – to study so I could move to London. So I got a place on a PGCE (Post Graduate Certificate of Education) at Goldsmiths College and I did that for a year and I hated that as well. And then I went to Drama School. My parents thought I was a teacher. Really I was secretly going to Drama School, I paid for it myself for three years. While I was at Drama School I was writing comedy."

Nuala McKeever

"I went to Queen's University Belfast and studied Spanish and English. I would be the first generation going to university, and education was free and Catholics really pushed that for their children – education, education, education. Now the huge Catholic middle class is very well educated and that is finding its voice for the first time really."

Lorraine Benloss

"I went to Crewe University to study Drama and Creative Arts and I took a writing option. The roles for black women were so limited at the time, mostly hookers and junkie's girlfriends. I wanted to learn the formulas so I could start writing more positive roles for myself and for other black women."

Lydia Nicole

"I won a scholarship at UCLA (University College of Los Angeles) for writing and took a few years off from comedy and got to Associate Produce a movie about black comics. I still survive as a producer in the comedy world."

Jo Brand

"My mother enjoyed the psychiatry side of social work and this probably rubbed off on me. I went to do a degree in nursing when I was twenty-one and did a four-year nursing course at Mordsley and Bethlem Hospital (one of Britain's first psychiatric hospitals)."

Was university the point where changes started happening with opportunities for self-expression? Remember how we saw that girls were outperforming boys educationally at secondary education? Another element of self-expression that needs to be considered is how women's language is belittled and trivialised and that according to men, that's all we do is talk all day.

Dr. Ruth Woodfield and Professor Pete Saunders's 1998 work at Sussex University on the differences between men and women's performances at University, showed that men did a disproportionate share of the talking in seminars (Kingston, Guardian 08/12/98) Another conclusion to this study, was that women were outperforming men in education and the reason for this was seen that, on average, they work harder.

An interesting finding is that not only do men do most of the talking in University seminars, but that men interrupt far more than women. This was also found in studies of secondary school children. Donald Zimmerman and Candace West's 1975 research showed that in mixed sex pairs, up to 97% of the interruptions are men interrupting women. In same sex pairs, women and men are about as likely to interrupt their partner. They concluded that 'men's dominance in conversation via interruption, mirrors their dominance in contemporary western culture.' Interruption is 'a device for exercising power and control in conversation'. Men also tended to control what will be talked about in conversations, also a finding of the Sussex project. So if you see this happening in your own life, and you will if you're a woman, my advice is, be strident and take control of conversations – otherwise you won't get your views across.

As a conclusion to this chapter, looking back on the most important formative years, although there isn't an 'Identikit' of a prospective future female stand-up comic, there are still some patterns that have been established. A lot of transient childhoods, quite a few youngest children or only children, all working class or middle class (or not privileged or privileged) , a lot who were tomboys, either very close to their Dads or no Dad present. Some of these women had discovered the power of comedy as a way of dealing with some of the flotsam life chucked at some of them or to fight back against repression whether that was from their culture or from religion. But the one thing that was amazing was the number who had actually gone to a single sex school, over half of them. Many found that being an outsider helps you to observe and to find the funny in the mundane. Many of these women were drawn to performance as a life choice, but strangely enough not stand-up comedy, that could be because of **THE BIG MYTH** (that women aren't funny). Until recently, there were few accessible Role Models who had actually succeeded in stand-up and those that had, hadn't had many opportunities to show in print how they had done it.

Brenda Gilhooley – Gayle Tuesday, because of the depressing statistics about the lack of work opportunities for actresses, which are still the same in the second decade of the twenty first century, uncovered in the course of writing an essay for her university course, made a conscious decision to go into comedy from a performing background as did Jo Enright who knew that it was exactly what she wanted to do.

Although Rhona Cameron knew she was going to perform at an early age, by the time she left school she didn't really have much of a clue as to how to set about it. Helen Lederer also knew she wanted to perform at an early age but didn't know what form that would be. For all the others, they all became accidental comics for various reasons whether that was the lack of good roles for women or just drifting into it because they couldn't think of anything else they wanted to do. Evidently there was no clear female comic career trajectory, Sat nav *or map to refer to. So after all these serious and grim issues – here's a bit of frivolity for you*

Q. Why do men talk about football?
A. Because it would be boring to talk about tits all the time! (Venge 2002:112)

Joan Rivers also noted their infatuation with this part of the female anatomy in her book about plastic surgery entitled 'Men are stupid..... and they like big boobs'. (2009)

Comedy delivery is not a gift given to everyone and comedy 'timing' is something that you either have or you haven't got. With some people it's a God given gift – others seem to take to humour like a duck to water and for some it just 'aint going to happen!

Looking back it seems that as there's lots of ways to skin a cat there are also many ways, from what the comics told me, to learn how to be funny. Some, like Jo Brand, Nina Wadia and Julia Morris came from environments where being funny was central to their family life, or Sioned Wiliam who unwittingly analysed the structure and make up of comedy from practically her cot and watching comedy programmes on the television with her family.

Others like Angie Le Mar, Nina Conti, Jenny Éclair, Jane McKay, Brenda Gilhooley, Julia Morris, Michele A'Court, Shazia Mirzah and Wendy Kane became 'comic junkies' and class clowns at an early age. Oddly enough, most of these all went to all girl schools where there were no boys to compete with as 'class clowns' otherwise it is unlikely they would have had an opportunity to become funny.

You may show talent in one direction as many of my interviewees did at an early age, but everyone knows you don't become an expert in anything without a great deal of study and application – an apprenticeship for want of another name so let's move swiftly forward to see what sort of form this took for my FSUCs.

Tŷ Elinor Pierce, Llanddarog
Tua 1968

CHAPTER 3

APPRENTICESHIP OF A CLOWN

In which I find out how they honed their funny bone!

In this chapter I wanted to see how my Interviewees developed their comedy potential – was it by chance, by watching, by copying, by using it as a survival technique? Where did this power come from, who spotted it, who nurtured it and who or what gave them the confidence to think they had something worth developing? I was a comedy junkie from quite early on in my life and one of the earliest photographs I have of myself is of me puffing on a pipe and pretending to be an old man! You've got to start early in this business! I failed my Scripture A level because I was too busy perfecting the 'one handed matchbox trick' which would in time become one of my most celebrated party pieces as was the 'be cool with a matchstick in your mouth then up your nostril trick'! I loved having comic roles in school plays and always got the comic roles in the predominantly female drama class at college. Christmas was always 'Morecambe and Wise' and comedy was what I loved on the telly, whether that was politically correct or not, such as Benny Hill and the 'Carry On' clan. Was my comic background in wild and windy West Wales similar to any of my Interviewees? What was happening at that same time when I was breaking in my palomino pony and riding him bareback, directly across the pond from the last radio signal point for planes leaving Britain (my square mile North Pembrokeshire's claim to fame!!) in the real Wild West of America, land of cowboys and culture?

Lynn Ruth Miller

"I started 'entertaining' by trying to amuse Holocaust survivors. I was very, very, good at telling jokes. I've always been a writer and a teacher and used to write funny columns. I then made a compilation of my columns. It started there really."

Bollywood Actor and Trainer, Harry Key has developed a form of Coaching, which he calls 'Provocative Style' and he says "If we laugh while we think about a problem, the laughter changes our current and future emotional responses to that thought."

Comedy and tragedy have often been called the two sides of the same coin, Woody Allan used to say. 'Comedy is tragedy or pain plus time'. If you're not right in the trauma it is easier for people to deal with it and for them to actually deal with it in retrospect, but when you're actually going through all that stuff, the pain is too much.

Thinking about three women in particular that I interviewed, Thenjiwe Tay Moseley, Lynn Ruth Miller and Lydia Nicole, they all come from backgrounds where existing and the boundaries of existence are really pushed as far as possible. Thenjiwe was brought up in a South African township where violence, death and destruction was all around and formed her normality. Lynn Ruth Miller started her performing career trying to make Holocaust survivors laugh. Lydia Nicole's mother was a prostitute and her father a pimp, and grew up in a New York environment where women were sold for sex by men and drug use was also a normal day to day reality for those in her environment, a world of daily challenges and difficulties.

Edith Piaf, my lifetime Role Model was one of eighteen children, had a tragic life full of violence, poverty, grief and despair but she loved to laugh. It is a coping mechanism for adversity, what used to be called 'gallows humour' and it's how gravediggers, doctors, undertakers, soldiers, and those who have to deal with challenging and emotionally difficult situations on a regular basis, are able to cope. Were there any other difficult environments where my Interviewees found their funny bones?

Mandy Knight

"Because I was fostered so many times, I've blocked out so much of my early life. I think I very quickly developed a way to appear 'alluring', so that I wouldn't have to leave somewhere so I suppose humour was my defence, my safety. I think it was always my way to be slightly lippy, slightly humorous, and comedy was always there."

Spring Day

"I grew up in a very tense household and I had to be funny to break the tension between my parents. My Mum hates to laugh – it's the 'loss of control' which I just couldn't understand. She was my toughest audience which egged me on. I have always thrived on negatives and negative notions such as people telling me, 'You can't do that.' "

Other ways of promoting comic growth were experiences of humiliation in the form of bullying as we previously saw, because of being 'other', whether that was about height, like Tanyalee Davis and Michele A'Court, looks like Shazia Mirzah, size like Lorraine Benloss, Dyslexia like Josie Stuart and Angie le Mar, having a Canadian accent like Jo Jo Smith, being fostered like Mandy Knight, adopted like Rhona Cameron or as a release valve for tension in Spring Day's household.

However not all homes and families were full of tension, some were full of laughter, banter and the breeding ground for future funnies. I had a wonderful Uncle, Owi, who used to put empty egg shells upside down on egg cups and do all sorts of silly and magic tricks just to get a laugh out of us kids. I loved him to bits because of this and always laughed a lot in his company. Were some of my Interviewees funny from really early on in their lives?

Amy Schumer

"Comedy was always a part of my life. I was always a funny kid. I tried stand-up after college and got addicted to it and then finally, after years, I got good. You don't learn. You just are. You can become a better stand-up, but you're either funny or you're not. I think there is a sadness to people who want to be funny but aren't but they try to learn it."

Susie Felber

"I was always entertaining kids. In the school playground I achieved fame starting at age 5, for making up parody songs and teaching them. I did one called "I dig you" set to the tune of "Tea for Two" and called it "The Hippie Song". I'm ashamed I still remember all the words. I dreamed of running away to audition for Annie on Broadway. We didn't live far but my mother was against showbiz kids. I dreamed of being on the cast of SNL (Saturday Night Live) I was in every school play and I did imitations of Madeline Kahn and Gilda Radner. And at home – well my parents were comedy freaks, so I my earliest memories were Monty Python, SNL, Mel Brooks, Peter Cook & Dudley Moore… I knew it all."

Nancy Witter

"My Father was the Chairman of a small bank and he was hilariously funny. People would never see his jokes coming and he kept them enthralled. I learned very early on about the power of rhythm, timing and how deliver a killer punchline. My daughter Annie is 31 years old, is naturally funny and is just starting out in stand-up. I think she has more talent than me, and I hope her road is easier than mine was. I actually told her how difficult this business can be and she said:"

Annie Witter

"You know, I see my world through a funny lens, just like you did. It's fun to share it on stage. I guess I got those funny genes from you and Grandpa."

Sioned Wiliam – BBC Radio 4's Commissioner for Comedy

"I was always interested in comedy when I was a child, because my father was a playwright, so we watched every new comedy show going. People like the 'Pythons', when I was a child, 'Do not adjust your set' and I was fascinated by English comedy especially, and I think I must have watched every sit-com and comedy that was around really. Without realising it, without a doubt, I was analysing and breaking comedy down to its basic components. It's given me a real grounding and provided a context for the work, so when I meet writers I know what they've done. I'm familiar with their work and it's the same with actors really."

Sian Parry – Ex Comedy Club Booker. Music Agent & Manager

"My Dad was a very well-known Welsh medium playwright, Gwenlyn Parry and he contributed to the Welsh cult film *'Grand Slam'* as well as the long running television soap, *Pobol y Cwm* (People of the Valley). We were big fans of comedy in our house and I often frequented the comedy clubs when I started looking old enough to be let in. It wasn't until years later, when I decided to branch out by myself, rather than work for soul destroying establishments, that I saw a gap in the market and decided to take the plunge in Cardiff and set up Poncho Comedy Club."

Joanna Quinn – Oscar Nominated Cartoonist

"Both my parents were funny people. My Mum was known for her wit and was a brilliant storyteller. She was a teacher and was therefore constantly performing. There was always much laughter in our house. My Father met my Mum when he was a teacher but then he left teaching and went into the world of advertising as a copywriter. He was Irish so again a great storyteller and had the gift of the gab. So I think I absorbed their love of telling a funny story by osmosis."

Nuala McKeever

"I was always a show off and a chatterbox when I was a kid. Up until I was seven I thought my name was 'Stop That!' I remember playing out in the garden one day and my mother called me in and she said 'Nuala, the only voice I can hear is yours', so I was probably quite bossy. We Catholics also have more of a tradition I would say of playing music and doing a 'party-piece' when you stand up and entertain the family."

Rhona Cameron

"In Scotland there's a great tradition of story-telling. When my family got together, my Dad's brothers, they'd all sing and play the piano and we'd all sing together. They had a wonderful sense of humour so I was brought up in a place where performance was encouraged in a social environment."

Being a Celt myself, I can relate to their experience as it's also a regular occurrence in Welsh families to have a 'party piece' for family occasions. Fortunately my party piece was singing and not like one of my cousins who played a full-size harp. All I ever had to do to access my instrument was open my mouth.

Nina Wadia

"My entire family have very good senses of humour. My brother's, because he was more wit based, was very, very witty like my Mum, my sister is laugh-out-loud funny, she was the joker of the family, and Mum and Dad – Dad being an air steward, he was very hysterical. I remember the parties they used to have when I was very young, you know, Dad used to be the clown of the party, everyone would say, if Minoo's coming to the party, it will be the best party in the world."

Sindhu Vee

"I always loved telling jokes. I was telling jokes when I was 4, watching and reading comedy whenever I could…even if it was stuff I wasn't allowed. That I was, or tried to be funny wherever and whenever I could, wasn't taken seriously and at times it didn't go down particularly well when I was growing up. But I certainly didn't connect my innate pull to comedy with a career. Not once."

Michele A'Court

"Despite the serious face at university, I was always the joker in my family, and often in class. My maternal grandmother had a wicked sense of humour, and she and I cast ourselves as the life-and-soul of family gatherings for as long as I can remember."

Jane Mackay – Owner of 'The Stand Comedy Club', Edinburgh, Glasgow

"I always had good friends and we used to make up plays and such like and have a laugh."

Nadia Kamil

"Being the only girl in my immediate family. I lived with my father and three brothers. I became funny to try and keep up with them and get some attention."

Ronni Ancona

"I've got two brothers who were very funny so humour was quite important in my family. I remember my Grandma saying. 'She doesn't really have a sense of humour' and to me this was the worst possible thing in the world because it was so important."

Angie Le Mar

"Humour is such a powerful thing to have. If you look at any singles column, the first thing they'll say is somebody with a sense of humour. That's what everybody wants. In the gift of it all, I have got that thing that everybody wants. I have got a sense of humour. So much so that I am using it to make money. I am funny. If you are a dramatic actress or whatever, when you perform, if you are not good they'll clap at the end. If you sing they'll clap at the end even if you had a terrible voice. If you didn't make them laugh, it's quite clear from the beginning that it's not working. And they are not going to clap at the end. Because your qualification is the laughter. Once you've proven that, it's so powerful to know."

Ronni Ancona's grandmother had bought into **THE BIG THEORY** *that the 'fair sex' didn't have a sense of humour. She'd have to eat her words now Ronni wouldn't she? If you're looking at the lonely hearts section in newspapers, everyone's looking for a 'good sense of humour' as Angie Le Mar says, and I have to say that I look for a good sense of humour in most of my female friends as well, and usually find it!!!*

This seems to reiterate what Lynda Lee Potter said "Nothing is sexier and more attractive to most females than men who make them laugh. So why do men hate jokey witty women?" (Potter, Daily Mail 28/01/04)

I personally think it's just that they're so insecure of themselves they can't stand the thought of someone else being the centre of attention. It could also be to do with the fact that when a woman has a real 'belly' laugh, the involuntary shaking is similar to that which happens when a woman has an orgasm – and men always want to control that too! To take this further he may be showing that as he can make her shake involuntarily with his jokes he may be able to make her shake involuntarily with another tool in his tool kit!!! (Now I am getting carried away!) But less of this smuttiness and back to my Interviewees formative years and Angie Le Mar again.

Angie Le Mar

"When I was about 7 years old, I used to call in to LBC Radio. They had a programme called Jellybones, and kids could call up to crack jokes. And I used to sit there on Saturday just ringing the number trying to get through to get my joke on the air. I remember one day I got through and it was like, 'We have Angela in Lewisham' and I was like, 'Knock knock – who's there – Annette – Annette who? – Annette is good for fishing!' Wow! He chuckled – and that's enough for me! And my brothers used to say that I used to stand in front of the television and pretend to be my Mum or pretend to be my Dad. I was always impersonating somebody in the family. She told me at 8 that I was going to be a stand-up comedian!"

JoJo Smith

"When I came here from Canada for good I was then like 9½ at that time. And I went to a back street school in Preston and I had a Canadian accent so from day one people would pick on me and bully me. It would always be like, 'Say some'at, go on, say some'at'. I suppose I used humour at that time to fend them off."

Jo Caulfield

"We moved around a lot as a child, because my Dad was in the army I changed schools a lot and had to learn to make friends very quickly and I'd go into a school and think 'Oh I'll do my funny thing then'. I used to do these impressions for my Mum of the officer's wives, who were quite posh and didn't work with their high faluting voices – 'Oh did you really! How marvellous! Ra ra bla bla' and my Mum would just be in fits and then she's say 'Do the officers wives, do the officers wives', and it was a really nice feeling because she enjoyed it so much and I used to feel special because I could do that."

Jojo Sutherland

"I started by doing shows for the Armed Forces at RAF Lossiemouth trying to get the officers wives to laugh."

Jenny Éclair

"In Germany when my Dad was in the army, we did shows in the cellar, we'd get mates around and charge them a pfennig or whatever and they'd go on for hours. We could sort of do a nine – hour show once we'd got going, we'd keep going. I always dressed up. I was always putting on hats and my Dad's army stuff. My Mum had to have certain clothes for functions so there were always a lot of clothes to dress up in and there was always a lot of role-play stuff going on. I knew from about eight that I was funny. I knew I could pull funny faces from about six. I knew that I had an expressive face."

Lorraine Benloss

"When I went to Secondary School I started doing drama. My sister Maxine was also at the school and she was very attractive and popular. I'd always sort of lived in my sister's shadow. I was the dumpy little sister. I soon realised that humour made me different and popular."

Jo Brand

"Well my Mum and Dad were always quite jokey people and they played sort of tricks and jokes on us and we'd all muck about a lot. My brothers are both very funny so I discovered comedy quite early on I think really."

*The evidence so far seems to point to the fact that many of my Interviewees have had a lifetime of funniness to draw upon, so much for **THE BIG MYTH,** that gets blown way out of the water!! Someone who has had a longer lifetime than most of us, now entering her early nineties, is a very funny woman who does not and has never actually done 'stand-up', the legendary June Whitfield. What drove her to choose comedy as a career?*

June Whitfield

"When I started out my career I didn't particularly intend to go into comedy but right from the time I was a child and went to dancing school I was always given the comedy roles and I think I sort of grew into it. When I went to Drama School at RADA (Royal Academy of Dramatic Art) during the war, because there was a great shortage of men, I was given roles like Peter Quince in *Midsummer Night's Dream* and the second grave-digger in Hamlet."

The great shortage of men during the war also allowed many women opportunities of doing work that had previously been considered 'men's work' such as Hattie Jacques working as an arc-welder and all those women who worked in armaments and as land girls. When the war ended many of these female workers returned to their homes and gave up their new-found activities so that our 'boys' could have their jobs back. Some didn't and thank God for that eh, otherwise we women would still be tootling around in our allotments or in the kitchen with our arms up to our elbows in soapy water. Let's move from the military to the 'Millies' – the sketch group Donna McPhail performed with for several years.

Donna McPhail

"I suppose I did become funny when I left school as a way of meeting people. Writing and performing the sketches with 'The

Millies' was a good experience for developing my comedy muscle. But the way I got into stand-up was purely accidental. This was back in around 1984 and there was a scheme available from the Government, I think it was called the Enterprise Allowance Scheme. Stand-up was one of the things you could do. So for my first year I had dole and I had an extra £40 a week and they paid my rent, so in effect I was paid to have an apprenticeship. But it only took a year from my first 'Open Spot' to being fully booked on a full time basis. Now it can take a lot more than that because there are fewer 'Open Spots' so the apprenticeship is quite a long one. At the time no one had any money and everyone was miserable and it only cost four quid to get in. It was really cheap, there was a need for it so in fact stand-up suffered least of all the jobs I could have done during the eighties recession because everyone was so miserable."

It feels as if this country hasn't ever been out of recession these days. During the last few years of this present recession we are now seeing female 'yo-yo' workers returning to hoovering and hovering over the kitchen sink in droves. Women have been the real victims of the world-wide recession as they are the ones who do the majority of part-time work and also areas such as training and educating which have shrunk. They have also been seriously affected by cuts in social security benefits. Women have had to look at other career options. Had I told my careers officer back in the early seventies that I wanted to be paid money to make people laugh and clap, he would have squealed with laughter, clever cookies went to be teachers or nurses. (You had to be an exceptionally clever girl to become a Doctor) I just wouldn't have known where to start – comics just appeared 'on the telly' and I had heard of the testosterone charged working men's clubs 'up North', where Marti Caine was plying her trade, but we didn't have them in Fishguard so that was never an option for me. Nowadays there are other ways of getting into a comedy learning process, such as improvisation and university courses as well as competitions, which have proved incredibly successful in developing and channelling comic talent. So finally we have a situation where comedy is really been taken seriously and even taught in our esteemed universities. But are they as accessible to women as they are to men I wonder, are there any differences in male/female behavioural patterns and what sort of outcomes do they have?

Improvisation Courses

Rigby Jones – Opera Singer

"There's a misconception that Improv is always about making people laugh but it isn't, it's about making a cohesive scene, comedy just takes it that step further so that the outcome is laughter. Nowadays opera is really big on television with opera being broadcast live from the Metropolitan in New York with close ups and singers can now no longer just 'park and bark' – they need to be able to act. Interaction is essential and it's taught me to play off my partners. Improv is the best acting experience you can get. You are really in the moment. I have been fortunate enough to work with some amazing Improv Coaches at places like Los Angeles's 'Second City' and 'Groundlings' such as Matt Craig (who used to write for Saturday Night Live – SNL), Katie Wilbert and Heather Morgan.

Betsy Salkind

"I've been doing comedy in America since the mid 1980s. I was always clowning around in my M.B.A. class and I used to be a volunteer comedy tutor for kids who were wards of the state."

Dana Goldberg

"I ended up teaching as well as bar tending for 11 years. The interesting part of that is those 11 years behind the bar gave me a tremendous amount of improvisation skills, not to mention material. I always had to be on my feet bantering with the customers, often they were a little bit intoxicated much like a comedy club."

I worked in the Frenchman Motel, Goodwick behind the bar for several years as a teenager and Dana has just made me realise that that was how I also learnt to banter and become really witty (as well as organise a strike on behalf of the cleaners for better pay conditions at the age of sixteen – yes I didn't mess about in those days!)

Susie Felber

"Stand-up exploded in the eighties in the States with all the new network channels but Improv. really looked down on stand-up. I started out in Improv. I ran a show in Manhattan for seven years in a place called 'Ye Olde Tripple Inn'. Storytelling is now exploding in the States and it's held in some really cool venues. 'The Moth' is probably the best known venue."

Mandy Knight

"Roundabout 1987, 1988 I started doing this improvisation workshop at the Comedy Store on a Saturday morning where I met Kit Hollerbach who was the founder of 'The Comedy Store Players', and in a very short time I was asked to guest with them in the performances, so I worked with them and through that I found out that there was this alternative comedy circuit."

Jojo Sutherland

"I trained as an actor. I had a brain haemorrhage which changes your priority and I wanted to go back to performance and did a ten week Improv course on stand-up to do my 5 minutes on stage, fell into it and loved it."

Sindhu Vee

"I got into stand-up formally in May 2012. Just for the fun of it and because a friend had done it, I did a four hour (Funnywomen UK) Improv workshop on 'Are women funny?' and two months later walked into a bar in Soho as an entrant to Funnywomen UK's heats for the 2012 Awards. At that point I had never even watched any live stand up myself. I won and went on to the semifinals. Then I took Logan Murray's course for 8 weekends on 'What is stand-up' and began going to Open Mike nights in London from October 2012 then I was invited to perform at the Edinburgh Fringe Festival in both 2012 and 2013."

Kate Smurthwaite

"I did a Logan Murray course in Camden from March 2004 – June 2005. I left my banking job which was a brave move but I had no regrets at all. I started out co-presenting a radio programme and it just grew from there."

Logan Murray – Leading Comedy Improvisation Guru

"I've taught: Greg Davies, Josh Widdicomb, Rhod Gilbert and Kate Smurthwaite amongst others. There's a whole new bunch of female alumni to look out for such as Diane Morgan (Philomena Cunk on Charlie Booker's Weekly Wipe) Andi Osho, Anna Crilley, Jessica Knappett and Luisa Omelian who are doing quite well. Ex-students of mine have gone on to win every major award in the industry; do radio and TV and some choose to travel the World doing comedy."

Holly Burn aka Kirst Kay

"I did a comedy course with Logan Murray before I went into comedy. I also studied theatrical clowning in Paris and trained with Phillip Gaulier – I found that I fitted in there more than with straight acting."

Lynn Marie Hulsman

"I am the Artistic Director of Comedy Sportz in New York. I teach people to tell the TRUTH – that's where the pain and common understanding comes together, when women tell their TRUTH that's when they relate to each other. We do Improv shows in New York once a week with colleges, corporates, religious groups, team building and coaching."

This is what Roseanne Barr had to say about 'truth telling' in her 1990 book:

"One day I read a quote: 'If a woman told the truth about her life, the world would split open'. I found a stage where I began to tell the truth about my life – because I couldn't tell the truth off stage. And very quickly, the world began to blow apart."

This element of truth telling is one that is reiterated by Kathy Najimy, a feminist stand-up comic in an interview in 1992 with Brenda Gross.

"I think it's easier for women…to deal with truths. And the truths for women are the obvious truths…But women are getting to the point where we have all this rage, and it is personal, so we turn the rage into comedy."

Roseanne Barr

"It is a place, perhaps the only place where a woman can speak as a woman…and what excited me finally, was the thought of a woman, any woman, standing up and saying NO…a huge cosmic 'NO' and the first time I went on stage, I felt myself say it and I felt chilled and free and redeemed."

Rigby Jones tells of her own experience with seeking the truth in her Improv classes and also about some of the differences between men and women on those course.

Rigby Jones – Opera Singer

"The first rule of Improv that you are taught on Day 1 is that sex and fart jokes are cheap laughs and men would always go for the cheap jokes straight away. Women choose more universal topics, tell true stories based on their lives and tend to play more on stage. Men are always making inappropriate suggestions and phallic jokes to women straight away. So even in a public sphere, men think they have a right to make unacceptable suggestions, it's as if they think they have a right for them to do them and not be tackled."

And my advice on that is – tackle them! You will undoubtedly be told 'You don't have a sense of humour', so be ready for that and get yourself a quick retort such as 'If you were funny, I'm sure I could bring myself to laugh'!

Logan Murray – Leading Comedy Improvisation Guru

"Usually, the ratio of women on my courses is 25 to 45%. Occasionally, more. I've only had one course in 12 years that was entirely men. I haven't really noticed a divide in behaviour along gender lines, but I suppose there is a degree of self-selection that goes on when people sign up for my workshops. They all tend to be extroverts, with some more than others!"

As I mentioned previously, you can even find comedy as part of an University Drama or Performance Module and author and lecturer Dr. Oliver Double has expertise in this particular field.

University Courses
Dr. Oliver Double

"I've been teaching stand-up comedy in universities for about 15 years now, and in that time I've probably taught roughly the same number of women as men. Certainly it's been better than the ratio of women to men on the comedy circuit. *(A consistent 10 – 15% over the years in the UK, maybe slightly more in the States, it's very difficult to find the exact percentage.)* Male stand-ups working professionally have always tended to outnumber female ones, from the time the form was emerging in Music Halls and Variety Theatres. Is this because men are inherently more suited to stand-up comedy than women? I honestly have seen nothing that would suggest this. The women I've taught have been as likely to be gifted as the men, in terms of material, performance, persona, imagination and even the cold, hard measure of laughs-per-minute. **Some of the very best ones I've taught have been women.**"

Thanks Dr. Oliver Double, I am going to quote the hell out of that last bit! So no substance at all in **THE BIG MYTH!**

Jo Enright

"I did a BA Hons. degree in Performing Arts (Major in Drama) in London and I studied acting at the HB Studio in New York. I didn't 'fall' into stand up as such. One of the modules on my degree course was Stand Up Comedy and it was taught by a wonderful teacher called Huw Thomas. He taught me so much."

Another way to grow as a performer and where talent scouts find potential is through comedy competitions. When I started researching this book I entered one just to see what it felt like and to push myself to write some material and have a deadline. It's easy enough to flounder around in a vacuum where you don't have to push yourself very hard to develop and a competition is a way of forcing yourself to literally 'get your act together'. Had they had any impact on my Interviewees?

Comedy Competitions
Rhona Cameron
"I won a competition the first night I ever did stand-up."

Jane Mackay – Owner of 'The Stand Comedy Club', Edinburgh, Glasgow
"I had always been funny, that is, the usual thing of people at work telling you that you're funny and because of this I entered the BBC Avalon competition in around 1995."

Thenjiwe Tay Moseley
"I entered the 'Golden Jester' and 'Laughing Horse' competitions. As soon as I got on stage I didn't want to come off. I also entered the 'Funny Women' competition and made it to the final and got a tour out of it. A friend I had gone to school with, Celeste Ntuli is called 'The Queen of Zulu Comedy" and I went and did support for her for three months. I started working professionally in 2012."

Lynne Parker – Founder of 'Funny Women' UK's leading community for female comedy
"I set up 'Funny Women' because a man told me that 'women aren't funny' and that there 'aren't any funny women'. I have proved him wrong several thousand times over during the last 13 years. Our Awards struggled for 70 entrants in our first year, 2003, and I found that this was more about women's lack of confidence in their comedic ability than the actual number out there performing. This year we've had over 400 entries in the Funny Women Awards across three categories – live performance,

comedy writing and comedy shorts for film makers. Some of our past alumni are household names such as Katherine Ryan, Sara Pascoe, Bridget Christie, Zoe Lyons, Susan Calman and Sarah Millican."

Jane Duffus – Director Bristol Based Women's Comedy Club

"The 'Funny Women' award has been going now since 2003, and the only other award just for women is our 'What the Frock Comedy award'. The waiting list for this year's award was **four** times bigger than those who could take part. So many women came down from London to take part in it. I get so many women who are trying to get Open Mike spots."

Sindhu Vee

"In September 2014 I got to the 'Funny Women' UK Final and had an audience of 400 in stitches and now there's no looking back. I've gigged in Delhi and Mumbai's Comedy Store. I had my first show at the Piano Man Arts Café in New Delhi in February 2014 with several more gigs in the diary both for India and the UK."

Bethan Roberts

"I entered lots of competitions including the 'Welsh Unsigned Award'. I got to the final in 2013 and won it in July 2014 (beating six men!!) It's given me a big boost."

Lynn Ruth Miller

"I was a contestant on 'America's got Talent' with Tanyalee Davis. I have to find my own gigs as no manager will take me on because of my advancing age (*80 at the time of interview).*"

No matter how much potential or talent a funny person has, they have to eat the frog, bite the bullet and mosey on out of their comic comfort zone making their pal laugh in the pub or work environment and actually go out there and do it, climb the rickety steps, take the mike and see if you can get others to laugh. This was where my curiosity led me next. My first time doing 'stand-up' was when I organised a women's comedy night to launch the book 'Cartooning for Equality' in Cardiff about seventeen years ago. They laughed in places is all I can say!! (but I did actually enjoy it quite a lot) It was incredibly scary but I did it and it gave me some confidence to do it again.

Donna McPhail was incredibly lucky to be the only person who was actually paid by the Government to learn how to become a comic in the form of the Enterprise Allowance Scheme, one thing we should be grateful to Margaret Thatcher for. But having learnt their 'trade', these other comics needed to get their tools out of the box, as it were, and venture on stage, and for most of these comics it was the biggest and most frightening step of all. Were there other ways to serve an apprenticeship than just to do it? And what force of circumstances launched them on to the stage that very first time and even after that very first time, what made them think they could do it? A lot of my Interviewees hankered after the bright lights and entered competitions or 'Open Mikes', others didn't know how to set about it and were 'pushed', some literally some figuratively on stage. But once they had made the first tentative steps on to the stage and they knew there was no going back, there must have been something that kept them going, that made them think that they could really make a go of it. How did my Interviewees feel about their initiation into stand-up and why did they do it? That's what they told me next.

'Taking the Mike'
What made you get up on stage the first time?
I lived in Belgium for five years and was a busker there for nearly four years, that was tough, but stand-up can be to a certain degree, tougher. It was really hard standing on street corners and trying to

draw your audience close to you so that they'd stay long enough to give you some money. I learnt an awful lot then that has been very handy when I've done stand-up and also throughout my performing life: how to read an audience, how to feel and gauge them, how to make eye contact, know when you need to do something different, learn who isn't paying attention and being engaged. That was where I really learnt how to perform and I only did it because I wasn't making enough money Teaching English as a Foreign Language to survive. Why did they do what they did?

Helen Lederer

"I was in a double act for nine months. I procured my partner from another partnership. I met her in an audition and knew that we'd work well together and we had a great nine months, which was a great way in. We wrote stuff every week, and that's how I started learning how to write. And then she couldn't make a gig and I thought 'I'll go on my own then' and that was my first time and of course the first time went really well because I'd already had nine months of doing it with Maggie (Fox). I just talked about being in denial of not being lonely, as I referred to myself as not being with her, but it got laughs, so it went fine for a bit but then you get to the point where you go 'Ah, I need some really decent material'. It's almost the more you know the more you do, the harder it is. My first experience wasn't as terrifying as it became, paradoxically."

Fortunately for Helen Lederer the fact that her working partner couldn't turn up, forced her to contemplate working on her own. She probably wouldn't have had the confidence to go it alone otherwise.

Sioned Wiliam – BBC Radio 4's Commissioner for Comedy

"My first real experience of performing comedy was at Oxford as one half of the 'BoBo Girls' with Rebecca Front who you may know from 'The Day Today', 'Alan Partridge' and 'The Big Train' (2002). We used to do songs and sketches in a way that seems very old fashioned nowadays actually, but we had quite a bit of success at the Edinburgh Fringe Festival and had a residency in a comedy club in London called the 'Canal Café'. We also did a couple of series for Radio Four of songs and sketches and worked together for about five to six years, and then I became a producer and Rebecca carried on acting. We weren't stand-up per sae, we were more interested in character comedy. There's hardly anybody around doing much of it now. Mel and Sue might be a bit close I suppose."

Sioned is now in the enviable role of poacher turned gamekeeper and is now commissioning comedy programmes for BBC Radio 4.

Maureen Younger

"The first time I did it, I did a really good five minute set. I was going to give up after the second time but I sort of just kept going."

Ronni Ancona

"I always really wanted to perform when I was a child but I was very, very shy and I was not confident of myself at all. When I went to Art College I ended up in a drama class by mistake and was too shy to walk out so I had to read and got a part in one of the Art School Pantomimes and I did loads of them so that's where it began properly I suppose."

Liz Carr

"I had done years of sketch comedy in a disabled women's comedy group called 'Nasty Girls' – I co-founded it with Ann Cunningham in 2001. Stand up though is very different and when I began, my first gig with AFP (Abnormally Funny People) was at Soho Theatre and my dark and sarcastic tone and demeanour and even my black clothing plus my crip appearance were clearly too much for the audience and at times I performed to silence."

Spring Day

"My first time on stage was in September 2001. I was fired from my first job in the Japan countryside because of my cerebral palsy. I was out of work and I saw an advert in the Tokyo 'Free English Magazine' and felt 'I am now ready for more rejection!' It was a little pub called 'The Fiddler' – I did 5 minutes, got a few giggles. A comic called 'Cloudy Bongwater' and another comic told me I had a lot of spark. I was shit in the beginning but I eventually 'got it.'"

Keep going, be persistent and focussed seems to be a recurring theme here.

Nadia Kamil

"I tried stand-up once, very briefly, at university. It went ok but I was more interested in doing characters and sketches at that time so I didn't really do stand-up again until around 2010. After years of doing sketch comedy, I wanted the direct conversation with an audience that stand-up provides. I had more I wanted to say as an individual."

Joan Rivers

"I fell into stand-up by accident, there was no work as an actress. No work at all in fact."

Nina Wadia

"I didn't plan on going into comedy as such, I had planned on being an actress or a dancer. Comedy came about because of lack of work for Asian actors. This was in '94 or '95 I was very, very frustrated with the kind of work I was getting. The theatre in Stratford East had this variety night on a Sunday night. Stand up was always something I'd wanted to try but had been too scared to do. So within the context of a show, if I did it, it might work and not be too scary. I went away and put together a stand-up piece, and did it, and it went down a storm on that night, and we were then booked for three weeks, straight after that."

Shazia Mirza

"After leaving Drama School I did supply teaching, and I started writing loads of material whilst I was looking for acting work and stuff. I enrolled on a comedy writing course at the City Lit. I started doing stand-up and doing the circuit only because I wanted to be on the stage every night. I didn't realize that I would be as successful as I have been."

Rhonda Hansome

"I started out in stand-up comedy in 1980. It was a conscious decision because of a lack of parts for black women. My look was not popular! It felt like it was the only way I was going to get ahead as I didn't have a guitar, a car or a dick! I needed representation and to get a higher profile, comedy did that."

Lorraine Benloss

"The first time I did stand-up I literally had to be pushed on stage. I was on a stand-up course because I was disillusioned after Uni because everyone else was getting acting jobs and I wasn't. I had an argument just offstage that people could see and they heard me swearing. I eventually walked on really angry because I didn't want to do it and said 'Yeah, let's talk about supermodels then, and I'll just move Kate Moss aside here'. (I moved the mike stand away) The whole act came over as really angry and everyone just really loved it."

Susie Felber

"In my promo you'll see just a few of the many hookers I played. Yes funny enough all the writers were men, how'd ya know? That said, I'd happily play a hooker any day if that's what a job called for. I am fine with playing a hooker. I started performing to get into writing without going to Harvard or writing for Lampoon which are the two other main ways of making it in comedy in the States."

Michele A'Court

"I watched Carol Burnett on tv when I was a child in the 1960s and 70s, and particularly loved her monologue segment – which was stand-up, but I didn't know then what it was called. There was no stand-up in NZ until the late 1980s, just character and sketch comedy. So when I finally saw it live on stage in 1991 in NZ, I knew what I had been waiting to do. All the theatre and tv and radio and writing had been a kind of apprenticeship for this thing, which finally had a name. But it took me about 4 years of dabbling in it to get brave enough to refer to myself as 'a stand-up comedian'." Before that I quietly mumbled 'I am a performer.'

Tanyalee Davis

"Becoming a comedian is just sort of something I fell into. I had only been to a comedy club once before my first time on stage. It was more of a dare after I saw a guy I knew doing an Open Mike and he sucked, so he challenged me to go onstage myself. I wanted to get into acting and/or dealing with the public."

Wendy Kane

"I was singing on stage one night and the straps on my halter neck dress broke. I used a four-letter work and the audience laughed hysterically. I was made to stand there and finish the song off by my manager (Ron Williams) who was also Bonnie Tyler's first manager. It just progressed from there really. I didn't actually sit down and write a show, it was mostly ad-libs that stayed and it just grew."

Something that has happened to a lot of female stand-up comics is that they came to it accidentally because of lack of work for them as actors. Joan Rivers told me that there was no acting work available for her at all as a Jewish actor which propelled her to give stand-up comedy a try so she was someone who came accidentally to stand-up, as did Tanyalee Davis, and Michele A'Court.

Women like Nina Wadia, Lorraine Benloss, Angie Le Mar, Rhonda Hansome and Shazia Mirzah were in an even worse situation because there's a tremendous lack of roles for Black and Minority Ethnic women full stop. I think nowadays, women realise that there is less work for them and are more willing to create their own work. But to do that you have to be generally more confident in your abilities to not only create work but also to sell it. Nina Conti was in a similar position when she realised that there was a gap in the market for a female ventriloquist but that she had to get out and create the show herself.

Another accidental comic was Ronni Ancona, who mistook an audition for a life drawing class. (A friend of mine similarly really impressed her hard of hearing sister, who thought she was attending 'knife throwing' classes!) Thank God Ronni did, otherwise the British public may well have been deprived of her outstanding mimicking talents. Wendy Kane's talents also 'emerged' (as the same time as her boobs!) accidentally as did Nina Conti whilst trying to create a voice easy on the ear for her drama lecturer.

Nina Conti

"I was terrified when I did my first stand-up with Monk my monkey hand-puppet. I drank about two pints of lager before I even did it. And there wasn't a big audience; it was only about 15 people in the audience. But I was terrified. But once I started to get the laughs, I recovered my presence of mind and got to the end of my five minutes.

I had a similar experience to Nina Conti myself about having to create some work when no work existed. Someone saw me in a stage show (with about five other actors) about Edith Piaf and asked me to come and perform in a theatre in North Wales. As the rest of the Company had disbanded I had to come up with something and that's how I came to write and perform a one-woman show about Edith Piaf. It was a bit scary and I didn't know if I was going to be able to pull it off, and a lot of 'blag' was involved. I also did something similar to JoJo Smith when she was asked to perform at the Palladium right at the beginning of her career when I agreed to do stand-up at St. David's Hall, Wales' biggest venue. 'It'll look good on the c.v.' is what I thought, rather than 'What do I do when I die on my a****?!'

Brenda Gilhooly aka Gayle Tuesday

"I'd decided, 'Everybody tells me how funny I am in dinner parties, so I'll do this'. Of course it didn't work out quite like that, because being funny at dinner parties isn't the same. Being comfortable with people in a friendly environment is really different to doing stand-up so I got really scared because they weren't all my friends. I just thought 'Oh I'll give that a go'. Of course it was the stupidity of youth because I don't think I'd have kept going with it if I hadn't been young. I mean if I started stand-up now and it was awful, I wouldn't keep going. But I was about twenty-four, twenty-five and it was really, really hard. And I thought it was going to be easy and it wasn't, and everybody was going to be really nice and they weren't. I did stand-up for three or four years as myself and then I decided to do something different and that's when I thought up the character Gayle Tuesday. Everything's easy after stand-up."

Some of the women I've interviewed have used stand-up as a transitory phase, and that was something they probably didn't want to be doing for a long time. French and Saunders did it for a very short time. Whilst writing this book I have also done several stand-up performances, some as myself and some as 'Bodicea Queen of HRT' on about three occasions, one of which was an Open Mike at the Laughing Cows Comedy Club at the Frog and Bucket in Manchester in 2008 when I was the first Welsh woman to perform there and I did find it incredibly liberating to hide behind a wig and costume. You may have heard the word 'Open Mike' mentioned previously, what it means is that anyone who feels they are funny and want to appear in front of an audience books themselves an 'Open Mike' slot for which they are not paid and which will be either at the beginning or the tail end of the night. The more Open Mikes you do the more chance there is of being seen and being booked and paid.

Jo Caulfield

"Getting the first 'Open Mike' was not difficult. It was in the Comedy Café, East London. Every Wednesday they have a new act competition. You just phone up and get yourself a slot. That's the great thing about stand-up, it's so immediate, even if you have to wait six months to have a slot it's not long. It's a great leveller – it doesn't matter what size, shape, sex or colour you are, all that's important is whether you're funny or not. It's very democratic and doesn't discriminate. The first 'Open Mike' after college was terrifying. I was really drunk and very scared. I didn't really think it through what I was scared of, maybe that I'd be humiliated or that people wouldn't laugh. The alcohol helped. I didn't do stand-up night after night which I think I should have done to get the experience. It was more like once every two or three weeks."

Hattie Hayridge aka Holly Red Dwarf

"Alcohol and desperation about still doing secretarial work played a big part in my first time on stage."

Mandy Knight

"There were two reasons why I made the leap from writing poems to my first real stand-up gig. The first is that I met Jo Brand. I've always sort of sat in her shadow, and just been overwhelmed by her stuff but we actually got on very well. She was very encouraging. I said 'I can only write jokes that rhyme' and she said 'Don't be silly, just sit and write some of the things you've said to me'. The other is that an ex-boyfriend of mine really made me feel rock bottom and that I had nothing at all left to lose. So I went out and all my first routine I don't remember it really, but it was just a complete letting rip about eating disorders it was just all the bile coming out and I don't remember any of my first gigs at all. I just completely got through them on fear, adrenaline, anger and that sort of real kamikaze 'Well, what the fuck does it matter' sort of attitude. What was quite sweet was a year later I got my first encore at the club where I did my first gig and I think it was around Christmas time, and then my ex-boyfriend went on to do a double act which was really shit and just got booed off everywhere, so really he got what he deserved!"

It's called karma Mandy and it's got a nasty habit of biting people in the ass!

Bethan Roberts

"I started doing stand-up at the age of 26, two years ago. I had depression and ended the pastry making course I was on a year early. I was at rock bottom and really missed performing. A friend randomly suggested I should try 'stand-up' , 'cause you're so funny'… I entered the 2013 'Funny's Funny' – Bobby Carroll's comedy competition on my first outing and found it difficult, I was scared but very excited!

Hitting rock bottom like Hattie Hayridge, Mandy Knight and Bethan Roberts gave them the impetus to give stand-up a try. What did they have to lose – absolutely nothing? Why not take a chance – just like Julia Morris did.

Julia Morris

"After Drama School in Sydney I went to work for Club Med, and when I came back, some friends of mine asked me would I like to host a stand-up night for them and I'm like 'Yeah!' And I hosted their stand-up night and they said 'You should go down to the Comedy Store'. And I went down to the Comedy Store and I hadn't seen stand-up live ever before. I sort of remember vaguely seeing it on the television. I thought if it's standing on the stage and just talking, I've been doing that forever, so I went and gave it a go and the manager of the Sydney Comedy Store that night ended up becoming my own personal manager and agent for eleven years in Australia. I was twenty two, back in the nineteen nineties. I actually started compering before I did the stand-up comedy, which is not the way it's usually done, but hey, I never do things the normal way."

Even with a belly full of beer you still had to be quite brave to step up on to that stage and some were incredibly brave or was that incredibly foolish, like Julia Morris compering at Australia's best stand-up venue even before she had done any stand-up herself as Nina Conti did, booking herself a show where she knew she had to perform an act of some sort.

Angie Le Mar

"When the Bemara Sisters broke up, because I was always the funny one, it was a make or break decision. So I went to a club and I thought if I can get black people and bring them together, turn on the light and tell jokes and make them laugh, I am so funny. So I went to a club, that happened, and it was, you know, we've got a girl who wants to tell jokes. In the black community at the time, there were no black female comedians, so it was like this novelty. So I started telling jokes and they were in stitches and I thought, 'Actually I can do this'. I could do this wonderful thing that I dreamt about years ago, it didn't have to just be acting now. So when I went in for stand up, as a novelty you know, if you want a black person and a woman – you get Angie. It was my first kind of make or break situation – like, 'What am I doing?' I thought I had to do it coz there's no longer the Bemara Sisters. Acting work, you know, you go along for an audition and you can't read it because of the dyslexia so you don't get it. So you lose out. So you've got to find a way of being able to be consistent and get work. So it was make or break."

Shazia Mirza

"My first gig was in Brixton at 1 o'clock in the morning in some rough pub. There was no microphone, there was no stage, there were about 200 men in there and I just had to stand in the middle of this room at 1 o'clock in the morning and make everyone laugh. And I stormed that gig. I just couldn't believe it."

JoJo Smith

"My first real gig was in a tatty little pub in Hammersmith,

London, called 'The Hop Poles', July 1993. I chose it 'cause if it was as bad as I anticipated, I wouldn't have far to get home! I was pretty rubbish and extremely drunk, thanks to my pals buying me triple vodka to steady my nerves. But I was hooked on the power of having a mike and making people laugh. Though to be fair, at that first gig I reckon they were laughing at me. An act called 'Buddy Hell' was top of the bill!"

Fern Brady

"In 2009 the magazine I worked for asked me to do an article where I tried stand up. After my first gig I couldn't sleep because I knew I was going to do stand up as a job. I can only describe the feeling as comparable to realising you love someone, which sounds fucking ridiculous, but anyway, it was dead profound. So I told my boyfriend at the time and he said "You definitely shouldn't do it again." which was nice of him. This discouraged me so much that I didn't gig again for a year but secretly I started to book in a lot of gigs. I broke up with that boyfriend and once I started gigging in May 2010, I never stopped."

Donna McPhail

"I was down at Jongleurs in Battersea a bit pissed, Arthur Smith was compering and he said: 'Come on, get up and do that thing you do in the show' (with the theatre group 'The Millies'). Having had a couple of pints, I thought that would be a good idea. I was drunk. That's the only reason I did it. And I stormed it. I thought: this is a piece of piss – well, I'll do this then!"

Jo Brand

"It was about 1986 and I was moaning to a mate of mine David, that I hated my job as a psychiatric nurse. I'd been in it for too long and that I wanted to do comedy and I just didn't know how to do it and he looked at me and said 'I know it's a cliché, but this is not a rehearsal, this is it! If you don't do something yourself, you'll never do it, so get your finger out!' That was a real turning point for me. Funnily enough, David's girlfriend set up a benefit in the West End, a sort of Greenpeacey sort of thing and she'd booked some comedians. She phoned me up, said it was a perfect opportunity, I could go on at the end and do fifteen minutes. So I had no excuses but it was a dreadful experience. I was pissed out of my head. I had to wait the whole evening before I went on and by that time I'd had seven pints of lager. I didn't go on until midnight and every comic that had gone on before me had died on their ass really badly. It was just that sort of a night, the audience weren't really interested. So, because I was so drunk I had this idea that I could go on and save the evening, which was stupid, 'cause I'd never done it before and I think I got booed off after about three minutes. Afterwards I was sort of semi-conscious really because I was so pissed, so it wasn't too bad. I think it would have been incredibly humiliating if I'd been sober but when you're drunk, you get this sort of false confidence, but it was good in a way because it made getting up again not quite so bad."

Thank God for the 'demon drink' which seems to have functioned quite strongly in several women's first experience of doing 'stand-up' and took the edge off what could have been a very humiliating experience. Once they'd had a taste it seems they just wanted more.

Liz Carr

"I had done sketch comedy. I had done acting work. I was doing a comedy / disability podcast for BBC Ouch! And all these things gave me a profile and so when Abnormally Funny People (AFP) formed and were looking to take a group of disabled people to Edinburgh Fringe – some experienced and some newbie comedians – they asked me, as someone who had stage experience but not as stand up as such. Accommodation and decent gigs in

Edinburgh for the month of Fringe? Chance to perform at Soho Theatre? Being filmed for a Sky Tv. fly on the wall doc of our experience? I decided to just go with it. I said yes. I do that a lot. Say yes. Drift into things. See what happens."

Nina Wadia

"The first time I did stand-up in the Asian Variety night, I was terrified. Something really funny did happen with it actually, because, I was backstage, my mike was switched on, and I was waiting to go on, and I remember standing backstage with Paul Shama, and I was saying, 'I can't do this, I can't do this', and the mike was on, and people heard that, and they started giggling, they thought it was part of the act. The minute I heard the audience laugh, my confidence went up, and I went out on stage. And I actually thought, 'Oh, I could use that!' It was the most terrifying thing I've ever done in my whole life. And yet, the biggest buzz that I ever got from a performance."

Dana Goldberg

"There was a show in Albuquerque, New Mexico called "Funny Lesbians For a Change." It was a variety show that raised higher education scholarships for women in the community. They gave me a 7 minute set in front of 650 people in a sold out theatre. I practiced in front of my sister and all of her friends. I did my set in the living room with a lint roller as my microphone, and they were stoned out of their minds so they thought I was the funniest person on the planet. I got onstage for the show and I remember looking down and I could see my heart beating through my shirt. I didn't touch the microphone. I thought I was going to turn it into an amplifying vibrator! I hit my first big joke that night and heard the most deafening laughter I had ever heard, and that was it, I was hooked. That was the only encouragement I needed!"

Ooooh! All very scary stuff then with a lot of alcohol in the mix. Once could have been enough to put them off for life but these fearless females had some payoff for all that adrenaline coursing through their veins – laughter! Washing over them like a big West Walian winter wave. Was there something or someone inspirational other than laughter which gave them the impetus to carry on?

Harnessing the demons –
Who or what made you think you could do it?
Who has given you a helping hand?
Nina Conti

"Well I think secretly that I had always wanted to do stand-up and I was much more drawn to comedy than to serious acting. I just saw the power that this monkey had because I had to do a couple of promotional shows in Edinburgh to promote my show. I took the monkey along and I just did five minutes of chatting with the monkey. And when he got laughs I realised that this was going to work. At the same time I was aware that no one else was doing this; no other women have done this for years and years, so there was a huge gap in the market."

Aditi Mittal

"I've been doing stand-up for the last three and a half years. We've always had comedy in India but always in Hindi and it was always dominated by men. Hindi comedy is very dependent on mimicry and making fun of others. The population of India is 1.2 billion and of those about 30-35% can be said to be Hindi speakers I recently did a 'Celebrity Comedy Roast' on Comedy Central. I was the first woman and only one in fourteen men. There were no holds barred. That really made me feel great. I met Kate Smurthwaite in the BBC's '100 Women Conference' in 2013. Kate became my Mentor and I have really grown over the last few months because of Kate's mentorship."

Sioned Wiliam – BBC Radio 4's Commissioner for Comedy

"I went to Ysgol Gyfun Rhydfelen (Rhydfelen Comprehensive School in Pontypridd, Wales) The drama teacher was immensely inspiring. I then went to Aberystwyth University and was very lucky to have Emily Davies teaching me, another extraordinarily inspirational character who was an Internationalist and made us feel that even though we were in this tiny little country with this tiny little language, that we had a contribution to make. She was a huge inspiration."

Ronni Ancona

"After leaving Art College, I got in with a group of people who loved comedy and I learnt how to do comedy improvisation and it was fantastic. Noel James, a Welsh comic set me off on stand – up. He was terrifically supportive and very helpful. This was about nineteen eighty nine. Noel had persuaded me to work as a compere at the Tatershall Castle, which was a paddle steamer boat on the Thames, because the club wasn't making much money, they needed a regular compere and it would be a very good experience. Around that time at the Tatershall Castle, there were a lot of people starting out who are huge names today. You had Eddie Izzard, Lee Evans, Mark Lamarr and Jo Brand and God man alive I was a dreadful compere, probably the world's worst! Then I went in for the Hackney Empire 'Time Out New Act of the Year' and I won that in 1993. I'd had a bad day at work teaching so I was a lot calmer than I normally was and it went really well and I won. I was absolutely astounded so that gave me a bit of a foot up as regards the circuit."

Lorraine Benloss

"After the comedy course 'Showcase', I started getting bookings, mainly on the black cabaret circuit. I was working in a theatre and in a clothes shop at that time. I needed to because each show I did there would be a promoter there who would ask me to come along and do an Open Spot, but that was their way of getting me to perform without paying me. Keith Palmer (Zoom Vision Entertainment Agency) then stepped in and started helping me with fees and bookings."

Jo Enright

"Huw Thomas, who taught the stand-up module at Uni, was, and still is, an incredible performer. He knows how to hold an audience in the palm of his hand. He taught me to see stand-up as a craft. He taught me to give all of myself to the pursuit of excellence in that craft. He introduced me to the work of people like Robin Williams (I watched 'Live At The Met' over and over) and other important political voices in comedy like Alexei Sayle. He taught me the importance of learning how to 'play' on stage, to serve the audience and not your ego. So working with Huw made me realise that much of stand-up was similar to acting, particularly if your act involved going in and out of characters like mine does. I learnt that both acting and stand up needed be rooted in truth. Having been so inspired by Huw, even though my initial desire was to do straight acting, when I left my degree I decided to dedicate two years to writing and performing stand up. I hoped that perhaps the stand-up would lead me into acting roles but the stand-up was never inferior to acting in my eyes. Fortunately I have been able to move between acting and stand up for the majority of my career. I love them both and when I am doing one I can't wait to switch to the other."

Liz Carr

"Abnormally Funny People (AFP) brought me into contact with the wonderful Tanyalee Davis who took me under her mini bingo wings and helped me develop my style and content. Through AFP,

ve minutes. It's the theatre, you're charging good money,
o respect the audience and give them a good show. My
she works with) is also a tremendous help to me, she
ent honest feedback, is incredibly supportive and
e only person I will always listen to."

ourt
ork from Mike King – a Kiwi comedian who made
the 90s. Mike took me under his wing and gave
o-one else much trusted a woman to be funny. We
t comedians, but he gave me huge opportunities,
rough pubs where we'd turn up and the punters
as the stripper."

erry Davey and I met as finalist in "Nick at
Funniest Mom in America". We performed
d the country for 5 years as the comedy trio
We created it ourselves because we weren't
ducer to do it for us."

rters male and female, but when I look
got was via a lady comedian. A woman
elped me get my first job at Comedy
s open. Another lady performer helped
roducing promos for another TV net.
authors. Other women hired me to
ople got me TV work."

of the *Pacifica Tribune* and it was
lumn. From that came the content

I had the chance to work with Huw Thomas who at the Kings
Head in Crouch End, London – a club which supports new acts
like no other I've ever experienced by giving them a generous place
to play and try things out. And then there's Steve Day, he says he's
Britain's only deaf comedian and if there are any others, he hasn't
heard about them! He says I have funny bones. He's taught me a
lot, particularly about enjoying yourself on stage and if you're
doing that then the audience will most likely enjoy it too. And
then there's my partner Jo – she likes to think she writes all my
material!"

Tanyalee Davis
"I have never had a mentor but I have a few close comedian
friends whose opinions I value."

Hazel O'Keefe – Laughing Cows Comedy Club and Women's Comedy Festival
"Donna McPhail really, really, supported us as a club and
headlined the opening night (Nov 1998). Donna was a comedy
purist cos she was gag after gag after gag. Comedy and the triple
gag was like an embedded language for her."

Shazia Mirzah
"Christine Collins was my acting teacher and she became my
mentor and she has really guided and supported me in my whole
life. My manager, Vivienne Smith, who also manages JoJo Smith
is brilliant. She's a hard Scottish woman and a very good manager
and I have got a very professional hard-working relationship with
her. She's very tough and very protective. I have never had a male
mentor ever. I suppose that's because I was kept in the dark about
men because of my religion – don't go near men, don't talk to
them, and they're evil. Which is true! It's ironic really I should end
up in a white working men's club with 200 men every night."

Rhona Cameron

"My manager, Jeremy Hicks is quite a mentor to me. I've been with him since the beginning and we're very close. But in terms of another comedian, who gave me my first break on t.v., who has been incredibly supportive to me, and who's helped me out of even financial problems in the past is Eddie Izzard. He's been very good to me. And I think he's the best comedian in this country."

Jenny Eclair

"My manager Richard Allan Turner has been more or less solely responsible for getting me to where I am. My boyfriend has been very supportive and always there. My agent *(at that time)* Vivienne Smith is also very helpful."

Jane Mackay – Owner of 'The Stand Comedy Club', Edinburgh, Glasgow

"Whereas most of the acts I have worked with have been helpful (though, in some cases, that may be because I own a club) my mentors throughout have been my partner Tommy Sheppard (all the more valuable because he has no desire whatsoever to perform himself) and my daughter Eva Mackay who found us our first premises in the tiny basement of a pub in Edinburgh's Grassmarket – near the School of Art – where she was then studying and who still does the door at the Edinburgh club at weekends."

Ashley Storrie – World's youngest FSUC and daughter of Janey Godley

"My Mum, comic Janey Godley is my mentor and she used to call me her 'muze' *(from amusing?)* and I have performed with her in the past."

Angie Le Mar

"I once met Whoopi Goldberg and it was just like meeting a sister,

she was really wonderful to me, we r
she pulled me in especially to have
in the press. Since then I have co

Nuala McKeever

"I met Shaun Carson (Frank
to write and that's when I s
up in my own voice and
then formed the basis o
Ulster television, called

Mandy Knight

"Jo Brand is not o
friend and the gr
been to places
experiences an
on her show
need one p

Nadia K

"I met
were
soon
her

seventy fi
you have
sister *(who*
gives excel
probably th

Michele A'C

"I got a lot of
it big in NZ ir
me gigs when n
are very differen
sometimes in ver
would assume I w

Nancy Witter

"Karen Morgan, S
Nites Search for the
in theaters and tour
'Mama's Night Out'.
going to wait for a pr

Susie Felber

"I have had many supp
back, nearly every job I
who was an improviser
Central by telling me it w
me get a job writing and
Both those women are no
perform and lady casting p

Lynn Ruth Miller

"Chris Hunter was the editor
he who gave me my weekly co

of my comedy and also my confidence that I had something to say that people wanted to hear."

Dana Goldberg

"I had the pleasure of working with David Brenner before he passed away. He was such an incredible man. He taught me not to be afraid of the silence in between jokes. The silence means I have them, the silence means they are listening and waiting for the next thing I say."

Betsy Salkind

"I worked in the Comedy Store on Sunset Boulevard for about ten years. Mitzi Shore was very supportive to female performers and had lots of us in all the time."

Lydia Nicole

"Mitzi Shore really nurtured women and brought them on. Most would come through the Store in L.A. I heard the voice of God from the age of four. I love God and try to be a good Ambassador for him. He always gave me direction including going to Los Angeles when I had no money and no contacts but God opened the door for me. It used to be a conflict (God and comedy) because I kept them separate. People used to tell me that I couldn't do comedy and act because it wasn't a Godly thing to do, until I met a minister who told me that God wouldn't have given me comedy if he didn't intend me to use it. I brought Mitzi Shore to God in 2001.

Betsy Salkind

"I got a job writing for Roseanne (Barr) She came looking for me and I worked very closely together with her and did six episodes of 'Saturday Night Special'."

Lots of different people have been very helpful and supportive, both male and female to my Interviewees. Some male comics were very supportive to women like Noel James (who I ended up 'supporting' on stage in the Wharf Comedy Club in Cardiff a couple of years ago and who also got me a gig when I decided that Bodicea Queen of HRT was ready to be unleashed on the world) who spotted the inherent talent and urged 'cooky' Ronni Ancona to try her hand at stand-up and compering on a Thames paddle steamer. Ronni Ancona was a student of Mandy Knight who was very lucky to work alongside a very supportive Jo Brand. Ben Elton was very encouraging to Jo Brand, and also a comic called Ivor, with whom she shared a flat. He gave her a lot of practical advice, such as how to hold a microphone properly, what sort of material to use, which way around to do a joke and how to make it work better and most important of all, how to deal with hecklers. I was never very good at asking for help from anyone, I was too independent, but age has made me realise that two arms can row a boat quicker than one so find someone who believes in your talent and allow them to help you with your development. Donna McPhail also had a lot of support from males, especially male promoters of small clubs on the lower levels of the circuit. You can never be too small to pack a punch as Tanyalee Davis can testify whilst mentoring Liz Carr and even those in the minority such as Sioned Wiliam, a first language Welsh speaker have an important part to play in the world and thanks to her drama teacher and university lecturer, Emily Davies, the importance of minorities on a world stage became evident.

The entry level to the world of comedy are the unpaid 'Open Mikes', and Angie Le Mar and Lorraine Benloss both did a lot of free gigs performing on the London black circuit, which gave them both the experience and the payback of laughter that they both desired. Mandy Knight also did a lot of 'Open Mikes', the more you did, the more experienced you became and the quicker you moved on to paid gigs.

Such a variety of people or circumstances that have given these women the confidence to carry on after stepping out with some trepidation on to the stage. Sometimes, like Nina Wadia, all they needed was the laughter and the applause, for others like Ronni Ancona, Rhona Cameron, Sindhu Vee, Bethan Roberts, Jenny Éclair it was, competitions that were the springboard to greater confidence and future success. Jenny was in good company at the time, with people like Eddie Izzard performing in the same competitions.

However, having served their early 'apprenticeship' in life as a comic, the nuts and bolts had to be put in place to support this passion. Practical advice on how to flex and develop the comedy muscle is also just as important, if not more important, as recognising the desire that comedy is something that pushes someone's button. Where this practical advice came from is what I was told next.

Gwenno Dafydd & Jo Caulfield, Glee Club, Cardiff

CHAPTER 4

LAYING THE FOUNDATIONS

In which I find out about Role Models, Battling with Bears & Alter Egos

Build your house upon the sand and it hasn't got a cat in hell's chance of withstanding the spring tides let alone any stormy weather that comes its way. Build your house upon a rock with good foundations and it'll weather any conditions it comes across. And as anyone who hasn't had any building experience would either get themselves some expert advice or a 'How to' book, aspiring FSUCs need as much practical support as they can muster. Someone who has already built a house is an obvious person to mimic and so my next step was to look at those women my comics looked up to or drew inspiration from.

Who were my Interviewees Role Models, who were they inspired by, who did they draw sustenance from? My own Role Models growing up in Fishguard, would have been the feisty Jemima Niclas, a local cobbler who took on the whole of the French battalion with a pitchfork when they tried to invade Britain over two hundred years previously. I always loved Joan of Arc for her fearlessness, perseverance and belief and I also had some very positive female Role Models in my own family, for example my maternal Grandfather's mother who ran a farm in mid Wales after being widowed in her forties with seven children to feed and clothe. All the boys went to universities and had very successful professional lives whilst all the girls went to London to be in service for the upper classes. My maternal Grandmother was also left a widow with seven children as was my paternal Grandmother. One thing that I decided from their stories was that I certainly didn't want to have seven children – it seemed to have a very detrimental effect on the man of the house!!! I think that as women we tend not to have as much access to heroines for two reasons, the first one being that their lives consisted mostly of bearing children and the other was that as history was for the most part collated and collected by men throughout the ages, women's achievements would not have been considered worth noting by men, therefore few of these achievements have been recorded for posterity.

As a singer I was very influenced by Edith Piaf. I'd heard about her when I went to live in Belgium and her rags to riches story really gave me the impetus to become a singer. I thought if she could do it so could I, and it's odd how she seems to have followed me on the trajectory of my life. I became fascinated by her life and wrote, performed (and later published and re-published with Parthian Press) a one-woman show about her. In the course of my research for my show, I ended up meeting Eluned Phillips, the only woman to be crowned twice as a Bard in our annual cultural binge, the Welsh National Eisteddfod and who was a friend of Piaf's for over a quarter of a century. I was very proud to be able to call Eluned a dear friend of mine and in fact she became a mentor to me for over twenty years until she died in 2007. She was always extremely supportive of both my singing and my writing and continued to write herself, until her death at the age of ninety two. I had an idea commissioned for Welsh television about her 90th Birthday which she chose to celebrate in Los Angeles. I did an interview about her life with a film crew out in Los Angeles, then sang some Piaf songs in her birthday party and then stayed on for a few days and spent several evenings in the world famous Comedy Store on Sunset Boulevard where I met resident pianist Jeff Scott, so it was through my Mentor and Role Model that these things happened.

The Comedy Store, on Sunset is the starting point for my comic *journey, as it was here that Don Ward saw what living legend Mitzi Shore had established and came away with a vision of establishing a similar venture in London. Having met Jeff Scott back in 2004, I kept in email contact and through him tried to persuade Mitzi Shore to give me an interview. She is quite a private and reclusive person and even the 'fabulous ferret' was not able to cajole her into giving me an interview.*

Returning to the issue of Role Models, if you look at the books available about comics and comedy up until very recently, you'd think that women had never made anyone laugh. When I started my research in 1996, there were countless books on comedy in which women were always either invisible, peripheral or mentioned in passing. The books tended to be written by men and the comedy scene looked at through their eyes, which didn't always match up to the information I was looking for. For example, according to William Cook in his 1994 book 'Ha Bloody Ha – Comedians talking', stand-up shares fiction's first commandment: write about what you know – which for women 'aint the same as for men, although in his defence, I will say he did include Jo Brand, Jenny Éclair and Donna McPhail, three out of a total of thirty one comics.

This is less than 10 % of the total comics featured, a figure consistent with the percentage of female comics performing on the London 'circuit' according to figures produced by top London comedy club 'Jongleurs' both in 1986 and 1996. There has been some improvement in the last few years. Women account for approximately 15% at present (although it's devilishly difficult to find the exact percentage.) There are more and more stand-up comics overall so that means there will be more women performing stand-up comedy even though the percentage is not greatly different to when I first started doing this research. One of my Interviewees, Mandy Knight became the first ever female Compere at 'Jongleurs', who was her Role Model?

Mandy Knight

"Jo Brand is a great Role Model. I think we share a very similar sense of humour but I think our execution is very different."

Jongleurs, surprisingly enough was set up by Drama teacher Maria Kempinska. 'Jongleurs', Britain's biggest chain of comedy clubs was started back in 1983 by her in an old roller-skating rink in South London on a push-bike and a £300 overdraft. She was very lucky to have been granted an overdraft as at that time, banks were very reticent to lend money to women at all, I know, I bought my own house in my own name around 1985 and it was hard work. The late seventies and early eighties was the time of the Alternative Comedy Scene. Some of the women that developed successful careers as a result of this were: French and Saunders, Victoria Wood, Helen Lederer, Jenny Lecoat, Ruby Wax, Tracey Ullman, Julie Walters, as well as Jo Brand, Jenny Eclair and Donna McPhail. Morwenna Banks and Amanda Swift wrote an excellent book back in 1987 called 'The Joke's on us', documenting some of these early pioneers.

However, nearly thirty years later the vast majority of books available about female comedy are scripts of popular shows as opposed to information about their lives. Mary Ann Rishel, Ithaca College, author of 'Writing Humor: Creativity and the Comic Mind', goes on to say "A...... study of stand-up comedy performed by females is long overdue, and its importance for understanding power structures in our society cannot be underestimated." However, up until very, very recently there were no books whatsoever about the lives of present day female British comics, or for that matter FSUCs from anywhere in the world. This is surprising, as whenever I have spoken to people, both men and women, about my book idea, whether in public or in private, I have constantly been surprised at their enthusiasm and interest in the project.

In the last two years there have been three books, the first by Viv Groskop; 'I laughed, I cried', is an account of Groskop performing one hundred comedy gigs in one hundred nights. It is described as "an experiment in doing what you want, even if it is terrifying, without giving up the day job". It was published by Orion in 2013. It's interesting to note, that yet again, Groskop is another female stand-up comic who went to an all-girls school (Bruton School for Girls) and then went to Cambridge. More recently in May 2015, 'The What the Frock! Book of Funny Women' written by Jane Duffus, who I also interviewed, which was published by BCF books.

Jo Caulfield says, "It was quite difficult when I started out, because there were no other real Role Models to aspire to. Therefore, many aspiring female comics had to be content with male comic Role Models when they were growing up. This book will change that scenario!"

The other aspects of their lives I wanted to look at in this Chapter were what they did before they launched themselves into comedy on a full time basis – how boring did their job have to become before they made a commitment to comedy? I was also interested to hear about the actual practicalities of life on the road, how they managed to keep a home life going and also to take a peek at their on and off stage characters and how they were able to make a shift between one and the other.

Articles have regularly appeared in the Press every year or so since I started working on this project asking why there were so few FSUCs? There are – it's just no one had brought them all together before, so here's the book to fill the void, full of positive and successful Role Models

Role Models
Ava Vidal

"I think it's a great idea to write a book celebrating female comics, I'm sure it'll be a big help for comics starting out."

Naomi Paxton

"The lack of amalgamated knowledge about female comics is because of their perceived scarcity in the 'canon' and histories of comedy – and that's about who is 'allowed' to be successful, who progresses in the mainstream hierarchies and who becomes a curator of their own work. Are they given the same opportunities to be visible on large stages and screens? It's also about their relationships to male colleagues and collaborators as well – even when their creative input has been equal or more prolific, the male names often seem to come away with the credit and longevity."

Jo Caulfield

"When I first started doing stand-up in the early nineties, I didn't really know how to do a comedy act, how to set about it. At that time there was French and Saunders but they didn't really do stand-up and there were no other real Role Models to aspire to. There were other women who did stand-up then but because no one had written a book collating all the information, you just didn't hear about them. There are an awful lot more women doing stand-up than are given credit for. My favourite female comics are Rhona Cameron and Joan Rivers."

Rhona Cameron

"I came from a small Scottish fishing town and it was quite unusual to go even up to the (Edinburgh) Festival. I remember having to go to the library to get a festival programme and I went on my own up to see Victoria Wood. And I liked her because not only is she very funny, I think probably the funniest woman in Britain, but I identified with her because she was androgynous, not pretty and she kind of laughed at herself. I related to all that. I related to women who were not necessarily conventionally attractive but I found the humour very alluring, very seductive."

Helen Lederer

"Victoria Wood was already established as a proper person when I started out and I think she's fantastic, I always have."

It's big responsibility to be the first in any new arena – you are creating a benchmark for the future. History in the making can only be seen in retrospect and lucky Helen Lederer, whether she was aware of it or not at the time was definitely in the right place at the right time, in the company of such comic legends as Alexei Sayle and Ben Elton. She may also not have realised but by virtue of doing 'stand-up' at a time when women were a rarity she, and other women she shared the stage with, such as French and Saunders became 'Role Models' for all future aspiring female comics.

Holly Burn aka Kirst Kay

"My Role Models were: Victoria Wood, Julie Walters, French & Saunders, Black Adder and Woody Allen."

Victoria Wood was a comic who had been immensely successful over the last three decades and one who was often named as having been a positive Role Model for many up and coming female comics. She did a drama degree with a strong emphasis on writing scripts, wrote all of her own material and as a result retained a tight control over her work and its content. What couldn't this woman do? She sang, she wrote lyrics and music, she created characters, sketches and musicals. She was, to me, the ultimate entertainer and a phenomenal performer and Role Model.

Victoria Wood I feel, was a total one-off, part of the Music Hall tradition of the all-round entertainer with her funny songs, her sketches and her characterization, but at the time when she came to the attention of the British public with her first few appearances on 'New Faces' and 'That's Life', in the late seventies, she was one of the very few funny women on our screens. Women had to look further afield to find inspiration and Joan Rivers was already making noises so loud in the comedy world in America that we could practically hear her in Fishguard! I would never have ever believed that I would have the honour of meeting Joan Rivers backstage with her entourage in Saint David's Hall when she performed in Cardiff in 2004, but meet her I did. She was very sweet and lovely and gave me a pack of mini lipsticks with her name on them and pulled me in close to have some photographs. She had just come off stage where she had performed a highly physical and dynamic set, even though at that time she was a phenomenal seventy one years of age. It took me a whole week of emails and phone calls to meet up with her and many thanks go to Gareth Griffiths, Manager of Saint David's Hall for organizing it for me. I also met her regular accompanist Will T Hall in New York's 'Don't Tell Mama' Piano bar in 2012 when I was in New York with the choir I sing with. Joan was probably a Role Model to more aspiring female comics than any other woman, she was larger than life and as bawdy as they came. Her fame spread all over the world, including the Far East.

Nina Wadia

"When I was in Hong Kong, the first stand-up I ever, ever saw, and I didn't know what a stand-up comic was until I saw this, was Eddy Murphy on the television, then I saw Robin Williams and then Joan Rivers performing. I thought she was brilliant, absolutely brilliant. I thought 'Oh my God, women can do this, women can do this'. So it had always been in the back of my mind, but I never had the courage to think 'I can do this', until that Variety night at Stratford East when I thought 'Actually, why don't I try it. I've always said I've wanted to, so why don't I try it', and it went down a storm, and I thought, 'Hang on, I can do this'. But I wouldn't have considered it something that a woman could do, if I hadn't seen the Joan Rivers set."

Nina Wadia would not be doing comedy were it not for Joan Rivers and likewise Aditi Mittal, a pioneering Indian FSUC, would probably not be doing comedy were it not for Nina Wadia's pioneering work with the ground breaking cult 'Goodness Gracious Me'.

Aditi Mittal

"My Role Models were Meera Syal and Nina Wadia in 'Goodness Gracious Me' – they set the bar very high and it's a question of sharing culture. I love doing characters, because I can hide behind the character and say things I might not be able to say otherwise in my culture. One of my characters is a sex therapist who only talks about sex in a well-meaning way and discusses things like vaginal tightening creams, which I could never talk about as me."

Joan Rivers' talent has inspired women worldwide from Fishguard to the Far East and I believe that she was an immensely brave woman in what was at that time such a heavily dominated male environment. She not only inspired FCUCs but also women such as Hollywood Film Director, Sara Sugarman.

Sara Sugarman – Hollywood Film Director

"Some women are very funny, Joan Rivers, I really love her and Sarah Silverman, for me they're comic geniuses. Marilyn Monroe was brilliantly funny and she had a tremendous amount of feminine energy. I love Melissa Macarthy, but I also love gentler underdogs."

Lynn Ruth Miller

"I owe Phyllis Diller and Joan Rivers big time – they suffered because they were women. I am able to do what I do because of them."

Cathy Ladman
"I watched the Ed Sullivan Show every week and loved 'I love Lucy', Carol Burnett, Lily Tomlin, Joan Rivers and Phyllis Diller. I also loved watching male comics."

And who inspired the grand old Queen of Comedy herself?

Joan Rivers
"Jackie Moms Mabley has been lost somewhere in comedic history. Nobody looks at female comedians as ground-breakers or as commentators on what's going on in the world because we do it with comedy. All she was, was a lady standing up there telling the truth."

*Here we go again, that word **TRUTH** keeps turning up all the time. Moms Mabley was a feisty old black grandmother with no teeth who had been performing from 1927 to at least 1963. Moms came out as a lesbian at the age of twenty-seven in 1931, becoming one of the first openly gay comedians, an extremely brave thing to do at that time.*

Jeff Scott – Resident Piano Player and M.C. at Comedy Store Los Angeles
"Phyllis Diller, Moms Mably, Carol Burnett, Joan Rivers, Totie Fields and Rosanne Barr have all paved the way in America for women to become successful as stand-up comics."

Sindhu Vee
"In comedy my role models are Amitabh Bachchan (his comedic timing is amazing), Guthhi (from Kapil's show), Bill Burr (a US comedian) and Carol Burnett.

Naomi Paxton aka Ada Campe
"I've always loved the naughtiness, versatility and physicality of

Carol Burnett, Josie Lawrence, Victoria Wood, the Topp Twins, Catherine O'Hara and Patricia Routledge in particular. Most of those I've only seen on screen. Live performers who have inspired me recently include Zoe Lyons, Sophie Thompson, Tameka Empson, Adrienne Truscott and Josie Long.

Adrienne Truscott

"When I was really little I loved Carol Burnett, re-runs of 'Laugh In'. I always stayed up late and watched Letterman and Joan Rivers on the Tonight Show. I LOVED Lily Tomlin, Original Saturday Night Live cast, Richard Pryor, Andy Kaufman. These days there are so many!! But in a sort of inverse way, my Dad (and family) was a real influence on what comedy could mean or what it does for people."

Rhonda Hansome

"I didn't really need a Role Model – I just did my own thing but Carol Burnett had a tremendous influence on me and of course the legendary Moms Mabley was a real pioneer and was called the 'Funniest Woman in the World' at one time. Whoopi Goldberg was knocked out by her when she was a kid and she's just done a fantastic documentary on Moms Mabley's life. Moms was totally fearless and that's what you have to be in life. I also watched any woman that came on the Ed Sullivan Show."

They would have been as rare as affordable dentistry so she must have had to wait a while for that to happen!

Amy Schumer

"I liked Whoopi Goldberg, Margret Cho, Lucille Ball, Gilda Radner. They were funny people. It wasn't because they were women. They were human beings and they were unapologetic about being funny."

Angie Le Mar

"When I was growing up, my idol was Whoopi Goldberg who I saw when I was 14, at a theatre down the road from me, when she did her one woman show with Fontaine and all the rest of the characters, and she just blew us away. I thought if I could do half of what she does I'll be great. And then I read that she is actually dyslexic. So then I thought I can tell the whole world, 'Guess what I am, dyslexic. By the way so is Whoopi Goldberg.'"

Lorraine Benloss

"I worship Angie Le Mar because she was one of the first British black stand-up comics. She has that kind of power thing, as soon as she comes on stage you can see how powerful she is and that's what I always want. I am also a big fan of French and Saunders. A lot of people say I come across a bit like Dawn French."

French and Saunders have inspired so many over the years and Dawn French's enduring popularity, not only with female comics but British women in general, was highlighted in a 2004 poll to find the personality who has most inspired Britain's young women. She was named the ultimate Role Model in a survey of 1,000 schoolgirls aged 16 to 18. (Clark, Daily Mail 08/04/04) At the same time as they were treading the boards in London, Lydia Nicole was trying to find a comic direction in Los Angeles.

Lydia Nicole

"I've been doing stand-up professionally since 1988 when I went to L.A. I always wanted to perform but I couldn't sing or dance so I became funny. There weren't many women doing it at that time, I did characters and stories and Richard Pryor was my Role Model because was the closest comic to what I wanted to do."

Richard Pryor also had a very similar background as Lydia Nicole, a Mother who was a prostitute and a Father who was a pimp. Another FSUC in the early stages of her comic career in Los Angeles is Welsh born Nadia Kamil.

Nadia Kamil

"Josie Long, who I was lucky enough to support on tour recently, encouraged me to actually do stand up and seeing what a wonderful, warm, creative environment she could create with her shows, really opened my eyes. I also like really silly absurdist stuff like Vic & Bob."

With the advent of the web and Youtube we now have an opportunity to see comedy from the comfort of our own homes and computers. Once we hear recommendations from others we can do our own research, nowadays all we need is a name, Google will do the rest for us and within seconds we have our own personal film archive to keep us laughing for the rest of our days. So here are some eclectic names from the present to the past who you can check out, all highly recommended by my Interviewees, starting with Blod Jones who until she started Googling, was inspired by her Grandfather.

Blod Jones

"I think in the world of comedy there is a vast landscape of male performers and growing up there were hardly any women on the TV that were funny. I really looked up to my Grandfather, who was very funny and cheeky. My ABSOLUTE comedy idol/heroine is Amy Poehler and I also love Tina Fey. Amy is not only one of the funniest performers I have seen but she also is so gracious with her time and nurturing of girls and women, be it in comedy or just within life in general. She makes me want to be a better funny person and her website 'Smart girls at the party' is encouraging a new generation of girls that they can be anything they want to be."

Fern Brady

"I loved Doug Stanhope and I used to watch Father Ted and Black Books on repeat when I was younger so I guess Graham Linehan would be my biggest influence. I loved Limmy from before he was even famous or had a series. It's exciting though, to see how things will be for the generation of girls after me. I remember when I was hoping to get into stand up, watching Sara Pascoe clips, loving her then thinking "Well, she's great and I really enjoy her so she probably won't get on telly." And now she's everywhere! I've never been so happy to see her and Katherine Ryan everywhere as they're what I wished I had had growing up."

Spring Day

"Most of my comedy influences are British live comics – Brendan Burns and Andrew Maxwell – what appeals to me is that they are foreigners – the ultimate outsiders. Both are very good story tellers and honest. Pamela Poundstone – she does a lot on the University circuit. I really identified with her, she's very good at banter. She would grab people's cell phones and phone people's friends."

On a Sunday afternoon when I was growing up, if was raining (and it usually was!) we would sit down to watch black and white American musicals and movies on the telly together as a family and I was mesmerised. I'm sure they inspired me to become a performer, let's rewind to see which other cinematic idols inspired some of my other Interviewees.

Roy Hudd – World Expert on British Music Halls

"'Burns and Allen' was an American comedy duo consisting of George Burns (1896–1996) and his wife, Gracie Allen (1895–1964). They worked together as a comedy team in Vaudeville, films, radio and television and achieved great success over four decades and I think that Gracie Allen and her 'Illogical Logic' did a lot to change the way that people saw women as being funny. George Burns was the straight man who fed Gracie the lines so she could be funny, which was a big change to what had happened in the past."

June Whitfield

"I think my Role Models were female film stars. It was Judy Garland and people like Eve Arden and Rosalind Russell, those sort of people, who weren't necessarily funny. Yes, they were funny because they were rather sophisticated and witty, I mean not Judy Garland but the other two, and I rather liked that."

Rigby Jones

"My Role Models were Debbie Reynolds, Gilda Radner (Partnered with Gene Wilder and was on Saturday Night Live) and Bonnie Hunt. I loved the fact that they were fearless and that they could play anyone and just had fun. Gilda Radner worked with Steve Martin."

Kate Smurthwaite

"I am the world's biggest fan of Joyce Grenfell and I loved the original Saint Trinians, which is all about an all-girls school. The slapstick acting going on in it is brilliant. They were fun Role Models."

Katerina Vrana

"Well, I've definitely been influenced by Greek actresses in Greek comedy movies from the 50s and 60s but I think my strongest influence and role model is Miss Piggy and 'The Muppet Show' in general. All my humour can be traced back to the 'Muppet Show'. I love it."

Nina Conti

"There aren't many female ventriloquist Role Models that I could have emulated really. Only one, her name is Shari Lewis and she's American and her puppet is called Lamb Chop but I had never seen them, I had never really seen any ventriloquism when I became a ventriloquist. Since I became one I have looked at videos and started watching. It wasn't something that I was inspired by as a child or anything; it really came later."

Nina had so few female Role Models to pattern herself upon and here's what pioneering New Zealand FSUC Michele A'Court says about that.

Michele A'Court

"I have been wildly inspired by American comic, Maria Bamford, and Australian comics Fiona O'Loughlan and Kitty Flanagan in the past 12 months, and it occurs to me that *women are different* and I want to have a jolly good look at that!"

Kitty Flanagan

"Ellen Degeneres has the most laid back brilliant style when doing stand-up, she is the master of the throw away. I think she throws away so much of her stuff you have to listen to it several times to make sure you didn't miss anything."

Which is what you can do with youtube – play it back as many times as you want! Here's another woman who recognised Edith Piaf for the incredible Role Model that she was.

Wendy Kane

"I was always very influenced by the French singer Edith Piaf. I love her. I think she's amazing. Strong women, I love strong women. I've often been told that I'm a bit like Ethel Merman. She has been called 'The Queen of Show Business' and 'The Loudest Woman in the History of Musical Theatre' – I like that. Piaf was also very funny and laughed a lot, which was probably her way of dealing with all the misery that she had in her life."

A theory explored in Harry Key's 'Provocative Style' work and one which Thenjiwe Tay Moseley is testament to.

Thenjiwe Tay Moseley

"I had no Role Models in comedy. All the stand-up comedy in South Africa was done by white people and the jokes, cheap jokes, were on us and they were doing what the audience wanted to hear and it was within the law. Now racist humour is against the law which is a good thing, but there still aren't enough black male or female comics."

JoJo Smith

"I was described in one of the papers as a feminist icon in South Africa. It was one of the papers. I can't remember which paper it was. It wasn't *The Gay Argus* coz they called me the 'most dangerous woman in Britain', even though I was in South Africa at the time. And I thought Myra Hindley might want to have a bit of a look in and Rose West. But it was some little paper, like a local thing. There were no women stand-up's in South Africa in the mid to late nineties. They thought Victoria Wood was new! And it was refreshing for me, because you know I do get the Jo Brand thing all the time. *(JoJo was often confused for Jo Brand at this time because at that time she was quite a large woman)* And it was great to go to a country where they had no idea who Jo Brand was. So I mean, it was very odd. The first time I went out there, I did this little club in Johannesburg every night for three weeks. The local acts were doing racist stuff. And there'd be black people in the audience and they'd laugh. And this one night I went on, and there was quite a lot of black people in and the compere was going, oh you know, 'All smile so I can see where you are' – really hateful, horrible stuff. And they laughed at all that; and they were offended by me. And that kind of hurt, but I was just that much further ahead you know. I suppose in the way that a black man would go and see Bernard Manning to prove that he didn't have a chip on his shoulder in the 70s." *If you want to find out more about this sort of behaviour read about Social Scientist J.M Suls's work about Field Dependency.*

Nuala Mckeever

"There's this dubious thing, the *Goodness Gracious Me syndrome*, you know, the Lenny Henry making jokes about being black. I mean why is it ok for me to make a joke about being black if I'm black, or Irish if I'm Irish? I know that the whole idea of making fun about people is about the fact that they are in a weaker state than you are, I'd say the Irish joke has died a death."

This could be about taking control and re-appropriating a concept or a word as both Adrienne Truscott does with rape and Richard Pryor did with the N word. This is what self-deprecation is – making fun of yourself before someone else can do it. Several studies show that women find this an empowering thing to do whilst men do not.

Rhonda Hansome

"This is what my Mama says about me 'Rhonda Hansome is One Funny Negro'. Richard Pryor was probably the first comic to use the N word on stage in around 1967."

When there is no-one to show the way it can be a long and rocky road to travel. Some Interviewees had no-one to set them on their way and for them they had to carve out a path of their own making.

Joanna Quinn – Oscar Nominated Cartoonist

"I was inspired by Posy Simmonds whose comic strips really influenced me. Her wonderful observation and drawing skill inspired me to look harder and always try to create characters that are based in truth. There is one woman animator who inspires me now above all and that is Michaela Pavalova from the Czech Republic. Her work is beautiful, funny and fearless. We only met for the first time about 6 years ago but we are now best of friends. There were no women animators that inspired me when I started out – on the contrary it was the lack of women animators that inspired me to fill in the gap!!"

Having seen who are the people that have inspired my Interviewees, we now have a whole raft of new names to look at, to be inspired by, and whose work you can check out. It's never been easier to see people's work – thank the Lord for good old Google and youtube. It's interesting to see the same names popping up, Lucy, Joan Rivers, Victoria Wood, French & Saunders, Whoopi Goldberg, Carole Burnett. Future generations of funny women will have so many more fabulous Role Models to inspire them.

So many of the women I interviewed were doing something in a comic environment that others of their gender, race, religion, culture, physical ability or nationality had never done before. They had few females to show them how to create their working lives and their hard work benefited those that followed in their tracks and showed them what was possible. These women are a true inspiration and deserve a section solely for themselves.

Pioneers
Maria Kempinska –
Pioneering Female Comedy Club Brand Owner

"I started Jongleurs in Edinburgh in 1983, I used my bike as collateral. Jongleurs also did Music Hall. I created a system, have

20 minutes of material and be funny. Lots of women started out in Jongleurs, Donna McPhail, Helen Lederer, Jenny Lecoat. I still believe that Jongleurs can be the world's biggest brand of comedy. The bookers are the powerful people in the industry and it's often a woman and both men and women flock to please her."

Hazel O'Keefe – Laughing Cows Comedy Club and Women's Comedy Festival

"Laughing Cows started in 1998. I had learnt all sorts of skills in event management and wanted to combine them with my passion for women's comedy. It was all very grass roots initially. I used to manage girl-bands and lug P.A.'s. around. It's a struggle to make a living and I still can't make a living from just the comedy but I do have a very rich life. I am determined and passionate. I am chartering uncharted waters. 'Laughing Cows' was always a safe place for women to talk. I've always been very particular about bringing bisexual, hetero and lesbian communities together. Initially we didn't make many ripples but we are now being seen as an absolute threat. I have created the UK Women in Comedy Festival – the last two weeks of October. 2015 was the third one. Europe's only women in comedy festival – in 17 different venues around Manchester, including the Frog and Bucket (*where I performed as Bodicea Queen of HRT*).

Jane Duffus – Director Bristol Based Women's Comedy Club

"I run 'What the Frock'. The idea of creating a space for women's performance came to me in January 2012 and the first event was in May 2012. In the last eighteen months I have created 26 events of which 22 have been comedy shows. I also run comedy workshops. I've had about 100 female comics through this year and I have a regular monthly night in Bristol and want to expand. Everything tends to happen in London so I was keen to develop a scene outside of the metropolis."

Sian Parry – Ex Comedy Club Booker. Music Agent & Manager

"I ran Poncho Comedy Club from about 2003 to 2007 in Cardiff. We opened at Sam's Bar in the centre and following there, we were mainly at Chapter Arts Centre. Elis James (Crims BBC 4) was a regular at Poncho when he was starting out." *(and I also had a little dabble there as well.)*

Jane Mackay – Owner of 'The Stand Comedy Club', Edinburgh, Glasgow

"When we started in '95, there genuinely was not one comedy club operating in Scotland, and if there aren't any clubs and there aren't places for people to learn what they're doing, they just can't do it. Because it's not something you can do overnight; you have to learn how to do it. We opened in March 1998 as 'The Stand' Scotland's first purpose-built comedy club. In April 2000 we opened a bigger club in Glasgow."

Joanna Quinn – Oscar Nominated Cartoonist

"I'm very aware that I am perceived as a very positive Role Model and a pioneer in my field for women in cartoons and I get a lot of emails every week from young women all over the world asking for advice, helping with dissertations or simply telling me I'm the reason they are doing animation! I enjoy the contact with them and always reply if I am able, as I feel I have a responsibility to do so. I also love teaching so I am quite used to trying to inspire and nurture young animators. The older I get the more I am regarded as a wise old bird of animation! However I still feel 18 so it's all a bit odd!!!"

Nuala McKeever – Pioneering Northern Ireland FSUC

"I think one of the problems I've had all my life as a comic, is thinking I can't point at anybody and say 'That's what I want to do when I grow up', there were no powerful Irish comedy female Role Models. The thing that I like about what I have done is that I get a lot of young females who say I've been a Role Model to them. Just in the simple sense that they see somebody doing it, you know. Coz there isn't really anybody else in Northern Ireland doing it at the moment."

When I went to America, for the very first time to Los Angeles I was really amazed to realise that there was such a high percentage of people living there with roots in South America. I knew so little about a Latino presence in America and the way so many of them were treated like second-class citizens and was delighted to be able to interview two of the Latina comic pioneers.

Lydia Nicole – Pioneering Latina FSUC

"The very first Latina comic was Liz Torres, back in the 70s. She was a good friend of Bette Midler and her stuff was very gritty and about the pain in a very funny way. How do you find the funny in your pain? Laughing at the horrors – nothing was off limits. I was one of the Latina pioneers. The first female stand-up show I co-produced was in 1991 called 'The Funny Ladies of Color' with Cha Cha Sandoval (Mexican American) who was the only other Latina in LA doing stand-up and we approached a variety of female comics to be part of our show such as Sherri Shepherd (African American), Lotus Weinstock (Jewish American), Karen Haber (Jewish American), Alexis Rhee (Korean American), Christy Medrano (Filipino American), Cynthia Levin (Jewish American), and Carlease Burke (African American) and we started doing the show on Tuesday night in Encino at the LA Cabaret. The following year, in 1992 we invited Dyana Ortelli to join the show along with Jackie Guerra another new Chicana comic. And that year we moved the show over to the Comedy Store on Sunset. I did the 'Hot and Spicy Mamitas' from 1994 to

2000. Dyana then joined Mamitas in 1995 when Debbie Guttierez dropped out. It was the first of a kind but male bookers wouldn't book us. We were five Latinas who were spicy, hot and motherly, I took what I did as a mother and made it sassy, funny and on the edge. We promoted ourselves, booked the shows, we had to create our own publicity and there was no social media at that time. We did a lot with a little, were very savvy and travelled across the country. At that time there were hardly any Latina stand-ups."

Dyana Ortelli – Pioneering Latina FSUC

"When I started doing stand-up, back in 1992, there were maybe just a handful of Latina comics performing in clubs in L.A. There would be a line-up of 10 to 12 comics on "Latino night", and only one or two of them would be women. I joined 'Funny Ladies of Color' in 1993, with Jackie Guerra. Then in 1995 I joined 'The Hot and Spicy Mamitas of Comedy' – we were: Lydia Nicole, Sally Diaz, Ludo Vika, Marilyn Martinez and myself. Five Latinas banding together as a group. We produced and secured our own venues; we hustled to sell tickets and get industry members to show up. Finally, we got enough attention to sell out the hottest comedy club in L.A. at that time — The Conga Room — two nights in a row. And we released our self-titled comedy c.d. in 1998. That's a pretty big deal for Latina stand-up comediennes!"

The two countries in the world where stand-up has really flourished and created comic heroes and heroines are America and Britain with Canada, Australia and New Zealand following suit. There has been a cross pollination of Role Models between these English speaking countries.

Angie Le Mar – First Black British FSUC

"When I started out doing stand-up I didn't think I was a pioneer. I knew that there was nobody here influencing me that I could refer to and say 'Well how did they get through?' There were people like Kenny Lynch, but there were no women in that scene; I don't know if there were on the cabaret circuit. But when I started, I was still looking to the Americans, people like Lily Tomlin, Joan Rivers, and Whoopi Goldberg. And that's where I was drawing my inspiration from. That was in the early eighties. But I think I've inspired the likes of Gina Yashere and Lorraine Benloss and I mentor quite a lot of young women, such as Donna Spence, who I also now manage.

Thenjiwe Tay Moseley –
Pioneering Black South African FSUC

"There are three black women doing stand-up in South Africa including myself, so you could say that Celeste Ntuli, Tumi Morake and I are leading the way."

Shazia Mirza – World's First Muslim FSUC

"When I started out in around 2002 I was often referred to as 'The World's first, probably only, Muslim Female Stand-up comic'. I have done TV all over the world and I have done press interviews all over the world and they have all said the same thing. 'We haven't got one over here, we haven't got one over here'. It's like America, Germany, Denmark, Sweden, Holland, Finland, all over the world. It makes me feel quite isolated really being a pioneer. I just think I am so glad I have got the courage to do what I want to do. But I know there are probably so many women out there who don't have that courage and probably want to do it. I think that I am taking a lot of stick simply for choosing to live my life the way I want to. I get attacked for doing stand-up. Some girl who works in an office, she doesn't get attacked for working in an office. But I am getting attacked for doing stand-up because I am standing on stage, I've got a voice, I'm making people laugh. And men don't like it. Joan Rivers who was one of the first Jewish women to do stand-up, now there's loads of Jewish women doing stand-up. Maybe in 10 years there'll be loads of Muslim women doing stand – up. If somebody doesn't do it and lead the way by being a strong Role Model, then how are the rest of them going to do it?"

Having Googled 'Muslim female stand-up comedian' in 2016, Shazia Mirza's name comes up as most of the top ten but she is now being followed by some American names such as New York based Aizzah Fatima, Fawzia Mirza in Chicago and L.A. based Mona Shaikh who has been banned in Pakistan and received death threats because of her website muslimsdoitbetter.com. Mona Shaikh, in raising her voice has exposed herself to a lot of hatred not dissimilar to that of Ayaan Hirsi in Holland, thirteen years previously. The "Dutch Salman Rushdie', Ayaan Hirsi, a 32 year old Somali Muslim immigrant and a political advisor to the Dutch Labour Party, who took on the mullahs, was forced to flee her adopted country under threat of death because of her stinging attack on Islam, a religion she herself rejected. Calling Islam a 'backward religion', she claimed that 'Orthodox Muslim men frequently indulge in domestic violence against women as well as incest and child abuse,' and said 'I had to speak up because most spokesmen for Muslims are men and they deny or belittle the enormous problems of Muslim women locked up in their Dutch homes"(Osborn, The Observer, 10/11/02) Ayaan Hirsi may be a little bit more extreme about her political beliefs about Islam and the reactions she gets for voicing them than Shazia Mirzah and the new Muslim FSUCs, however, what is similar is that men don't like them voicing their beliefs and women who do so are still very much in the minority and lone voices crying in the desert.

Sometimes it's not about raising your voice to be heard, it can just be about creating something where nothing existed previously as Katerina Vrana and Michele A'Court have done in their respective countries.

Katerina Vrana – Pioneering Greek FSUC and Promoter

"Hmmm… I'm not a pioneer because I'm a woman, I'm a "pioneer" (am I a pioneer? That word always makes me think of people battling with bears in woods in order to build a settlement) because I brought the experience I gained in the UK comedy scene over to Greece. So I started things that didn't exist before, like the first Open Mike night and a comedy club which runs like comedy clubs in the UK and the States."

Michele A'Court – Pioneering New Zealand FSUC

"You don't have time to think of yourself as a pioneer – you're too busy getting on with it! But I do realise that I'm one of the first generation of stand-up comedians, let alone *female* comedians here. And yes, you get to set the agenda in a sense – we created the Comedy Guild to look after ourselves and each other, for example, and that would be difficult to do in a country that already had an established industry. I was one of the first female stand-up comedians in NZ – stand-up comedy only really started here in the late 80s – so there were no 'sisters' to show the way. With the odd exception, the boys have been supportive and encouraging. And the ones that weren't probably would have been arseholes regardless of my gender. And the NZ Festival has worked hard right from the beginning to raise the profile of women comedians. There's been a showcase for women-of-the-festival every year called "Divas" – and it always sells out fast. Like most comedy festivals, the staff are largely women *(isn't that interesting?!)* and Hilary Coe, the NZ Festival Director, has been incredibly supportive of me specifically, and women in general."

And I was incredibly lucky to have the views of (probably) the world's oldest and youngest FSUCs.

Lynn Ruth Miller – World's Oldest FSUC

"Women love me cos I've got lots of opinions. Lots of young people want to be me when they 'grow up' because I'm over eighty and I don't give a shit!! I am sailing uncharted waters as now, since Joan Rivers died, I am probably the world's oldest female stand-up comic. She was six months older than me."

Ashley Storrie – World's youngest FSUC and daughter of Janey Godley

"I'm probably the world's youngest female stand-up comic, I started at the age of 11 and carried on until I was 14. Now in my twenties, I have recently made a comeback!"

No it wasn't child labour, Ashley Storrie's Mother Janey Godley is herself a FSUC of note and ran a comedy club and Ashley's childhood was one where she was constantly surrounded by comics who came to stay with the family and work locally so it was a very natural thing for her to do. Janey Godley is a very strong and positive woman and a force to contend with. Finding few strong female Role Models in the animation world she was working in, Joanna Quinn decided she was going to create them. I was lucky enough to be cast as one of the raucous and rebellious friends of the main character Beryl, in the Welsh version of her award winning film 'Girls Night Out', and if I hadn't been Directing Theatre in Education in West Wales at the time, I would have also been in the English language version too.

Joanna Quinn – Oscar Nominated Cartoonist

"My first film 'Girls Night Out', won 3 awards in the 1987 Annecy Animation Festival in France. I was particularly struck by the lack of strong women characters portrayed within the films and noticed how 'Girls Night Out' stood out as a funny film for women by a woman. It was this experience at Annecy that made me think seriously about the responsibility of the film maker as communicator of ideas and particularly the responsibility of women film makers as portrayers of positive images for women. Being nominated for two Oscar nominations with films 'Famous Fred' (1996) and 'The Wife of Bath' (1998) as well as winning the Leonardo Da Vinci award in 1996 for 'Britannia', a biting view of British Imperialism, (which ironically enough was presented to me by Prince Phillip!) made me very aware of what I needed to do. I was extremely proud to become the recipient of the 2013 ASIFA (International Animation Journal) Laureate Prize and was delighted to receive a framed drawing created especially for me by noted Czech animator Michaela Pavlatova who is my own Role Model."

So many pioneers making tentative and then confident steps for the future of worldwide female comedy. Betsy Salkind, Lydia Nicole, Cynthia Ladman were also in a very privileged position on the other side of the Atlantic working as they were under the wings of the Mother of all Comedy, Mitzi Shore, who has probably done more than any male of female in the world to develop comedy and comics from her enclave in the Comedy Store on Sunset Boulevard. Looking towards the hills of Hollywood, both Welsh born Film Director Sara Sugarman and Welsh based Animator Joanna Quinn have also both made inroads into what have previously been a very male dominated film industry.

Nina Conti has been a pioneer with her cutting edge work in Britain with ventriloquism, another pioneer undoubtedly is Michele A'Court who was one of the very first female stand-ups in New Zealand. Her role in the development of the New Zealand Comedy Scene was pivotal and again can only be recognized in retrospect.

The work done by Latino comics such as Lydia Nicole and Dyana Ortelli, black comics like Rhonda Hansome and Angie le Mar and disabled comics such as Liz Carr and Spring Day have created some pretty awesome Role Models for younger women to aspire to. And we have some tremendously funny women making huge strides in India with Aditi Mittal and Sindhu Vee, Katerina Vrana in Greece, Spring Day in Japan and Thenjiwe Tay Moseley in South Africa.

Another pioneer carving a new comic direction for people of restricted growth and those with disabilities is Tanyalee Davis. She works and travels literally worldwide and gets everywhere she needs to on her scooter on trains, planes and all forms of public transport. She appeared on the John Bishop Show in Spring 2015 to great acclaim and I'm really hoping that will be her break into the 'big time'. She is not an overnight success by any stretch of imagination, having been working clubs all over the States, Canada, Britain, Japan and worldwide collecting more air-miles than even Andrew Lloyd Webber has ever done when popping into the House of Lords from New York to vote for austerity cuts!

Before the break – Life before stand-up

Performance is a career with many pitfalls and lots of unemployment and many of the comics I interviewed had a life before they ever came to stand-up which may have given them an abundance of experiences they could feed into writing their acts or given them certain skills which enabled them to deal with their raucous and unruly audiences. Jo Brand was a psychiatric nurse and Ava Vidal a prison officer. So if men say women shouldn't be working in stand-up comedy as it's too aggressive and violent, then if you follow that argument through, women shouldn't be working in psychiatric nursing or behind bars or in Accident and Emergency areas.

Jo Brand

"Incidents of violence in an outpatient clinic in a hospital are high. I was a psychiatric nurse in the emergency clinic at the Maudsley Hospital, which was a twenty-four hour self-referral clinic for people with acute psychiatric problems so basically anyone could come in through the door and be psychiatrically assessed. So a lot of people would come in with weapons, with knives and guns on occasions. I did it for six years. Probably the worst incident I had as a psychiatric nurse was being karate kicked against a wall by a very hyper maniac patient who was a bloke, six foot four and a fair bit stronger than I was."

Stand-up comedy must have been a walk in the park after psychiatry for Jo Brand. What other work experiences did my Interviewees have? What did they give up to become FSUCs?

Sindhu Vee
"After finishing my Masters in Chicago I became an investment banker in London. I loved my job but quit banking after I had my first kid because I missed him too much while I was on business trips. Then I was in Mom mode for a few years. After my 2nd child was born in 2006 I decided I was too bored to remain in Mom mode all the time so I started the UK's first online ethical luxury fashion boutique called DeviDoll.com It brought the most chic ethical fashion and lifestyle labels, from around the world, together under one roof. Ethical fashion is, broadly speaking, fashion that is as much about style as it is about environmental and social responsibility and sustainability. I was named as one of the 11 most inspirational women in ethical and sustainable fashion in the UK. There is no doubt that DeviDoll.com put me in touch with my creative instincts and reminded me that they were there and to take them seriously. I'm pretty sure that I made the move into comedy because I had already spent some time with my creative self through DeviDoll.com. We were a luxury brand for sure, so I could see the writing on the wall. So I downsized and ultimately called it a day when the recession really started to bite. In 2006 I decided to volunteer with "Room To Read". It was an honour to be asked by them to join their Advisory Board in 2008. My volunteering work

with this amazing charity has continued alongside everything else I have done since."

(*Room to Read is a global organization seeking to transform the lives of millions of children in Asia and Africa through a focus on literacy and gender equality in education. Founded on the belief that 'World Change Starts with Educated Children', Room to Read works in collaboration with local communities, partner organizations and governments to develop literacy skills and a habit of reading among primary school children and to ensure girls have the skills and support needed to complete their secondary education*)

Kate Smurthwaite
"I worked in a bank for eight years and that sucked – I was just a bit of a misfit."

Maria Kempinska – Owner of Jongleurs Comedy Chain
"I taught English and Drama and Old Tyme Music Hall."

Naomi Paxton – Aka Ada Campe
"I did a drama degree, then went to drama school in Glasgow, then worked as an actress, doing theatre and radio. I was involved in a couple of sketch comedy groups on the radio, which was really fun. When 'resting' I worked backstage in the West End, predominantly in Wardrobe although I've also worked Stage Door and Box Office at a number of venues. I've just finished a Ph.D. on the 'Actresses' Franchise League'."

Rhonda Hansome
"I was a puppeteer when the Muppetts appeared on Saturday Night Live, my character was called Vash."

Cathy Ladman

"I went to college at the age of 16, went to teach English then went to California to do stand-up at the age of 25.

Julia Morris

"I got a job for six months in the Club Med Village in New Caledonia which is a French settlement in the South Pacific, then Bali Indonesia for a year, then I lived on the North Island of Japan, singing and dancing and performing in the shows for Club Med and then just hanging out with guests all day and tanning. It was heavenly."

Nuala Mckeever

"After university and doing some work as a temp I then became a researcher at the BBC for about eight years. I was also in the 'Hole in the Wall Gang' then came my t.v. break. 'Two Ceasefires and a Wedding'. A piss take of love across the divide in Northern Ireland. I then got offered my own show."

Angie Le Mar

"I had an A level in Sociology so after leaving school I went to do social work working with young juvenile delinquents. I used to traipse them down to Drama Club and you'd just see a change in children. You know I really think drama is a healer even if you don't want to be an actor."

JoJo Smith

"While I was still at college, just before I left actually, I started my own fanzine, called 'The Ligger' as this character called 'Gaye Abandon'. The success of 'The Ligger' led to my first professional journalistic engagement when I was invited to write for the now defunct 'Pop Star Weekly'. This was followed by stints on *Record Mirror, Smash Hits, NME* and 'The Face'. I also used to be a bingo caller at Butlins and what that did teach me was to focus on what I was doing and not be put off by the audience whatever they did."

Jo Caulfield

"I passed my English A level then I left school and went to London where I worked as a waitress. I bummed around, sold vintage clothes on a market stall and travelled quite a bit. My sister was a writer and I'd always fancied acting so I did a post graduate acting course, having not graduated! It was a year-long course and I had to do a stand-up slot as part of it. This was in the early nineties. I left it for a long time because I was really working hard on my stand-up and then when I did it I thought 'Oh this is a bit of fun' and then I went out and started getting some Open Mike spots. When I left college I had no real plans, I just drifted. I was still very shy, I didn't really know how to do a comedy act, how to set about it."

Hattie Hayridge aka Holly Red Dwarf

"I did my A levels and failed them and went to a Further Education College and did a secretarial course and worked as a secretary. Later, when I was 25 I went to university to study 'International Relations'. I wanted to be a war correspondent. Secretarial work only gave me one joke to use in my stand-up routine so it obviously was not a rich seam to mine for comedy!"

Jenny Éclair

"After I left Manchester Poly, I was in a band, 'Kathy Crème and the Rum Babas.' I'd always done a few poems within this band, like punk poetry. It was in the late seventies, early eighties. I came to London to be a waitress and luckily for me by the time I got to London in around '82, there was a very small London comedy circuit building up. 'The Comedy Store' was up and running and there were all these little rooms above pubs, it was the 'alternative cabaret' it was called. I think a lot of it came out of the poetry and folk circuit really. It was the days of the GLR and people got funding for these things, it was all quite supportive and optimistic those days in the eighties."

Donna McPhail

"After school I tried to get a job as a librarian but I was told I was overqualified! We lived in St. Neots. The nearest town was Cambridge and I worked as a waitress. I was sharing a house with some students. One of the girls said 'Let's do our own comedy revue – do you want to be in it?' and I said 'All right'. I had never written anything like that before but I went home and wrote 'Cover Girls' which was a magazine format with song lyrics and sketches etc. We were called 'The Millies', the students approved, we all moved down to London, got our Equity cards and did that for a few years. 'The Millies' were a successful touring company but there was no money in it."

Lorraine Benloss

"I worked as a shop assistant in Evans the Outsize for quite some time. I got some great material there such as the stuff I do about communal changing rooms. I also worked at a theatre at the Stage Door. I worked in the shop because it paid for my travel. They used to give me a travel card, a 1 to 6 Zone on the Underground which helped a lot with my comedy as so many of the clubs were really off the beaten track."

Wendy Kane

"I sang in various bands and duos for about ten years altogether, mainly in working class clubs but I also travelled around the world to Miami and India and worked with people like Bernard Manning and Chubby Brown. Chubby Brown refers to women as 'split asses' which I think is disgusting. I broke away from home at the age of sixteen and had five years of freedom. Then at twenty-one I met a very domineering man, he was a detective inspector. The relationship lasted twelve years, it should have lasted four! I was stuck in a rut. He treated me as an interviewee. I never had access to money, although I was working. If I wanted anything, I had to ask for it, even when I was thirty. I feel very bitter about it. And this is what I try to get over to every woman when I'm on stage, you don't have to stay. He even dictated what I could wear. I had two children by the age of thirty – where could I take them, what could I do? He was extremely manipulative. I came out of that relationship with nothing, not even the kids beds."

Michele A'Court

"Stand-up was a part-time thing for a few years. Before starting with stand-up, I worked as a presenter on a children's tv show. Then in 1998 I got rid of my husband and took sole responsibility for a massive mortgage, and had to turn this "comedy thing" into a career that paid some serious money. As desperate as I was at the time, it was a huge gift (cheers, buddy) because I had to start doing *every* gig, not just the pretty ones, and I had to start valuing my work so I could afford to keep the house and eat. That's when Mike King's support and work opportunities became so valuable. Also, every overseas Festival (Melbourne in 1997 and 2004; Edinburgh 2004; Adelaide 2006) has been an inspiring experience, with moments where you finally see that you're quite good! It can be hard to see that when you're working in such a small community in NZ.

Although there is a London 'circuit', a lot of stand-up involves travel, as noted by Michele A'Court, mostly in this country but also more and more around the world. Doing stand-up comedy can often involve working away from home for quite long periods of time depending on whether it's a tour or a single night's gig, especially so in America. Life on the road can be quite gruelling for anyone, but has additional practical 'challenges' for women who tend to be the ones who do the washing, ironing, organising and 'caring' on behalf of men who are on the road in whatever capacity, whether that's because they're a long-distance lorry driver, in computers or a stand-up comedian.

My working life was like that for a good three years (late nights coming back on trains) when I used to busk and sing in restaurants and bars all over Belgium. I wouldn't go out to work until half past nine then I'd often be home at 2 o'clock in the morning and then I would go for a drink because, you know, you could go for a drink at that time in Belgium, and sometimes catch the first Metro home at about five in the morning!

The practicalities of life on the road need to be accommodated even before these women are able to get up on stage and need careful organisation, even when there are no domestic responsibilities such as caring for children or in some cases, parents. Women are still the main carers in society and this is the biggest invisible barrier to women whatever sort of work they may be seeking. And what about those with families, there's even more to think about at that point? Childcare is less accessible now than it was ten years ago and the cost is yet another barrier to working women.

Living in the fast lane – Reality of gigging away from home.
Donna McPhail

"Male comics have that home life when he'll come through the door knackered and she'll have something on the table for him. Not that I'm heterophobic but that would help. But having to come back, pay all your bills on your own, do your washing and then pack again. And then of course women have to take so much more gear. You have to take your make-up, your hair products etc. Men can go on stage in a manky t-shirt that they wore to bed two days ago, they'll play football and then just walk out on stage and do a gig in what they are wearing. Women can't, they have to make an effort, whether you're going to a board-room or onto a stage. When I go away for four or five days my case is very heavy. It's got three suits in it, your clothes you wear the rest of the time, your make up etc."

Dana Goldberg

"Not gonna lie, the last 8 days have been awesome, but they kicked my ass. 600 driving miles, 5 flights, three shows in three different states. Living the dream but I need a massage, some bourbon, and a three day nap. Next stop…home in LA."

Dana Alexander

"I work in 27 countries world-wide and organise all my own gigs. I don't have any children."

Jane Duffus – Director Bristol Based Women's Comedy Club

"I have a husband who is immensely supportive and no children. I also have a very small handful of friends who are willing to help out who believe in what I'm doing and want to be there from the start."

Mandy Knight

"I don't have any children, I have a partner who is supportive of what I am doing. I don't think many men would put up with what we do – you know I can never go to weddings, no social events, you don't have any weekends together like you would with a normal job. I'm always travelling back from wherever I've been performing on a Sunday. I am frankly tired of going out every night every single weekend and not having a life. I have two holidays a year and that's it. I don't get to hang out with anybody.

I have very few opportunities to fuel my life in order to be able to write about anything. All I do is live in a hotel and I go from total isolation in front of four hundred people back to total isolation and then I've got to reconcile that with Monday, Tuesday, Wednesday being a housewife and a normal person."

JoJo Smith

"No children. No partner. No personal life. You know, I have friends and I hang out and do stuff. But obviously it's very difficult coz, you know, a lot of my friends, my old friends from my journalism days and stuff like that, when they are out to play I am working. Having been an only child, I was never lonely as a child. You know, I am quite happy with my own company."

Nina Conti

"I have a boyfriend who I have been living with for a couple of years. He's an actor, he's Irish, and he spends a lot of time in Ireland because he gets a lot of work over there, both theatre and television. Yes, he's very supportive of me – he knows what it's like, the travelling and everything."

Kate Smurthwaite

"My boyfriend works full time for me as my P.A., he sorts out my diary and makes packed lunches for me which is highly unusual in this business."

Jo Caulfield

"I'm married to a comedy promoter. He understands the working lifestyle I have. It would be hard to do this sort of work if he didn't understand the lifestyle. There's never been any of that 'Oh you're never here at weekends.' I don't know what he does but I'm never here and he doesn't seem to mind. When we go on holiday, say in New York we'll go and buy comedy tapes and go to comedy shows. I think in that way for men and for women it's an incredibly hard life, it can cause rows about the fact that you don't see each other."

Nuala McKeever

"I was married to a comedy writer, Shaun Carson. Comedy brought us together. We were married for three years then split up."

Julia Morris

"I do all my own washing, ironing and prepping. I wound down my touring so I don't tour as much anymore, as I used to. I mean, you know, what is a 34-year-old woman doing in a hotel on a Saturday night by herself across town. Like no thanks. I try and mix them both. Like if I am going to play an away game, what we call it, then I try and organise it so that my partner can come with me. It definitely helps that your partner understands what you are doing really. As a life, stand-ups keep pretty strange hours. Because you're working until 11 and then you think 'I might just go out for one', and then you're up till 1 o'clock in the morning and then you get up at whenever during the day. It's a totally different sort of life, and there's another whole set of people living at that end of the day as well."

I can really relate to that – my life was like that for a while and I still prefer the later hours of the day, which drives my husband nuts because he's an early bird.

Shazia Mirza

"I don't have a boyfriend, I was brought up and I am a Muslim – I am not allowed to have boyfriends before marriage, but my parents have tried to arrange a partner for me on numerous occasions."

Hattie Hayridge aka Holly Red Dwarf

"Well I live on my own so I don't have many domestic commitments really. It's much harder for women with partners and kids definitely. I can very much go anywhere at the drop of a hat. I'm not dictated to by anybody or anything. It's a very free falling type of situation, which is good and bad."

Lynn Ruth Miller

"Even though I'm over eighty years old and don't have any kids I'm known as 'The Stripping Granny'. I don't mind being alone. I've always been alone and drove once from the East to West America. I never get lonely or frightened."

Cathy Ladman

"I don't travel as much as previously when I used to go to New York, Seattle, Austin, Texas, Cambridge. I was single or without kids at that time, staying in cruddy hotels but I loved exploring new cities. Touring is very challenging if you have kids – you have to have a lot of support."

Personal Life

Michele A'Court

"I have a daughter, Holly. I've been with my partner, Jeremy Elwood, for 7 years. He is a comedian, actor, musician and writer. I have had huge support from retired parents who live next door – for short and long-term babysitting. The rest of it is organized chaos. Jeremy cooks, I clean. It's difficult finding a babysitter. Especially one who understands that the gig might finish at midnight, but you haven't wound down till 2am. And getting enough sleep between the end of a gig and the start of a child's day."

Jenny Éclair

"I have a long term partner art director Geoff Lowell and a daughter born in 1989. He's more than ten years older than me and he's always been there for me. That sounds very crap but he has always been very supportive – despite not having seen me perform live. There aren't that many men who would take on the babysitting role quite so willingly. I think he's secretly quite proud but not overly impressed. I think there's another direction he'd like me to go in. I think he'd rather that I swaned around in caramel cashmere."

Janey Godley – Prolific Scottish Blogger & Scottish FSUC

"I have one daughter, Ashley Storrie who is also a comedian."

Jane Mackay – Owner of 'The Stand Comedy Club', Edinburgh, Glasgow

"I have a daughter Eva Mackay whom I had at 17. I like my home comforts so I don't fancy being on the road, sleeping on floors or in grotty B&Bs with a bunch of lads in their mid-20s. Luckily, I have never had to do much of this."

Joan Rivers

"I have one daughter Melissa." *(Who used to work very closely with her.)*

Lydia Nicole

"I'm a single mother, my daughter was born in the early nineties I had to take her to the clubs with me if I couldn't get a babysitter. I took her to the L.A. Comedy Store once and her father filed a complaint once saying I was an unfit mother."

Victoria Jordy Cook

"When I split up with my daughter's Dad I had a genuine

problem in that as a single parent with no additional help – just getting gigs would be a logistical nightmare, who would look after my daughter while I was out working? I tried strapping her to my back but every time I turned around she'd get whacked in the face with the microphone stand. In the end I realised I'd have to take a break from stand up while I got us sorted which was heart-breaking but had to be done. Luckily around this time I started getting work in TV which kept me in the game."

Nina Wadia

"I have a partner, his name's Raiomond Mirza, and he's Canadian, we've been together for a long time since 1998. We have two children and he's very supportive of what I do."

Brenda Gilhooly aka Gayle Tuesday

"I'm married with two children, two daughters."

Since having their children, their working lives have taken a slightly different direction, Helen Lederer, Susie Felber, Victoria Cooke and Brenda Gilhooley all write far more at this point in their careers than they did when they were footloose and fancy free. When I interviewed Jo Brand in 1996 she was single. Since then she has become a mother herself, not once but twice, and also married. She still manages to tour so it's obvious that she has found some way of accommodating her working life with the demands of motherhood. She is also now focussing more of her time on writing and has published two novels.

Jo Brand

"As a female stand-up work wise, you'd need to have a bloke that was very supportive or a very good babysitter that didn't mind being out all hours of the night or being on tour, but I mean Victoria Wood's got a family. She takes her kids on tour with her and seems to manage perfectly well."

Angie Le Mar

"I've got three children. I'm married to an I.T. specialist who also does music, he plays keyboards, sings and does music production. He's got a studio downstairs. He's extremely supportive of me. He's been there when I used to do the gigs up and down the motorways sometimes when I wasn't even getting paid. He would put the petrol in the car, get in the vehicle, do the gig, and buy me a kebab on the way home. I was gigging around when I was pregnant. I'd be on the stage and say, 'Well I couldn't get a babysitter, there you go!' They'd go like, 'First of all we've never seen a black woman doing comedy, and now she's pregnant.' Two weeks after I had the child, I was back on the circuit. And I just went, I just kept going. My baby was with my Mum because I was at home at the time. At the time when it happened, I got pregnant, my Mum said to me, 'Don't take it as something you have to stop for, you just keep going and I am here to support you. You know every setback is a springboard to success.'"

Sindhu Vee

"I've got three children, I'm married to a Dane. I'm very lucky to have a lot of practical support as I certainly wouldn't be able to gig in India as I do."

Wendy Kane

"After my disastrous first relationship I met someone else and married him in 1993. There's a new basis for this relationship, one of equality. He's also my manager. I've had so much support from him that my career's taken off at a hundred miles an hour. I can't work enough, there aren't enough days in the week. My husband is in the business. He used to be in personal security for big bands. When we got together he decided he wanted to manage me. I'll never go to work on my own – he'll set the gear up. It's a partnership. We're both together twenty-four hours a day. I've got three children. I have an A level student who babysits and during the day I'm with them. I'm up at seven. I do get very tired."

Jojo Sutherland

"I have four kids and my husband is either their father or their uncle because I married then divorced his brother! He's incredibly supportive, I couldn't do it without him."

I have yet to find a comedy club with a crèche. When my daughter was born I used to find flexible childcare incredibly difficult to find for my career in television and performance. I had no close family who were able to help and my husband was working away all the time during the week. That's when I had to seriously think about finding work I could do which didn't include any extensive travel and where I could be available for school holidays, after school and childhood illnesses. It's interesting to note that most of my interviewees had either no children at all or one, those who had more than one did have a very good support system. I was delighted to see two sets of inter-generational comics, Nancy and Annie Witter and Janey Godley and Ashley Storrie – what a rich apprenticeship they must have had. As in the days of the old Music Halls, the acts would circulate and a present days FSUCs life involves an awful lot of travel, sometimes internationally, staying in hotels of varying standards of cleanliness, sometimes away from home comforts for weeks at a time, always eating on your own, a lonely existence and if children or caring responsibilities are included in the mix, it's a lifestyle that women might not be able to manage without a great deal of practical support. But manage they do and out on the stage they go to strut their stuff, larger than life itself!

When I met Jo Brand I was secretly terrified of the prospect – she scared the s**t out of me on the television but when I met her I found her to be almost on the 'shy' side, something I simply hadn't anticipated. Another person who I thought was going to be terrifying *was Joan Rivers – meeting her was one of the highlights of my working life and certainly one of the times when I felt most nervous – but again – she was such a sweetie! More like a pussy cat than a tiger! And as I continued in my quest to write this book and got to know more and more female comics, I also realised that a lot of them were not what I expected at all, that the scary 'Larger than life Luurvies' and 'Bitch Goddesses' on stage were in fact constructions and creations, a bit of blag to overcome the stage fright. I was quite interested as to how they formed these 'characters' and images and how my Interviewees would describe themselves on stage.*

Larger than Life Lurvvie? Bitch Goddesses?

Donna McPhail

"I always dress so that I'm confident and I've also learnt to dress up because that's what people expect. On stage I am up front – it's more aggressive than honest, I like to push people to the edge. I'm confident, entertaining and thin – undeniably thin! I am actually quite shy off stage."

Lorraine Benloss

"The persona I have on stage is of a woman on the edge. It's almost like I've had enough, it's like you've caught me at the end of a bad day and I'm just going to let it all out. It's like I'm still there, I'm still intact but I'm very angry, almost like the views you have in your head but you keep them up there. On stage I'm very much 'Don't mess with me' and I can deal with everything and I'm in control. Off stage I'm pretty quiet. I have my loud moments and I'll have a laugh. My friends still see me as the life and soul of the party but I am quite quiet. I'd describe myself on stage as: Mad, cynical, in control / controlling, angry and bitter."

Helen Lederer

"You need a huge amount of energy as you know, strange energy to harness to do it and a belief that you want to do it. You've got to believe in yourself, I'm probably quieter with friends. It's just a louder version of me and on stage I'm slightly mad without being incomprehensible."

Hattie Hayridge aka Holly Red Dwarf
"Slightly less grumpy on stage is how I'd describe myself and I wear a black chiffon dress but I wear flat shoes with it to make it look quirky. I've got six dresses all the same so I don't have to worry about what to wear, it takes far too long otherwise."

Betsy Salkind
"I wear a dress on stage to be disarming and I look like a Sunday School teacher."

Tanyalee Davis
"The only thing I would say is different about me onstage as opposed to off is that I over exaggerate my movements onstage. I try to be as big as possible when acting out my "bits". Personality wise I am the same on as offstage. Onstage I'm energetic, animated, charismatic, inspirational and real."

Nina Conti
"Well, my act is shocking I suppose: Monk, the monkey I would say is quite charming. Silly, unexpected, and maybe a bit whimsical. In a funny way I suppose that is quite a good description of me. But shy I would say. I think there's a definite outlet there in Monk, being able to say things through him, which wouldn't come out as well from me. I'm not sure I am that shocking but I am quite irreverent and I don't believe in taking anything too seriously."

Brenda Gilhooly aka Gayle Tuesday

"'Gayle Tuesday' came about because I just felt that I wasn't really getting to grips with stand-up as myself and I thought, if I can't be me, I'll create somebody else to be me."

Naomi Paxton – aka Ada Campe

"Diva Magazine said about me 'Ada Campe resembles an unhinged super-villain' but I think that quote has a lot to do with the costume, wig and make up – and I love it! Ada is flamboyant and larger than life. I worried for quite a long while about the potential negative reinforcement of women that I might be engaged in – for example a 'hag' character who wears too much make-up, is portrayed as middle aged, drinks on stage, refers to her sexuality and is in many ways a type of grotesque or misogynistic figure of failure. This didn't bother me initially, but the more I did gigs at feminist events the more I worried about it… but as Ada kept and keeps getting booked it's been more about learning to pay attention to how audiences react to her rather than trying to create a problem where there isn't one. People react to her really well and find her fun, which she is. Any sense of menace is connected to (hopefully) a sense of anarchic freedom and of laughter – audiences don't know what she might do or say next and in theory, anything is possible. So now I don't see Ada Campe as a 'harridan' – she takes control of the stage, hence the rather overly assertive opening, she isn't going to let anyone else be in charge but has no axe to grind with audience members. She looks harsh and is fizzing with energy but wants the audience to like her and enjoys playing with them. As far as the dressing up goes – I love drag costumes and panto dame costumes and want that flavour for Ada, so she's entirely theatrical rather than attempting to be sexy. It's important to me that the audience has a good time. Eye contact is key – and allows me to make a connection and let them know that they can trust me to play with them but not to humiliate them. I decided on the name 'Ada Campe' because it's sort of silly, a bit drag and also old-fashioned. I liked the idea of the militaristic reference mixed with the silliness of 'Campe' and, for me, she had to have a first name that evoked an earlier period of time. Ada frees me up to play, react, speak and be a different part of myself. Ever since I was a child, my love for acting was about not being myself and about escaping myself. Ada Campe is entirely herself and is very comfortable with that – I get to enjoy that confidence and also to hide beneath it…I write her, dress her up, buy her props and then let her get on with it!"

I really loved Ada Campe when I saw her – she really reminded me a lot of my own character Bodicea Queen of HRT – an absolute cauldron of bravery and 'couldn't give a f**kness'. Naomi refers to Ada as a 'harridan' which is how men used to portray women but in the same way that Richard Pryor and black people re-appropriated the 'N' word, this I feel is a significantly positive move on behalf of Naomi and one that shows confidence in women's ability to take control and to laugh at themselves.

Wendy Kane

"I'm like two different people on and off stage. I'm like Jekyll and Hyde. I'm a totally mad, loud off the wall person when I'm on stage. I think I'm everything that everyone wants to be. My stage persona is confidence incarcerated. It's a mask, it's a costume. On stage I'm loud, truthful, emotional, constructive and false as in acting a role."

Jane Mackay – Owner of 'The Stand Comedy Club', Edinburgh, Glasgow

"I'm pretty much the same on and off stage and on stage I have been described as: intelligent, incisive, iconoclastic, droll, witty and wonderfully offensive! That will do nicely!" [Sunday Herald]

Julia Morris

"I've always presented myself in an expensive frock and high-heeled shoes on stage, and that comes from the old expression of 'dress for the job you want'. Well no stand-up looks like they're going to walk straight onto the television – I do!"

And it seems that this approach worked extremely well for Julia who by now has starred in 'Australia's Got Talent', 'House Husbands' I'm A Celebrity Get Me Out Of Here etc.

Angie Le Mar

"I'm sharp, stylish, sexy, funny and cool, but no words to do with aggression or anger because I'm a devout Christian so that's not my tone."

Jojo Sutherland

"My Stage Persona is that of a 'Bad Arse Mama'. I bust all the stereotypes and use my kids a lot in my act, it's a 'Thank God someone else wants to choke your kid.'"

Nuala McKeever

"I'm friendly, sharp, impatient, funny and confident. I wouldn't be angry. You know, bafflement maybe, slightly baffled, you know – what the hell's this about kind of thing! But fairly pleasant."

Shazia Mirza

"Strong, deadpan, funny, frightening. That's how I'd say I was onstage. Offstage I'm quite gentle. I'm only five foot five inches tall and I'm quite skinny and that's not a very frightening physicality for the audience. I am very hard-faced when I am onstage. I think I put on that front to protect myself because it looks like I am in control. But when I speak, because I am so direct, I feel that yes, they know I am in control. I wear the hijab on stage, the same 'lucky' pair of trousers and a plain black shirt. I deliberately dress down. I want people to listen to what I'm saying."

JoJo Smith

"I've grown up while I've been doing this. I've been doing it for a long time now and I've changed a lot but when I started, it was a toned down version of me pissed in a pub. I'm a bold, brash, foul-mouthed slut. It's still that 9-year old that was getting pushed around; I'll make people laugh and they'll instantly like me and everything will be ok then."

Nina Conti

"There's that awful thing of wanting to be liked which I am really trying to fight at the moment, because I think what other people think of me has nothing to do with you but you know I am just trying to get rid of the wanting-to-be-liked thing. So the monkey can get away with being downright shocking, that's all right, because I can still play the bashful, apologetic, smiley one."

Ronni Ancona

"My Mum always said you've always got to be nice and polite to people so I found it very hard to be aggressive back to people so my heckle put downs were useless."

Nancy Witter

"Women try too hard to be liked."

*Ronni Ancona really wanted to be NICE, as does ferocious Ada Campe, foul mouthed JoJo Smith and smiley Nina Conti! Here's a lovely 2015 Facebook update that I stole – "A real woman always keeps her house clean, the washing basket is always empty. She's always well dressed, hair done **nicely**. She never swears and behaves gracefully* in all situations. She has more than enough patience to take care of her loved ones, always has a smile (and lipstick) on her lips and a kind word for everyone. Post this as your status if you, too, suspect that you might be a man!

It's interesting to see that many of these FSUCs still want to be liked, which is really another way that society brainwashes us into releasing our power to others. Soraya Chemaly in an online Forum called 'Films for Action' in an excellent article which has collated information on language similar to the information that I have collated, suggests that the most empowering way we can help our daughters to challenge sexism is to teach them these ten little words:

"Stop interrupting me."

"I just said that."

"No explanation needed."

And I would also add, very loudly, if it was, – 'That was my idea, not yours'.

"That's an excellent suggestion, Miss Triggs. Perhaps one of the men here would like to make it."

*My favourite cartoon in 'Cartooning for Equality' is the one above about men appropriating women's ideas. I have had that done to me so many times in the past and maybe you have as well, but no longer – make sure you have a good old paper trail noting any great ideas you have, and preferably some magazine articles giving yourself the credit. Tell people about **YOUR** great idea before someone else claims it as their own. (Remember your new mantra – 'I just said that'!) It feels very unnatural, not **NICE** and very uncomfortable to begin with but you will get used to it! Come on – you know you want to do it – you little Rebel!*

Jenny Éclair

"In terms of my image, I buy my own clothes and do my own hair and go along to photo shoots and may be encouraged by my agency's choice of photos. Sometimes I think I've encouraged an image but I've been quite happy with it. But now the thing is that my age counts for me now because I'm not a threat, because although I come across as vaguely glamorous from a distance, when people get close up they realize quite how raddled I am as a caricature. My age has become a safety net for me. Because it is a cartoon, so it's safe for everyone to laugh at as much as with. It's obvious that I'm not taking myself seriously. How you look on stage is actually quite important. I went through a very bad phase when I thought you had to be fat to be funny. I thought, when I was really confused about stand-up maybe I should just get very fat and then people would just relax more. That was when I was in my twenties. I thought 'Fat, jolly person on stage, that'll work. I flayed around for years. You eventually find your own thing.'

Joan Rivers – St. David's Hall, Cardiff 14th October 2004

An incredibly energetic performance from a 71 year old woman. On stage for a good hour and a quarter. She seemed tall on stage (although off stage she is barely five foot tall) Moved around a huge amount. At one point she lay on the floor and did a very laboured 'getting up' although even that seemed well rehearsed. Wore a flamboyant sparkly blue top, stilettos and black trousers. Very charismatic.

Two other FSUCs who are vertically challenged; Kitty Flanagan coming in at under five foot and Tanyalee Davis barely reaching three feet six high, also take great care with how they look on stage:

Kitty Flanagan
"Suits and boots make me feel like I'm the Boss of everyone. I like to feel tough and I'm in control on stage because that works for my act."

Tanyalee Davis
"I dress sexy onstage but I believe in general I am not seen as a threat by the women even though most men fantasize about being with a little person."

It's intriguing that Mandy Knight, who acknowledges Jo Brand as her Role Model has such differing views to her on how to look on stage.

Mandy Knight
"This guy who owns the 'Comedy Café' says to me 'Show business is the business of show', and he said to me 'You're a good looking woman, so don't you ever dare to come on in a pair of baggy trousers ever again' so that's why I always dress in Chinoiserie. *(Chinese fabric)* I do think it actually is important that you don't look like everybody else. Red is for on-stage, blue is for off-stage and my character on stage is really just an extension of me."

Jo Brand
"I think to be on stage you have to make yourself look as neutral as possible, particularly if you're a woman. I've always tried to wear

kind of baggy, kind of non-committal clothes on stage so that it's not the focus of what I'm doing."

A lot of variety in the stage personas, some kept it simple with the focus and attention on their content whilst others used clothing and or make-up that they could use as a way of developing a character that they could hide behind. What I found was really intriguing was how many of my Interviewees said that they were shy and that the character on stage was an exaggerated version of themselves. And we have seen that even before they get to the thrill of the performance, lots of practical problems have to have solutions. However the foundations have been laid to start treading the boards. If you thought that was difficult, next you'll actually hear about their working environment and the barriers and difficulties they have all successfully overcome to become FSUCs.

CHAPTER 5

WORKING LIFE ACHIEVEMENTS

In which I find out what life is like for a working FSUC

In this next Chapter I was curious to find out what sort of environments my Interviewees were working in and what sort of challenges these environments were presenting for women. I wanted to know what did my Interviewees find 'funny', what made them laugh, what or who was the subject of their comedy and was it different to some groups or audiences? Rose Laub Coser in a 1960 study about comedy in a state psychiatric hospital concluded that in that particular working environment, senior staff used humour to mock junior staff and thereby humiliate them into being in their rightful place. Less frequently, those at the bottom used humour to express rebellion against instructions from managers, though never when they were present. So humour cascades downwards in society. A waterfall and not a fountain as I mentioned in Chapter 1. You could poke fun at the Boss – but not when he or she was around to hear it happen, no, that was taboo. And talking of taboos, were there any taboo subject areas that were off limits to my Interviewees for whatever reason? Topics such as rape which in the last few years has become more and more prolific in comedy both in Britain and the States.

I also wanted to look at the power of comedy. What did it look like, what could it achieve, what could it change – for better or worse? Russel Brand for example has over twelve million Twitter followers – that's a great deal of influential power. How far is too far in comedic terms? The Burmese comic Zarganar, active in Burma's democracy movement, who for organizing private deliveries of aid to cyclone victims, has been sentenced to 45 years in jail by a Burmese court. Also as we saw the death threats delivered to comic Mona Shaikh and also Ayaan Hirsi when they dared to raise their voices.

One of the first people I saw doing stand-up on the television was Irish comic Dave Allen who sat on a chair, drank scotch, smoked a cigar and uttered Irish profanities under his breath. Did my Interviewees do this? Could they do it? Did society 'allow' them as women to do this or did they just stick one finger up and do what they wanted anyway? What style did their comedy take and was it different to a man's style of comedy. Jo Brand is famous for her self-deprecating humour, that is, poking fun at herself before anyone else does it – is this the norm for female comedy or are present day comics experimenting with other forms of comedy? And once they have mastered this live medium what other performance environments and opportunities were awaiting them and did they actually want to go in that direction?

Helen Lederer

"When I started out performing stand-up in the late seventies, there weren't a lot of female or middle class stand-up comedians around so I was quite unusual."

Hazel O'Keefe – Laughing Cows Comedy Club and Women's Comedy Festival

"There are about five to six thousand female comics in Britain. They are not invisible – just not collated. I could name about 800 off the top of my head. I get hundreds and hundreds of requests from women who want to perform at Laughing Cows."

It's not surprising to find that the percentage of FSUCs has not radically improved in Britain since the time of the Music Halls, there hasn't even been any improvement since the development of the

Alternative Comedy scene and interesting to note that in America the figure is somewhat higher, although it may not be as high as Jeff Scott thinks it is when we hear about the experiences of some of the American FSUCs I interviewed. It's good to know that according to Hazel O'Keefe there are at least five to six thousand FSUCs in Britain – this book could be a great little seller!!!

As a professional performer of over thirty five years I have worked in all sorts of environments: bars, clubs, terraces, restaurants, stables, churches, castles, crematoriums, streets, concert halls, front rooms, open air venues with sheep penned just across from where I was singing, old people's homes, hospitals, television and radio studios, film locations in disused cottages, chateaux, chapels, rivers, motorways, forests, moors in the lashing rain; the variety has been surprising as has been the reaction from the audiences, some of whom are often drunk, who may or may not become violent, some not totally compos mentis and the changing rooms have usually been the toilet – ah the glamour of show-business!!! What sort of variety of locations did my Interviewees have and what sort of audiences?

Welcome to the piranha pool!
Venues & audiences?
Betsy Salkind

"Venues in the States back in the 80's – bookstores, café's, private parties, any venue that was willing to take me. I was being banned from comedy clubs because I was being too challenging. There was a time when I was so filled with rage about the oppression of women and children. I cannot express that rage on stage."

Naomi Paxton aka Ada Campe

"I have been very lucky to have been able to perform in Wilton's Music Hall *(Mentioned previously in Suffrajests – The History Chapter)* and I was very much aware of its historical significance and it was a total thrill to perform there. I first went to Wilton's

Music Hall in 1997 to see Fiona Shaw in 'The Waste Land' and since then have seen comedy and theatre there and have always loved it as a performance space. For the show I did there, I invented a distant relative for Ada who had performed there in the Edwardian period so she could tell the audience how thrilled she was to be there too! There have been a couple of other venues steeped in performance history that I feel honoured to have played as Ada as well – the Royal Vauxhall Tavern and the Garrick Theatre spring to mind."

Hattie Hayridge aka Holly Red Dwarf

"I usually perform in Theatres, Art Centres and I still do rooms above pubs now and again so it's still a complete mixture. I work internationally, mainly theatres or someone abroad has set up a venue so it could be anywhere, where they've changed something into a comedy club, a restaurant or something. Usually you'll do one club. A promoter has got some sponsor that pays your fare and you go over to do that place so it may be three nights and then you come back. It's mainly British ex-pats in the audience."

Donna McPhail

"I work a lot on the British circuit but I've also worked a lot 'daaan unddaaaar' in Oz, but it's so scary to do that, because you never know if your humour translates to another culture."

Kitty Flanagan

"The best thing I did was move from Australia to the UK and work heaps, it meant I didn't have time to dwell on things, if I had a bad gig, I just went and did another one straight away and 'fixed' all the stuff I did wrong."

Blod Jones

"Having moved back to Cardiff this year, I certainly think it is easier to get your career going in London. There are more opportunities to perform every night of the week. There seems to be more bounceability there, you can die hard one night and perform the next and completely turn the room around."

Dana Goldberg

"When I went to perform in the UK, I still felt comfortable. Those were definitely some of my most challenging shows but they went well. In order to make a crowd laugh, they have to be able to relate to me. Since there weren't any other Jewish lesbians from the United States in the crowd that night, I had to find another way to get them…and I did. Traveling is one of the best parts of my work so it's never been a problem for me."

Katerina Vrana

"I'd say the only difference in audience reaction is a matter of how familiar the audience is with stand-up comedy. In Greece, they have very little experience with stand-up so they take a little bit longer to warm up and some jokes just don't work, like anything that is self-referential to the forms and tropes of stand-up. I do little variations that have to do with local references or cultural signifiers. And of course there is material that only works in one place because it is entirely about that place. The biggest difference is when I change the language. Swearing in Greek is a sheer delight that cannot be replicated in English. At all."

Sindhu Vee

"I've performed in the UK and India, at the Comedy Store – both places love comedy, love stand-up and have been hugely welcoming. I grew up in India. I love gigging there because I can use a lot more Hindi in my act than in the UK and a lot of my life experience resonates with the audience. For example, my struggles with fobbing off an arranged marriage – almost every middle class Indian woman my age can identify with that."

Katerina Vrana

"The first guy to do stand-up in Greece was Harry Klynn. He did stand-up with a Music Hall / Variety note to it. He was huge in Greece in the 70s and 80s. Huge. Bizarrely, no one followed him. Then a comedy club opened in 1995 in Athens, "Comedy Nights", but it never quite created a 'scene' though a lot of the comedians still performing today started out there. Greek stand-up comedy developed a scene I would say in late 2011 – early 2012, with the first 'National Stand Up Competition' and the first Open Mike night."

Angie Le Mar

"Before I went onto the mainstream circuit. I did the fashion shows, anywhere there were groups of black people for two years doing free gigs. Then I worked on the mainstream circuit and did quite well there. I didn't stay too long on the mainstream circuit, because by then the alternative, which was black comedy, emerged. So the black comedians were filling out Hackney Empire, you know, filling out the Crucible, filling out the Nottingham Playhouse. We were hiring big venues and filling them out. So we didn't necessarily need the mainstream circuit at that time, places like Jongleurs. The black comedy circuit could quite happily have existed on its own."

Nuala McKeever

"There is a very small circuit really of three or four venues in Northern Ireland. There's Derry and Belfast and maybe some of the smaller towns have little theatres and they would put on a comedy night. We performed at 'The Empire' Belfast a few times, it's a bit of a bear pit, loads of students. You know a lot of the time they just want the usual kind of bigoted stuff, you know, Catholic/Protestant whatever. I just can't be arsed with it really. We would do places in Derry, Dublin local clubs, theatres and bars, cabaret type places like that. They were quite rough and full of drunkards."

Hazel O'Keefe – Laughing Cows Comedy Club and Women's Comedy Festival

"If you took alcohol away – the comedy would collapse!"

Lynn Ruth Miller

"I hadn't been in a bar since the 1950's and didn't realise you could do stand-up in bars."

Lydia Nicole

"I couldn't get into the black or white comedy clubs at the tail end of the eighties in L.A. so I did stand-up in prisons, hotel lobbies, bars, anywhere really that would let me perform."

Jeff Scott – Resident Piano Player and M.C. at Comedy Store Los Angeles

"Before finding salvation at The Comedy Store, I played for 'The Sirens Of Satire' (an all-female comic evening, but at another club), for four years so I mostly know female comics (Sherri Shepard, Pam Maddison, Kelly Kirsten, Lotus Weinstock, Penny Wiggins, Janice Hart, Cynthia Levin, Judy Gold, Lydia Nicole, Rhonda Shear, Beth Lapedis etc. etc.) I got to open and play piano for 'Saturday Night Live's Victoria Jackson several years ago, which was a big treat! And I always love working with such talented and generous female comics as Janice Hart, Pam Maddison & Penny Wiggins over the many years I've known them."

WOW – Now that's one long list of fabulous FSUCs to check out! Thanks Jeff Scott.

Cynthia Levin

"I had to adapt my material a little when I came here to London from America. People do like to hear you telling about what you know and it's good to make fun of the audience. An outsiders experience as an American reveals the nonsense of their behaviour."

Tanyalee Davis

"I perform all over North America with residencies in Vegas, all over the UK and further afield. I find British audiences to be far more uptight than North American audiences. The audiences/venues vary from comedy clubs, theatres, bars to posh lounges."

Ashley Storrie

"Doing comedy in America was so easy. Los Angeles was dire and the comedy was weak, generic and by numbers. The perception of women in the States is that they're snazzy, sexy, feisty, and powerful like Sarah Silverman and American sit-coms are all about putting down men – men are just as disenfranchised as women."

Nadia Kamil

"Coming to Los Angeles from London to develop my comedy may be a terrible decision! When I first came out here I experienced a whirlwind of excitement. I performed some really excellent shows which were received so well I didn't really think it was happening. I got an Agent straight away and I thought "America loves me!" so it seemed obvious that I should move out here and start making a go of it. I do miss London's comedy scene. I find it much more experimental and varied than LA which is very angled towards television. Also I miss squash, electric kettles, decent tea and Nando's!"

Susie Felber
"'Don't tell Mama' is a very old comedy club off Broadway in New York with a great back catalogue and it's around the corner from Letterman and it's a bringer show – that is, you bring your audience along."

Nancy Witter
"I worked in the back room of 'Don't tell Mama's' for ten years. We did 'The Pool Party' every Saturday night for 10 years."

I love 'Don't tell Mama'. I have sung there on four occasions – it's also a very famous piano bar with a little theatre out in the back. I didn't realise at the time when I was there, that it was also a very famous comedy location. This was where I met and sang with someone who has become a very dear friend, the fashion designer Malan Breton and also the very talented pianist William TN Hall who was Joan River's stage pianist for several years. Another one of my interviewees Rhonda Hansome also performs there on a regular basis.

Audiences
Spring Day
"I do 5 to 6 shows a month – mostly for an U.K. ex-pat crowd and Japanese wives. Before the earthquake there were more bankers and financial people (who then went to Shanghai and Taiwan) People are still dealing with the aftermath of the earthquake. The audience would be mostly ESL (English as a Second Language) and Japanese people who have studied abroad. There is a traditional Japanese comedy culture called 'The Manzai', which is one straight person and one idiot and it is quite formulaic and a little bit physical using silly names. The styles of

comedy I personally use are 'Release' and 'Incongruity' but I don't do 'Superiority', that is kicking someone's butt. I am almost allergic to authority. My comedy is about taking something painful and making it beautiful – making a flower out of shit."

For those who are particularly interested in comedy, there are three main theories that go way back to Freud and even further to the time of Socrates and Plato. I am sure if you want to know more about them you are perfectly capable of Googling them yourself, but for the time being and in a nutshell here are some examples:

Incongruity – When you're expecting a different answer to the one you get:

I said to the Gym Instructor: "Can you teach me to do the splits?" He said: "How flexible are you?" I said: 'I can't make Tuesdays!

Release – When you let off comic steam in a tense embarrassing situation.

A woman tells her friend: "For eighteen years my husband and I were the happiest people in the world! Then we met!"

Superiority – When you make someone else feel inferior – the butt of the joke!

A woman goes into a café with a duck. She puts the duck on the stool and sits next to it. The waiter comes over and says: "Hey! That's the ugliest pig that I have ever seen." The woman says: It's a duck, not a pig." And the waiter says: "I was talking to the duck."

And whilst we're doing jokes the following was voted the world's funniest joke in the world on Richard Wiseman's 'Laugh Lab' website and in fact contains all three theories:

Two hunters are out in the woods when one of them collapses. He doesn't seem to be breathing and his eyes are glazed. The other guy whips out his phone and calls the emergency services. He gasps, "My friend is dead! What can I do?" The operator says, "Calm down. I can help. First, let's make sure he's dead." There is a silence, then a shot is heard. Back on the phone, the guy says "OK, now what?"

Michele A'Court

"There is one fulltime comedy club in NZ – the Classic in the main street of Auckland, our biggest city. I perform there often, and at various pubs around the country that have weekly or monthly comedy nights. I also do corporate entertainment, host conferences and awards nights, do "celebrity" debates, and I have some regular gigs on tv and radio. In my head, all these jobs are the same – it's the same process, the same approach, and they all use the same skills."

Thenjiwe Tay Moseley

"My first language is Zulu but I can switch from Zulu to English depending on the audience. Afrikaans is the language of oppression and I refuse to speak it. We did a gig in the Lyric Theatre in Johannesburg with an audience of around 2,200 Zulu speaking people, which would have been the biggest gig we did. The first six rows were all white people so the only way I could communicate to Celeste Ntuli, the headliner, that she might have to vary her set was by doing the set totally in English."

Aditi Mittal

"I do lots of pubs, clubs and sometimes auditoriums, which are edgy but not 'dirty' so my audiences would be anything up to 1,000."

Dana Goldberg

"I do stand-up, hosting, and a ton of live auction work in the States. I seem to have a gift for all three. My audience range from 100 to 3,500 people. I can perform in small black box theatres and clubs, or in a giant ballroom depending on the event or crowd. I love working with major charity organizations across the country. I've helped to raise over 3 Million dollars for HIV-AIDS research and prevention, women's health and LGBT equality. The audiences range in age, gender, sexual orientation and ethnicity. I love the diversity of my audiences."

Cynthia Levin

"Stand-up in bigger venues will change to be more receptive to women's comedy."

JoJo Smith

"I performed live on the internet back in 2002. It worked by standing in a basement room at the BBC, with a load of other newish comics and a guy with a camcorder. They would film you, so it wasn't actually 'live-live' it was 'as-live'. So they'd film you doing your bit of material, and then run upstairs to somewhere in the IT department and put it straight out. It must have been a digital camcorder he used, you know. Somehow they film it and, you know, two minutes later, it was out on the Net. Yes, we had 1100 hits from Rumania for my bit! I'm big in Rumania!" *They'll be putting pictures of you at the side of their stoves like they did for Lydia Thompson in every kitchen in Riga!*

There are a huge variety of venues for these woman from the room above a pub in Camden to luscious gigs in swanky hotels for Brit ex-pats, cafes, prisons, libraries, in fact anywhere that could be turned into an area to capture some people who wanted to be entertained. There are festivals worldwide including expensive gigs in the

Edinburgh Fringe that cost a fortune to put on, to big theatres holding several hundred people and big auditorium gigs in South Africa, America and India holding thousands of people. Another myth doing the rounds is that women can't handle big auditorium type gigs – we aren't authoritative enough! Well, I'd say, Thenjiwe Tay Moseley, Aditi Mittal and Dana Goldberg disprove that theory, and if you don't believe me, Google it, there you will see undisputable evidence. The world wide web gives a fantastic new platform to create new audiences but the one thing you can't do with a web audience is hear them laugh. You need to be in closer proximity for that to happen and now I was told about their interactions with the audiences.

Who is in the audience and how do you deal with them?

Katerina Vrana – Comedy Promoter & FSUC

"In my experience, it's usually half and half gender-wise. It's the age and nationality of the audience that can vary drastically. In central London, for example, in the club I used to run (Angel Comedy) we used to get maybe a 60/40 men to women, 25-35yr olds, but from a spectacularly wide array of countries. In Greece, I tend to get equal split of men and women in the audience but the ages range from 30 – 85!"

Jane Duffus – Director Bristol Based Women's Comedy Club

"My Bristol audiences are very mixed and I'd say that 10-50% of the audience are male although all the acts are female. It's not a 'girls night out' and I actively discourage hen nights."

Hazel O'Keefe – Laughing Cows Comedy Club and Women's Comedy Festival

"My audiences now would be 50/50 male/female and 15% with a disability. I really want to have an integrated mainstream audience. My pledge is to make all my comedy venues much more accessible and to that end I have created 'Comixlive' which is a website showing accessible venues and 'a practical approach to solving the problem of discrimination in the comedy world' as the 'Telegraph' says on my website."

Michele A'Court

"The range of audiences is vast – students, business people, small towns. The lack of stand-up history in New Zealand has meant for a long time that the audiences were young (the ones who might otherwise be going to a music gig) but more and more middle-aged people (like myself) are starting to see stand-up as an entertainment option – 'Movie, dinner, theatre or comedy tonight, darling?'"

Angie le Mar

"At the beginning I did the London circuit. But then it just became the black comedy circuit. I think they were two different audiences at the time; I think the mainstream lot (on the London 'circuit') were talking about bras and periods and babies and stuff like that. But on the black comedy circuit they talked about everything. You know, the male audience were happy to hear us talk about anything. Our audience was 70% black women anyway. There wasn't as much sexism in the black comedy circuit as in the mainstream. Yes I think because I was the pioneer and I could, to a certain degree, really set the agenda. You come out with all the other black guys that are doing it and I am on a par; there are no apologies there. And our audience is not drunk; they are very sober so you need to be very funny. It's a culture thing really that there's no drink available. It's different venues as well. In theatres you don't actually get drunk, you see what I mean; in a comedy club that's the whole point of them being there is the drink. So there were two different things happening. And you know, I have always said I have tested my performance on a sober audience whereby you better get it bang on."

Spring Day

"The audience would be stag weekends and weekend rugby clubs with men dressed as vaginas. Men liked to be treated like shit and they are not intimidated by you. Japanese men don't date as they don't date Americans, others date Asian women. Tokyo audiences – 20% of them will have seen you last week so you'd better have something new for them."

Jo Caulfield

"Generally I think a female audience will try harder to understand some material. Men are just much less willing to make an effort to understand something that is not in their world. But that's because men will put themselves first and if they don't get the joke straightaway it's not worth bothering with. Whereas women have always had to be in second place and we pander to men don't we."

Jane Mackay – Owner of 'The Stand Comedy Club', Edinburgh, Glasgow

"We have marginally more women in our audience than men overall. We keep kind of membership and audience figures – 52% of our audience overall in Glasgow anyway are women. That could perhaps be because 52% of Glasgow's population is women. But I know that there are some clubs that are quite male.

Jo Caulfield

"I've done several years of sell out shows at the Edinburgh Festival and often I have groups of straight men in the audience. They haven't been dragged along by wives or girlfriends; they've come because they want to see a comedian. (Obviously some of them come because I throw in a free laundry service!)"

Jane Mackay – Owner of 'The Stand Comedy Club', Edinburgh, Glasgow

"The Edinburgh Festival has a kind of mixed impact on 'The Stand' comedy club in the sense that there is I think an element in Edinburgh of a bit of resentment sometimes about the Festival and the way it's now, in terms of comedy anyway, become a very, very big industry. And it's very expensive. And people are placed by the big agents by spending an awful lot of money on publicity and spin and all that kind of thing. So obviously, we are a comedy club in Edinburgh, it would be perverse of us to fuck off and not do anything doing the Fringe – it's a busy time of year for us. We put on about 14 shows."

Spring Day

"I've performed at Edinburgh four times, every year since 2010 and have done a one-woman show. I've always had a lot of men enjoying my show. Edinburgh is the family reunion I want to go to. I consider Edinburgh to be the slightly abusive boyfriend – he keeps beating me up but I keep coming back to him. It's a great 'crash course' in comedy. I felt like a fly on the wall and learnt a lot. By being a teacher I've always got an audience."

Tanyalee Davis

"A turning point in my career was when I performed at the Edinburgh Fringe Festival in 2003. I was picked up by my UK manager and have been back and forth to the UK since then. I have had many great opportunities from that one experience."

Most audiences are mixed these days, even those with just females performing so at least women are now being seen by more men than they used to, which is a very good thing in my mind, as their laughter will be all that's needed to show that women are funny. The Edinburgh Fringe Festival is one of the most well-known if not **THE** *most well known* *comedy festivals in the world (amongst Melbourne International Festival, the Montreal and New Zealand Comedy Festivals) and doing well there gives great exposure. Comics will pay thousands of pounds to have a gig there which may only be frequented by five or six people in the audience if you're lucky. I had a guest slot in a friend's show several years ago and I think we might have made it up to double figures in the audience, so we did well. Edinburgh is a huge financial risk which may or may not pay off. Edinburgh did turn out to be a turning point in Tanya Lee Davis' career when she attracted the attention of a Manager and since that time she has had tremendous opportunities from that one experience, so for her it was definitely worth the financial investment, for others, maybe not. Visibility and exposure are crucial to the development of a comic's career and the person who has more time on stage than any other is the M.C., The MASTER of Ceremonies – as women obviously aren't capable of taking control and leadership in this very important role! (I'm being very sarcastic at the moment, thanks to my Uncle Ifan for the lifetime Masterclasses he has given to me in this skill!)*

Taking Control – Mistress of Ceremonies
Jane Mackay
"The M.C. is the second most important person on the bill after the headliner, you do as much as the headliner in terms of time. You can go and do the same stuff as a set if you like."

Jeff Scott – Resident Piano Player and M.C. at Comedy Store Los Angeles
"We have an MC/hosts for our Open-Mic amateur shows on Sunday & Monday (usually an up-and-coming comic that Mitzi Shore gives hosting work to for the learning experience). The rest of the week I provide piano music as the guests enter the club, then a welcome speech and then I announce the first comic. After that, the comics tag-team introductions, but I am responsible for letting them know which comic is next."

Jojo Sutherland

"I do a lot of M.C. work. I improvise and interact with the audience a lot. I think women make much better M.C.'s in big rowdy places. Lots of men have told me that their worst ever event would be hen-parties. Women are not confrontational so can deal better with these types of events. Bookers have realised that women can control a drunk room, especially an older woman. And what has tended to happen over the last few years is that more people are having positive experiences with female performers and they are coming back to see them."

Thenjiwe Tay Moseley

"My manager is a film producer Zamo Missie and she negotiates my fees. Performing in Britain I have been very lucky and have already had some tremendous opportunities like being the Host M.C. of the Berlinae in Berlin which was a huge honour."

Maureen Younger

"I've been doing stand-up for ten years. I do mostly M.C. work throughout the UK but if I work abroad I do sets. I am the resident M.C. for London's 'Laughing Cows'. The brand is now growing and also going to start up in Birmingham and Coventry. You talk to people as an M.C. and you have to be warm. I think that being an older woman can be much easier than if you're a young man. You have more life experience on how to deal with people. It's very empowering being a women on stage and it's good for other women to see you there."

JoJo Smith

"When I did my first MCing at the (Comedy) Store in London it was like my first open spot; I have never been so scared. I was nervous for weeks before. I was only the second woman to have MC'ed the London Store and the first and only (*at that time*) who's ever done it at the Store in Manchester. I'm the only woman to MC (Master /Mistress of Ceremonies) 'Up the Creek' probably because a lot of women don't play there, because it does have that reputation of being a very tough gig. It took me 18 months to go back, and I sat there waiting to go on thinking, 'I don't need to do this; I can go'. And of course by then I was getting twenty minutes everywhere else. So I was a lot more confident; I knew what I was doing. I felt like I had to conquer it. And I just had the most fantastic gig and you know they just started booking me in straight away. And I didn't ever have a bad gig there ever again. So far! And yeah I started MC'ing at other places; one of the first places I was regularly doing it was the Glee Club in Birmingham. Because I loved playing there so much, I worked out that if I compered it I could do it more often because I wasn't doing so much material."

Liz Carr

"I perform occasionally with AFP (Abnormally Funny People) but I'm more likely now to be found MC-ing cabarets and performing at camp cabaret nights like 'Duckie' at the Royal Vauxhall Tavern. I love live performance but I don't do it often anymore."

Many of these women, especially in the last few years, had taken on the role of Master or Mistress of Ceremonies – a very important role where they spend more time on stage than any other comic and it can be quite a challenge to control rowdy audiences.

Kate Smurthwaite

"I do a lot of M.C. work and political comedy."

My personal has always been political for my entire life and at the tail end of my twenty year comedy project, I have come to realise that stand-up comedy and politics are really the only two places where women are able to publically talk and exchange ideas about what matters in their lives. The world wide web is now quickly becoming another forum where we can talk about our lives and there we see on a very regular basis how 'trolls' keep trying to shut women up from talking about their experiences, their 'TRUTHS'. I am intrigued to find out, as to how if you're the 'court jester' – a professional buffoon, how did someone like Jo Brand manage the transition quite so easily, to jump from comedy to politics? And for that matter Boris Johnson is recognised as a professional buffoon but he has no qualms at all in stepping onto the political stage. Jo Brand is often asked to be a political commentator and pundit, but that may be because she has always been involved in politics, as have Jane Mackay and Kate Smurthwaite.

In June 2015, I had the greatest pleasure of meeting one of my all-time political heroines, Julia Gillard, in the Welsh Assembly Government. Julia Gillard was the 27th Prime Minister of Australia, and the Australian Labour Party leader from 2010 to 2013. She was the first woman to hold either position and was born in Barry, South Wales where I trained as a teacher. She feels passionately that women in public life deserve a standard of behaviour better than which they are getting. Sexism is NEVER acceptable and this is discussed at great length in her world-famous 10th October 2012, 'Misogyny Speech' which you can see on youtube.

She has had some really vitriolic attacks on her, such as placards saying 'Ditch the Witch', articles in the press criticising the way she dresses and looks and personal pornographic cartoons being mainstreamed. Politicians such as Nicola Sturgeon (SNP) Natalie Bennett (Green Party) and Leanne Wood (Plaid Cymru) all had to put up with personal attacks in the media in the run up to the 2015 Westminster election and Liz Kendall has also being subjected to almost misogynistic bullying in her pursuit of the Labour Leadership as has Hillary Clinton for many, many years. The history of sexist attacks against Clinton is well documented. A recent analysis found *that "bitch", "c*nt" and "slut" were the three most common insults directed at Clinton on social media. In a political rally a 'heckler' (just like in stand-up!!) harassed her by shouting out 'Iron my shirt. Iron my shirt' non-stop until Hilary Clinton got the lights put on in the auditorium and he was disarmed verbally by her and ejected from the building accompanied by rapturous applause from Hillary's supporters.*

Gillard said it often felt quite lonely being the only woman in the room, and that if you're a female politician you couldn't win at all on the family level: No children – barren bitch, kids – why aren't you looking after them? She felt that women were never received as full human beings but that they were constantly being categorized as 'Mary' or 'Magdalen' (Lying bitch, vile harridan) She had had to harden her heart in politics and felt that women needed to have a very strong sense of purpose and not allow it to bother you. Dealing with things such as sexism and gender early and comprehensively was essential, self-protection was crucial and she was a great supporter of naming and shaming.

Comedy and Politics
Naomi Paxton

"There is a strong connection between comedy and politics. You're given a voice and a platform from which to show and represent ideas, values and communities. If the persona is robust enough you can include political ideas and comments within your work without making them the focus. I'm really aware that so many issues – much of the sexism women face, the racism in our society and the 'I'm alright, Jack' attitude of the right wing, for example – are underscored by the language we speak every day, our habits of behaviour and culture and our very skewed view of history – and it's those assumptions and casual slights that reinforce prejudice. Comedy can be a great tool for showing these things up and for challenging them."

Betsy Salkind

"The first time I was on cable comedy television in the States, all the politics had been removed so it was all pretty bland really. Why? So that it would appeal to everyone, but surely when you remove the politics there's nothing left. It's great now with the internet and the new uncensored possibilities that are available. It's another great way of getting stuff out there."

Adrienne Truscott

"Comedy is a very strong vehicle for engaging with people in a public arena, a bit like politics."

Jane Mackay – Owner of 'The Stand Comedy Club', Edinburgh, Glasgow

"I try and break down stereotypes about expectations on stage, for example if I talk to a woman in the audience and she says she works in a hospital I'll ask her if she's a Doctor and not if she's a nurse so there's an opportunity to raise a bit of the audience's awareness because a male comic might just take for granted that the women would be a nurse."

Donna McPhail

"I've had men come up to me and go 'I never thought women were funny but I enjoyed you – and that's brilliant and they don't know that you're a lesbian. Half way through you tell them, they still laugh and they go out thinking 'I wouldn't have gone if I'd known, but I did and enjoyed it' and what does that say about what they think about lesbians and what they think about women and it's not the material within the show that counts it's the fact that people go away with that changed opinion. That to me is how I'm political, not what comes out of my mouth so much but the fact that I'm there and I'm doing it and I'm doing it well."

Rosie Kane – Scottish FSUC & Previous Member of the Scottish Parliament

"I realised I had immense power when I became a Member of the Scottish Parliament, but I feel that there is more freedom of expression in comedy than in politics."

Dr. Jane Davidson – Former Cabinet Minister, Welsh Assembly Government

"I think I've been very lucky as I have never felt constrained in what I say in the political sphere. I think training in front of an audience, getting used to barracking or heckling and being confident enough to articulate what you want to say is really helpful. Having acted professionally for a short time (despite having a face for radio!) I certainly found drama training really useful in Politics."

Sian James – Labour M.P. for Swansea East 2005 – 2015 & Women's Activist

"Dennis Skinner calls the House of Commons, the 'Palace of Varieties' – he is correct. Every day, things would happen or comments would be made that were comical. Often, these incidents would be played down or whispered about in case the Press got to hear about them. It was as if we could only display serious, rigid images of ourselves. This has got worse at Westminster over the years. The Press can pick up on stories now so quickly, printing small incidents as major faux pas. No-one wanted to be part of a story which drew attention to the lighter side of Westminster life. Humour is a great pressure valve. *(Relief Theory)* Telling funny stories, relating personal anecdotes are the norm in society but at Westminster this was frowned upon as not being, 'serious'. Another example, of where politicians are forced to create public images of themselves, images that meet the needs of others or the Press. I had one MP colleague who every time we saw each other we told jokes that our partners, children and friends had told us. These were lighter moments in a serious day and were moments that I appreciated and I hope he did as well."

Katerina Vrana

"The political situation definitely helped to promote the comedy scene in Greece. In the crisis, people couldn't afford to go out the way they used to. Stand-up is cheaper than other forms of entertainment (both for the punters and the people producing it) and it cheered people up at a time when they sorely needed laughter so I think it most definitely gave it a helping hand."

Which is exactly what happened in London in the early eighties recession as mentioned by Donna McPhail.

Jane Mackay – Owner of 'The Stand Comedy Club', Edinburgh, Glasgow

"I came to stand-up late, I started at 38, as a result of disillusion with my former political path. I had been an active member of the Labour Party from 1975 until Blair and most of my work – in press and publicity – had been political. But I really wanted to be an MP for the Highlands. I got very near a selection; I was an Islington Councillor at the time. The tube broke down so I missed my flight and I missed the selection. I mean thank Christ now. I wouldn't want to be a representative of Labour you know. I vote Nationalist now. I think it's not an accident that what we started doing, does in one way coincide with a Scottish Parliament and a true Scottish 'voice' developing."

Professor Christie Davies in his 2004 study for the Social Affairs Unit, called 'The Right to Joke' (Davies, Daily Mail 17/02/04) maintains that 'True comedy flourishes where freedom is at its strongest.' If you look at the other side of the coin does that then follow that where there is no comedy (or a comedy scene) there is suppression? It's interesting to note that the Scottish comedy scene's growth was at the same time as power was being devolved in favour of the Scottish people and which has kept on devolving with Scotland now calling for independence.

If the Welsh Assembly were to have the same sort of tax-raising and law making powers (WATCH THIS SPOT!! Things are starting to happen!) as the Scots, who knows what would happen to our comedy circuit, which consists for the most part of an imported-English-comedy-over-the-Severn-Bridge-Cardiff-based Jongleurs and Glee Club scene. Very little has changed in the last fifteen years or more apart from the occasional appearance of Rhod Gilbert on national television and of course the imported-English-comedy-over-the-Severn-Bridge Machynlleth Comedy Festival or 'Mak' as it's commonly known to those who can't get their chops around the rest of the tricky Welsh consonants. And here is what Jo Brand says about comedy and politics, which brings us neatly to the next part of my research which was to examine closely **THE BIG MYTH** – 'Are women funny or not?'

Jo Brand

"Either you make people laugh or you don't. If you're a comic the most important thing to be is funny and make people laugh so if you can do a good joke with your political view in it fair enough but if you can just get your political view across and it's not funny, don't bother being a comic."

Hysterical – Am I funny or am I not?
Joan Rivers
"Funny is funny"

Janey Godley – Prolific Scottish Blogger & Scottish FSUC
"Guys, have you ever walked on stage and heard people groan because they feel cheated that the headline act is a woman? 'But

will she be funny?' you hear people say. If I was a lawyer/brain surgeon/politician/nurse it would be illegal to question my ability to perform my job based on my sexuality. Only in comedy is it acceptable. Well it's fucking not – so quit it!"

Julia Morris

"I know that one thing for the female comedy industry, is that a lot of people get a real look of disappointment when a woman walks on the stage. Girls only started doing stand-up in around the 80s in Australia, and that's when they did all that tampon stuff. And I think that's all that people were used to and they haven't given women a chance to see that they've come on in leaps and bounds since then."

Maureen Younger

"It always surprises me that comedy is always singled out as why there are few women. Most films have more men in the cast – they don't say women can't act. Sexism is 'Women are not funny' – would you say 'Black people are not funny? I refuse to answer the question 'Are women funny' – it's a non-question. Lots more women are now doing Open Mikes (*which is the entrance level to getting paid gigs*). More women are giving it a go and coming through the system. Many think that stand-up comedy is a short cut to stardom which it most certainly isn't."

Hazel O'Keefe – Laughing Cows Comedy Club and Women's Comedy Festival

"How can people say that women aren't funny? It's lazy stereotyping. It's unfair, unfounded and there are lots of legal issues linked in with it, Employment Law for example. We know that women are funny, why do we keep examining this issue? 'Funny is funny' (as Joan Rivers used to say) although I've never had a Tory comic on the Laughing Cows stage for some strange reason! Comedy is a very powerful vehicle for positive change.

When you're on stage you have to read a room and use what tools you have. The comedy I am fighting for is comedy as an art form. Zoe Lyons, Barbara Nice and Jo Enright are brilliant comics and suitable for all ages and they work in every context. Zoe Lyons should really have her own television show."

Dana Alexander

"I sat in the audience before I went up and when the MC said, 'She' and the Yorkshire rugby stag do guys all went 'Ugh' I shot the ring leader the filthiest look, had a good show and then in the break he felt so bad I let him buy me drinks in the break even though all my drinks are free. Why? Because I am an asshole."

Jo Caulfield

"Sometimes when I'm announced as a woman there is an audible groan of disappointment, but I don't blame them for that it's only because they haven't seen many female comics. But if you're good they'll laugh. If they don't laugh at you purely because you're a woman who cares – they're idiots."

Spring Day

"I'm not keen to advertise that I'm a woman because I don't want to emphasise that I'm a woman for the same reason I don't want to emphasise that I'm disabled. Both things are parts of me and I address them as such but they do not represent the whole package. I've never heard of a guy emphasizing that he's a guy in the promotion of his show (That doesn't stop him from talking about his dick). A promoter in Asia told me I inspired him to start an all women show. Something about the way he said it sounded like I had inspired him to start the Special Olympics. Comedy is not a physical sport, there is no need for the separation. We are all human. As Joan Rivers said, 'Funny is Funny'."

Ronni Ancona

"I'm as vain as the rest of them but I find actually comedy terribly liberating because when you're getting dressed up all you think about is 'Am I funny?'. That's the great thing about comedy. You don't have to be particularly anything, just funny. You can be any shape or size. It's not a job that requires a certain look. You do have to have a presence on stage. It's very powerful. I'm aware of that when I see other people on stage. It's usually charismatic."

Tanyalee Davis

"By many people (usually men), women comics are seen as not funny so that may dissuade some women from giving it a shot. But if you're good, you're good!"

Blod Jones

"There will always be people who say that women can't be funny but of course women are funny. It is just a sad factor of a generation brought up solely on male comedians."

Kitty Flanagan

"I've never thought about it but now that I do, I think when I worked on the comedy circuit, I always had a weird subconscious motivation of 'I don't want to be the un-funniest act on the night, otherwise people will think that all women aren't funny.'"

Michele A'Court

"In the early days, there was a perception that women did period jokes and just weren't funny, and low expectations on the part of the audience. (Though that's gone now.) I do a lot of corporate work, and there used to be an assumption that a woman couldn't command enough attention and respect to control an evening, but I think we're all over that now. And fairly often these days, I get corporate gigs *because* I'm a woman – maybe the guy they had the year before offended too many of the wives, and they want a turn at being represented."

Sioned Wiliam

"The most significant female stand-up that I've ever worked with is Victoria Wood who is just one of the great comics of Britain. The fact that she's a woman is interesting. We recorded her stand-up show in the Albert Hall. She was doing material that was very specifically feminine, it was about menopausal women and the quality of her performance had a very kind of feminine slant to it. However, it didn't make it better or worse because she was a woman, it just happened to be that was the stuff of her material. As far as I was concerned she was just a brilliant comic and I didn't commission it because she was a woman."

As William Cook maintains in 'Ha Bloody Ha – Comedians Talking' was that you should 'write about what you know' so that you retain your authenticity. Women's experience in life is entirely different to a man's experience so that will have an impact on the type of material they will be writing and delivering. 'Truth' is a word that keeps coming up, that is, a true account of your reality, and I found that honesty, authenticity and integrity was central to what all the comics did.

Donna McPhail

"People always judge. A man comes on and people ask 'Is he funny?' A woman comes on and their immediate thought is 'Would I shag 'er', the women go 'Would my boyfriend shag 'er', what's her hair like, do I like her clothes, is she attractive?' All these judgements are made before you even get to the microphone. And the women, if their boyfriends like you too much they don't bloody like it. However, I don't try to get the women on my side. I'm either funny or I'm not."

It was felt by ALL my Interviewees that you were either funny or you weren't – it was that simple, and in that way it was the most egalitarian form of performance possible, accessible to anyone from any class or background. If the audience didn't laugh – then you just weren't funny at that particular moment. An audience's reaction to the fact that a performer was female was a potential contributory factor to what was a bad gig. My worst gig ever was when I did an all-male after dinner event when the audience talked the entire time I was speaking. It really gave my self-confidence a good old thumping. I wanted to find out what made a gig 'bad' for my Interviewees.

Lorraine Benloss

"A bad gig is one where no one listens to you. If you are not heard you are powerless."

Michele A'Court

"I had some really bad gigs, especially in the first few years, like all comics, male or female. The gigs where everything is wrong from the room set-up to the PA not working… The odd gig where the MC has just done a raft of nasty anti-lesbian jokes and then intros me with, 'And speaking of women, we've got a little lady coming on now.' The one where one of the punters, who was royally pissed, got his cock out and came on stage to show it to me, and told me that would solve all my 'problems'. But thank God, all that seems to have gone in NZ. Mostly, people have heard of me or seen me on t.v, and think I might be all right at this thing. Which is all you need to get through the first 30 seconds."

Lynn Ruth Miller

"The art of comedy is to get an idea from your head and get it into the other person's head and to get them to come to the same conclusion – that it's funny! Comedy is a lot of rejection and I'm used to that. I've only bombed twice but nothing in life is failure, everything you do is a building block to something better. At the age of eighty, I'm learning how to hoola – hoop at the moment."

It's also a very age resistant form of performance, you can keep doing it until you draw your last breath, which is what Lynn Ruth Miller seems to be intent on doing, because if you are talking about truth in the content of your act, that is, your true experiences – then your experiences of life are going to be changing anyway as you grow older.

Dana Goldberg

"Nothing is a mistake. My Jewish Mother would say differently. She would say I should have gone to medical school."

Shazia Mirza

"I feel that a lot of men try to shut women up and demean us anyway don't they? I think one of the reasons why there aren't many women doing stand-up is that we are generally not encouraged to have a voice in society."

Kitty Flanagan

"I think women often bow out sooner. If they have a few bad nights early on, they might call it quits and go 'Oh well, that was hateful, I'm not funny, I don't want to do that again'. Whereas (in general) men tend to think 'Wow, what was wrong with that audience?'"

Nadia Kamil

"A promotor once tried to make us do our 2 person show to an audience of 2, even though there were parts where we needed 4 people in the audience to join in. Another bad gig was when I did have a breakdown during the Edinburgh festival once and had to cancel a show. We didn't really believe in the show, so took a day off, made some changes and made a show we loved and I stopped crying on the rainy wet cobbles every day."

Tanyalee Davis

"When I was in the finals of the Seattle Comedy competition I developed a terrible stomach virus which caused my potassium levels to drop almost causing organ failure. I was vomiting for days and I had to perform. I took a plastic bag onstage with me in case I got sick. I placed 2nd overall but ended up in the emergency ward 2 hours after the competition ended."

Nuala McKeever

"A guy came up to me in a bar; and accused me of criticising Sinn Féin and he was very belligerent. And then he opened his jacket and he stuck his hand inside his jacket and I thought he had a gun or something. And then he kind of pushed me out of the way and pushed past me and walked out. It was a bit frightening."

Rhona Cameron

"I had a really unpleasant experience in Ireland once. Only because Patrick Kielty used to be in a club there and they only just wanted him on and they never wanted any of the other acts that came over from Britain. And before I could even speak somebody threw a bottle and I just left."

Betsy Salkind

"My worst gig was in the Comedy Store in Leicester Square at 12pm on a Saturday night. Within five minutes of me getting on stage people were throwing pints at me."

Helen Lederer

"I think this was at the Comedy Store. This guy said to me. 'Let's see your clit', and I said 'Let's see my what?' not being familiar at the time, believe it or not, with the term. And I went home and I thought 'Www' (*reflective self-questioning*) I remember buying chocolates from a garage, eating a lot of chocolate and I just thought 'Www' *(more like disgust this time)*"

Kate Smurthwaite

"A guy was smoking in the front row. I asked him to use an ashtray, he chucked the cigarette at me and I walked off. The cunt word gets chucked at me all the time."

Maureen Younger

"My worst working experience was when I was in a private party and the room was totally wrong. I was separated from the audience by a dance floor and it just didn't work at all. The space that you're in is really important and has to work for you. The worst heckle I got was – 'Show us your cunt'!"

Hattie Hayridge aka Holly Red Dwarf

"I had an egg chucked at me once and had the cunt word chucked in my direction, but it was the same club which was notorious for this sort of treatment. It was called 'Up the Creek' and the one before that was called 'The Tunnel'. I don't have lines ready to counter this sort of incident I just react to what they've said. The guy who threw the egg, it hit me in the face. And with that you just see red really and I went over to where he was sitting, because he was sitting at the front. So it was quite easy to see who it was and I picked up a tray of empty glasses and stood with it over his head and I was truly deciding whether to smash it down on his head or not because I kind of have a bit of a temper, which most people don't expect because my act is quite gentle and you could have heard a pin drop but I put it back on the table, went back to the mike and carried on and then people weren't heckling me then, and then I said, 'I'm getting off , I'm getting dizzy', because I obviously was. And the compere said 'Who thinks we should throw this bloke out' so we all said 'Yeaaah.' So we all made a grab for this bloke and as he got dragged past me I punched him in the face so it served him right really."

Aditi Mittal

"I've had a few dangerous situations but when that did happen alcohol was always involved. There was a guy yelling throughout my set on New Year's Eve trying to shut me up. They had to escort him from the building."

Shazia Mirza

"I was attacked physically, on stage when I did an all-Muslim gig on Brick Lane. I was on a bill that night with 5 other Asian men, one of whom was Muslim. Everybody laughed at them, they thought they were great. But I was told I was a disgrace, a disgrace to my culture. I thought, you haven't even heard my jokes! I'd only done like the first two lines, and they grabbed me by the neck and threw me backstage. It was these Muslim men taking control of women again. And I thought, that's exactly why I did stand up in the first place. Because I didn't want to be like them. I wanted to do what I wanted to do regardless of what people thought of me. They think it's not good for me to be doing stand-up because it's against Islam. Well attacking a woman – isn't that against Islam? So I just thought, you're all just hypocrites."

A bad gig for some of the comics would be when they felt they weren't being listened to. Wendy Kane was booked into a male only working club and she 'died a death'. Her comedy does not work with male only audiences, this could be because her material is mostly centred around women's issues and men are not interested in listening to what she says. From the above responses I would imagine that what they are trying to say in a comic way is sufficiently powerful to provoke all sorts of responses such as sexual name calling, violence, beer and flying ashtrays. What is the power of comedy and is this why **THE BIG**

MYTH prevails – so that women don't get their hands on it?

Power is the ultimate aphrodisiac – and what of humour?

Hattie Hayridge

"It is men that get the continuous stream of groupies when they come on stage. I think blokes are a bit scared of a woman that goes on the stage and does stand-up. I mean lots of blokes have said to me 'I would chat you up but if we ever went out, you'd talk about me on stage.' A woman might think she's a fat and ugly and got fat legs or something but I think a bloke's main insecurity is that a woman will say 'He was so shit in bed.'"

Brenda Gilhooly aka Gayle Tuesday

"On a Friday night if you're a male comic, blokes get groupies, it's an authoritative and powerful position to be in, in front of a microphone and none of those things are what is supposed to make up a really **nice** girlfriend. Arthur Smith calls them 'Gag hags' and says that men, bye and large, are terrified of funny women. Females never get groupies, apart from possibly lesbian groupies."

Nancy Witter

"Women being funny or too witty is not considered sexy. Not like it is for a male. A funny guy on stage, no matter what he looks like, will always score with a chick after a show. Not too many men come looking for the funny chick after the show!"

Michele A'Court

"When men are asked what they want women to be, they rarely say, 'Highly opinionated with an ability to always have the last word,' which is what a comedian is."

Maybe one of the reasons men keep perpetuating **THE BIG MYTH** *that women aren't funny, and don't want women to do comedy could be is that they are scared we're going to make fun of their willies! Why aren't women scared that men will do that to them? Being 'crap in the sack' (Because we just sit back and lie there, bottom line, 'and think of Engerland') – they actually have to 'perform') If you believe that men will shag anything, then a woman can't be a bad shag as they're just a receptacle. Simone De Beavoir said that no one was more arrogant towards women, more aggressive or scornful than the man who was anxious about his virility! – aha – wee willy winkie syndrome!*

All stand-up comedy, humour and laughter in general are about building up a story of tension, step by step with the audience until the 'climax' and release or the 'punch line' is delivered and the pay-off of hopefully hysterical laughter comes as a reward. This is not so different to sex, call the story the foreplay (if you're lucky!) when there is a build-up and a 'climax' when we involuntarily shake and lose control – just like laughing at a great story. Historically women have had to depend on men to bring about this situation but not any longer…. Bless you Saint Ann of Summers – you have put the way of happiness in the palm of our own hands!!! Now, if you combine attractiveness, the one area of power that women are encouraged and indoctrinated into thinking is one our main powers, with the power of humour, what happens then?

Hey good lookin – what ya got cookin?
Shazia Mirza

"If you see an attractive woman who's also very funny, that's dangerous and that's very powerful."

Tanyalee Davis

"I've found that some of my good looking female comic friends dress down on stage because they believe female audience members find them a threat and don't laugh and those same female audiences members will not let their male partners laugh because they think that their men most likely want to screw them."

Liz Carr

"I do remember another woman comic telling me that as a traditionally looking woman she thinks that in terms of the audience, the men want to fuck her and the women hate her. I think disability transcends all that into pity and wonder and 'awwww isn't she amazing?' If men do think about fucking me then they're more likely to think 'Is it possible? How the hell…'"

Julia Morris

"If I looked like Catherine Zeta Jones I wouldn't have to be funny. You don't have to be funny because things do come easier to beautiful people."

Lydia Nicole

"Audiences didn't know how to deal with a good-looking funny women when I started out."

Jo Caulfield

"I did have a man come up to me after a gig and say 'I thought you were really funny. But why do you do it cos you're quite pretty.' Quite! Really! Women in any situation are judged on their appearance more than men. But as a comic what you look like is only important in terms of how it helps set up your persona."

Julia Morris

"Staying fat helps me, because I am quite attractive and if I was slimmer, the women would see me as a threat. The way women judge each other is 90% based on size. So the girls are quite happily laughing at me and thinking I'm great because, 'Oh well she's fat so he won't fancy her'. You need to be careful you don't isolate women in the audience because they can be your greatest ally in a crowd without a doubt. But as soon as you lose them you've lost everyone."

Jenny Éclair

"For a long time, I always perceived that it was dangerous for a female comic to be attractive."

Lynn Marie Hulsman

"Women got by more on their looks in the 80s and didn't have to focus on any other aspect of themselves. I've got lots of quirky and funny friends, but women knew they weren't going to be Steve Martin. There were no women to model themselves on. It was very threatening to be funny and female and even more so if you looked fabulous. It was not accepted. With women like Amy Schumer we are finally at an age when her looks are not important and that she is 'allowed' to be funny."

When I asked Amy Schumer the following question: As a very attractive young woman in comedy which is very unusual, what sort of impact has this had on your type of comedy and how you are perceived by your audience (both men and women)?.... this was her answer!!!

Amy Schumer

"Thank you. I wanna answer but I'm just so excited that you said I was young and attractive! I can't focus!"

So that put me firmly in my place!!!!
Amy Schumer leads the way in 'allowing' good looking women to also be funny, in fact, very many of my Interviewees are very, very

good looking – what is being challenged is that this doesn't have to be enough, that they have other attributes other than the way they look that are powerful and empowering. Interviewees like Nina Conti, Lydia Nicole, Ronni Ancona, Dana Goldberg and Dyana Ortelli to name but a few and others I didn't get to interview such as: Sarah Silverman, Amy Poehler, Tina Fey, Nicky Glaser, Aisha Tyler, Natasha Leggero etc. in the States and Shappi Khorsandi, Ellie Taylor, Sarah Hadland and Sally Phillips etc. etc. in the UK !!! Embrace your funniness you fabulous and gorgeous females. You can be both!!

JoJo Smith

"I was having my photo taken by this really famous photographer, and I was going, 'Do them pictures like you do with Dawn French'. He went 'What do you mean?' and I went, 'The one where she puts her hand under her chin to hide all the double chins'. He went, 'Well, what do you want to look like?' and I went 'Like Kate Moss'. And he said, 'I'm not a fucking magician'."

Myfanwy Alexander – Writer of BBC Wales Sony Award winning comedy 'The LL Files' & member of BBC Radio 4's 'Round Britain' quiz

"Women are still being selected to appear on panel shows because of their appearance, rather than their comic genius. As a result, inexperienced women are sometimes there for decorative reasons: who can then be surprised if they die on their feet? Before rushing to say that 'woman are just not as funny as men', observers should note how twenty something men picked mainly for their looks would fare against razor sharp experienced female comics."

Kate Smurthwaite

"Panel shows will have a token pretty woman and she will have lots of close ups of her laughing at the blokes and she will often be the butt of the humour. It creates this impression that she's a bit of fluff. Women are not taken seriously and we can't be experts on subjects on the television. Submissive women are usually picked and by doing this the television industry supports and promotes Patriarchy."

FSUCs prod and poke Patriarchy, that is, a society run along male rules, by challenging unspoken rules and empowering women in a new environment. What other power did comedy enable my Interviewees to access?

Rhona Cameron

"Comedy had a place in the eighties, had quite an important place in the Arts where before it was normally Oxbridge review types from the fifties, sixties, seventies, who had previously achieved success, it became a kind of wider forum. People have gone into chat shows and films and all sorts of things and so I think the growth of comedy has made more people want to get into it. People saw comedians moving through the media and arts into quite powerful positions, with their own shows and not necessarily about comedy."

There's a British comedy 'Rich List' and in the 2013 one Sarah Millican was the only woman in the top twenty! She did earn over two million squid that year and came in at position number nine. No wonder people like Peter Kay and Michael McIntyre are literally laughing all the way to the bank. Peter Kay earned a whopping £32 million from comedy that year and Michale McIntyre £21 million.

Ronni Ancona

"I like bringing pleasure to people. I genuinely do. I had this letter from a woman who said 'I don't know who the hell you are but my husband's very, very ill. He's in hospital and you really make him laugh'. It made me feel very humble, very moved, and in darker moment felt well yes it is worthwhile actually."

Dana Goldberg

"Comedy gives people an outlet to let go, to laugh, to forget about everything else for an hour while they sit in a theatre and listen to me say all the things they want to, but don't give themselves permission to."

Hattie Hayridge aka Holly Red Dwarf

"Some people, because I've been doing it for a long time, come up to me and say 'Oh yes, I've grown up with you.' Which kind of brings tears to your eyes really. I think 'Oh I wish I'd said something more important.'"

Michele A'Court

"The feel good factor. I love it when people tell me they still think about something they heard me say years ago – that it made them think differently about something. I woman who saw my recent show about depression says it 'changed her life' – which felt good!"

Lorraine Benloss

"I think I have influenced some women's lives positively by talking about being big and being happy with yourself no matter what your body shape. Like my boyfriend said 'Don't you think you should lose some weight' and I said to him, 'Don't you think you should look like Denzil Washington!'"

Tanyalee Davis

"I have been told I am very inspirational. There are a few people that think I should be very insecure with myself because I am a little person and then they see me onstage being full-on and self-confident. I love proving people wrong. I believe my shows give people an insight into my life and allow my audience to see that I do not let many things slow me down."

Wendy Kane

"It's my space and I'm in charge. Every woman in that room is talking through my mouth."

Shazia Mirza

"I have people stop me all the time to say to me, 'I think what you are doing is really inspirational'. I have had a Muslim woman come to one of my shows who told me that her husband used to lock her up in the house and treat her really badly. And she said, 'When I heard about you, I thought God I must go out and see that woman. If she can do stand-up comedy then I can go out and get a job in an office or do what I want to do.'

Lorraine Benloss

"I wouldn't say that all my humour is fuelled by black messages or black information. I do think I am a voice for black women but I don't even know if it's through my material or the fact that they're just seeing a black woman on stage. I think that's enough. Black women are pretty much invisible in British Society."

Kate Smurthwaite

"The history curriculum doesn't talk about women in history so we are still largely invisible. Having strong Role Models is crucial for women."

Jane Duffus – Director Bristol Based Women's Comedy Club

"The reason I started 'What the Frock' comedy club, was because I realised that female comics are scarce but this could be because no one has noted them. Saying that, there's no history of women being composers. However in May 2015 I published 'The What The Frock! Book of Funny Women', when I profiled 70 female comics."

Maureen Younger

"As a rule, women who have spoken out have been castigated as witches, and to a certain extent written out of history. History is usually written by the victors, that's why it's 'his' story not 'her' story."

Dana Goldberg

"If I kill at a club, usually I'll hear 'that second comedian was hilarious!' If I bomb, I'll often get 'that lesbian comic wasn't very funny.' Suddenly my sexual orientation comes into play. I'm not sure why that happens, but I think people's prejudices and opinions come more into play when they don't like someone as opposed to when they do and feel totally comfortable with them."

The power of comedy (apart from the very obvious financial aspect if you become successful) and it's impact on my Interviewees as individuals varied from person to person but what they all had in common was a voice that was amplified in front of an audience. What I wanted to find out next was what they talked about and what they felt was a 'no go' area. I was particularly interested to see what was taboo for my Interviewees. Marti Caine was the first comic to break the 'Sanitary Towel' taboo which was considered highly shocking at the time in the seventies. Here was a woman talking about a woman's body and not just about her body but about how we deal with what comes out of our bodies. It was quite a radical and empowering thing to do at the time and she was incredibly brave in retrospect as she had to put up with a lot of flack for it for a very long time. And for many years there was a perception that women are going to be doing those jokes. This may have been because it was empowering at that time, but material is now becoming much more universal and varied. Nowadays I think women can actually talk about whatever they want to and the taboos are of their own making rather than society telling them you can't talk about things like that because women don't or aren't 'allowed' to. Women have certainly moved on in the Western world; women don't need to talk about things like that because they're not relevant anymore. When you see adverts on the television about Tampax, what's the point of talking about it in public? What is really interesting is to see pioneering comics such as Aditi Mittal talking about the truth of the situation in India, that is, that young women have been raped on their way to a toilet to change period products and how it can potentially be a very dangerous experience for young Indian women. Raising awareness on these matters is a very powerful forum and could eventually lead to legislative and policy changes, although with the October 2015 debacle about retaining VAT on period products as a 'luxury' item may mean that this subject may yet return to many a FSUC's set. The first person's set I examined was the FSUC who had been doing it the longest, Joan Rivers.

Old wives tales –
Where do you get your material, what's taboo and how do you deliver it?
Content of Joan Rivers Act – Cardiff – October 2004

- How she kept a Tampax visible in her handbag to make it look to prospective suitors that she could be impregnated! She was 71 years old at the time!
- Her Plastic Surgery – a lot.
- How growing old 'sucked'
- Her daughter Melissa and her grandson – being present at his birth.
- Winona Ryder gave her the clothes she was wearing (Winona had recently been convicted of shoplifting!)

- Stealing things from mini bars
- Cliff Richard and 'girlfriends' – is he gay?
- Giving advice to young women not to marry for love but for money – a lot of the content of her act
- Very self-deprecating and irreverent.
- No taboo subjects – death, cremating her mother in law (whilst still alive) Twin towers, Michael Jackson, bitching about Barbara Streisand and Julie Andrews (two of her closest friends)

Lynn Ruth Miller

"My themes are my age, I'm eighty – you look in the mirror and you don't like what you see. I'm not clean and I use a lot of double entendres. I talk about mammograms, bikini waxes and how we women are so ashamed of our bodies. I talk about senior-driving, on line dating. I haven't 'dated' for fifty years and I certainly don't have to worry about getting pregnant! Most men of my age are too 'dead' for me and can't keep up with me. People are afraid to laugh when I talk about sex. No one steals your comedy like you can! Your interpretation of any material will always be original and yours only. It all comes from the same pool – that of humanity."

Nancy Witter

"In 2008 after I was downsized from my job at a bank, I went to New York University to get my professional certification in Life Coaching. With what I learned from my clients along the way I wrote a self-empowerment book with women over 50 in mind. 'Who's Better Than Me? A Guide To Living Happily Ever After' It includes exercises, quotes, and has advice on dating, job hunting, confidence and courage. You can take more risks after 50. Every decision you make as a young person will influence the rest of your life. When you are over 50 it's very freeing, because you have less time, you actually have much less to lose. My newest production is with Karen Morgan in "Hot Flash Laughs" We created this show especially for those of us over 50 in New York."

Dana Goldberg

"I think I found my voice by honouring who I am. I've always been out as a lesbian, so that was established early in my career, but over the last few years I've really given myself permission to be bigger on stage, go to places I wouldn't let myself go to in the past."

Sindhu Vee

"My life is the hugest source of material for me I am drawn to very everyday topics, to things that are happening around me which I think are funny. Like parents, spouse, dog, kids, traffic. Just everyday things like being confused for a doctor on a flight and having no way to really get out of that situation without looking dodgy. Nine hours of having to lie through my teeth to keep the illusion alive! I jot down ideas or record them on my Iphone all the time. Then I write them out and try them when I do Open Mikes in London (and in Delhi). I refine and/or add with each performance."

Victoria Jordy Cook

"Another challenge I suppose is not using my daughter as a constant source of material."

Ashley Storrie

"My Mum, Janey Godley gets away with a lot of stuff because she's older. The older she becomes the more endearing she becomes. My parents ran a comedy club and the acts would come and stay with us. I have seen nearly every live act on the circuit and have noticed all the female content trends as they have come and gone over the years, from the period jokes and husband as the butt of the 90s to funny songs and ukuleles, twee girls with knitted jumpers and clunky shoes. My stage persona is angry and sexually threatening. I do a lot about sex. I'm not going to sleep with your boyfriend. Is your husband cheating on you?"

Rosie Kane – Scottish FSUC & Previous Member of the Scottish Parliament

"I'm really angry about many of society's ills, especially women's issues. I've suffered with anxiety and depression all my life and stand-up is a great outlet for the anger as long as it's funny."

Tanyalee Davis

"I talk mostly of my life and experiences. And my perspective on things. If it's regarding my life I don't consider anything taboo. I found my voice after being on stage for many years. I talked more about my life experiences and my perspective on things."

Liz Carr

"I talk a lot about my life and the ridiculousness of life as a disabled person. I go to places that I think many others avoid and I don't believe I have many / any taboos. I actively enjoy pushing those buttons and hearing the gasps of shock from an audience – and I love nothing more than when an audience laugh despite themselves. I know when I'm on stage talking about sex that there can be a feeling of shock and that's really just about the fact people have such low expectations coupled with many assumptions about disabled people and sex. So when I talk about my own sexuality, I can almost feel a roll of the eyes in a 'pc gone mad' kinda way at some gigs."

'Nice' women, let alone women with a disability, didn't used to talk about sex, let alone admit to actually enjoying and being an active participant in it. Think about the expression 'Lie back and think of England' – What was that all about???? Social control of our bodies and minds. I do believe that the most important women in the entire history of women's development were Margaret Sanger and Marie Stopes, who brought contraception to the masses and allowed us as individuals to make decisions about when pregnancy was going to occur and thus enabled sex not just to be a way of reproduction but also to become a source of joy and fun. Comedy usually involves a fair smattering of talk about sex or possibly sexual innuendos (the great Marie Lloyd used to 'tease' her audience) and therefore this is not an area 'nice' girls should be involved in. Tanya Lee Davis, all three foot six inches of her is incredibly raunchy and talks a lot about sex which is quite shocking in a way as she is almost childlike in her appearance so in some ways she rips apart the taboo about sex and disability, as does Liz Carr.

Shazia Mirza

"And for getting good material, I'd say, be funny and sleep with the right people. I'm a virgin so I don't have sex with them, just sleep! Also when you asked about material – tell the truth. The truth is funny, look at your life. Look at and observe everything you do in your everyday life. Observe the people around you – you don't have to make it up."

Sian James – Labour M.P. for Swansea East 2005 – 2015 & Women's Activist

"My Mother is the person who taught me to speak out, whenever or wherever I saw injustice. She always said, that speaking the truth could never hurt you."

Jo Enright

"I don't deliberately not talk about sex. I'm happy to write routines about any subject as long as I like the routine and it's in my 'voice' so to speak. It's not that I've deliberately avoided it. When I write something on that theme, that I think is genuinely funny enough, I will happily bring it before an audience."

Katerina Vrana

"I talk a lot about my experiences as a Greek living abroad and cultural differences and stereotypes and now I'm doing a new show about sex. So I talk a lot about that. No subject is taboo. It's always in the way you handle it."

Rosie Kane – Scottish FSUC & Previous Member of the Scottish Parliament

"My comedy slags off the right wing and I give a working class woman's perspective. I describe myself as a raconteur and 'story teller' and I've been doing it since May 2012."

Betsy Salkind

"I used to say I became a comic so I could be myself without being institutionalised."

Sindhu Vee

"Women were silenced in my family and as a result of my upbringing in a culture where our family driver had a daughter who had been married off at the age of eleven, this sort of material which forms the basis of my stand-up has enabled me to empower others by raising awareness of other ways of being."

Aditi Mittal

"Topics I talk about – I have had friends from school and college who have had to suffer immensely. Only 2% of the population in

India use sanitary towels, they are very, very expensive and I talk about the shame of it. Most women will use old sari blouses and end up with violent lacerations by the steel hooks. Women are being raped on their way to the toilet. This happened to a friend of mine who was so ashamed and embarrassed she hid it for five months. This was a huge, huge, taboo and I broke it. Older women were very suspicious of me because they thought I was giving away women's secrets. The 2012 gang rape in Delhi has triggered a wave of feminism in India and things are slowly changing – we are fighting back."

Michele A'Court

"No subjects are taboo – I think anything and everything must be talked about by comedians – that's our job. We're the jesters in the world's court, and comedy is the most powerful way to find the truth. But it has to be funny. Race, gender, religion, social issues, politicians – all of it is fair game for comedy – ridiculous anti-smoking laws, the culture of fear that has us joining AA after a glass of pinot noir, constructing Bird Flu Pandemic survival kits, the lunacy of the War on Terror."

Betsy Salkind

"I presented 'Ann Frank Superstar' – a one woman show of Ann Franksploitation. Done in 1998, it was very well received."

Jo Caulfield – Material

"What has been really impressive in the 'Time Out Stand-Up' competition is the range of different styles. Hopefully this will help to dispel the myth that women all do the same material. There are women doing observational humour that is not gender specific, there's a couple of very surreal comics, some are more intellectual and some are very silly. And it's not just stand-up, there are songs, poets and some 'Smack the Pony' style sketches. There is also a wide age range, it's so refreshing to hear from a Mother of four; we hear plenty from male comics about having kids but not from women. Mainly because the women are at home looking after them, while the men are on stage, talking about looking after them."

Sara Silverman – Film Director

"The stories I like to tell are about outsiders, often women, or men who don't act like men. For me, comedy always comes out of situations, you write the character and that's whatever's in your soul But my perception of comedy is that it has to be authentic and the truth, yes a hundred percent, whether it's stand-up or situation, that's what's funny is when it's truthful. With my film 'Very Annie Mary' I just listened to the stories of that village (Pontycymmer) and tried to harness the stories of the village into the craft of screen writing, but all the little anecdotes shaped into the story came from the village and what had happened there."

Hattie Hayridge aka Holly Red Dwarf

"As a general rule I'd say that any subject that is done well isn't taboo, even material about things like September the 11th. If something is someone's true view then nothing is taboo."

Shazia Mirza

"People were scared to laugh after September 11th. I think they thought I was going to blow them up. I was scared to do gigs for a while. Then I thought, well people are going to attack me or not laugh. I did a clever joke about the pilot's licence which fortunately was very funny and which people really enjoyed. 'Hello, my name is Shazia Mirza. At least that's what it says on my pilot's licence'. The whole room erupted, they were really relieved to be able to laugh at it."

Now, that, is one of the best examples ever of the 'Release Theory of Comedy'.

Helen Lederer
"A lot of my material was about relationships, we just reflect back the life that we are experiencing. I think it's the mundaneness, the true, the embarrassing, those things, people stuff."

JoJo Smith
"I do all that getting older stuff, you know, it's very close to my heart. Now my material mainly comes out of the compering coz you adlib stuff. And I like just talking to the audience. I enjoy bouncing off them."

Cathy Ladman
"I'll often use stuff from the audience."

Julia Morris
"I have found that my material has changed over the years, depending on where I am in my life. I also just basically tell stories like an Irish storyteller. I just basically do stuff that's happened to me, my own personal experiences."

Nuala Mckeever
"I'd have a mixture of observation, topical material of what's going on politically or in the news, observations of the way people behave, things that people say and a little bit about growing up as a Catholic girl, puberty and the Virgin Mary – how did she not realise she was special? You know, everyone else in Palestine at the time was looking like a cross between Woody Allen and Yasser Arafat; she has blonde hair and blue eyes. Did it never occur to her that she was born with something a bit special? I suppose I am self-deprecating. I've got a good line that Northern Ireland

men aren't very romantic. A Northern Ireland man's idea of foreplay is, 'Have you finished that gravy chip yet big girl?' And then I would always add, 'As you know, I was that big girl'.

Sioned Wiliam

"Women are more naturally self-deprecating aren't they? Men are almost too insecure in a sense bizarely to do that."

Jo Brand

"Male humour is confident and up front, female humour is self-deprecating."

Rosie Kane – Scottish FSUC & Previous Member of the Scottish Parliament

"Humour can be a huge release, self-deprecation humour is very comforting to those with low self-esteem."

Blod Jones

"Although my mother-tongue is Welsh I don't do my set in Welsh as the course I attended with Logan Murray was in English. I feel that at the moment my set wouldn't work through the medium of Welsh as I am quite self-deprecating about my Welshiness."

WARNING! – Serious but useful bit coming up.
Several studies have been done to find out if there are any major differences in what sort of humour men and women prefer. (Chapman & Gadfield 1976, Zillman & Cantor, 1970, Zillman & Stocking 1976, Levine 1976 & Easton 1994). The biggest finding was that both men and women like to have women as the 'butt' of jokes. However, Zillman & Stocking's (1976) work about self-deprecating humour suggested that women did not view the person who placed themselves as the 'butt' of the joke in a negative light, although men did. Additionally, males did not enjoy women making fun of

themselves, as in the past this was done by men towards women. In fact, when this happened it was quite liberating and empowering for the women as they saw themselves as being in control. What is interesting is that over the last twenty years I have seen men becoming more self-deprecating – which I think is a very good thing!

Wendy Kane

'I talk about things in my life – childbirth, men. I tell it as it is and women go 'You're talking about my husband' and women come up to me and ask me if I'm having an affair with their husband, because I describe him to a tee."

Angie Le Mar

"And then I started telling the truth, about everything; you know, this is how I feel about racism, this is how I feel about abuse, this is how I feel about my weight. And I just started being honest."

Maria Kempinska – Owner of Jongleurs Comedy Chain

"Jongleurs policy is non-racist and non-homophobic but not non-sexist as men were also being affected."

Jeff Scott – Resident Piano Player and M.C. at Comedy Store Los Angeles

"Since we have no censorship as to what the comics can say and/or talk about (like most other clubs), thanks to Mitzi Shore seeing a need to nurture young comics no matter what language is used. Therefore, our female comics are already more blue than most on the circuit. When you have to follow Joe Rogan (TV's "Fear Factor" host), you gotta be tough & funny...or at least learn how to become tough & funny quickly!"

Rhonda Hansome

"I talk about race and gender inequality, relationships in general. In fact I'll talk about anything but rape which is hurtful and malicious."

Rhona Cameron

"People who have become comedians have got certain personality traits and therefore they've probably got quite a lot to say about life and usually have not had a conventional life or a conventional outlook therefore they would have more to write about. I do observational stuff, mostly self-referential observational stuff, how I see life. I wouldn't tell a racist joke but I do detest political correctness also. My criteria is if something is funny enough I would do it. Obviously, there's no question I wouldn't do rape jokes, God it would be ridiculous.

Nadia Kamil

"I consider myself to be a totally political comic, particularly social justice, especially women's issues. I also like to be silly and whimsical and physical and playful. I have done a sketch about rape which challenges society's perceptions that the woman is always to blame."

I went to New York in March 2011 and went to numerous stand-up comedy clubs around Times Square. I was astounded at the amount of rape jokes doing the rounds and also a lot of racist hatred being proliferated. There was a time on Facebook as well, when there seemed to be a lot of jokes about Rohypnol and in fact I got rid of a Facebook friend who I was quite fond of, because he had put up a joke about rape and Rohypnol and couldn't understand why I was so angry about it. No part of rape is funny from any perspective. To all those who don't think the rape joke was a problem, or rape jokes are a problem: A lot of people accuse feminists of thinking that all men are rapists. That's not true. But do you know who think all men are rapists?

Rapists do. *They really do. In psychological studies, the profiling, it comes out* ***again and again.***

Virtually all rapists genuinely believe that all men rape, and other men just keep it hushed up better. And more, these people who really are rapists are constantly reaffirmed in their belief about the rest of mankind being rapists like them by things like rape jokes, that dismiss and normalize the idea of rape'. So the more we raise awareness that rape jokes aren't funny the more we will isolate those who think that they are. Sharing laughter with others means that you share the same values as well and as I said previously, there's no part of rape that's funny for the victim! If you have an opportunity, read a brilliant 2009 online article in the Washington City paper called 'Rapists who don't think they are Rapists' by Amanda Hess.

I was incredibly fortunate to have an Interview with Adrienne Truscott who makes no bones at all about tackling this subject head on. She turns the 'rape joke' on its head and uses it in an incredibly positive way to empower women and challenge and raise awareness about this issue.

Adrienne Truscott

"My show, 'Adrienne Truscott's Asking For It: A One Lady Rape About Comedy' was already in the development phase in July 2012 when the American comedian Daniel Tosh flippantly responded to a heckler at a show who disliked his jokes about rape. His comment — "Wouldn't it be funny if that girl got raped by, like, five guys right now?" — set off a firestorm in the comedy scene about whether rape was an appropriate stand-up topic or whether this was a line that shouldn't be crossed.

I'm a firm believer that you shouldn't censor comedy in any way. It's a subtle form to comment on the absurdities of life and comedians have frequently done that. When you say the words 'comedy' and 'rape' in the same sentence people will often have a very strong reaction – because there's nothing funny about rape –

the notion that you would take it light heartedly is shocking but satire is an incredibly useful tool and certainly I think the way we talk about rape, the way women should or should not walk in order to avoid it, the way we legislate women's bodies in the aftermath of rape and what the choices are, that is all completely available to the wildest of satire.

In my show I don't wear pants (*knickers*) on stage, I wear a jacket and shoes – I'm not ridiculous, I wouldn't go out on stage barefoot! I don't feel at all vulnerable on stage – in fact I feel very empowered by being half-naked on stage. In some ways it's the audience that feels very vulnerable. I feel that nudity provides us with elements of great surprise and comedy.

But as a performer I am taking this notion wearing an 'asking for it' outfit to what I think is a comedic extreme, because it looks really silly as well as taking that logic, that the way that a woman is dressed affects the way that she is treated and possibly invites violent assault. So I am in a room, I drink gin and tonics during my show, I'm a very approachable and friendly gal and I'm not wearing pants, and there's not much more of an 'asking for it' outfit that you can wear than that, and I don't get raped every night in my show. To me that act only happens when somebody's willing to rape."

In May 2014 in a BBC television programme called 'Blurred Lines' Produced and Directed by Gaby Hornsby and introduced by Kirsty Wark, looked at how sexist jokes reinforced sexist behaviour, the way that the web has promoted hatred of women, and how it was now making a huge contribution as to how we create our society and values. The 'Everyday Sexism Project' mentioned a 14 year old girl who had noted three jokes made about rape by teenage boys towards her in school in one single day.

How does that make young girls feel – valued, safe, equal, protected? I think not, and when we start questioning women's self-confidence issues we need to dismantle this sort of behaviour, draw attention to it and proclaim once and for all that we will not tolerate it any longer. Korean American Comic, Margaret Cho, who is herself a survivor of abuse, latest 2015 single is called 'I Want to Kill My Rapist'. In the video, Cho and a band of 20 young girls, all armed, chase after a rapist to exact their revenge. Let the naming and the shaming begin and not just in Britain – it's a world-wide problem! In January 2015, a video of men in Lima, Peru being tricked into catcalling their own mothers, started to become a global viral sensation, raising awareness for a campaign to end the sexual harassment of women in public. I think the video is ultimately very funny and the reason for that is because it is based on truth – there are two sorts of women – the Madonna (Mother) figure and the Magdalen (Slut) figure. What is very interesting in this film is how the perpetrators confuse the Madonna for a Magdalen. It challenges the stereotypical assumptions that we have, that all women are either one or another.

Jane Mackay – Owner of 'The Stand Comedy Club', Edinburgh, Glasgow

"I also have to say that I detest having to laugh when men backstage say of course birds/women aren't funny'. And that is one of the biggest myths; women are bloody funny. It's just that we are not funny in the way that they are funny."

Wendy Kane is the only comic I interviewed who works specifically in working men's clubs with a working class audience. She often performs in women only nights such as hen nights. She also noticed that women waited for a cue to laugh or not from their male partners. If the men did not laugh then they also would not laugh. She was able to see the reaction to the same material in Ladies Nights when they would laugh raucously, not caring what men thought (as they weren't there to stop them from laughing), which seems to back-up what Suls found in 1983 about women being field dependent (seeking permission from others before laughing) and which Roseanne Barr also mentions in her 1990 book. Wendy Kane had previously worked with both Bernard Manning and Chubby Brown, both immensely confident and misogynist performers. However, Wendy Kane believes that women are their own worst enemies when they sit there and laugh when women are obviously the 'butt' of the joke but this could also be linked to the above phenomena, or fear of men's disapproval. If a woman is economically dependant on a man then it's likely she won't laugh at something he doesn't find funny. No change there since Music Hall days then!

Kate Smurthwaite

"When I've run clubs rape jokes are always taboo however, as an M.C., you have no control on the content of other comics jokes. All you can do if they say a rape joke is to respond with humour e.g. 'Give it up for Fred Blogs – recently voted 'Boyfriend of the year'!!"

Briget Christie in her 2015 'A Book for Her *And for him, if he can read' talks extensively about a subject which you would never think would be funny – that of Female Genital Mutilation, (FGM) as does Thenjiwe Tay Moseley.*

Thenjiwe Tay Moseley

"I will talk about FGM in my set, different lifestyles, the experience of living in different countries. My job is to heal people through laughter but not to open wounds so I am now steering away from jokes about rape victims as I have met too many women who this has happened to."

Susie Felber

"The worse the comedian the more often the rape jokes."

Maureen Younger

"I personally don't like rape jokes and perpetuating blaming the victim."

The most horrible, creepy joke I have ever heard.

"I've had a lot of luck with the women – yes, so far none of them have ever identified me!"

Yeeeeeuch! I mentioned in the previous section the way that women are 'defined' in a biblical fashion as either a Madonna or a Magdalen. In all my life-long exploration of religion (including the two years I spent perfecting the one handed match-box trick in Trevor Phillip's A level Scripture class) I have to say that the perception that I had of the Madonna was that of serenity and joy and that she was controlled, constrained and contained. Her lips were closed at both ends of her body – both traps were shut! She looked too demure and never looked like she could be 'avin a laugh. Magdalen on the other hand, always appealed to my rebellious nature, she was the non-conformist, the rampant one, the raucous sociable one who could make great connections with all and sundry and both traps would be open. I could imagine going on a good night out with her to a comedy club and with Jesus turning all the water into wine, it could turn out to be a very jolly night indeed!

Comedy clubs are quite 'loose' relaxed places, there's usually alcohol involved, and as Hazel O'Keefe said, 'if you took away the alcohol, the comedy would collapse'. When I interviewed a lot of these women the anti-smoking laws had not kicked in and smoking on stage and off stage was a regular occurrence. Quite a lot of crude language and swearing was used in the acts, sometimes to accentuate a 'butt' and other times just to shock. What makes me laugh at times is when men tone down their language when there are women present as they are concerned that our little ears and sensibilities will be offended. I personally choose my time and place to swear, you won't catch me swearing in chapel – yes I often go to chapel because it's a central part of my Welsh culture and I'm a Christian, (not a very good one – but

I try very hard!) but you may well find me swearing like a trooper in company where it would be acceptable. Swearing, drinking, smoking – some may find this behaviour to be quite 'masculine' rather than 'feminine' but what I found to be reassuring was that none of the comics were particularly concerned about these issues apart from Sindhu Vee, whose act talked a lot about smoking and it's connection in her culture with being a 'loose' woman, which is not something we would consider in Britain. Shazia Mirza's family perceived her as a tart because she talked freely about all sorts of issues that 'nice', (ooo there's that word again) girls just didn't talk about.

'Impropriety is the soul of wit' – back to dainty or dirty
Shazia Mirza

"My family perceive me as a bit of a 'loose woman', that women who have a voice are slappers. I am a virgin and I am a stand-up comedian. Because it's against my religion to have sex before marriage so I disprove that theory."

Aditi Mittal

"The perception in my culture is that if you're funny you're either crazy or slutty. I'm both!"

Nuala McKeever

"A woman can be a Madonna or Magdalen and if you side with the whore side, you might entertain the chaps but none of them is going to want to take you home to his Mummy. It's hard for a woman under 50 to get away with being very crude."

Jane Mackay – Owner of 'The Stand Comedy Club', Edinburgh, Glasgow

"You can talk to older women and older men about sex, so I don't think sex is so much of a keynote thing. I flirt a lot with older blokes. And I suppose that's semi-political too in the sense that young people think they've invented sex but we are the pre-Aids sexually liberated sixties swingers."

Hattie Hayridge aka Holly Red Dwarf

"I think if they're believable a raunchy, earthy woman on stage is really good. But it's got to be genuine."

JoJo Smith

"Lucky for me I like talking about sex anyway, because that's a universal thing. So you know I can go and stand on a stage in Johannesburg or Melbourne or anywhere, and people have had sex. If you're playing in a club where the audience is 18 and over, the chances are everybody in that room has had sex, and I happen to find it funny you know. When I started I was told I was too dirty. And Mandy (Knight) I remember seeing Mandy when I was about to start and I was like – 'God and I've been worried about being too shocking'. And that's when she was doing the real hardcore stuff. But you know she made a decision; she sat down and wrote a clean set. So that she could break into Jongleurs and start earning some money. And then the thing is, it's kind of people like her I suppose that blaze the trail. So it was easier for me because people like her and Donna (McPhail) were already doing Jongleurs. And even Helen (Lederer) people always think oh Helen's quite straight, but you know Helen sings about vaginas for twenty minutes. And there was a time when that was considered shocking."

Mary Whitehouse must be spinning in her grave by now and Helen Lederer leads the way in finding out about bits of her anatomy she didn't even know the name of in the seventies!

'Don't knock me, I can do it better' – Self-deprecation.

My 'day job' as a 'Leadership and Public Speaking Coach' brings me into contact with a lot of quite powerful people both men and women, and I am interested in seeing where humour functions within this arena. Numerous studies have been conducted in this realm with various outcomes. A study by Bell Leadership Institute found that the two most desirable traits in Leaders were a strong work ethic and a good sense of humor. You'll note that there is no mention of ability or experience. It's as if humour, to them, already indicates leadership.

In another piece of research conducted by Forbes the American business magazine in 2012, this was the top ten list of requirements of a great leader:

1. Honesty, 2. Ability to delegate, 3. Communication
4. Sense of humour, 5. Confidence, 6. Commitment,
7. Positive Attitude 8. Creativity, 9. Intuition
and 10. The ability to inspire.

However, in a 1980 study conducted by Seattle University to investigate leaders' use of humour found that the leaders who poked fun at themselves and who didn't take themselves so seriously were preferred to the ones who poked fun at others.

This should be really good news for women who as we have seen, have always tended to use self-deprecating humour and we don't take ourselves too seriously anyway. When Jo Brand started out on her comedic journey, she was very self-deprecating and I have found that women are quite happy to take the mickey out of themselves but not so much out of other people, the 'Superiority Theory' of comedy was not as popular with women. Whereas with men – men are mostly quite happy to make a butt of anybody. Just to reiterate the serious bit we saw earlier. Research has shown that men appreciate jokes with a 'butt' or victim, that women appreciate self-deprecative jokes and view it as a positive thing and men view it as a very negative thing. It's also ok to make jokes about Jews if you are a Jew (e.g. Woody Allen, Joan Rivers) or mental health issues if you have had to deal with them yourself like Fern Brady.

Nuala McKeever

"I saw Billy Connolly and the guy beside me was about 15 or 16 stone. And Billy Connolly was going on about fat people. It was funny, you know, about people saying, 'I'm retaining water'. And he says, 'No, you're retaining chips!' And this guy is killing himself laughing beside me but I felt quite uncomfortable with this thing. Well I mean everybody told sexist and racist jokes I suppose in the days gone by and still wish they could get away with it. Again a prime example of Suls's 'Field Dependency'."

Jeff Scott – Resident Piano Player and M.C. at Comedy Store Los Angeles

"Sometimes we have a special guest just pop-in (like Andrew "Dice" Clay, Chris Rock, Martin Lawrence, Robin Williams…) Dice is a living legend in the world of stand-up comedy (having sold out Madison Square Gardens and other venues, more than any other comic), but he's not everyone's idea of funny. On the other hand, without the freedom to experiment on stage (which The Comedy Store supplies 7 nights a week in 3 show rooms), you'd never have a Dice, or David Letterman, Robin Williams, Jim Carey, or Sam Kinison! And as EVERYONE says, the sign says COMEDY STORE, not the 'Take this shit seriously store' (lol). And if you don't like one of our comics, wait fifteen minutes and they'll be a new comic on stage, every night!"

Cynthia Levin

"Jeff Scott is a really good friend of mine and I'm also big buddies with Andrew 'Dice' Clay. He will always be there as that's where he works out his material. He is nothing like the character he portrays (misogynist, racist, homophobe)"

Andrew 'Dice' Clay is not 'nice' at all and is the antithesis of Political Correctness and is based (very loosely!!) on Luke Rheinhart's Cult figure 'The Dice Man'. He is a 'man's man'. He smokes and drinks on stage, he uses expletives all the time, he is a hateful, shameless, misogynistic racist homophobe who says things that no one else will. I saw his show at the Comedy Store, Sunset Boulevard, back in 2004 and walked out!!

The Dice Man' by Luke Rheinhart (aka George Cockroft) was first published in 1971 and since then re-published countless times. This was at a time when women were even more firmly tied to the sink and saucepans and a career woman was a dried up asexual prune. Time of mini-skirts, free love and the dawning of sexual liberation always instigated by a man. When I read this book in around 1980, before I really understood how patriarchy and misogyny worked, I was intrigued by the way it challenged conventional behaviour by allowing important life choices to be decided on the throw of a dice and to some degree, it has formed the way I live my life by challenging expected behaviour. Having read the book again very recently, I see it with a fresh pair of eyes and realise that patriarchy and misogyny still create and form very strict boundaries of behaviour. In an article in the Independent in 2013, Richard Branson spoke about how he was inspired by the Dice to make decisions in the early days of his Company 'Virgin'. Luke Rheinhart was described by Loaded as the 'Novelist of the Century' so I will leave you to make your own conclusions!! However I was very fortunate to be able to talk to George Cockroft (aka Luke Rheinhart) about some of these issues:

George Cockroft – aka Luke Rheinhart – The Dice Man

"I couldn't have written a good book about a Dice-Lady back 45 years ago. The only good book I could write about a person surrendering to chance had to be based on my life and my own weaknesses and obsessions. Simon de Beauvoir's THE SECOND SEX had inspired me, but my knowledge of the massive limits put on women's lives then (and now) was more from books than experience.

About twelve years ago a long-time UK friend, Peter Forbes, wrote a screenplay entitled DICE LADY. I found it too dark and misogynistic for my taste but wanted to help Peter get it filmed so wrote a long short story entitled DICE LADY, which I could claim as a sequel to THE DICE MAN so Peter could get permission from Paramount to option my "sequel." Later, I and a UK writer-producer, Ellen Taylor, collaborated to revise Peter's screenplay. Our version got rid of most of the darkness and misogyny, but it is a very imperfect script."

It looks like we have made some progress (if not much) from the time of the 'Dice Man' but Madonna and Magdalen were in conflict at that time and still are. The unspoken rules about embracing our sexuality are not the same for men and women in society with women not 'allowed' by society to talk as freely about sex as men. There appears to be an idea that if you had a loose mouth you also had loose morals, and in some ways that is why women are discouraged from 'having a voice' as to use your voice in a funny or political way allows you to challenge and break down the walls society place around us woman and to finally break out of those moulds and limiting roles. 'Nice' women didn't drink, smoke, swear or be excessively loud. What did my Interviewees think about this and what other 'rules', if any, were these rebellious women breaking?

Fishwives and street hawkers
Just 'cos I'm a woman don't mean I can't swear.
Michele A'Court

"I adore swearing. Explosive consonants are very powerful and satisfying. I never swear at a corporate gig, so after a few of those, I can sound like a sheep-shearer down at the comedy club. I swear when I *think*, so it would be weird not swear when I talk. I've never separated male and female comedians in my head – we're all just comedians. For a lot of years, it was just me and the boys in NZ, so I assumed we were all subject to the same rules. I didn't have a group of women comedians to place myself in. (Though punters and critics sometimes treated me differently – for example, noticing *my* swearing, but not the boys.)"

Tanyalee Davis

"I think I play by my own rules. I don't smoke… hate it! I do drink by not usually before I go onstage. I do cuss in my show but I can take it out. I get away with cussing and talking about sexual stuff onstage more than most people. It seems funnier hearing "fuck" from a little person."

Dana Goldberg

"I think the only way I "play by the boys rules" is that I sleep with women!"

Sindhu Vee

"I'm a heavy smoker. A woman smoking in public in India is two steps from being a prostitute."

Hattie Hayridge aka Holly Red Dwarf

"I don't smoke and I don't drink on stage, that's what used to stand me out at the beginning, because I was different. But women shouldn't be excluded from these things anyway."

Lynn Ruth Miller

"I started drinking at the age of seventy, stand-up comedy at the age of seventy one and burlesque at the age of 73, which is extremely funny but not at all sexy. I'm four foot eleven inches tall (*same size as Edith Piaf and Joan Rivers*) and weigh 95 pounds. I do a lot of observational comedy."

Liz Carr

"I don't drink or smoke but I compensate by swearing a lot and talking graphically on stage."

Kitty Flanagan

"I swear more on stage when I'm nervous, that's how you can tell if I'm nervous during a gig, there'll be a few more random (and unnecessary) 'f'k'n's thrown into my stories. My accent is always a lot broader when I perform but I noticed that with Irish comics and Canadians too, I think it's a subconscious defence mechanism – don't mess with me I'm tough (as opposed to tiny which is what I really am!)"

She barely makes five foot in height.

Jane Mackay – Owner of 'The Stand Comedy Club', Edinburgh, Glasgow

"Swearing I think is slightly culturally different for us Scots. One of the things we get a lot of stick for is, Scottish people swear a lot and are not as shocked by women doing it any more. I remember once doing a gig in Newcastle, and some blokes came up to me afterwards and they were appalled that I'd been swearing and they didn't think that women should swear on stage."

Julia Morris

"I swear all the time off stage but not generally on stage. Not unless there's an aggressive feeling in the room and I feel 'Oh God I'm going to have to go hard to hold this.'"

JoJo Smith

"As a jobbing comic I'm the one that's mostly like the lads in a way and I think it's because I don't make a big deal about being a woman. I just go out there and do the job and make people laugh. And you know to me it doesn't really matter what sex you are. You know – you're an entertainer. Jo Enright is a comic who is very lucky because she can act as well. So she gets acting work to supplement her comedy work. But if she was trying to make a living off the circuit, she wouldn't make a very good living because the managers won't take a chance with her. Because they think, well she can't go out on the late show because she's too clean."

Jo Enright

"One of the reasons I don't swear in my act is because when I went full time as a comic in 1994 I did several high profile TV shows so several of my routines were written with TV in mind and that became a lasting habit. At that time producers were asking comics to decrease or remove swear words for certain shows. As it happened I didn't swear in my act anyway. I had been very influenced by Jerry Seinfeld and Ellen Degeneres. I loved the way both these acts worked their routines so that there was no need to swear. As students we were taught by Huw Thomas to use swearing sparingly, to choose those moments carefully."

Aditi Mittal

"I'm very conscious about my language and the way I talk on stage. I don't swear."

Angie Le Mar

"I don't smoke, drink or cuss either on stage or off, I just don't. I was brought up in the Church – Pentecostal; and I have had this religion, my Mum was an evangelist, my father was a deacon."

Lydia Nicole

"Working as a Christian comic I don't necessarily do 'clean' comedy and I have learnt new 'spicy' ways to not use profanities."

The percentages of FSUCs as we have seen previously are very low, and it will often be the case that they will be the only woman on the bill. Is this just to do with percentages or was there something else at work?

Jojo Sutherland

"I have been involved in stand-up comedy for the last twelve years and in all that time I have never been on the same bill as another woman. One of the biggest clubs, Jongleurs, their thought process is that there's only room for one woman on a bill. Audiences get used to seeing just one woman on the bill, we have to change that so that we aren't exceptional. The irony is that comedy is run and booked by women, they are the gate-keepers."

Maria Kempinska – Owner of Jongleurs Comedy Chain

"Yes of course we have female comedians on our bill and often two in a night. We have some great female Comperes. I have always organised the bookings and the principle is the same – Are they funny? I have also been more inclusive than other clubs as a matter of procedure regarding race, colour and creed."

Shazia Mirza

"A really bad gig for me was when there were 200 white men in the room. I was the only woman on the bill. I was the only person of colour in the whole room. It was a hard gig."

Liz Carr

"You're usually the only woman on the bill. Male comics varied – some were lovely and some pretty much ignored me. When I did women only gigs however the other acts were on the whole, much more friendly."

That is, more encompassing and not as isolating as with all male comedy.

Dana Goldberg

"It is rare you'll see two women on the same bill and rarer still to see a woman headlining. This may not hold true outside of the US, but that's my experience in the comedy clubs circuit for sure. I think there is still that stigma that women aren't as funny, but there are incredible women breaking those barriers down every day."

Kitty Flanagan

"When you work the circuit in the U.K, when I was doing it, you rarely had a second woman on the bill."

Lorraine Benloss

"I was the only female comic on last night which can be hard."

Betsy Salkind

"Typically American clubs will either have one woman or no women and I find it much healthier to go to all women's clubs when I'm on the bill with many women on it because I don't have to represent all women. If there's multiple women on the bill there's more freedom."

Aditi Mittal

"We have two comedy clubs here in Mumbai and I'm always the only woman on a bill. It's a very low cost form of entertainment, a person and a mike."

Jane Duffus – Director Bristol Based Women's Comedy Club

"Female comics who gig with me tell me that other bookers when they contact them they say 'Oh no, we've already got a woman on that night's show!'".

Hazel O'Keefe – Laughing Cows Comedy Club and Women's Comedy Festival

"People were not taking the risk of more than one woman on a bill. The comedy circuit has changed over the last five to eight years. Now there are so many female comics. Some of the female bookers are now starting to book more women. They do want things on a plate and some of them are too lazy to think outside of the box. Now if you book a diverse line-up then your audience will reflect that. It doesn't make sense not to."

Betsy Salkind

"Many bookers say that women aren't funny. Jerry Lewis also went out of his way to say the same thing and got a lot of press for it."

Lydia Nicole

"The comedy world is predominantly male with never more than one female comic per night as the norm."

Holly Burn aka Kirst Kay

"Comedy's a boy's club and we have different voices which they don't particularly want to hear."

Dana Alexander

"I think the most difficult thing for me to combat when it comes to sexism, especially in comedy is the sexism that you receive from other women, you know, women holding each other back. The problem with this ethos is that we're looking to curry favour with men which I think is the mistake. I find it very interesting when you look at the commissioners and producers of 'Dapper Laughs' and things like that, these are all women and they're going 'See, see, we're not going to be offended by your rape joke, don't worry, we can denigrate women just as good as you can – and we're trying to curry favour with people who don't necessarily see us as equal human beings which is the biggest problem which I think we have."

Nadia Kamil

"There's constant sexism but nothing huge. e.g. people assuming I'm the comedian's girlfriend instead of the actual comedian."

Fern Brady

"I do get mistaken for the comedian's girlfriend when I arrive at gigs over and over again. But this is sexism in society, not sexism in comedy. I wish people would stop thinking it's a thing in comedy. I get more TV work for being a woman."

Sara Sugarman – Hollywood Film Director

"I'm not going to compete with the lads, I don't want to, I don't want to tell your stories. I don't care about big cars and shagging women and who gets the girl with the blonde hair. I think it's always better to go under the wave (rather than challenge patriarchy) and I think it can work for your benefit. I have directed female-led stories and they think politically that they have to get a female director. I like being in the margins I've always found that that's the way to fly your flag and to say I'm a female director and I'll make my own rules."

Nowadays, some stand-up comics have found nationwide fame by progressing from the comedy gig to television or even films, in the case of Amy Schumer's 2015 hit 'Trainwreck', which can deliver some phenomenal money making possibilities such as panel shows, voice-overs, comic pundits on a huge variety of programmes and have the added benefit of creating ready-made audiences for larger venues and dvd spinoffs and very large bank balances for some! My favourite mechanical performance medium was always radio drama as it gave you much more of an opportunity to play around with characters. I also did a year and a half on Radio Cardiff every week presenting a half hour radio programme called 'Mack and Welshy Woman' where I was baptised as the 'Welshiest Woman in Wales' by my co-presenter Neil McEvoy. What did my Interviewees feel about other opportunities to perform? If you remember well, the talent scouts used to trawl the Music Halls is search of content for the BBC's brand spanking new radio and television shows.

Fifteen minutes of fame – Radio, Television, Film and Online
Lydia Nicole

"I worked at a radio studio as a teenager. Start as early as you can!!"

Victoria Jordy Cook – Radio

"Radio is something I've dabbled in for years but only recently have absolutely fallen in love with it. I have a show every Saturday 6-9 on BBC Newcastle. I write topical material the night before the show or a few seconds before I deliver it and the satisfaction I get from it is great! I can't tell people's reactions over the radio so I listen back with my head under a pillow usually and see what worked and what didn't, then write some more of the good stuff. If the joke dies the problem is I can relive it over and over again when friends listen in on Iplayer and slate me for it."

Ronni Ancona

"I had my two separate careers. I had my stand-up and then I had tv and radio where I was basically using my capacity and versatility to do voices, to do lots of parts in radio and tv I got asked to do a tour with Rory Bremner and I did a big tour with him and that must have been in 1994 and that's when it all started.

Brenda Gilhooly aka Gayle Tuesday

"I did stand-up as me for almost three years. I did Gayle Tuesday and within six months I was on British television and I think what it was, was that she was very visual. It was a gimmick, it suited t.v. slots on comedy shows, five minutes at the start of her routine, gag, gag, gag off. It was just a media idea you know, it's a comedy Page Three girl. That's all it was, whereas what does Brenda Gilhooly do? Well she chats about bla bla ... but a blonde silly comedy Page Three girl is just so much easier for people who work in television, who watch television to just get it quickly in five minutes. It really surprised me how quickly it took off. I started getting booked for nearly every comedy show that was on."

Julia Morris

"Stand-up is not the sort of job that's so overpaid that you can put money away and make sure you're covered for the bad times unless you get onto the television. Television is like a stand up's pension plan."

Liz Carr

"I never imagined 5 years ago that I'd be in a prime time BBC drama *(As Clarissa Mullery in Silent Witness)* so I have no idea what the next 5 years will bring. More acting opportunities I hope. The odd gig or cabaret spot where I can do all kinds of things and not just comedy. Being in a sit com? Who knows?"

Hattie Hayridge aka Holly Red Dwarf

"I would probably say the turning point experience in my career was being spotted being 'Red Dwarf', which is a t.v. sci-fi sit-com."

Lorraine Benloss

"My television appearance on 'The Real Macoy' made me realise I could do something well. I didn't have any self-belief previously, I just thought all these good gigs were just flukes."

JoJo Smith

"I had my break with the telly; my own T.V. show with *Funny Business*. I was so lucky, it was brilliant for me because, being new, I got to talk to all these people who were successful and find out the tricks of the trade. I had something like 70% of the market share, but you know the fact that I got all those viewers for *Funny Business* didn't stop 'em sacking me and replacing me with a boy who wore trendy glasses, who ended up pissing everybody off and wasn't funny and got the series cancelled. And the *Mail* said that I'm an intelligent interviewer and everything else but that doesn't count for shit. They want people who are twenty years old with perky tits, not a forty year old fat bird. Or they want laddy blokes who jump in and not let the guests answer the questions. You know, my face didn't fit and neither did my genitals! Grenada didn't see me as a future star and it suddenly went from 2 million viewers to 80,000. That's what the new (male) presenter brought it down to."

Aditi Mittal

"Comedy came to television about five years ago in India and when stand-up started, all the material was self-deprecating initially. The present art-form is a combination of English and American humour."

Maria Kempinska – Owner of Jongleurs Comedy Chain

"Those who were any good in Jongleurs were snapped up by television which ate up material."

Julia Morris

"Working as a television 'Warm up' act has taught me lots of good lessons that I'd kind of forgotten about. One is how really important your warm up artist is. They are one of the most important people on the night. They are the first face of your show; they get the people in the mood, or they get the people aggressive, or they get the people offended. They can drive your crowd away from you if you're not careful."

That's where I saw Rhod Gilbert working for the first time as a warm up artist for the BBC in Cardiff – you could see he was going places. He probably had his ticket to London on the Megabus tucked carefully into his pocket! He also had a blue car the same make as ours (similar to a hedgehog!) and lived in our street for a while (useless piece of information which you might be impressed by!) Jo Caulfield was a regular warm-up artist and writer for Graham Norton for several years. As far as I know she did not live in our street but if she did, she'd be welcome to join the road's running club which after five years, still consists of just the two of us!

Sioned Wiliam

"On the whole stand up is something we don't use a great deal of on ITV. *(in 2002)* But often a lot of people who have been stand-up comics are turning to writing situation comedy, performing in it, performing in comedy drama and that's the point where I'll meet them. I think fifteen or twenty years ago I may not have been so lucky as a woman producer. I don't think I would have been accepted quite as easily. Things have changed dramatically in the last twenty years. But there's still a long way to go. Television now for young people feels more that the women and the men are doing the fun stuff together, you know at one stage the women would be doing the cookery demonstrations, the men would be doing the fun stuff and now you do feel that there's that difference, in terms of performance. The men and women have equally dramatic roles and occupy as much screen time as each other. I think things have changed a lot actually."

Television is still very much a young person's game with a very long hours culture that is exhausting and not particularly family friendly to anyone. Over the last few years there have been several high profile court cases involving attractive well maintained fifty something female presenters who have been sacked from their television programmes because they are deemed too old, whilst men can literally go on for ever, their craggy complexions and heavy lidded eyes staring into the lens with no regard for sensibilities. Look at Attenborough – national treasure that he is – he'll still be on the telly when the postman will be bringing him his telegram from the Queen. Panel shows are another challenging area for females with cut-aways of them laughing at the male jokes and far fewer women on panel shows in the first place, as I mentioned previously.

Angie Le Mar.

"Who knows why I haven't got my own TV show or the accolades that I should be getting by now. I've had t.v. executives who've said 'Angie we really think you are funny but we don't know what to do with you'. And I say, 'Well do the same as you do with Jo Brand, or French & Saunders'. They all say, 'But is there an audience for you? Can you make white people laugh?' And I say, 'Well if they've got a sense of humour, yes I can'."

Angie took her work 'Direct to Audience' and created her own work and audience, way before anyone else was really doing that. Now with so many other web based platforms available to use, it really is possible to connect directly with your audience.

Lydia Nicole

"I now direct and act. I have a lot of friends in L.A who don't have a lot of common sense. I'm very busy at the moment doing my 'Common Sense Mamitas' blogs which runs on latinheat.com and I'll be self-publishing a book before long on this. I've been approached by 'Latina' magazine to prepare a column based on them. I'm also working on a programme where I meet people over a table for a meal and I find out more about them. 'Breaking Bread' is going to be about funnelling Latina talent through by allowing the public to find out more about them by asking personal questions."

Susie Felber

"Television is going away. Netflix is streaming services and commissioning live sites. These are attracting 18-35 year old men who have got the most money in their pockets and programmes are being created for this demographic. I'm now working on a comedy video game with Simon and Schuster then working with Audible on an eleven month contract on audio books."

The comedy industry has many different facets and now new outlets and some women have made it in an entirely different capacity than performance. As Jane Mackay notes, most of the bookers are female and have a lot more power than you would imagine.

The Power behind the Throne?
Jane Mackay

"What I think is interesting is if you take comedy as an industry, a lot of the key management players are women. Many of the most powerful behind the scenes people in stand-up comedy are women. And the people who book comics have immense power over the live acts. 'Jongleurs', which was started by Maria Kempinska and is booked by Donna Burns, who is therefore, the single most powerful person in the UK in terms of giving acts live work. Many comedy agents and managers are women. e.g. Dawn Sedgewick or Vivienne Smith, they are the people who make money out of this not the people who perform. So it's not quite supportive in that way, it's more of a kind of powers behind the throne sort of thing.

It's interesting that they are women though. And sometimes I wonder if that is because women do like comedy and they appreciate it as an audience or whatever, but for some reason they won't do it themselves.

Jojo Sutherland

"It is mostly women who are behind comedy ventures throughout the UK. All the big agents are women. Julia Chamberlain is the booker for Highlight and then there's Jane Mackay, who ran and compered at 'The Stand' for years, and, of course, Karen Koren of the Gilded Balloon."

Michele A'Court

"I find it fascinating that most of the world's comedy festivals are administered by women – they stay in the business, but do something more practical than performing."

Sioned Wiliam (Interview conducted in 2002)

"I was the first female Controller of Comedy at ITV although there's a very, very experienced and famous Commissioner for Entertainments, who's a woman called Claudia Rozencrants *(ITV 1995 – 2005)* who does things like 'Popstars' and the Brian Connelly show and things like that. Sophie Clarke-Jervoise became a comedy Editor at BBC before me I think and Myfanwy

Moore was certainly running BBC Choice before me and Dannielle Lux and I are roughly the same time, I'm amongst a crowd of women involved in television comedy production.

But back in 1995 there were no Commissioners for Comedy. I mean I remember going to see the actual Commissioner for Comedy at ITV twelve years ago to talk about a pilot I made for LWT with two women in it and I remember a conversation about , because we had a problem with the casting and I remember that Commissioner, ironically, I ended up having his job, I remember him talking in a slightly old fashioned and rather sexist way about who we could have in it so much so that I was struck by it and thought that I hadn't really come across that before or even after. I think that's about the only time I had come across it. And that would never happen now. You wouldn't start talking about 'who's that little brunette' and that 'little blonde' and he actually used those terms, which is just looking back, is hilarious. So I think things have changed in that sense and with more women in power, things we accept as pretty normal and natural, that of more as perpetrators and less as victims should become more the norm."

Sara Sugarman – Hollywood Film Director

"Hollywood has always been about making money ever since it was set up by glove makers in the early part of the last century. Once you realise that, it becomes much easier to deal with the financial aspect of it. They're just traders and once they see that there's money to be made from positive females, they will be more accommodating."

Joanna Quinn – Oscar Nominated Cartoonist

"Disney's smash hit *Frozen* featured a prince-less feminist cartoon hero who sings, 'Yes, I'm alone, but I'm alone and free!' This signalled an important break in the traditional princess genre, equally important, the blockbuster became the highest-earning animated movie of all time, proving that children, and grown-ups will pay to watch complex and strong female characters. And it was written, directed and composed by women! Currently, only 1 in 4 speaking animated characters are female. The success of *Frozen* is expected to change the way we think about gender at the movies, which can be nothing but a good thing."

Looking back through this chapter I was interested to note that there was a cross fertilization of British and American working locations and that the content of the acts was vast and varied and reflected the life experience and perspective, or 'take' of the performer – anything goes at all in the personal choice about subjects and that also taboos were of their own choosing. What was interesting to see was that the taboos were to do with what was happening in their society at that time. e.g. Aditi Mittal talking about period products as it was a real taboo in India. Bad gigs varied but not being listened to was a bad gig for most as were sexist attitudes and language, including powerful and threatening rape jokes. There was a strong connection between comedy and politics with the personal being very political. Television was seen as a hindrance to stand-up comedy, eating up material but also presenting other opportunities and boosting self-confidence. Jo Brand admits that the transition to television presented her with massive problems, especially with 'Through the Cakehole' which was a big learning process for her. She admits to having made a lot of mistakes, too many sketches which weren't funny enough. As Jo Brand's strength lies with her 'stand-up' it seems unfortunate that she was side-tracked into areas which she feels dissipated her power. However, she has over the last ten years or so slipped easily into panel shows where she can be more spontaneous.

Many of these women, especially in the last few years had taken on the role of Master or Mistress of Ceremonies – a very important role where they spend more time on stage than any other comic and it can be quite a challenge to control rowdy audiences. Jo Jo Smith, who became an M.C. quite early on in her career, had the most amazing opportunity – all she did was interview comics about their working lives. This was at a point when she had only been doing stand-up for a couple of years, a relative unknown, soon after she had started doing twenty minute sets. What a gift! What was also interesting to note was how many women were involved behind the scenes in the comedy industry. Perhaps having realised what a lonely and challenging life it was to be perpetually on the road, they appreciate that they can be based more in one place rather than have the transient lifestyle which goes along with being a jobbing stand-up. Perhaps they realise that as a producer, dealing with people on a one to one basis, which I think women feel more comfortable with, they realise that they will have a longer career and make more money than if they were performing. So now that you've had a taste of what their working lives consist of – let's look to see what barriers and difficulties my Interviewees have overcome in the pursuit of their dreams.

Gwenno Dafydd. Welsh 400 metres, 800 metres,
1,500 metres 3 kilometer walking race
Championship medals 2012, (50 – 54 age group)

CHAPTER 6

STAND-UP AND BE COUNTED – BARRIERS AND DIFFICULTIES OVERCOME

In which I get my chisel out to chip away at the glass ceiling

Sticks and stones – Dealing with drunks and hecklers.

All working environments have certain elements which may be unpleasant, you may have to travel long distances, endure a long ride on the underground, be bored stiff out of your mind, share an office with someone who has bad B.O. or smelly feet but most people do not work in environments where alcohol and the effects it has on those who imbibe it are a constant presence. Alcohol can have very unpleasant effects on those who have too much of it and can make usually nice and unassuming people into belligerent arseholes whose next action you may not be able to identify. These women work late at night, which also has its dangers, they travel in lonely places and are often on their own.

When I worked as a busker in Belgium I sang in the Galleries (Arcades) in Brussels or on the terraces in Knokke, Gent, Brugges or Oostende during the day. My only real issue with my own personal safety was if someone was drunk that they would accost me – as someone did and wacked me on the nose in Dusseldorf. I was also picked up by the police for busking in what was at that time Beograd, kept for a few hours, was told not to do it, and then asked to move along – which I did – to another pitch just around the corner!

The evenings would be the time when it was more dangerous as I used to sing in restaurants which were usually along cobbled lanes with very little lighting and had to catch the late train back from Antwerp or Brugges or wherever. I don't know how many flashers showed me their appendages in those years, in fact my record was once on the train to Brussels from Gent (in broad daylight) and again on the way back to Gent on the platform at Brussels Central Station! Did my Interviewees have to deal with these sorts of issues?

Heckling is a form of verbal aggression as we saw with Hillary Clinton and the 'iron my shirts' incident. What other issues, barriers and challenges have my Interviewees encountered and what did they have to do to get over, around, through or under to get past these obstacles? We have seen what a bad gig was, what did a good gig feel like and how did they measure success? Were there other issues at play – a comedy glass ceiling they had to take a pick axe to? What were those invisible barriers that were stopping them and how did they get to where they got? But firstly heckling – verbal challenges, confrontational and threatening behaviour all trying to shut us up and stop us talking about what we want to talk about.

Michele A'Court

"Being very small is possibly an advantage for me. I don't look very threatening and men don't seem to mind losing a verbal battle with me. I don't look like I could back that up with a punch".

Angie Le Mar

"There was one guy once who was really abusive and confrontational, I really don't know why. So I got off stage and was going to punch him in the mouth, he was like, 'I don't like you'. So he stood up really quickly like 'Ok I'm going to challenge you Miss Le Mar'. And everybody was like 'wooooooooo'. And then I said to him, 'Just like a dick – you stand up for no reason'. You know he sat down quietly and I never heard from him again. And then you realise you've got to be so on the ball because they are going to heckle you."

Hattie Hayridge aka Holly Red Dwarf

"Usually men are all right with my act. Sometimes the worst audiences are women. Blokes find them harder to deal with. A woman heckler is much harder to deal with because a bloke doesn't quite know how hard to come down, like in a hen night. The blokes used to quake at the thought of a hen night, more than a stag night."

Jane Mackay – Owner of 'The Stand Comedy Club', Edinburgh, Glasgow

"I always had a predisposition to tackle hecklers, perhaps more than some other people. I'm never frightened of hecklers, I first spoke in public in 1975 at a Stirling University general meeting when people used to throw bottles at us in the Labour Party and, in 1991, had to stand up and speak in front of hundreds of all-male direct labour organisation workers (builders, plumbers etc.) and tell them most of them were going to be made redundant. When you have done that sort of thing some arse of a student calling you fat or whatever pales into irrelevance. However, it was probably very useful experience having to stand up and talk. I haven't got a ready-made list of put downs I just usually say whatever comes into my head at the time."

Rhona Cameron

"You always get heckled if you're a woman but that's fine because I can deal with that."

Maureen Younger

"I don't do Jongleurs and I don't get heckled."

Lorraine Benlos

"I'm polite but in control and if that doesn't work I threaten them with violence."

Jo Brand

"The only thing to do with heckling is to take the specific heckle and use that to do a put down, but you can't always think of one so most comics have a bunch of heckle put downs that they'll use depending on how bad the situation is, that will go from quite nice ones to really horrible ones to shut them up and make them cry! I use put downs and 'If you can't beat them, groin them'."

Someone said to Helen Lederer at the Comedy Store, 'Let's see your clit', That must have felt quite physically threatening and very upsetting in retrospect for Helen. In some ways he attacked her very being by reducing her as a person to just one part of her anatomy. He discussed her in public as if she were an object, no more than a Page 3 girl. So there it is again – the biggest insult, or is it a threat, made by a man to a woman in a comedy club is to objectify her and demand that she shows the audience her sexual organ as we saw with Helen Lederer, for what purpose, so that she can be conquered, so that she can be impregnated, so that she can be raped, so that she knows where here place is, to show her who the Boss is? It's an intriguing question. Men on the other hand seems to have no problem in whacking their tackle out as was offered on a plate (well maybe not quite literally!) to Michele A'Court. Malcolm Hardy of 'Up the Creek' notoriety (and I actually saw him do this on stage in Cardiff), was notorious for doing this and JoJo Smith was also told by him that he would fuck her. I rest my case!!

It must have been very hard for Helen, Michele and JoJo to put themselves in a position where they triumphed in this situation. Ready prepared 'put down' lines in a comedic set of skills can sometimes be a way of defence in these really difficult situations.

Jo Brand likes nothing better than a good battle with a heckler. She has had food thrown at her, during a performance, by drunk students at 2.00 am. She also had a very unpleasant experience after performing, in a hotel in Belfast late at night. A very drunk man that she did not know, shone a torch in her face and went 'oh look it's her', sat down on her lap and started kissing her on the ear, a situation which would not be tolerated anywhere in every day society.

Wendy Kane has a stock of about 100 one liners, mostly aggressive, to silence the hecklers and protect her verbal space. The power of a heckler should not be underestimated. On the night when I went to see Wendy Kane's show a very drunk woman came on, grabbed the mike from Wendy Kane's hand, tried to take over and eventually did. She had to abandon her set two thirds of the way through as she was so drunk Wendy was worried as to what she might have done. She had an ashtray thrown at her once whilst she was on stage. She picked it up and used it to stub out her cigarette. Although she took control of the situation successfully she admits that it was an unnerving experience, and seemed to underline her physical vulnerability as a woman working in a so called 'man's territory'.

Donna McPhail likes to use her wits and enjoys rising to the challenge. She also stated that women also heckle. Her advice is: "develop a thicker skin and get better quickly." Ava Vidal used to be a prison warden. Jo Brand's worst experience as a psychiatric nurse was being karate kicked against a wall by a patient. Being heckled and having food thrown at her pales into insignificance by comparison.

It seems that the larger the physical frame, the readier the female comic was to use it in launching themselves at unruly punters. There were several short FSUCs like Tanyalee Davis, Kitty Flanagan, Mandy Knight and Rhona Cameron who is only 5ft 2inches tall but who appears much taller in her posters and Michele A'Court whose height is not a problem apart from possibly reaching the microphone!! To get to the microphone in the first place the starting place for life as a professional comic, you have to put your name down for an Open Mike spot which is not paid and which you may have to wait a few months for. They are on at very unsociable hours, that is, very early in the morning when the audience is usually very drunk, do not listen and are an unknown quantity, they may or may not become violent or abusive. So you'd better have some money in your back pocket from somewhere to pay for your travel there and back as many of the comedy clubs on the London circuit are spread out throughout London, with no coach and horses to get you from one to the other as in the time of the Music Halls.

An iron hand in a velvet glove – Safety and control
JoJo Smith

"I don't drive, I am totally at the mercy of the trains. It was always fairly easy to get an Open Mike spot, but it wasn't very easy to get booked. Because basically you'd have to do half a dozen or so. They try you out before you get booked. I did some and I had various friends who had cars who would take me. Anything like Home Counties, I mean just doing an Open Mike spot in London used to cost me a tenner. And I was only getting 50 quid a week, so I had to pay to get on the circuit. Where I live now I am very safe and where I used to live, where I wasn't very safe, I used to get a tube so far and then get a cab the rest of the way home. So I was never walking around late at night, you know, unless it was in a busy area. And also coz of my size you know I don't look like a victim coz I am bigger. I mean Jenny Éclair has been mugged twice on the circuit – if you haven't heard her speak, you'd probably think you could have a go at Jenny. But if I'd heard her talk I wouldn't want to take her on!"

Bethan Roberts

"I did loads of Open Mikes in the beginning. The atmosphere is tough and very often there were no audiences. It was a lonely experience and I always made sure I was with a friend. I haven't really thought why I didn't want to be on my own but I suppose deep down, the reason was the fear of being raped."

Jojo Sutherland

"I would sometimes drive to Leeds (from Edinburgh) for an Open Mike – You've got to be committed in this job."

Jenny Éclair

"One practical drawback, unless you've got a car it's dangerous. I think that's something people don't think about, is that there are women traipsing around London in the middle of the night trying to get home after gigs. I got mugged twice on the circuit."

Lorraine Benloss

"So I've got to take 2 or 3 trains. It's just making sure I get the connections, that's my only worry because if I don't get my connections then I'm stuck in some place I don't know. I'm often the only female in a club which can feel isolating and I often feel threatened. Blokes don't have that fear so that's why they get out there and do more gigs, therefore they get to do the paid gigs a lot quicker. Men get attacked but they don't get raped and that, deep down I suppose, is my major fear. I know that that would probably be one of the things that would stop me going on stage. I don't know how I would be able to recover from that."

Tanyalee Davis

"I've had some terrible experiences travelling to gigs in the UK. I travel with my 3-wheeled scooter so therefore I need accessible transport or assistance. I've had a platform operator refuse to let me back on a train at midnight after a gig."

Liz Carr

"As a wheel-chair performer, I have almost been dropped whilst being carried upstairs to do a gig. I have had acts struggle to get me on stage at the start of my set so the audience, hell all of us have been heart in the mouth to see if I'll fall out of my chair. Not a great way to start a gig. And then there are the panic attacks that I started to have on stage – outwardly doing my material whilst inside I'd be thinking 'I'm going to fall off the stage' or 'How am I going to get off the stage if I want to?' Being trapped on the stage, unable to get on or off independently was incredibly stressful. The gain was not worth the pain."

Jo Caulfield

"You have to be really careful to be safe. I'll park my car somewhere and I'll ask one of the guys to walk me there."

Donna McPhail

"Although I've done judo since I was a child it's just not funny being on a night bus in London on your own. It's a safety thing… purely about being sensible, being a woman on your own, out late at night in London. You need a car, it's anti – social hours. You also need a car that's reliable because if you break down on some dark stretch of the M1 on the way back from a gig then you're not safe either."

When I interviewed her (in 1996), Lorraine Benloss was still doing 'Open Spots' but says that it is very difficult for women, they have to be twice as good as a man to get one.

Having to work for nothing initially until one establishes oneself, means that you have to have some form of other income, hence Benloss' two other jobs. Her free travel card, which she has from her job in the clothes shop, is essential for travelling to and from clubs which can be spread right throughout London. She does not have a car, she can't afford one and is heavily reliant on public transport and taxis. Most of the clubs are based in North London and she lives in East Ham.

If she has 3 or 4 gigs in one week she could be spending most of her earning from comedy on taxis. The reasons why she pays out for taxis is fear of violence, whether real or perceived, especially sexual violence. Research has pinpointed that although young men between the ages of 18 and 25 are most likely to be the victims of violence, women's perceived fear of rape and violence is far higher than actual occurrences. This is as a result of the social conditioning of women and the fear of rape and violence as a form of social control. (For Academic proof to this little nugget of information – have a look at the following work – Stanko (1987), Radford (1987), Green, Hebron and Woodward (1987) all in Hanmer and Maynard (1987))

Before Lorraine Benloss contacts any club to see about the possibility of working, she works out the travel arrangements to see whether they are feasible. To get all her connections she needs to have finished performing by 11:00 p.m. which is often impossible as Open Spots are generally only after midnight. Thus women's fear of rape and violence obviously is self – limiting with actual access to working opportunities, and women are forced to modify their behaviour and activities through fear of attack. We need to grab 'em by the goolies, shout 'fire', stick your fingers in their eyes, get some pepper spray and reclaim the night Sisters!!!

We forget these days that everyone has their own mobile phone. Less than ten years ago they were actually quite expensive and out of most people's budgets. When I interviewed Donna, back in 1996 she had a mobile phone to give her the added safety factor that we have come to rely on them for. I used to have to drive regularly from north to south Wales late at night over very desolate areas such as Snowdonia and the Brecon Beacons when I used to film up in north Wales and yes it could be scary at times, especially when my Volkswagen camping van ground to a halt half way up a 20% incline in the hills outside of Machynlleth (or Mak to my non Welsh speaking readers!!!) at half past eleven one night. The same Volkswagen had a puncture on the M4 coming back from London one night and I had it jacked up on the hard shoulder at around twelve that night.

It's never usually vocalised, rarely recognised but that's what lurks beneath the fear, that is women's fear; of the dark, of being alone in a park, of running along a river, of travelling on their own, when you dig deep and find out what the source of the fear is, you will find that it's the fear that control of their own body will be taken away from them.

It's interesting to note that British comic and founder member of the UK Comedy Guild, Sara Pascoe wants comedians to join with her in making the comedy circuit fairer for all. She points out that logistically things are different for men and women, for example, travelling home late from a gig, an area where women become very aware of their vulnerability, something reiterated by JoJo Smith and Lorraine Benloss.

The Comedy Circuit Manifesto consists of five clear points:

- *Fair pay for all*
- *Safe working conditions*
- *Protection from harassment and discrimination.*
- *Fair treatment in the workplace*
- *A standard contract for comedians.*

Equity Magazine Autumn 2015.

So if this is what they are asking for in 2015, it's safe to say that not even these simple elements are in place. Contrast this with the list of desirable working conditions that Amy Schumer has put together in the States and there are strong similarities. This is what she says about the 'bad' gigs.

Amy Schumer

"There are too many bad experiences to list. Traumatizing, embarrassing, horrifying, humiliating, the list goes on!"

However towards the end of her January 2015 appearance on the Brian Koppelman's Grantland Podcast 'The Moment', Amy Schumer went off on a bit of a rant, when she called for a 'Comedians Bill of Rights' or 'Comedy Club Commandments' that every booker should heed. This list gives some sort of indication as to some of the bad experiences she may have been talking about in the States.

- *Just pay another $100 so the comic can stay in a nicer hotel.*
- *Just splurge $20 for a cab so that the comedian doesn't have to get picked up in some car that doesn't have a bottom to it, by the dishwasher that you just hired, who has like eight priors.*
- *Don't make them do morning radio when you know it's not going to pull even one more person into the club. It's just to promote your stupid Thursday-night show that it's your fault you couldn't fill.*
- *Don't have your child in the green room.*
- *Don't invite your friends back to the green room.*
- *Don't make them get to the club an hour early and do a sound-check.*
- *Don't make them stay after to take pictures with the staff. Don't give them a discount on their meals – just buy them their meals. Your disgusting basket of onion rings from the fryer you haven't washed. You're just lucky that Jon Taffer hasn't come in there. You would get a Z on the health code.*
- *We're not your friends. Don't make us feel bad if we don't want to stay and drink with you.*
- *Just pay us at the end of the weekend. Don't make us sit there in your cold, smoke-filled unventilated office, with*

> *your shitty carpet and your space heaters, and make us wait*
> *so you can piece together if we're getting an extra $9.99.*
- *Give the comedians a bonus if they deserve it. Don't make*
  us stand in the back with a clicker to make sure.
- *Don't make us do four shows on a Saturday.*

The above list gives a pretty clear picture of what the reality of Amy
Schumer's life on the road is in the States – but what about my other
Interviewees?

The buck stops here – Practicalities and realities.
Donna McPhail

"It's a bloody hard job and very lonely. It's horrible. Men can go back to the hotel bar and they'll just sit there. Chat with a couple of other guys or go to the pub or something like that. Women can't do that. You can't sit in a hotel bar without being hassled. Or you go out when you're touring and you stop somewhere for lunch, you're a woman eating on her own…it's extremely hard. I've stayed in more than my fair share of grotty dirty hotels. I was put up in Middlesborough once in a sort of pub, they had rooms upstairs basically for all these alcoholic old men who didn't have anywhere else to go. It was awful…with the men coughing up and down the corridor. This was about 15 years ago and now I'll try and drive home any distance overnight because the whole hotel thing for a woman is unbearable. And women have to make an effort, whether you're going to a board room or onto a stage. It is very hard, like any job where a woman is working in a man's world and working on your own, and you do feel isolated and the pressure is all yours. It's 24 hours a day. There's always something you can be doing, admin, writing and it's always your responsibility. You direct yourself, you produce yourself, you drive yourself and it's really tiring."

Jo Caulfield

"Some women can get scared about doing stand-up. Some completely irrational reasons. The comic's lifestyle is ideal for men or women under 30 who want to get drunk, sleep around and talk endlessly about themselves."

Kitty Flanagan

"Touring can get desperately lonely – occasionally I could get to do a weekend with someone like Jo Caulfield because she Emceed a lot and it was always great to have a girl to hang out with on the road."

Lorraine Benloss

"It can be quite a lonely existence."

Tanyalee Davis

"I work in Britain and the States and in the US many comedy clubs put the comedians in apartments or flats. These apartments are usually quite disgusting. Even though the flats are supposed to get cleaned I've seen more pubic hair on the bathroom floors than a CSI scene. I never sit on the floor (which I usually do in most places) in a comic's apartment for fear of getting pregnant."

Susie Felber

"The comedy centres in the States are flights away and men will usually have a woman who has the kids and looks after them. It's tough to go on the road for a woman if you have a kid. Most women who make it in comedy have either one kid or no kid, Joan Rivers had one, Melissa. You'd be better off leaving comedy until you're a Grandma like Pat Candaras who is an older woman in her seventies. Children and comedy – the reality is if you're divorced you can at least do gigs every other weekend when the Dad's got visiting rights! Maternity leave is better in Britain.

Childcare is more expensive in America, it's $20,000 a year. Women drop out of the workforce. It's more expensive than being an undergraduate. I expected to go back to work immediately after giving birth. My husband is an editor for a newspaper but at that time he was between jobs and I also had to look after my mother who had cancer. Pay for stand-ups is low pay or no pay. I was paying $80 to the babysitter and earning $50. Nothing is impossible but male comics have no idea of the challenges we female comics have to overcome."

Rhonda Hansome

"The hardest thing for me was to leave comedy and the return is very hard as the whole industry has changed. It's really hard again now to get paying gigs. I came back about four years ago and I'm very happy. It's very slow and very challenging because I'm older and I have a different energy but I'm making friends with new comics."

Dana Goldberg

"I'm the only one who can make this happen. Sometimes it's really difficult to organise my family and domestic commitments. I travel so much so I do miss out on a lot of social functions I would love to attend. I think it's the nature of the work though. I just need to accept that this is going to happen. My family understands my schedule and is insanely proud of me. I think a lot of people believe it's hard to date a comedian because we are on the road so much. I don't have any children, but I do have a wonderful partner right now who sometimes acts like a child!"

Nancy Witter

"While touring we typically would leave New York on a Thursday night and come home Sunday morning. Sometimes we did two or three show in different theaters if they were in driving distance.

Then we might not go away again for another two or three weeks. We'd work from September to end of November and then January to May. I loved traveling with the ladies. I wouldn't have wanted to travel on my own, touring as a group was much more fun and it was great to share the exciting experience."

Michele A'Court
"Tough things to deal with for me, have been being a solo mother/primary care-giver – working nights and making school lunches don't go that well together. I have huge support from retired parents who live next door – for short and long-term babysitting. The rest of it is organised chaos. Jeremy my partner cooks, I clean."

Angie Le Mar
"I think that's what women do really they come and go, coz other life comes up. Because if a man is on the comedy circuit and his wife gets pregnant he can still do the gig. So different lifestyles dictate how you operate, but saying that, if you want to do it you are going to do it. I don't think there's a gender on that. You've either got it in you to do or you 'aint. ..or maybe you want it like this or you want a very small circuit or you maybe want it international, it's the individual that makes the choice of where they want to aim to work."

Hattie Hayridge aka Holly Red Dwarf
"The changing room it's usually a toilet and sometimes the blokes will just sit in the Green Room, not getting changed, just sitting there and it's you that has to go and find somewhere else to change. I'm sure they would move if you just herded them all out of the room, and said 'Piss off, I'm getting changed' I think they would actually, but they never offer."

Helen Lederer

"If I hadn't done it then I wouldn't be doing what I'm doing now, and it is related. It's not something you do for a bit just to get your Equity card. I didn't do it as a stepping stone, I did it because I knew that that was what I wanted to do. I think it's as simple as that. However, I'm not one who can stomach the constant grottiness of the realities of life on the road. I need hot baths and niceness and I need my husband as well."

Donna McPhail was the most vociferous about the actual practicalities and realities of a 'stand-up' comics life on the road and the situation was even worse in the United States with many comics being away on tour for several weeks. A very isolated way of working with all the unpleasantness of being a woman on your own, staying in manky rooms, eating on your own, drinking on your own. You can't approach people as easily in a bar if you're a woman – men assume you're looking to pick someone up. People come up and harass you and then Donna's had people trying to break into her room. That would be a barrier to anybody. These are some of the invisible barriers – there are many, many more. Stereotypes means that everyone is lumped together for ease of identification – a group which will have certain recognisable attributes. But it is also a way of sucking away individual power. The media does this a lot and it's ever present in society, for example – all blondes are ditsy air-heads. This is the area I looked at next.

Stereotyping and Power Vampires
Ronni Ancona

"As a woman when you stand out on stage people subconsciously, I think they categorise you. They think what's she doing here? Is she blonde and ditsy? Is she doing a bimbo thing? Is she aggressive and gay? Is she being fat and derogatory? They kind of categorise you."

Donna McPhail

"People have to pigeonhole female 'stand-ups' to make them feel safer. you know Jo Brand's fat, Jenny Eclair's old and bonkers, I'm a lesbian. They say well she's very funny but she couldn't get a boyfriend or she's not normal in some way so I think it's quite a major part of the whole topic. And there's this element that women aren't funny unless they're fat, bonkers or lesbian… Yes comedy is very powerful and the ability to make people laugh is very powerful and people aren't comfortable with women wielding that amount of power."

JoJo Smith

"I get the Jo Brand thing until they've actually seen me, and then they realise that the material is actually nothing like hers."

Jane Mackay – Owner of 'The Stand Comedy Club', Edinburgh, Glasgow

"Some people have likened me to Jo Brand. I mean that's another thing that pisses you off: if you're a gay comedian, or a black comedian, or a woman comedian, you are like another gay, black, or woman comedian. Nobody goes, 'Oh here's another 21-year old bloke who's exactly the same as 2000 other 21-year old blokes talking about having the munchies and not having a girlfriend'. As soon as you're in the minority position, however much of a minority it is, it's a bit like only one lesbian can be funny, so Rhona Cameron fucks it up for the rest of them."

Rhona Cameron

"I feel I've have been pigeonholed as the gay, the lesbian comic *(as was Donna McPhail before her)*. But that's just the media. They need to label things, they need to simplify things."

Shazia Mirza

"Comedy is perceived as a male world. I have had people come up to me and ask me if I'm a lesbian because they think that to be a comic, a female comic, you've got to be fat and ugly or a lesbian. They pigeonhole you."

Julia Morris

"I get pigeonholed in London as 'that Aussie bird'."

Nuala McKeever

"Some people would say, 'Oh my wife loves you and my daughter loves you and my mother loves you.' And I don't want to be pigeonholed as a comedian for women, just doing women's things. Coz I don't think it is. And I like it when men come up, particularly if they're educated, and they say, 'Nice to see someone doing intelligent humour.'"

Michele A'Court

"I've often avoided working just with women – that kind of ghettoization of female comedians. It can make us too easy to dismiss and ignore, and I've always wanted to "make it" as a *comedian*, rather than as a *female* comedian – work alongside the boys, compete with them equally for gigs and for respect. However, recently I've become really interested in seeing how other women work, what they talk about on and off stage, and their different styles."

You'll have to buy this book, Michele – save you thousands of pounds in international travel and years of painstaking research!

Tanyalee Davis

"I feel my act crossed gender, racial and geographical boundaries and stereotypes. I have received a positive response from most men. My motivation is show the world that I am a big talent even though my exterior is small. I want to be an inspiration to people."

Rhona Cameron

"Comedy is quite a powerful thing like being a city trader for example, that was often a predominantly male job, a very powerful enigmatic kind of thing. Historically we were always the objects or 'butts' of humour or the straight people."

As I mentioned previously, Roy Hudd calls June Whitfield 'The Comic's Tart' as she has 'served' them all!! How did she feel about being the butt of so many jokes?

June Whitfield

"I've never really thought of it as being the 'butt' as I say in my book, which was called 'And June Whitfield' I've been an 'and' a 'with' and occasionally a 'but', but most often I don't think that feeding someone to do a funny line as being a 'butt', I mean I don't mind mother in law jokes at all. In fact I've thoroughly enjoyed it. Half of it is idleness I think, because the responsibility is with somebody else."

JoJo Smith

"It annoys me sometimes because some women do bleat on about, 'Oh it's so hard' but actually it's not. Because if you are half-way funny and a woman, you will get more breaks than a white, male, straight stand-up. They're the hardest done by coz there's millions of them, you know. We're still a novelty like the black acts are, like the gay acts, like the Asian acts, like the disabled. You know we're exciting, we're a bit of glamour on the bill. It's all those blokes talking about chopper bikes and football that are fucked."

Donna McPhail, when I interviewed her in 1996, used to get very angry when she was called a lesbian 'stand-up' comic by the Press. "I'm a 'stand-up' comic, who's a woman, who's a lesbian. I'm defined by my work, gender and sexuality in that order."

She felt very strongly that the press was dispersing women's power by pigeonholing them. Someone who could literally nearly be put in a pigeonhole is diminutive Tanya Lee Davis. She actually needs a step to get on to the stage and occasionally will sit on the step with her legs dangling over the edge if she feels like it. However, she shatters any previous assumptions any one would have of a person of restricted growth or the concept of 'disability' and maintains that you just need to be yourself, and as every human-being is totally different to each other, that means shattering stereotypes. Stereotypes and pidgeon-holing were seen as being ways in which women's power was being dissipated. Having one woman on a bill was also an 'invisible' way of 'dividing and ruling' and seemed to be a very regular occurrence.

What other elusive and intangible barriers had been recognised by my Interviewees?

Invisible Barriers
Maria Kempinska

"The whole structure of comedy is very masculine and men are better suited to the isolation of the job. The environment is very isolating and women give up. Men learn jokes and gain status by being funny. Comedy hasn't got a caring or nurturing environment (because it's male). This question will often asked in the industry: Who's the man with the money?"

Naomi Paxton aka Ada Campe

"Systemic sexism and lack of equal opportunities, influence and access to networks are some of the reasons why women are less prolific than men in the comedy world. The focus on heteronormative ideas of physical attractiveness and the idea that women should seek to maintain these at all times. The idea that funny women are more of a risk than funny men – and the persistent reinforcement of that inequality on very visible platforms like panel shows, talk shows, sketch shows, improv shows, gala nights etc."

Dyana Ortelli

"The biggest barrier for a woman to reach the top in the word of stand-up comedy is simply that we are greatly outnumbered by men. It's a man's world out there."

Dana Goldberg

"I think the biggest barrier is that we are out-numbered 3-1 in our field by men."

Logan Murray – Leading Comedy Improvisation Guru

"I don't really know what sort of ratio men to women would go on to become successful (that is make a living by working on the circuit) after my courses. The ratio (since the early eighties) always seems to be 1/4 women to 3/4 men. But I think that basic sexism reflects an ingrained sexism in society as a whole. I think the bar is set very high for women in Comedy. Unfairly so. There is an element of judgement going on with (mostly) male promoters that the male comic never has to put up with. There were some really hard hitting, clever women comics back in the 1990s, but it always seemed to me that the male 'knob-gag merchants' got a much easier ride.

Lynn Marie Hulsman – American Improvisation Guru

"One of the goals of the Improvisation that I do is to get a better gender balance and train women to become referees but women don't want to step up to the challenge. Our default mode is for men to take charge. Because it takes up space, because it was powerful. The biggest thing is that women look for 'Permission' from someone to take up the space. When we hold auditions our aim is to get diversity and a higher percentage of women."

One of my favourite expressions is 'It is better to apologise than to seek permission' – which roughly translates into my main life moto – 'Just get on with it!' – I have given myself permission to do whatever I choose to do in my life. My moral compass is sufficiently clear and strong to know that I will not hurt anyone on purpose in the pursuit of what I want to achieve from life and I would suggest that any woman do the same. Give yourself permission to succeed!!

Kate Smurthwaite

"The biggest barrier is the lad mags (porn) lifestyle and culture. Humour is considered a lad's thing. FHM runs comedy competitions. The Comedy Channel is even called Dave – a real blokey name."

Maria Kempinska – Owner of Jongleurs Comedy Chain

"Don Ward (Comedy Store) used to have a strip club – that's how blokey it gets."

Cathy Ladman

"There's a very close connection between sex and comedy. At the Riverside Comedy club in Las Vegas there were topless girls called 'Crazy Girls' to the left and the comedy room to the right. The mind-set was close."

Aditi Mittal

"For men, humour is about aggression and putting someone down, for women it's about taking people on a journey and getting others to understand your perception of the world. Humour is our currency but it is not yet considered mainstream."

Remember we found out that most of my interviewees didn't

appreciate the 'Superiority' style etc., as they found it too aggressive. Mainstream society has legislation to 'encourage' employers to treat their workers equally, one day, this may happen with comedy.

Jane Davidson (ex Welsh Assembly Minister)

"I think all organisations should be actively made to treat their workforce equally so there is a very clear message to the next generation that your gender does not affect your work chances – it has never affected mine – even though that may be because my family tell me I don't have an embarrassment gene! (Nor do you!) *(She knows me well!!!)*

Sian James – Labour M.P. for Swansea East 2005 – 2015 & Women's Activist

"The greatest barriers for women are our own self-doubts. We constantly strive as women to prove our value, whether on a PTA or as elected politicians. The men I have met during the course of my career, never display any doubts in their abilities. Even when they get things wrong (as we all do from time to time) they never seem to take responsibility and always have a reason or someone to blame for the error. This belief in their abilities and talents is overwhelming. It is to be seen in spades in Westminster, the word humility is just not in their lexicon. Words like service, community, consensus and partnership are seen as weak and are devalued by the system. Yet, if you speak to women those are key words in their vocabularies. We need to encourage women to participate more and speak out on issues that affect them. We are NOT noisy, strident harridans *(Here's that word again with all it's negative connotations!)* We are over 50% of the population with our own opinions and ideas. We should not be afraid of how others perceive us, or comment on our characters or physical attributes, we should get 'stuck in' and express our opinions. After all, that's how men behave and it hasn't done them any harm. An elite can only be an elite if others admire them and want to be one of them. We need to create our own support networks for women in the political arena not try to copy what the men rely on – TRADITION!!"

Eton, Eton, Eton, Eton, Eton, Eton – I could go on and on but what for – you know exactly what I'm talking about and in the States it would probably be the Ivy League Universities where your power systems are bred and nurtured. Just Google Eton and you will find that it has been the nursemaid for nineteen British Prime Ministers and if that's not a good enough reason to get rid of it and the elitism it promotes in the 21st Century I don't know what is. The thought that the only person who is capable of leading a country is one whose parents are rich enough to pay educational fees that could buy a small village in West Wales, is totally ridiculous and not democratic in any way.

Sian James – Labour M.P. for Swansea East 2005 – 2015 & Women's Activist

"It was quite a culture shock getting to Westminster in 2005. It's roles and functions were based on the lives of upper class men in the 19th century. Men, who would work in the city or in the legal profession during the morning, then walk the corridors of power in the evening. That was changing but the 'gentleman's club' atmosphere was palpable there. There were also far fewer women when I was elected. That year, because of positive discrimination (one of the Labour Party's bravest decisions) we saw the number of Welsh women MPs double from 4 to 8. Wonderful but still not enough, we were outnumbered in Wales by 32 male MPs."

If you have ever watched Prime Ministers Question Time on the telly you can see what a bear pit of heckling confrontation it is. It is outdated, old fashioned and not fit for purpose. Build a new transparent building such as the Welsh and Scottish Assemblies, have a more democratic seating arrangement and drag the whole lot screaming and kicking into the twenty first century is what I say, and whilst you're at it, let's have a bit of wealth distribution from the house of Saxe Coburg too with all their ridiculous but powerful paraphernalia and so much money in the bank they could alleviate world hunger in one quick sweep if they chose to. After that short sharp jump on to my soapbox let's go back to stand-up comedy!

Michele A'Court

"Doing stand-up goes against the way we've been socialised as women – it's about being in charge, being powerful, and being very sure of yourself, when women are generally encouraged to be attractive and pretty and soft, and to focus on making other people feel powerful and sure. I suspect a lot more women want to do comedy (women are funny – listen to a group of them in a bar or café and they're spending most of their time cracking each other up) but, being practical creatures, they often find easier and faster ways of succeeding. There are a lot of men in NZ who do comedy, but many of them are a bit shit. There are very few women in NZ who do comedy, but most of them are really, really good."

Brenda Gilhooly aka Gayle Tuesday

"I think one of the reasons there aren't as many female stand-up's as men is that of course humour is not biological but what puts women off from doing stand-up is that it is such a combative thing. I don't think that women want big rows as much as men do, we're not used to fighting, I don't think we want that, we just want to be listened to."

Maria Kempinska – Owner of Jongleurs Comedy Chain

"Comedy is very confrontational and women aren't particularly good in those situations. Men always know they will be in a battle – women are not used to it and are not combative."

Helen Lederer
"I cannot do aggressive confrontational stuff."

Ashley Storrie – World's youngest FSUC and daughter of Janey Godley
"There's a belief that women aren't gladiatorial, which isn't true."

It's interesting to note the difference in stand-point from older to younger FSUCs. I have also found that a lot of young feminists are quite feral and game to pick a fight – something which was quite rare when I was growing up. I did get into two scraps with two girls when I was young, once in primary school and the other time in secondary school, neither of which I instigated but I remember both were quite shocking.

Brenda Gilhooly aka Gayle Tuesday
"I don't so as much stand-up now because I've done telly, I've had kids and I'm doing a bit more writing. I stopped doing stand-up when I began to do telly, you get better money and I had a child at home and it just sort of happened naturally."

Ava Vidal
"I get a lot of racist and misogynistic comments. Men just don't want to see us there".

Rhona Cameron
"I did a gig a few years ago in Brighton and it was sold out, two shows and I got two encores and the editor from the *Guardian* was there and he wrote on the basis of what he saw, I didn't deserve to have a career. But what he should have written was 'although

the audience really liked it, I didn't'. I mean if you're doing an extra show because one is sold out and you do an encore and everybody's laughing in all the right places, it's not fair to have that reported differently. So an incident like that is probably one of the worst situations I've come across of subversive tactics, which is insane and a person like that does actually deserve possibly to have his fingers cut off."

Sian Parry – Ex Comedy Club Booker. Music Agent & Manager

"Poncho Comedy Club came to an end because we had to move venues because of organisational difficulties with the original location. A lot of time, effort and money was spent on marketing and promo of the launch and it was knowingly sabotaged by a man, who I won't name, and the launch night was pulled from under my feet the day before. It was the end of PCC. Gone was the capital and gone was the incentive. You'd think 7 years later I could forgive the guy, but I would happily torture him for hours to this day. When you put your heart and soul into something you've worked so hard to achieve and along comes one heartless git and takes it all away from you like a flash…it gets to you…big time…..but you brush yourself down and carry on with your head held high, it's the only way."

Thenjiwe Tay Moseley

"If you're a man and you say what you do, that's enough, if you are a woman you always have to prove yourself."

Wendy Kane

"It's still a very male – dominated career…they (*male comics*) won't let women in. I was once told by a famous comic, that women shouldn't be doing comedy because it's men's work. You're invading their territory. There's a lot of hostility from the men, they don't like the rivalry or that women take control. You have to have staying power or you'll stop doing it 'cause they've told you to stop doing it, once again male domineering tactics."

Lydia Nicole

"I've realised that if your name is not on 'the list' then you 'aint going to make it even though producers are saying there aren't enough Latino performers, truth is the they're too lazy to look further than the pool so get out there and create it yourself."

Cynthia Levin

"There is no respect or financial recognition for comedy performers in the States, we have no unionisation and no equal pay. It's the most respected when you make it but the least respected when you're at the bottom of the pile."

Shazia Mirza

"Some women criticise me but predominantly it's men who do. In the Koran, Islam gives women a lot of power. Women are supposed to be the equal half of men. But it's actually our culture that has come along and said that men dominate women. It's a very chauvinistic culture not religion. I think I am right and my parents were wrong. My Dad is a very chauvinistic man who didn't like my Mum working; even though she trained as a teacher in Pakistan, he wanted to control my Mum. Which is like a lot of Muslim men; all his friends and relatives were all like that. Especially my Mother's generation of Muslim women, they didn't have a life; they just had to have kids and that was it. And I am the total opposite of that generation of women."

Tanyalee Davis

"There also seems to be more of a "boys" club within the American circuit. Many club owners/bookers will take the male comics out golfing or to play basketball."

JoJo Smith

"The guys all get together and play football, they all go off to each other's weddings and everything else. And as a female comic I don't get invited to those things. I've got some really good friends on the comedy circuit and some that I occasionally socialise with. But it's not the same, it is quite a lads' club.

Julia Morris

"The thing that can get you out of the industry quicker than anything else is the freeze out from the guys. And I don't think the boys do it on purpose."

Susie Felber

"Most of my comedy performer friends are male and they would not tell me about a job that was going. These were liberal friends who always had less experience than me. They didn't intentionally leave me out they just wouldn't think about telling me. The way work is commissioned in the States is that a 'packet' of information is released by companies saying what the show requirements would be and I would often not hear about this until after the deadlines. American television shows have mostly male authors and it's for this reason, they just keep women out of the process. The people making the decisions are men and women are just not writing the shows."

Nancy Witter

"Comedy is a very misogynist business. The booking agent for David Letterman lost his job because he revealed in an interview that he didn't think women were as funny as men, and that they acted like men in an attempt to be funny. He was fired the next day after the article appeared in the New York Times. The men want to keep the power within male enclaves. There still isn't a woman on late night telly. The ones hiring are male. It's an old boys club. Johnny Carson made Joan Rivers the first permanent guest host whenever he went away on holiday (which he did for at least 13 weeks every year) She knew that NBC would never give her the permanent job. Joan Rivers said the three reasons were; because she was female, Jewish, and from New York. When she took a job as the first woman to host a late night television show at Fox, she called Johnny Carson to tell him first. He hung up on her, blackballed her, and never spoke to her again. I doubt he would have done that to a male counterpart. Jerry Lewis was also someone who said he thought women were not as funny as men."

Cathy Ladman

"Jerry Lewis has been saying that women aren't funny in public for at least the last twenty years and says can't bear to see women demean themselves on stage. One year, I took part in his telethon to raise money for Muscular Dystrophy. He proceeded to talk all the way through my ten minute set. He was so rude and unprofessional. He was giving me the stinkeye and I confronted him and played right down to him. I've had guys try to take my power away from me by telling me to take my clothes off."

You just got to talk LOUDER next time!! Ah that old chestnut again – I've got the right to tell you to take your clothes off!!!!! TWAT! (Totally Weak And Tedious) and there's me re-appropriating a woman's word.

Logan Murray – Leading Comedy Improvisation Guru

"Then there are loads of gigging women comics slogging away too, scrabbling for gigs, trying to get famous. I think one thing that works against the female comic is the belief among most promoters that the sky would fall if they put two women on a bill outside of International Women's week. This needs to change."

Hopefully this book will help to change that situation. 'Awareness Raising' of something and having hard and fast evidence in front of you about an issue is a very positive way of challenging and instigating change. Dana Alexander is one feisty and assertive woman and is constantly raising awareness of funny women.

Dana Alexander
An after show conversation I recently had:

Woman: "You are the funniest girl Comic I have ever seen. I hate women Comics.

Dana Alexander: You are a woman join us. There are a ton of funny girls out there.

Woman: I've never seen any. Who?

Dana Alexander: Allyson Smith, Keesha Brownie, Kate Davis, Nikki Payne, Debra Digiovanni, Zabrina Chevannes, Jen Grant, Kathleen McGee, Karen McOuat, Shannon Laverty, Janey Godley, JoJo Smith, Jojo Sutherland, Diane Spencer…I went on and on (as many more are on this list) just to annoy her.

Woman: All women Comics I see talk about their periods and do "women" jokes.

Dana Alexander: Really? Name 3.

Silence

Dana Alexander: (To the male comic beside me) Can you name 3?

Silence

Dana Alexander: Can you name any males that do period jokes?

Comic: Yeah a couple.

Woman: I was just trying to give you a compliment.

Dana Alexander: By telling me I am the best of the Comics you hate?

Woman: Yeah. Maybe we should go.

Dana Alexander: Oooh getting a bit testy! Are you on your period?

Ashley Storrie

"I feel that we are regressing. Women are not assertive enough on stage. Recently there seems to be a big infantilization. If you look adorable and non-threatening the people will accept what you say. Sarah Millican, who is probably the most successful of all British female stand-ups, is a bit dotty and not a threat, she's not going to sleep with your boyfriend!"

Sara Silverman – Hollywood Director

"As a Female Director, I don't compare myself to a man. I recently had a really unpleasant experience in Montreal, Canada when the Director of Photography treated me abysmally, it's funny, he has issues with his Mother, and was talking about her all the time, and he was so horrible and undermining and trying to divide and rule and he did and the men ganged up on me with him and they treated me as if I had absolutely no talent at all and I didn't dominate like they all did and also didn't wear make-up so I wasn't an object of desire for them either. Disgraceful behaviour against women and I used to find that in the early nineties here in Britain but I haven't found it since. I think things have really progressed here. But a friend of mine was a camerawoman, cute looking girl, she had to give it up because whenever she bent down to pick up a big box they would pinch her arse."

Sioned Wiliam

"The myth that women aren't funny, it's rubbish isn't it! Absolute rubbish, but in some ways women believe the myth. I mean, there may be fewer of us as performers but the quality of performances, somebody like Victoria Wood, is a one of the great comediennes of the Twentieth Century, French and Saunders are the same, yes there aren't that many of us but there's no question that their comedy is very feminine and very funny. Or people like Joyce Grenfell, you go back to the tradition of the Music Halls, Marie

Lloyd and you're talking drag artists like Vesta Tilley, there have always been funny women but society hasn't allowed them a voice really until the twentieth century."

And as I mentioned previously – don't ask for permission from ANYONE – just get on with it!

Janey Godley – Prolific Scottish Blogger

"Some men say some women moan too much about sex-equality. I understand that, but have they ever walked up to a comedy promoter for a gig and thought 'I hope they don't have a male comic on the bill as they won't have two.'"

Kitty Flanagan

"I'm sure you will have heard this answer from every woman you're interviewed. Invariably you get the backhander, 'I usually hate female comics but you were really good.' I think the problem is they haven't seen enough female comics. They probably hate a lot of male comics as well but they see so many of them and like so many of them they don't tend to notice the duds so much."

Yep, I did! They all said it in fact in various ways, but I find Dana Alexander's comeback pretty darn sharp!

Dana Alexander (Black Canadian comic)

Punter: I normally don't find female comics very funny but you were great.

Dana: I normally don't find white people very smart but you sir… are no exception.

Some other ways of undermining women apart from witty comebacks: Wendy Kane has had doors slammed on her professionally by both male and female comics. Working in the heavily chauvinistic working men's clubs she had encountered far more hostility about claiming a space on stage than the others. She also has been subjected to some subversive tactics to try and thwart her such as men making her perform later on so that everyone is drunk by the time she performs. She has had nasty phone-calls and letters to the taxmen from people jealous of her. Once her daughter was rushed into hospital and she wasn't covered for a replacement because she wasn't actually ill herself.

Another trait I have encountered from women is that we don't expect to be listened to. The studies I have looked at have looked at the way that women use language and they have all shown that women's use of language generally is not as powerful as men.

We are not particularly good at giving orders, using 'I' and have great difficulty with being assertive – I know – I run courses, mostly for women on the subject!! Use Dana Alexander as a great Assertiveness Role Model – she's very confident of what she wants and she usually gets it.

'The woman that deliberates is lost' – Self-Confidence.

Julia Morris

"When I left Australia to come to London I was one of the five top women in television, as famous as Davina McCall is here but I had a real shock when I came here and have to do what I would have considered in years gone by as the 'monkey boy' job of warm up. Sometimes it can just be a humiliating experience."

Cynthia Levin

"I moved to London in September 2012 and the world has just opened up to me. I'm the most excited and happiest I've ever been. I'm working downstairs now at the Kings Head Theatre pub in Islington and I teach acting. London's a great opportunity to work very hard and you can become part of the comedy community. I'm always writing new stuff. I feel great."

Jo Brand

"Well I think it's really a question of self-confidence, I think that women are getting a lot more confident now, but I think that 'stand-up' is a very specific sort of art where you have to be comfortable with everyone concentrating on you and I think that that can be quite hard for women."

Julia Morris

"The big thing about stand-up is that if you have any sort of confidence of being on stage anyway, then you are twenty miles ahead of anybody else. Cause they have to knock off stage nerves as well as well as the actual nerves of 'Is my stand-up funny or not?' That's a big weight to carry so no wonder new people always look so inexperienced."

Nuala McKeever

"Meeting Sean Carson, who I ended up marrying, he said to me the night we met, 'Why aren't you writing, you're the funniest one in the whole group *(Hole in the Wall Gang)*. That was a big turning point; a personal experience with one other person you know. Somebody giving me the confidence or allowing me to feel confident. And getting the first laugh obviously."

Dr. Oliver Double – Author of numerous Comedy books

"So why have men tended to dominate the profession? Lots of reasons I suspect, from lecherous comedy promoters to audiences that give women a harder time than men. Also, to make it as a comedian, you have to have a level of self-belief that borders on insanity. Maybe men have been socialised to be more prone to be that egocentric and cocksure?"

Yep – that sounds just about right! It's interesting that you bring their appendage into the equation – the thing that make them confident and 'cocky' takes away women's confidence – if you remember, the main reason why woman are loathe to walk around alone at night!

Jenny Éclair

"My barriers have just been self-doubt, lack of imagination and my own shortcomings really. I mean we're all captains of our ships. I think confidence in yourself is the most important thing. Boys are born with confidence. They're encouraged to show off, they're encouraged to have an opinion and to voice that opinion and girls just aren't."

Sindhu Vee

"All I've done in the past has given me an enormous confidence which is very obvious on stage. However, leaving my previous career of banking in 2003 had a devastating effect. My identity disappeared and my self-confidence fell to about zero at that time. I now think that I had to get to rock-bottom to really realise what was important to me."

Hattie Hayridge aka Holly Red Dwarf

"Sometimes the barriers and frustrations in the business are yourself. I suppose in a way there aren't any actual barriers, sometimes they're just in your own mind."

Nuala McKeever

"It's hard to break into something that is a fairly male dominated thing and the biggest issue is probably a lack of confidence; To stand up on stage and be heckled by mostly young male drunk studenty types is quite difficult."

Donna McPhail

"Confidence in yourself is the hardest thing…Men can take more heckling because of their inherent confidence."

Shazia Mirza

"I think a lot of women find stand-up really scary as they think that it's hard enough as it is to walk into a room full of people and talk to them normally, never mind make them laugh. I think it's a confidence thing; I think they just don't have the confidence. I think your book will be really inspiring to the next generation."

Helen Lederer

"I am a person who gets nervous before any performance. I'm just made like that and I get nervous before I get to a party, before I knock on the door of a house. That is something I have to accept about myself and it's a pain, I hate it and it's a weakness but that is me."

Ronni Ancona

"I was plagued with self-doubt for so long and always still am."

Lorraine Benlos

"I haven't pushed myself as much as I'd like to. My own lack of self-confidence is a big barrier."

Bethan Roberts

"The biggest barrier for me is my own lack of self-confidence."

Maria Kempinska – Owner of Jongleurs Comedy Chain

"I had no-one in my family to support me and I made masses of mistakes but I suppose my biggest failing was my lack of self-confidence."

Kate Smurthwaite

"Your average guy goes around feeling more important than a woman."

Angie Le Mar

"I think they think it's women themselves that stops women from doing stand-up. I think they've got a block there already. They start off going, 'It's going to be hard as a woman, it's going to be this as a woman'. They language themselves as 'woman'; they don't language themselves as 'funny'. And when you see yourself as funny, you go for the stage; when you see yourself as woman you go all the way back down and come on stage and apologize. It's about going up on stage funny."

Sioned Wiliam

"I think it's confidence that stops women from progressing in comedy. Confidence and feeling that they haven't got anything to say, which of course they have. I think it is that issue of women feeling they need to apologise for being on the stage, whereas men take it for granted. They do literally prance around as if they own the stage whereas women are much more apologetic about taking up even a small amount of space on the stage. I think that's a major difference. And I think perhaps that men are more political. I mean that's the joy of Linda Smith, (*who tragically died in 2006, several years after this interview*) is being someone who's got a real political perspective. I just wish there were a few more political comediennes out there."

Ronni Ancona

"I didn't have equal billing on the 'Alistair McGowan Big Impression' although I did perform a lot in the series. But that's never really bothered me, because it was more his show than mine. I mean it suddenly become a bit of a thing with a lot of women. I always think 'Oh what a relief. I can keep a lower profile', which I suppose, deep down, is a confidence issue."

Sioned Wiliam

"Lynda Smith who was an absolutely outstanding political comedienne, found a real confidence to come on and compete just as securely with men, if you heard her on the news quiz or watched her on 'Have I got News for you', you could see that she was really confident. She played the same game as the men, without being particularly aggressive, she just found the tone and the confidence to do that. Comedy is to do with confidence and irony, the men have been more confident and more ironic over the years, but I think women are getting there now. And people like Victoria Wood and Jennifer Saunders, Dawn French, people like that really did open the door for women by just allowing women to go on stage and be very confident."

Some Interviewees found confidence in becoming another character, such as Brenda Gilhooly, Holly Burn and Naomi Paxton and the incredibly talented Ronni Ancona, who although she appeared to perform as much as Alistair McGowan – she didn't have equal billing with him, although she said she didn't want to have that responsibility! Although Jo Brand did not mention her own lack of self-confidence as a barrier she believed that it did hold a lot of women back in 'stand-up' and many of my Interviewees believed that it was the one thing that really held them back – well 'Fake it till you make it' is what I tell my clients on my confidence courses. I tell them how you can trick the brain's limbic system into believing that you are supremely confident. Behave as if you are confident and you will start to feel that way. Were there other ways in which we behave differently to men?

Behavioural differences between men and women

Maria Kempinska

"Both men and women criticise women about the way they look and the language of men and women is different."

Jenny Éclair

"Men are much better at bantering. I firmly believe that men are wittier than women, they are. I'm not saying that they're funnier than women, they're wittier than women and this is because their wit has been sharpened from a very early age because men don't communicate with each other in the same way women communicate. When women talk to each other they talk truth and they'll talk from the heart and they'll actually confide in each other. Men tend to communicate in jokes. Women do comedy from the heart, men do comedy from the head. Female comics talk from experience. I feel that women are more likely to punish themselves if something goes wrong on stage. If you've had a bad gig a male performer will blame the audience, the female will blame herself. So how you work on stage might not look very different but what happens on the long ride home might be quite different."

If this is true that men are fluent in the language of wit, and women are fluent in the language of truth throughout their lives, something which I have realized is true since I started noticing it, then it will follow that men will become much more fluent in this language, it doesn't mean they are funnier than women, they just are wittier, which is one form, but not all forms, of funniness.

Jane Mackay – Owner of 'The Stand Comedy Club', Edinburgh, Glasgow

"Women are harder on themselves – don't be. If a night is bad a man will blame the audience. A woman blames herself. That's why most of the women who stick at it end up being better than men and are usually better at working with and judging audiences. This may be because they do not see the world through the white heterosexual male prism."

Jo Caulfield

"A group of men will sit in a bar and tell each other old jokes. Women never do that. You'll never hear a woman saying 'There was an Englishwoman, an Irishwoman and a Scotswoman and they all walked into a pub..' Women in a bar will make each other laugh by exchanging stories and intimate gossip. Also by drinking vast amounts of alcohol and singing karaoke."

Yessssssssssssssssssss! I'll drink to that. I LOVE karaoke. In fact that's what I wanted to do in my hen party but I got the night wrong in the Robin Hood pub, haunt of Charlotte Church and my closest karaoke club.

Jeff Scott – Resident Piano Player and M.C. at Comedy Store Los Angeles

"I definitely believe there is a difference as to how male audiences react to female comics and female audiences to female comics etc. but that's just society's perception of the differences between the sexes, no matter what job we're talking about."

Holly Burn aka Kirst Kay

"Society is deeply misogynist and we treat women differently and there are different expectations of how we behave in society. Audiences treat men and women differently. We live in a man's world and women are part of the problem."

Logan Murray – Leading Comedy Improvisation Guru

"There's no difference between men and women in any of the exercises I do. Everyone is pretty good at revealing their inner idiots."

Sioned Wiliam

"Yes, I think comedy is a very male domain, although bizarrely enough at the moment all the Heads of Comedy in English television are women. (2004) But in terms of particularly stand-up comedy, I think women tend to spend a lot of their performances apologising for being on stage and I think Jo Brand has changed things a bit, but there was a time in the early eighties with people like Jo Brand and Hattie Hayridge, Helen Lederer and the few comediennes that were out there, would come on and apologise almost for being fat or for being neurotic or for being a bit mad."

Hattie Hayridge aka Holly Red Dwarf

"A woman stands out more. If she's good she stands out more and if she's bad she stands out more. And if she's up there on stage, a woman is representing the whole of the female sex. Whereas a man's a man. A man also gets a bit longer leeway at the beginning for people to decide whether they like them or not."

Lorraine Benlos

"Males tend to be more aggressive, it is their whole persona. Men are much more relaxed and confident, it is their stage. Women are much more apologetic. It is unexplored territory for us."

Brenda Gilhooly aka Gayle Tuesday

"Another thing that women do and men don't do is women tend to go straight into their first joke. And the minute they feel the relief of the laugh they get from their first joke, they sort of settle down and start to enjoy it. I have really noticed that even the most superb female comics like Jo Brand will do their first gag as quickly as possible, she'll go into her first joke quicker than a bloke would. Whereas men faff about, talking about the curtains and this and that and that's a real confidence thing. They just tend to muck about for about five minutes before they go into their first proper gag."

Kitty Flanagan.

"I always think a male comic gets a five minute grace period when he walks out on stage. The audience consciously or unconsciously thinks 'Oh here we go, let's see what this guy's got' he can faff around for a while and get his jokes when he's good and ready. With women there is no grace period, the assumption is that you are going to be shit and you have to prove yourself otherwise. Immediately. It's a sort of the innocent until proven guilty argument, but with funniness. A woman is presumed unfunny and she must prove otherwise. Whereas a man is presumed funny until he proves otherwise."

When I went to several stand-up comedy clubs in New York in 2011 and 2012 I noticed that all the male comics did this and got a lot of material from this sparring with the audience, there were far fewer women appearing on the bills so I couldn't say if this was an American trend or a male thing but I have noticed that male comics in Britain have more of a tendency to 'play' and mess about with the audience than women do. This I believe is to do with their inherent and in built sense of self-confidence and entitlement – the same sense of entitlement which is at the core of 'manspreading' – the way they take up as much space as they feel like taking, whether that be on a stage or on the underground! Even when they went on stage several of my Interviewees didn't feel that they had a real right to be there and just rushed into their sets, rather than muck about as the men tended to do. Was there anything else? The list of invisibles is getting pretty long by now!

Helen Lederer

"Fear of failure and fear of being mocked stops women from doing stand-up Just not having the stamina to maintain that kind of exposed self, a sense of the unnatural, practical, emotional, sociological perceptions. It's a pro-active thing to do and women often have other areas of nurturing and money earning and stuff and you've got to be at the top as well. You have to be very strong emotionally."

Dana Goldberg

"I think it's the same thing that stops anyone from doing anything…fear. Fear we aren't funny enough, fear they won't laugh, fear we won't be able to make a living or pay our bills, fear we will fail. If we are all honest with ourselves, I think men and women alike both experience those same fears."

Victoria Jordy Cook

"I guess the barriers to starting up in comedy however are just the same as they are for men – finding spots to perform in and building a good name for yourself. These can both be overcome by getting up there time and time again, being prepared to fail and not let that stop you!"

Hattie Hayridge aka Holly Red Dwarf

"I'd say promoters are more willing to invest in blokes. It's just like every other job, in that sense of, they think a woman is just in it until she finds a husband and then she'll leave."

Jeff Scott – Resident Piano Player and M.C. at Comedy Store Los Angeles

"I would say what stops women from becoming successful stand-ups is bland material for one. You have to find your authentic voice, and just talking about 'guys do this and girls do that,' has been done to death! What can YOU say that hasn't been said to death, but that's any comics challenge."

Tanyalee Davis

"It seems more socially acceptable for men to be able to talk about anything without being chastised."

Jane Mackay – Owner of 'The Stand Comedy Club', Edinburgh, Glasgow

"Stand-up is probably a scary thing because you have nothing to hide behind. It's just you on that stage. I think being a bit older has always helped me. Because you know who you are by then; personal comments about how you look or whatever are not going to hurt you as much as I imagine they would have when you're a young woman. Women are constantly being judged on how they look, men will turn up in any old manky jeans and t.shirt."

Helen Lederer

"I think people give women a harder time as in all walks of life – sexism is as apparent now as it was in the times of the Bible."

Aditi Mittal

"Having an opinion in India as a women is considered very racy especially for a massive audience. There's another female stand-up in Dehli who is married but she won't talk about her marriage at all on stage. It's the Madonna v Magdalen concept."

You may be thinking by this point – this is not an easy path to choose in life – so why do they do it? There must be some very valid reasons.

'Curioser and curioser!' cried Alice – Why do they do it?

Betsy Salkind

"I'm a teacher a writer and a stand-up and I am totally unemployable. It's hard and I've been depressed when it's been too much, but I never want to stop performing."

Aditi Mittal

"Laughter represents togetherness and makes me feel good. It's high time that women had a share of the culture."

Donna McPhail

"I've had control of all my working life which would be very difficult to give up."

Thenjiwe Tay Moseley

"I was always making people laugh for free and I liked the thought of being paid for making people laugh. I had a lot of stage confidence and I was used to making everything funny."

Kitty Flanagan

"It's one of the few jobs where you have total control which is what makes it hard to do any other job."

Maureen Younger

"The hours are better than temping and I'm good at it. I like the fact that you have total control over your working life."

Lynn Ruth Miller

"I'm very determined which is probably to do with my OCD and I will stick to something until it's like a dead horse. My life is going to get bigger and bigger because I've decided it's going to be. I'm very conscious that I'm 80 and that age is not on my side."

Wendy Kane

"I love the buzz and I couldn't do anything else. I'm just telling it as it was, that is recounting my experiences".

Liz Carr

"I love the experience of making people laugh and the sensation of being in front of an audience when a gig or performance is going your way. There 'ain't no better feeling and I come alive on stage."

Lorraine Benloss
"It's a bit of escapism and a chance to say what I want to say. It's also a platform for my own ideas and writing."

Jojo Sutherland
"It's the best job in the world."

Rosie Kane – Scottish FSUC & Previous Member of the Scottish Parliament
"It's the first thing in my life I'm good at."

Ashley Storrie – World's youngest FSUC and daughter of Janey Godley
"I tried to avoid being a comic but it's the thing I do really well."

Jenny Éclair
"I feel extremely lucky to be doing stand-up comedy. I know it all sounds very actry/wanky but it's almost a blessing because there's so many awful jobs, so many dull, dull jobs. I'm never bored when I'm on stage. I can feel it in the wings, the beast comes upon me and I know when the beast is working and it's glorious, it's the most alive I feel."

Shazia Mirza
"God, I have got to make something of my life; I have got to do what I want to do. I saw my Mother just living the life of a Muslim woman and every woman of her generation, all the Aunties in the family – all the women have got exactly the same lives. They were doing what their husbands wanted them to do. They have just seen me on TV and think I have just arrived there.

They have got no idea at all about comedy because that's not part of their culture."

Rhona Cameron
"Being a comedian's a great thing. I feel just to be able to make a living out of doing what you want is very, very important. You know it's a great luxury in life."

Amy Schumer
"My ultimate aim with my career is that I wanna continue to make things that I'm proud of and work with the people I love. It would also be nice to be rich as shit too! Health. Natural disasters. Things beyond my control are going to be the only things to stop me from doing that. But I'm going to do everything in my power to create the best work I can."

Angie Le Mar
"Doing stand-up is an opportunity to have your voice and views listened to. It's like, I've got something that's important to say. And I like the power of being on the stage and being able to say it with humour."

Jane Mackay – Owner of 'The Stand Comedy Club', Edinburgh, Glasgow
"One of the most satisfying things about this job is that I can say what I like in my own way and you work alone so you are responsible for success or failure."

JoJo Smith
"Yes I like doing this; it's a great life. You know I worked in a chip shop when I was thirteen. And I had to scrub all the fat off the ranges twice a day. And you know this is fantastic; people fly me around the world to talk bollocks. It's brilliant. And it's something

I never thought I'd do and never wanted to do. I suppose I just drifted into it. It's the one area actually where you are not judged on your size, your sexual preferences or the colour of your skin. If you're funny, you're accepted."

Julia Morris
"To be able to make a crowd hurt, and just leave the stage makes you feel amazing. There's nothing to describe it. I couldn't even compare it with skydiving or sex or any of those things. It's a completely different feeling, although sex whilst you're skydiving? Now you're talking! Stand up's nowhere near that good!"

Nearly all the women I spoke to agreed that it was exciting and fun at times and for some it was the only thing they were good at! Both Jo Brand and Jenny Eclair agreed that it was an immense privilege to be able to do it, to 'stand-up' and be listened to. Apart from these elements there were also some special events and accolades that made it all worthwhile. This is what I heard next.

Some Highlights and recognition
JoJo Smith
"I was the first person (man or woman) to encore in Open Spot in Jongleurs, Camden and that felt incredible."

Jojo Sutherland
"I did a gig in 'The Stand' in Edinburgh at 12.30 at night and I had two in the audience and they laughed from start to finish. That was a real defining moment for me."

Cathy Ladman
"I've been doing stand-up for 33 years now and there have been some fabulous experiences throughout my career such as being on the 'Roseanne Show' and 'Tonight' Show nine times."

Susie Felber

"Sarah Silverman made it to the very top and then had so many years in the wilderness. It was very brave of her not to give it up. I was her vagina's dep once in the V monologues!"

Rhonda Hansome

"All the following comics were all in the clubs at the same time as me. Rita Rudner, Sarah Bernhart, Joy Beha, Margaret Chow and Rosie O'Donnell. I toured for two and a half years with Anita Baker, Arethra Franklin, the Pointer Sisters, Diana Ross and Smoky Robinson. We worked in the Catskills, in gambling resorts and in the Villa Roma, places like that. I also worked in New York's Radio City where I worked with Ruby Wax and was interviewed by Lenny Henry."

Jenny Éclair

"When I was pregnant with my daughter, the Perrier Award wasn't as big a thing then, it was in about 1988 and I got a special commendation, me and Eddie Izzard, which was like the forerunner of the Best Newcomer Award which eventually became part of the deal. There is now a Perrier 'Best Newcomer' which is feted in terms of the Press it's quite a big thing but in those days it was a sort of 'Well done' sort of certificate and didn't really amount to much. I was very thrilled when I got that and I got a Time Out Award."

Betsy Salkind

"For nine years I was the Chair of the SAG/Aftra Comedians Caucus and we got the very first official contracts at Comedy Central and BET. The best night of my life had to be when I sat next to Roseanne Barr and Jennifer Saunders at a gala event."

Cynthia Levin

"The highlight of my living in L.A. was working every night at the 'Comedy Store' on Sunset Boulevard as a paid regular from 1994-2000 and then again when I came back in 2005."

Shazia Mirza

"I've won the London Comedy Festival, I performed at The Palladium, I've done the Royal Albert Hall, The Palace Theatre, The Theatre Royal Drury Lane. Those were all major events and turning points because they were such big stages."

Maria Kempinska – Owner of Jongleurs Comedy Chain

"Men recognise other men and their achievements but not what women have achieved. I loved having the MBE for my contribution to comedy."

The highest accolade for me as a Welsh speaking woman would be to be received into the Druidic Throne 'Gorsedd y Beirdd' and I would dress up in a king size Egyptian cotton bedsheet, wear green wellies and have a crown of ivy placed upon my head. Don't laugh – I bet that Sioned Wiliam is also angling for that honour with her most recent novel!!!

To reflect on the invisible obstacles that all my Interviewees have surmounted they are numerous but hopefully once they have been identified they can be destroyed with a big huge wacking sledgehammer with a bit of energetic elbow grease behind it. We can all learn from history. That very first female star of Music Hall, Jenny Hill really put her heart and soul into her act. She was quite eccentric if you recall, dancing acrobatically, jumping from a kitchen table into a half filled bathtub and finishing off her act by cavorting around and playing the bagpipes. Certainly a 'one off'. Present day comics such as Naomi Paxton and Holly Burn are reclaiming that joyful inventiveness.

Confidence or lack of confidence is the one big barrier that can stop us from doing everything – it limits our potential and restricts our growth. I work with my clients towards transforming fear into fearlessness as that essentially is what confidence is – the knowledge that whatever life chucks at you – you will cope!

Be fearless to be funny! I bet Boadicea, that most famous Celtic warrior Queen had them rolling around in stitches with her jokes whilst she was giving the early Romans some stick! Boadicea was my alter ego for a short time when I devised a character to hide behind called 'Boadicea Queen of HRT' – she was totally fearless!!!! Fearlessness is not something we usually attribute to women, but if we weren't fearless would any woman have ever considered giving childbirth another shot? I speak as someone who had a 47 hour long labour, was eventually induced, baby was distressed and had to have foetal clips, the cord was around it's neck, had internal and external stitching by a student midwife who nearly stitched up the wrong orifice, had septicaemia, baby ended up in the Intensive Care Unit and then suffered the final indignity of being told that this was a 'normal delivery'! Thank God I didn't have one that had any complications then! Yes, of course we women can be fearless, and to quote a book whose title inspired me to go on a solo trip around South East Asia for two months. 'Feel the fear and do it anyway!' (the very best book about personal development EVER! (Susan Jeffers) This is the most amazing self-help book out there and I recommend it highly in all of the self-confidence courses I deliver, it is the Dalai Lama of self-helpery!

Something that has recently been 'identified', particularly in females is something called the 'Imposter Syndrome', most notably among high achieving women. Actors have a similar condition when they think that they will be found out of as not being capable of doing the job or that their last job is their last job! This is all to do with confidence but if we are constantly being told in the media that we are not good enough, not nice enough, not accommodating enough, not maternal enough, not thin enough, not young enough then how on earth are we expected to allow any good feelings to enter into our subconscious. I devised an image for my daughter when she was growing up to help her survive her teenage years. It was called 'Y Plisgyn Aur' (In Welsh of course, as that's my first language – it means 'The Golden Shell') and I tried to get her to imagine all the wonderful things that I and her Papa used to tell her and all the encouragement that people would give her and let all those things build up into a beautiful golden shell of internal protection so that all of life's ugliness and knocks would never enter in. Now I don't know if all my Interviewees had a golden shell to protect their fragile egos, but one thing is for sure, they have all succeeded in surviving the life of that rarest of breed, that of a Female Stand-Up Comic.

Have you been put off stand-up yet? If you're still with me at this point then we will now go to the really exciting part of the book when all these genuinely special women give advice to women who want to make their way in stand-up comedy. I personally feel that they have all got a lot to say about life in general whatever career path you choose and especially so if you are a woman. In my work as a Confidence Coach one of my favourite sayings is 'Life begins at the furthest edge of your comfort zone' and I can guarantee that all my participants will inspire you to want to push your comfort zone just that little bit further, so without further ado, let's hear those 'Tips for the Top'.

Stori Stori. 18. 9. 85.
Owenno Dajyáá.

CHAPTER 7

'TIPS FOR THE TOP'

In which I share with you, the reader, the advice I was given

Comic JoJo Smith's first television experience was 40 episodes of ITV's *'Funny Business'*, which she wrote and presented and which had an audience of around three million. The programme had three stand-up acts performing on every programme with Jo Jo Smith interviewing them. She had only been doing stand-up at that time for about two years and had just got her act up to twenty minutes in length. She got to talk to successful stand-up comics such as Lee Evans, Craig Charles, Joe Pasquale, Brian Conley and Jo Brand and found out some very useful tricks of the trade. I decided that I'd be daft as a brush if I didn't do the same, so I used the interviews as an opportunity to get some advice from all these successful women. Their experiences are extensive and highly varied and in the previous chapters you may have read how they overcame challenges that you have been struggling with. In this final chapter I will let them get on with revealing the precious nuggets of advice they want to impart about their own particular area of expertise. And don't forget that knowledge is transferable into your own profession. A brilliant work ethic is a brilliant work ethic in any profession and skills are transferable from one profession to another! As Joan Rivers used to say – *'Funny is Funny'* and in my mind *'Success is Success'.*

But for those of you who have a passion for comedy, as I do, then the world we are now entering into is the very peculiar male dominated world of comedy but I am sure you can all relate the knowledge to your own personal environment. Some of the advice is just applicable to future FSUCs but most of the advice is great advice for any person especially women who are often less self-confident and more doubting of their own abilities. We are still creating our own realities much more so than men, finding a way of accommodating care responsibilities, of creating a healthy work-life balance, of reaching our potential whilst the body clock ticks away in the background and other issues to do with safety, use of language and status that don't affect men in the same way.

In the ebook version of this Chapter, should you wish to buy it alongside this book, there are hyperlinks for your convenience to enable you to find more about the comics in question. I have included their Twitter details and some additional details, be that their Wikipedia page or website. You can hyperlink from the ebook to all their sites to find out even more about their work and their working environments.

I'm going to start this Chapter with advice from the latest darling and rising star of the American comedy scene, Amy Schumer, star and author of 2015's film 'Trainwreck' a very attractive and feistily funny comic and this is what she told me. I met her in the Cellar Comedy Club in Greenwich Village, New York, September 2013. Thanks to another one of my fabulous FSUCs Tanyalee Davis for suggesting I go and see her, and also thanks to that lovely doorman who sneaked me in when I came back pleading and begging to be let in, when he had told me and three of my friends ten minutes previously that it was a total sell out and we couldn't get in for love or money!

Amy Schumer

"I would give the same advice to an attractive women as I would to an ugly guy starting out in comedy. Just get as much stage time as possible and only do this if it's the only thing you can do."

Amy is constantly challenging and subverting sexist attitudes and female stereotypes in her work in America and another person who is pushing the frontiers of acceptable behaviour within her culture and conventional background and has found her comic voice is Sindhu Vee.

Sindhu Vee

"In 2003 when I left banking in the city my identity disappeared. I had to get to rock bottom, to lose everything when my self-confidence was zero to realise what was important to me. Women were silenced in my family, but I wasn't going to be. All I've done in the past has given me an enormous confidence which is very obvious on stage, so don't underestimate the importance of all your experiences.".

In my work as a coach and trainer I am constantly trying to identify 'transferable skills' on behalf of my clients who are looking for new opportunities in their lives. Victoria Jordy Cook has rechannelled her comic potential into a more stable radio environment for the time being in her role as the mother of a young daughter, rather than in the long distance land of UK wide comedy clubs. What skills make up her comedy kit?

Victoria Jordy Cook

"To have a successful career as a comic takes a whole host of ingredients, funniness, the ability to write and deliver great material, determination, a love of service stations and driving 10 hours for a twenty minute slot…but the quality I have found most consistently exists in successful comedians is – a brilliant work ethic. It's the guys who are working their arses off when they're not on stage or on TV that get to the places others don't. To actually love comedy makes this feel like the easiest part of it. Don't be scared to fail. You will. Like loads of times. Loads. Keep working really hard, enter competitions and put your name out there. Just bloody do it!"

A FSUC who works phenomenally hard and doesn't allow the grass to grow under her feet is Spring Day, who was born with slight Cerebral Palsy which affects the way she walks. However, this has not stopped her from re-locating to Japan and also performing every year at the Edinburgh Fringe Festival.

Spring Day

"You really have to decide that you're always going to have a great time on stage. I see a lot of people who move to New York without having a rounded unique personality and they all end up sounding the same. Develop your own voice. Watch two or three comics that you really, really admire and that you want to emulate not copy. Watch and learn! Keep writing, keep growing. Don't listen to criticism – I didn't listen to any criticism for the first two years. I never missed a show. Get as much stage time as possible."

Getting as much stage time as is possible is a central theme to all the FSUCs I spoke to, so you have to really wrestle with the devil and push that comfort zone to its furthest limits as this is the one thing that they were all scared of to start with!!!!!!!

Michele A'Court

"Get stage time, do every gig you can get your hands on, try not to sound like you're delivering a script, and write some stuff that is just about being a human being rather than a woman."

Ronni Ancona

"I definitely, definitely think you have to have as much live experience as possible. Whether that's through doing your own show or whether it's doing stand-up. I really do think it's imperative and we filmed things in front of a live audience. I still do a lot of radio stuff in front of live audiences and a lot of live work and all right, it's in a different context, but I still think it's terribly important."

This was certainly the case for Chrissy Rock who starred in Ken Loach's 'Ladybird, Ladybird', in which she plays the part of a woman, battered by her partner and Social Services. Chrissie, the story goes, was spotted doing stand-up by Loach and without previous acting experience played the leading role, winning an award for her natural passionate performance. Chrissie also made her mark in 'I'm A Celebrity Get Me Out Of Here'."

Hattie Hayridge aka Holly Red Dwarf

"Get out there and perform six nights a week, because then you get a complete momentum, especially if you've been thinking up things whilst you're on stage, and if you're doing it twice a week which is what I am now. You've lost that momentum even by doing it just twice a week. I should have had a whole spate of doing it continuously almost, which is what some of the young ones do now. Stand-up is not just about performing and performance skills, but about good material. It needs to 'bed in' like a pair of old slippers, nice and comfortable, but not too comfortable that it loses it's 'edge' or becomes an automatic response."

Maureen Younger

"Gig a lot and write a lot, every day if possible, and be professional. Don't ever be late, know where the gig is. Sometimes events happen so make sure you have plenty of time to arrive. Make sure you're doing something different. It's your personality that will sell your material so develop that and that will only happen if you gig."

Bethany Black

"I'm afraid I don't really have any advice specific to trans people in regards to performing comedy, comedy's a personal and subjective thing so the same advice works for everyone; go out there and perform and try and find the things you know are funny and make other people laugh, if you enjoy it then work really hard at getting better, most comedians are lazy, so every day you spend working hard you'll surpass someone who spent a day playing video games and eating trifle with both hands."

So get out there, gig as much as you can, take as many opportunities to perfect your craft whatever that might be. Put in the hours and get out from behind your hairbrush and mirror and leap onto that stage – that's the only place you will really learn as you need an audience to bounce off and to see if something is funny. Being on stage is a scary place to be, I know, I have been performing for over fifty five years now from my first appearance as the Virgin Mary in a Church Nativity play to my most recent forays as event M.C. and presenting a one person tribute show about Edith Piaf. From Madonna to Magdalen! I have appeared as myself and as characters as various as my alter ego 'Bodicea Queen of HRT' and 'The Ugliest Woman in the World' (which was my favourite character) and felt more comfortable with a nice wig and costume to protect my fragile ego should things go wrong. Some of the women I interviewed also found that their strengths in comedy were not in communicating directly with an audience as themselves, they preferred to hide behind a character like June Whitfield, Ronni Ancona and others do with such perfection.

June Whitfield

"I do admire stand-up comics tremendously, I really do. I could never, ever, ever do it. I'd be terrified. No, I need people around me. I think it's very, very brave thing to do, especially for women. But it's all really come the way of women since they started writing their own material, so I think probably the best chance is to write your own material and be seen, that's the difficult bit, then somebody might see you and think 'Oh yes, this person might be good for this'. It's so much the luck of the draw, but the main thing is to be seen."

Ronni Ancona

"I think that starting off as a stand-up is a very, very fine way to become a comic actress. I don't think it's the only way necessarily. There's a brilliant comedienne called Julia Davies who I really admire, she did 'Human Remains' with Rob Bryddon on BBC 2. She's very clever and she wasn't a stand-up. She actually did her own kind of character shows and Geraldine McNulty, (Mrs Raven in 'My Hero', Father Ted & Eastenders) she's very clever and there's a whole breed of comediennes and to me they are comediennes, just because they haven't done stand-up, they're still comediennes, but they went through putting on their own shows and things like that with a narrative aspect. Women genuinely make me laugh when they're doing stand-up. I mean Jenny Éclair I find so funny. Or Jo Brand or Mandy Knight or Rhona Cameron they just make me laugh so much. I love female stand-ups but for me, I'm not as happy being myself. I'm much happier being other people."

Brenda Gilhooly aka Gayle Tuesday

"What clearly works for me is I just put a wig on, and that changed everything. Yes, it wasn't me anymore. It didn't matter, it really didn't matter if I died on stage because it wasn't me. They don't hate me personally. It's just an act – they don't get the act. I can go to the bar, they won't know who I am. I don't have to leave the building because I feel so humiliated – all those things went out the window and then I started to go down much better than I had before. And don't compromise."

Naomi Paxton aka Ada Campe

"I do Ada Campe because it makes me laugh and lets me play with lots of people. I suppose the best advice I could offer would be: enjoy your time on stage, be nice to people, watch a lot of performers and note what works and why – and vice versa – and be critical of your own work. Also – you don't need to swear to be funny or assertive."

Talking to so many women from so many different perspectives and backgrounds meant that there were numerous conflicting views. Someone who doesn't think that stand-up should be used to hone acting skills is FSUC Susan Murray, she doesn't agree either with Naomi Paxton about swearing!

Susan Murray

"It really f***s me off when f***ing actresses oh sorry, they like to be called 'actors' these days, muscle in on our business cos they want an Equity card. It really f***s me off when comic actresses refer to themselves as 'comedians' too. Unless you've been stood at the back of a stage shitting your pants waiting to go on stage to tell jokes that YOU HAVE WRITTEN YOURSELF, you're NOT a comedian. We work so hard to do this job, we have to be funnier than the men just to survive because men and women in an audience just don't trust you despite there being many funny female comics in the last two decades. So here is my advice for new female comics – if you're shit, pack it in. Don't do long winded monologues with a few 'amusing' lines here and there because then we all get tarred with the same boring brush as you. If you're good, keep going, keep writing new jokes, get as much stage time as possible and don't give up the day job until you are more than able to do so."

Jane Mackay – Owner of 'The Stand Comedy Club', Edinburgh, Glasgow

"It's possibly true that women's use of language generally is not as powerful as men. We are not particularly good at giving orders and generally discouraged from using bad language. So buck that trend."

Comedy Commissioner, Sioned Wiliam, also did her apprenticeship on the stage to learn the nuts and bolts of the comedy machine. Sioned realised that performance might not have been her greatest strength but nevertheless that foray into performance gave her an insight into what works and doesn't work. Her comedy passion led her into another area, a new 'day job', where she had more opportunities such as producing and commissioning programmes, and she progressed from 'The Oxford Review', through 'The Bobo Girls' to eventually finding her comedy niche in Production and eventually the very First Female 'Controller of Comedy, ITV Network'. For her, as for so many of my Interviewees, integrity and being true to yourself is crucial.

Sioned Wiliam – BBC Radio 4's Commissioner for Comedy

"Always do what you believe is right. Always do what you want to do and care passionately about and don't try to second-guess other people. I think that's one of the most crucial things. If you second-guess other people what you do will never ring true. I think you have to do what you think is funny."

FSUC Liz Carr realised that she also had to tell the truth about her life and the effect her disability has had on it, a very unique perspective but one that had aspects that made her laugh.

Liz Carr

"Talk about what you want to. Do it. You have every right to do it. Don't let someone tell you they don't want to hear about women's stuff or that you have to be relate-able to the audience. I was told my material was too disability orientated but you know what, it's not like there's a whole load of disabled woman comedians on the circuit talking about the same old thing every night. We have a unique perspective – everyone does – don't underestimate that and don't become a conveyor belt comedian with no personality. Do what makes you laugh. Do what you enjoy. And most importantly, if it stops being fun, stop it – either give it a break or quit. I do a handful of gigs a year now and I absolutely love them – I gigged with Steve Day recently and he saw me do a 20 minute set. He thought I must be doing a lot of comedy because I was 'electric' – in fact, I hadn't done a show for 6 months. I felt funnier and more relaxed than I had felt when I'd been a full time jobbing comic. I'd begun to hate them, they were meaningless and comedy by rote. I was too scared to try new material in case I wasn't going to be booked again. I was bored by not doing new material. And then a producer of the comedy night 'Duckie' saw me do a gig at Soho Theatre and I told a story about an awful job I'd had. It was less a joke and more a catharsis. No one laughed at that material but the gig went well nonetheless. Afterwards, the producer, Simon Casson approached me and told me his favourite bit was the material about my job. He booked me there and then to do anything I wanted at his club. Stand up or not, he'd be happy. He offered me 8 minutes and a decent wage. Most importantly, he said that whatever happens, he'd book me again. That's the kind of gig I want now. That's the kind of gig I thrive at and I think I deserve now."

It can sometimes be difficult to turn down work especially in the early part of your career when you want the experience and to say NO to particular projects, especially for women who have a tendency to be people pleasers. At the grand old age of fifty eight and three quarters,

I have finally learnt to say NO and not feel guilty. I wish I could have learnt to do this earlier in my life, it would have saved me a lot of energy and time. Performers are constantly being asked to work for nothing and people will say 'Oh this will be good for your portfolio' – I'm nearly sixty years of age – I don't need to add to my portfolio any more thank you very much! You wouldn't ask a plumber to come and fix your drain just so that it 'would look good on your c.v.', which is what performers are constantly being asked to do. Nowadays I only do projects if they are paid or if I really want to do them and I would suggest that all women learn to do this and not be persuaded by people guilt tripping them into working and giving their energy and life force away for nothing. This is what Oscar nominated Animator Joanna Quinn has to say about that.

Joanna Quinn – Oscar Nominated Cartoonist

"Work towards having 'f**** off' money so you can be in a position so that you don't have to do jobs you don't particularly fancy, but that may take a few years before you're in that position. I'd rather be making films than any other sort of work. There are lots of women who make their own short films because unlike live action, animation is something you can do relatively cheaply and often on your own. It's an area where women can tell their own stories without compromise. It's all about confidence. The challenges that women have to overcome in animation are the same as in any industry I think – it's mostly men at the top, so you have to be strong, determined and very good at what you do. So work hard, be vocal and say what you think, be brave and ambitious, try and surprise people with your commitment."

Someone who is as passionate about comedy as Joanna Quinn, but who could never ever see herself doing it for any length of time is Comedy Promoter Hazel O'Keefe.

Hazel O'Keefe – Laughing Cows Comedy Club and Women's Comedy Festival

"I've never ever wanted to do actually perform comedy, it's way out of my comfort zone. I feel 10/10 sick just thinking about it. I'm much happier organising and managing events. That's my area of expertise, so stick to what you know and go with your strengths."

Jane Duffus has also found ways to be involved in comedy without actually stepping up on stage, but taking a background role gives her plenty of opportunities to see other comics in action and to learn from what they do.

Jane Duffus – Director Bristol Based Women's Comedy Club

"Gig as much as possible, watch as much comedy as possible (whether that's on the telly, radio or local clubs), and learn from what others do badly as well as what they do well. Always listen to the other acts who are on the same bill as you. Be prepared for some gigs to blow and learn from them. Record all your sets on your phone so you can watch them back and see what worked. Learn to read the audience – if you're bombing, don't drag your set out for the sake of it. Take it on the chin. Most of all – enjoy it. If you don't enjoy it, don't do it."

Lynne Parker – Founder of 'Funny Women' UK's leading community for female comedy

"Be creative with how you can build a sustainable business around your passion for comedy. I have developed a workshop and coaching programme to help women explore performing and writing comedy. There has been a constant demand for this kind of training since I first set this up in 2009. I have also gone on to adapt some of these techniques for coaching and training in the workplace and have worked with some well-known companies and organisations who want to confront diversity issues and encourage more women to 'Stand Up to Stand Out'."

Myfanwy Alexander – Writer of BBC Wales Sony Award winning comedy 'The LL Files' & member of BBC Radio 4's 'Round Britain' quiz

"Women need exactly the same attributes for comedy that they need for life: a strong nerve, a quick tongue, a sharp eye and a thick skin."

Sara Sugarman – Hollywood Film Director

"I'm not a tactical person but I would say that I try not to make enemies in this business, but if I do make enemies then I cut them out because I've found that that happens a lot in Hollywood. You have to find out what people's agendas are and how you can meet those agendas."

So don't compromise, stick to your guns, toughen up, don't be silenced, find areas where you can function without having to dance to someone else's tune and be committed and authentic. Authenticity is a concept that kept coming up on a very regular basis, authenticity and truth telling by telling stories about our lives and experiences, whatever our backgrounds, ethnicity, location, religion or physical capabilities.

Jeff Scott – Resident Piano Player and M.C. at Comedy Store Los Angeles

"As I've heard Mitzi Shore *(The woman who created the Los Angeles Comedy Store and who is probably the most powerful women in the worldwide world of comedy)* say on many occasions, don't worry about being funny, be authentic to who you are."

Jeff Scott, who I met at the Comedy Store, introduced me to the fabulously funny Tanyalee Davis, who I have now known for over ten years and have met on several occasions. She is now starting to make her mark here in the UK and you will certainly be hearing more about her over the coming years. Tanyalee Davis is a person of restricted growth and travels the world with her comedy and disability scooter. She has to vary her act depending on whether she's working in Las Vegas or Birmingham.

Tanyalee Davis

"My advice to other female comics is to be yourself and be persistent. We have to work extra harder to get respect in this business. Find your voice and make it relatable to everyone, men and women."

Katerina Vrana not only works in different countries but also does her act in different languages. My mother tongue is Welsh but I speak English quite well considering I only started speaking it at the age of seven! As a very curious and nosy person I also speak Dutch, French and a bit of Spanish. Last year I presented my entire Piaf show through the medium of Dutch in Antwerp and have no issue moving from language to language. Were there any issues that Katerina had to take into consideration with audiences from different cultures I wondered?

Katerina Vrana

"I do little variations in my act that have to do with local references or cultural signifiers. And of course there is material that only works in one place because it is entirely about that place. The biggest difference is when I change the language. Swearing in Greek is a sheer delight that cannot be replicated in English. At all! So I would say be aware of the cultural differences as something that works in one place or country won't necessarily work elsewhere. So be brave, be fearless and try things out."

Be fearless to be funny! 'Bodicea Queen of HRT' was totally fearless when she came to Manchester and entertained the audience at the Frog and Bucket with a slash of scarlet lipstick, red basque, horned helmet and mini pitchfork!

Nina Conti

"I am really sure that fearlessness is key to comedy really. To not be afraid to try and not be afraid to fail. You have to be fearless. You have to be fearless to be funny as well because if you try a joke out and you are not 100% in it then it won't work."

Brenda Gilhooly – aka Gayle Tuesday

"Don't be put off by the fact that you think everybody else is better than you – just have confidence in yourself. Practice makes perfect. Persevere and don't give up is my best advice. Nobody's a good stand-up comic straight away, get through those first few gigs and work through your fear."

My lifelong drug of choice and confidence booster is running and I really connected with Los Angeles based FSUC Lydia Nicole, who also loves to run.

Lydia Nicole

"Know your voice, be clear about what you want to talk about, develop your own identity. I love running, it clears my mind and connects me and God, so I'd say own your own lane (that is, as if you're running a race). Be true to yourself. Don't accommodate others, as women we tend to accommodate everyone."

Yep, we women are always trying to be nice, to meet everyone else's needs but our own. We are all too scared to be called selfish, not a particularly pleasant attribute, but one which becomes more comfortable as you move on through your fifties I have found!

Cynthia Levin

"Always be reliable for the audience but true to yourself. It's all about confidence and it's about trusting yourself. It's worthless to compare yourself to anyone else in the whole wide world, there's no one else at all just like you. If anything, it's going to cripple you if you constantly compare yourself to others. You should also feel less bitter about seeing others develop at a quicker pace. Run your own race along your own path."

Cynthia Levin, Lydia Nicole and Brenda Gilhooley all say it is crucial not to compare yourself to others, run your own race and keep on plodding at your own pace, whatever that pace of development is. However, the only place your act will develop is on stage, not in garden parties and networking events or drunken pub crawls, so get in front of that proscenium arch and give it a go. Try things out, find your own style and variety of comedy

Nuala McKeever

"I think the secret of any good stand-up is that you don't do the one thing to much; don't do too many reversal jokes, don't tell too many long stories, don't do too many quick one liners – you know, a bit of variety. Don't apologize. That's good advice, I watched an early Frank Skinner tape recently and he was sort of defending what he'd said and justifying stuff and it doesn't come over well. It makes you sound like you're not sure. You know you need to be very confident obviously when you do get up on stage and you're saying to people, 'I'm funny enough to be listened to'. So you can't get up and then kind of start backtracking."

Jojo Sutherland

"Do what you do and be proud of it. Don't take no for an answer. Don't apologize – you have every right to be up on that stage. Don't explain – just do it."

One of the things I notice a lot about women is that we constantly apologise – Sorry that I'm funny, sorry that I've challenged your sexist stance, sorry I'm not nice, sorry that I'm taking up space in society, sorry that I'm loud and opinionated. It's as if we are apologising about our very existence. A lot of women also have very tiny voices, not me – I learnt to shout from one mountain top to the next in North Pembrokeshire, telling my brothers it was time to come home for tea when we were playing hide and seek – you develop pretty strong lungs and voices like that. And growing up with so much physical space around you as I did, you also get pretty relaxed about taking up as much space in society as you want. This is what Nadia Kamil, another FSUC with Welsh roots, and Brenda Gilhooley say about taking up space, both on stage and in society.

Nadia Kamil

"Take up space because men do it all the time. They feel entitled to it, so they do it without thinking. It also took me a long time to realise that my voice was as worthwhile as anyone else's. Find your own voice. What's most important is that you believe in what you're saying and you enjoy saying it."

Brenda Gilhooly – aka Gayle Tuesday

"Relax and just enjoy yourself. Pretend that you do own the stage. Muck about a bit before you go into your first joke. Never go on too long. A comic called Ivor Denbino (yes, that's his real name) said to me once. There are two rules in comedy. 'If it's going badly – get off, and if it's going well – get off.' And I've completely followed that rule."

Similar to what I have always tried to abide by in my performing career, 'Leave them wanting more' if it's a good gig. So the same rule applies if you're having the gig from heaven or the gig from hell, this is what JoJo Smith says about having a bad gig.

JoJo Smith

"Don't ever lose your temper, even when the audience is being sexist or abusive. Once you lose your temper, your sense of humour goes and you've lost control."

Great advice JoJo, I'll have to remember that next time I'm in front of a Year 9 and they are provoking the heck out of me, and now here is some pragmatic and practical advice from Jenny Éclair before you go and claim your rightful place centre stage:

Jenny Éclair

"Always wear pants on stage – they act as a safety net. A tampon fell out of me once when I was working – it could only happen to a woman!"

What other attributes do you need to make a success on stage as a comic, what do you think Ronni Ancona?

Ronni Ancona

"I think you need stamina, something a little bit freaky about your personality. It's always nice in any comic to see an element of their personality shine through because that's what differentiates and that's what tickles some people and doesn't tickle others. I think you need to learn from your mistakes and bad gigs so much and have a self – belief but don't get too cocky."

In the Confidence Courses I deliver, one of the most important things I teach about self-confidence and self-belief is that it only grows if you push yourself to the outward reaches of your comfort zone as I mentioned, and do things that might really, really scare you, like getting on the stage in the first place or once you feel comfortable on stage, trying out new material. How do Nina Wadia, Shazia Mirza and Jo Caulfield do this?

Nina Wadia

"The best way is try new material out is on your friends. I mean that's how I've done it. If your friends laugh you know an audience will laugh. Because you're friends are a lot more difficult to make them laugh, because they know you. Hopefully you've got a good bunch of friends. The material that works for me was stuff that actually happened to me. People I've actually met. Because to me they were funny and I found a funny way of expressing that, but everyone is different. If you want to try a set, don't go out and try something that you've never tried in front of anyone. And if you bomb you just walk off. You just go 'Thanks for having me and you just walk off.' Give them a big smile and go. But don't ever, ever say. 'Oh come on, this is really, really hard, please laugh'. You know you just don't do that because that just makes the audience cringe, absolutely cringe."

Shazia Mirza

"To try out some new comedy material to see if it's funny, I just go to a comedy group where we try out material in front of each other and give advice on it. And we see if it works or not, then we go and put it in the middle of our set and do it on the circuit."

And if you can't find a group where you can do this then start one in your local area, meet up on Facebook first of all, then in your home and if it outgrows your front room then book a Church Hall – be pro-active!

Jo Caulfield

"It's a good idea to keep your material as fresh as possible. I know lots of other stand-up's who don't write any new stuff for years but if you come across any new stuff you think why not. You 'rest' material for a while, maybe six months then bring it out again, otherwise it gets boring. My biggest mistake was not gigging enough. Get out there and learn your craft."

I have been learning the craft of writing lyrics since I was sixteen. I still have some of the rubbish I wrote then hanging around in some old scrap books. I will recycle them one day when I have time. One thing I learnt on one of the numerous writing courses I went to was, it's not the writing, it's the re-writing which is where you find the magic. In fact I will always carry a little notebook with me to jot down some nice turn of phrase or some ideas for a song as I will find that if I don't write it down immediately, it will have just disappeared into the ether. So write as much as you can is what I would say as do Rhonda Hansome and Nina Conti.

Rhonda Hansome

"Write all the time, start hanging out with people who are doing it and you might want to become a manager or a promoter if you don't want to get up on the stage."

Nina Conti

"My mother, who is a writer, gave me some good advice. She said just write everyday; don't worry whether it's good or not, just exercise that muscle."

I have found that by exercising my writing muscle and a bit of 'chutzpah' (Yiddish for extreme personal self-confidence, courage or audacity (usually used approvingly). I ended up having some amazing work experiences such as being a temporary Press Officer at the BBC in Cardiff for about three months. Having been asked if I could write a Press Release I lied and said YES (I had never written one before but quickly learnt!!) and ended up writing articles for the Radio Times. I had to go and see the Boss every Friday and ask him if he wanted me to come in for work on the Monday and shared a room with the rugby pundit Eddie Butler for a while. So say YES and find out how to do something later!!!! Be brave and blag it! If you get offered something which isn't exactly what you want to do but it will stretch you, then say YES! As singer Rigby Jones says:

Rigby Jones

"My advice to any woman who want to make a success of her life is to keep your blinders on and charge ahead but also 'Blessed are the flexible for they will not break', meaning be a bit flexible with your goal and it will open other doors for you."

That most successful of Music Hall pioneers, the very first female star Jenny Hill was physically also very flexible and realised that all those muscles present in the human face could be contorted into a variety of grotesque shapes to milk the comic potential out of a situation.

Lorraine Benloss

"Facial expressions are so important. Sometimes you can't find that word which is just going to end a specific joke so it's just a facial expression that can do it. And getting the right material is crucial, I like doing universal subjects really that everyone can understand."

I saw Lorraine on television on 'The Real McCoy in around 1996 in what was her first tv appearance. Several of the comics I interviewed had entered a new environment, that of television, which required developing a new set of performance muscles. Television notices every muscle twitch, every nervous shift of the eye and it also gobbles up material so don't deliver your best stuff EVER on telly. Television can make a comic a household name and can be fraught with difficulties such as aiming the spotlight at someone before they're ready for that sort of attention. Television didn't do any favours at all for Hattie Hayridge.

Hattie Hayridge aka Holly Red Dwarf

"Don't do television too early on in your career. Appearing on 'Red Dwarf' led to difficulties in my work as a stand-up. I'd only been doing stand-up for about a year. I'd only been doing it without doing secretarial work for about six months. So in another situation that would have been great because then I was well known and that could have put me on theatre tours. But it was slightly too early along the stand-up scene to put me on big tours like that because I was still learning how to do stand-up but with some sort *of fame in a way.* I had to learn and develop my new material in the public eye as well, you know. I couldn't have been put on tour at that time because I didn't have enough material."

The way to do it to get the most mileage out of it is the following, as suggested by Nina Wadia.

Nina Wadia

"They're clever now those that put the stand-up on, they make sure that they tour the entire country first, then they do a big West End run and then they televise it. They get the best of all worlds. And then from that they get sit-coms and panel shows. It all seems to work out quite well. But never start off doing stand-up on television. It'll kill it dead."

Television is often the pinnacle of a FSUC's career. They may have been working in grotty old clubs up and down the M1 for the last twenty years but it's only when they get on television that they suddenly start to get recognised as a 'NEW' talent. How do these comics become really great at what they do? Shazia Mirzah, Dana Alexander, Aditi Mittal, Ava Vidal and Dana Goldberg shared their thoughts with me about the 'bad' gigs, they are the places where real growth occurs.

Shazia Mirza

"How does one become a great comedian? By facing the challenges instead of running away from them. I did 'Up the Creek' in Croydon last night. It was a really rough, working class gig. And I had a really hard time but I got £150 for it so it's all right. And there had only been three women in that club in the past three months. I was the only Asian woman on that bill in three months – well ever, because there's no Asian women doing stand-up now. *(Early noughties at that time – there are now in 2015)* But anybody would have looked at that 200 white male, drunken Croydon crowd that were there could have said 'I don't need to do this' – or go somewhere where they are going to listen to me. But then I thought what would that achieve?

The whole point is that I go to these places where they have probably never known or met a Muslim woman in their lives. And I tell them what it's like to be me. And then that is an achievement – giving these people something to think about and laugh about. It is easy for me to do London comedy clubs – it's very multi-cultural – I see Muslims in London all the time. They know what I am talking about. But to go somewhere where there's no person of colour in the audience, where it's racist, I felt very much it was them against me last night. I said to them, 'Are there any Pakistanis in here?' I was going to do some material about going to Pakistan, and this guy shouted out, 'No love, you're on your own'. And you know I felt it. It was them against me. But you know, I stood there for 20 minutes and they laughed. I mean I didn't storm them by any stretch of the imagination but I said what I wanted to say and people laughed. I got heckled left right and centre. And I have to do more of those because surely those are the ones that are going to make me. I always try to believe in myself. I know that some women take it personally if somebody doesn't laugh at their jokes. They think, 'Oh I'm rubbish, I'm rubbish', they take it personally, whereas guys don't take it that personally. You get some crap comedians going round who are male; that's because they believe they're good and they're so arrogant. They just don't care."

Dana Alexander

"It's the hard gigs that will make you a better comic. We have to do things for us, we have to impress ourselves as women. We have to stop trying to fit into someone else's box. Stop trying to get through someone else's door. Make it your own party, you don't even need to get into theirs, it's not even that fun anyway!"

Aditi Mittal

"Stick with it, when it feels awful, it will get worse and you will be your own natural enemy so what you should do is just shut up and get on with it. Don't take any notice of what other people are saying – there's lots of people you just aren't going to please so don't worry about them and what they think."

Ava Vidal was starting a tour and writing her own book so was snowed under with work when I contacted her in November 2013. When I asked her what advice would she write in a letter to her younger self, starting out on a career in comedy, she said:

Ava Vidal

"To be honest, the letter would be very short and just say, 'Don't bother'. I get a lot of racist and misogynistic comments. Men just don't want to see us there. I think it's a great idea to write a book celebrating female comics."

Dana Goldberg

"Get your ass on stage and do it. Period. That's the only way you're going to know if you're good enough. Try not to compare yourself to anyone else out there. You can be inspired by people before you, want to emulate their careers, but don't compare your career to other comedians out there. You'll never feel like you're accomplishing enough if you do that. Decide what kind of life you want, what kind of comedy you want to put out into the world, and go do it. It's the hard gigs that will make you a better Comic."

But to do the hard gigs, the ones where no one is listening, when the audience talks when you're speaking, they ignore you, they heckle and shout out at you 'Get your tits out' as someone shouted at me when I was making a speech in a 'Reclaim the Night' protest march in Cardiff, September 2015, what do they do to your confidence? (I shouted at him that he looked a bit old to be breast feeding in public!!!) Wendy Kane who has worked with the likes of Chubby Brown says:

Wendy Kane

"You have to have the guts to get out there and do it. I think the reason why a lot of women are scared to do stand-up is because to a certain degree it's unknown territory. But when I'm on stage, every woman in that room is talking through my mouth. They say to me, 'You say what we haven't got the guts to say'."

And to do that you have to have a certain amount of self-belief that you are funny enough to shout something witty back at your heckler. In my Confidence Courses I teach my clients to 'Fake it till you make it', that is pretend you are self-confident, something that Donna McPhail used to do.

Donna McPhail

"If you ever have a crisis of confidence, as I have in the past, the way I got around it was by pretending and acting that I was confident, then I get that first laugh and that would make me feel confident and then I'd actually become confident. Audiences smell fear and they can almost see it in your body language. They can smell it and they can see it and then they're on yer! You should never be scared of hecklers because brilliant things can sometimes come from these unexpected sources."

Shazia Mirza

"You have to believe in yourself no matter what. Because at the end of the day, you have to stand on that stage. You know in the times when my confidence has dipped, the gig hasn't gone very well, because I have stopped believing, and a lot of times it really is mind over matter. You know I thought I did badly last night. I went out there, I thought it was an awful gig, all the other comics were going, 'God, that was alright'. It's never as bad as you think. A lot of the time, some other comics are not that funny; they don't have that funny material. But they believe they are. And because they believe they are, they've got control. It looks like they know what they are doing and they don't. It's mind over matter."

Have you ever dreamt of something like doing stand-up or whatever? Walt Disney had a beautiful moto which was 'If you can dream it – you can be it' and I am a firm believer that that applies to anything in life if you want it enough and you are prepared to put in the hard work. This is what Jo Brand said to me about this:

Jo Brand

"I think if there's something that you really want to do, you should at least try to do it and if you fail, at least you've had a go. There's a lot of people who think 'I really wish I'd tried that when I was younger', and regret not giving it a go. My friend Helen Griffin, who I became friends with when I trained as a psychiatric nurse over twenty years ago, wanted to be an actress and I always wanted to do comedy. And neither of us ever thought we'd get anywhere with it but we performed 'Mental' together at the Edinburgh Fringe, a play we wrote together."

And if you're funny but there aren't any roles for you – you write your own material. That's what I should have done when I realised that there were no funny roles around for me, but I also wanted to sing and ended up creating a tribute show about the French singer Edith Piaf. Angie Le Mar has some great advice about creating your own work.

Angie Le Mar

"Create your own work and don't wait for permission to do it. I find I have been doing a lot of acting. I write and direct and produce and do everything. Now I have got my own company, 'Straight to Audience Productions', I actually manage comedians as well. That just came about through lack of TV progress. I had a meeting with a commissioning editor once and I remember saying to her, 'You know, you've got a contract that could last two, maybe four, years; I've got a talent that will last a lifetime. When your contract's up, I'm still talented.' I'm off to build my own destiny. When my last daughter was born I was very sick, I had fluid on the brain. And I read this book, *Conversations with God*, and in this book it was just saying about talking to God and I remember saying to God, 'You gave me this talent to make people laugh. I am Britain's first black female comic, why do I have to keep knocking on these doors?' And the response I got back from God was, 'Well because you keep asking for permission; I gave you the talent. Go straight to your audience.' So I called the company 'Straight to Audience Productions', I put our stuff on video and we sell it straight to audience – mail order. You know, if you want Angie in concert, of if you want Angie's T-shirts, Angie's CDs or Angie anything, it's just a complete branding, we sell it straight to the audience. Now we've got a radio show as well that airs twice a week that's called *The Ladies Room*. The room where women talk and men can listen. We sell it through a radio station. It's just a complete enterprise of a talent that I was waiting for people to give me permission to be able to do. Yes, life is too short and the worst thing that can happen is that you have an experience. And if that's the worst thing? Oh please!"

So create your own work, be seen, get out there, what about competitions? In the early stages of writing my book 'Sock it to them Sister', I took part in a few comedy courses and several local comedy competitions. I didn't get very far so I stopped. What advice was there to be had on competitions?

Jane Mackay – Owner of 'The Stand Comedy Club', Edinburgh, Glasgow

"Don't take part in comedy competitions. We have clubs, we book clubs, we have to have people who can do 20 minutes in front of perhaps a rowdy or difficult audience. Somebody who's done ten open spots in competition conditions, you know, where they're being judged on a variety of criteria like originality, or difference or whatever, can be just absolutely damn useless when they're booked. You know, in what other job would you decide who you were going to employ on the basis of a bloody competition?"

Fern Brady

"Never enter the 'Funny Women' competition. It's like the Paralympics and is just full of wannabe actresses. If you really want to be a comedian, compete against men and do 'So You Think You're Funny'."

What else could you do that would give you some experience in standing in front of people and talking, apart from a three year teaching degree? I learnt how to work an audience and play a room when I was singing on the street, in bars, restaurants and terraces all over Belgium, I learnt so much about performance just by being 'wallpaper music' in the background, but JoJo Smith's apprenticeship was as a Bingo Caller.

JoJo Smith

"A really good lesson I learnt when I was a 'Bingo caller' was to focus on what I was doing and don't be put off by the audience, whatever they do, even if that is hissing and taking the piss! And another lesson I learnt was not to do the big venues too soon. I did Battersea (Jongleurs) when I'd only been doing stand-up for about 6 months and basically I got ignored off. And at the time Lisa White was the booker and she spoke to me afterwards and she said, 'Look, 'Jongleurs' isn't going anywhere. Wait until you play in 'The Banana' (in Balham) and you play in all the other clubs and then come back. Because then you'll be confident; you'll be used to playing big rooms and your confidence will be up'. And that was brilliant advice. And I would give that advice to anybody starting: Don't be in a hurry to do 'The Comedy Store' and 'Jongleurs' coz they're not going anywhere."

If you're lucky enough to be given advice by a booker then it would make sense to listen to them as Maria Kempinska says –

Maria Kempinska – Owner of Jongleurs Comedy Chain
"The bookers are the powerful people in the industry and it's often a woman and both men and women flock to please her so it's worth bearing that in mind."

So according to JoJo Smith you have all the time in the world, that's good to know. Lynn Ruth Miller found this out at the grand old age of 81 when she embarked on a brand new career on television as the world's oldest FSUC (Now that Joan Rivers is no more) Joan was six months older than Lynn Ruth, so age is no barrier, what other advice does she have?

Lynn Ruth Miller
"Don't try to be a man...Come from truth...persist. Love what you are doing for the sake of DOING it. Listen to the audience – they're always right. If they're not laughing it's because you're

not funny. Learn how to construct a joke properly, watch how Joan Rivers does it. Have the courage to be yourself. You have a right to be unique. Be like you and no one else. There's no age limit for being funny!"

I had a Skype conversation with Lynn Ruth and we spoke for well over two hours. She is a young spirit, highly original, and reminds me very much of my dear friend and mentor, Eluned Phillips, who at the age of ninety was writing lyrics for a musical via email with a young man from Boston if I remember well. Originality, or lack of originality is something that bothered the very unique Mandy Knight quite a lot.

Mandy Knight

"Be inventive and be original. The standard of comedy is dying, because what's happening is that there aren't any more Eddie Izzard's around so all you've got are pale imitations of him. He did it when we first started and at that time there was no one to copy, there was no one to emulate."

Jo Enright

"I did one of my first open spots at the Comedy Store in London in the early 1990s. Eddie Izzard was on the bill and when I came off stage he was very kind to me. He said I showed potential and in order to develop that, he told me to do my act as often as I could, to play as many rooms as I could. That's the same advice I would give to a young woman wanting to build a career in stand up. I would also advise her to invest in a dictaphone and to record as many of her performances so that she can listen over and over and work to improve the act as she goes along. For most comics it's a very long apprenticeship but it's a fantastic journey. It can be lonely and it can be rejecting (especially when new ideas are being formed) so have at least a couple of friends who understand the creative work you are pursuing and who can be there to listen when there are difficult moments. Try. And if it doesn't work the first, second or third time, keep on trying. Be courageous. Because when the ideas do begin to work it is exhilarating."

Mandy Knight

"Stand-up comedy is quite an egalitarian platform actually because the better you are, the more you work and one of the beauties of stand-up is that it's not only judged immediately but it's also judged by the people for whom it's intended, which is the general public. On the record, I have to say, no bloke takes the food out of my mouth. Now you do have to have a greater resolve and work a bit harder to get to the top but Victoria Wood is the only person to have sold out the Royal Albert Hall for fourteen nights in a row. That's over and above Billy Connolly, so don't tell me it's not possible. It's totally possible. That woman works like a Trojan but that's why that woman has got there. I'm a big fan of motto's, some are the tools of my life, one specifically being 'The biggest helping hand you'll ever find is the one at the end of your own arm', and there comes a point where if someone throws you a life line and you go 'It's the wrong colour' – you're going to go under. You've got to find it within yourself to grab hold of it. So if you see an opportunity or someone tries to help you – grab it!"

That person who may help you out may well be in the audience. Without an audience a comic can't function and often they may give you a line which you can bounce something back on to, like my breast feeding incident. Julia Morris also reminds us to be mindful of the audience and what they do.

Julia Morris

"Listen to your audience is the only advice I have for new comics. If they're not enjoying it, or if they are silent for a long while, it's time to go. Don't wait for that great big thunderclap of a laugh.

Get off the stage in two minutes instead of doing your whole five. So it's listen to your audience and know when to go. Always leave them wanting more. If you choose to be a stand-up comic, all you have to be is funny and the rest should, in theory, fall into place."

When people are funny we laugh – it's as sure as if you eat too many chocolate hobnobs you will need fillings and a bigger pair of pants, but going on stage can be such a desperately nerve racking thing to do, why do it if you don't enjoy it, as Kitty Flanagan and Bethan Roberts say.

Kitty Flanagan

"Just say what you reckon and do what you do and let like-minded people find you. Don't try to do what you think people will like. Do what YOU like. Pack some top quality gear into your opening couple of minutes. Then once everyone's laughed a few times, you can take your foot off the pedal and relax. Walking out with a big smile plastered on my face reminds me to have a nice time and enjoy myself. It also makes the audience feel better if they think you're having a good time. It's just common sense. After all, it's supposed to be a pleasure doing comedy, not a battle."

Bethan Roberts

"Don't think about the negatives. I tend to think about things too much. Just do it and have fun with it. Don't be intimidated by big male personalities."

What are the negatives? They might throw something at you, like an ashtray, a pint of beer or a piece of pizza, they may take their cocktail sausage out in front of all those who are present, but worse far worse than that is – they may not laugh!!! But how will you find out? Helen Lederer and Kate Smurthwaite tell us what to do.

Helen Lederer

"Making people laugh off stage and on is a very different ballgame. If you are ever going to find out if you have potential, just having a burning desire to get up on stage isn't enough, you just have to do it. Unless you do it, how are you and other people going to know that you can do it. It's not going to happen unless you do it. I think the main thing is to be yourself and wall yourself off from other performers and other comments and just be funny, be funny. You mustn't give your energy and power away to the wrong people. Focus on being funny."

Kate Smurthwaite

"Just go and do it and make friends with some nice people. Run your own club, you'll get loads of gigs. Do lots of M.C'ing. You'll get loads of stage time. You could do festivals. You can be the sort of person to make comedy videos. Youtube is such an amazing place to grow your fans, then you can build up your fan base online then get a gig which will sell out. Accumulate fans. Not everything on Chortle *(The comedy website which has critiques of comic's acts by the punters)* is true – it's really easy to get sucked into the male hierarchy. Keep saying what you want to say and say it."

Jane Duffus – Director Bristol Based Women's Comedy Club

"I don't have time to go to clubs so I depend on word of mouth and youtube clips to book the comics for 'What the Frock'. I won't put on funny ukulele acts – there are too many of them out there. It takes 40 hours to run a show. I believe in paying fairly and on time."

I am a self-confessed Facebook Addict and really can't remember what life was like before Facebook. I have grown my 'Friends' to over 3,000 worldwide, which is nonsense really as I probably have maybe five or six really good friends that I would depend on if the caca hit the fan. However, I use it every day to raise my profile by pumping out stuff about what I am doing professionally, information about events that I have organised, gigs that I am singing in, political causes I believe in, especially issues affecting women and all in all, although I have had some unpleasant events with some horrible people over the last seven years or so, I do know that they are living in Facebook land and can't hurt me (unless they are a nutter and that's not an invitation to come and do something horrible to me by the way!!) So what have you got to lose by embracing and using these new technologies?

Susie Felber

"Social media is now enabling women to take their own marketing seriously and youtube is more democratic and fair as you are judged on the numbers that watch your clips rather than any other factor. This is highly empowering. So use these methods to be seen and heard."

One of the female comic pioneers you will have read about in the history chapter, 'Suffrajests', Jenny Hill, was a prolific self-publicist and we should take note of her pioneering marketing methods. As women we now have more ways of accessing, creating and noting our own stories and 'truths' through social media than ever before, which I believe is really being used in a very positive fashion by 21st Century women especially as a tool for raising awareness of world-wide issues in a very immediate way which is not censored. Janey Godley is a prolific blogger and someone who doesn't mince words in any way about her life and work as a FSUC, which she feels passionately about

Janey Godley – Prolific Scottish Blogger & Scottish FSUC

"I didn't know I was a female stand up until someone said 'next up is a woman' – turns out it was me. I want to get to a place where journalists no longer can say 'Can a female comic be funny?' when they aren't allowed to say 'Can a female pilot do her job? I'm in the only job where its ok to be openly sexist about my career choice. If you're a female comic and you're finding it hard and can't take it – give up! It's a tough business. If you don't like it, fuck off."

Likewise her daughter Ashley Storrie encourages women to be more honest and less apologetic in their approach.

Ashley Storrie
"I would encourage women to stop with the self-deprecation and balance with aggression."

The issue of authenticity and truth telling keeps coming up as Thenjiwe Tay Moseley and Dyana Ortelli tell us.

Thenjiwe Tay Moseley
"Don't listen to what people say. Go on your own to your first gig. Don't be afraid to make fun of yourself. Do not copy people and be honest and talk about your own experiences. Tell the truth, the audience knows when you are telling the truth."

Dyana Ortelli
"**First – Find your voice; who are you?** Define yourself. What do you represent? What is your unique voice saying, that is going to make you stand out from the rest?

Two – Be fearless. Go out on that stage and don't be afraid to try out new material. That's the only way to find out what works and what doesn't. Don't be afraid to fail. Every comic has experienced a bad set. A bad audience, maybe. You pick yourself up and you go back on that stage and keep trying.

Third – Be relentless. Keep going. Don't stop. Call the clubs. Make yourself available. Seize the opportunity to perform in lesser-known small clubs where you can test new material. The more you perform, the more you test out your material, the more comfortable and confident you will be in front of an audience."

Dyana Ortelli draws attention to your voice and what you have to say, what issues do you want to talk about, what riles you or makes you angry? Challenge those issues and find a funny slant to them. My French teacher in secondary school didn't particularly like me because I used to mess about in class and she used to bring me down to the front of the class and say 'Gwenno Williams, I don't like you but you've got a good strong voice'. Well that 'good strong voice' has stood me in good stead and has brought me 'mucho dineros' in the course of my life and enabled me to make a living. But it's not just how you say things – it's what you say is crucial as well and this is something really important to Blod Jones.

Blod Jones

"Find your own voice, because in that you will find your own originality, be kind to yourself – Rome wasn't built in a day and stick with it! Have faith in yourself and your message. You will get there one day… and if all else fails I heard Morrison's are hiring!"

Blod Jones started her comic journey on one of Logan Murray's Improvisation classes and he has worked with the best comics in Britain. What advice does he give?

Logan Murray – Leading Comedy Improvisation Guru

"Find ways of making money out of your craft as soon as possible. Don't get stuck in the Open Mike spot ghetto of unpaid gigs and stick to your guns. Once you realise how ridiculously easy it is to make other people laugh, then you have a choice of trying to please the crowd or to **say exactly what you want to say and assume there is a way of making this funny to most audiences**. It is a wonderful craft that you never stop learning from.

In any case, a book celebrating the excellent female comedians this country has produced will hopefully make an important contribution, by encouraging women to take up the mike."

When you 'take the mike' initially in your brand new 'Open Mike', the graveyard shift when lots of people are really drunk, you don't get paid and you still have to pay for a taxi home so it's really important to bear in mind what Betsy Salkind says

Betsy Salkind

"What you get paid and what your value is have no bearing on each other. The vast majority of female comics are supportive. If you are truly original you will need to create your own shows."

Yep we know we need to create our shows, do the marketing on Facebook and Twitter, what else do we need to do?

Cathy Ladman

"We women have to be more assertive, we're not taught to be assertive and we're often full of self-doubt. Go with your heart and don't let fear dictate what you can or can't do, either stay miserable at rock bottom or get out there and do it."

Victoria Jordy Cook has changed her working environment for the time being to accommodate her young daughter's caring needs. Is comedy a family friendly environment?

Susie Felber

"Learn that there is no place for children in comedy. Keep going. Hold on tighter to the women in your life than the male comedy buddies

405

– they will not call up their female comedy buddies to just hang out or tell them about some new work that's going. Band together and open the doors for each other. Not much of a place for straight girls in comedy. I used to pray that I would grow up to be gay!!"

Comedy clubs are not the place for children – they would probably get drunk on the alcohol fumes! Alcohol is the oil in a comedy engine. I have a personal policy never ever to drink before any sort of professional performance, something that Hazel O'Keefe agrees with.

Hazel O'Keefe – Laughing Cows Comedy Club and Women's Comedy Festival

"Don't drink when you're working – it's very easy to fall (off the stage). You have to be absolutely professional. It is very, very, hard work and you must be very, very focussed."

Annie Witter

"Stay focused, be sober (mostly) write everything down, write, re-write & re-write, perform as much as possible & don't compare yourself to others – especially your Mother!!!!"

Nancy Witter

- The best way to predict your future is to create it.
- Rise up and become comedy club owners.
- Appeal to baby boomers – they want to have a laugh.
- When you're grown up you can't make excuses. If you can't get in through the door then get in through the window.
- Define your own success and what it looks like.
- Don't compare yourselves to others and the success they are enjoying – your time will come.
- Just keep focusing on what you and no one else does.

- There's plenty of room for talent.

One of the places where talent can and does develop is in Improvisation classes which are very popular in the States with even singers being encouraged to take courses to improve their 'park and bark' techniques. Non – verbal communication is so, so powerful with as much as 55% of the messages we give and receive being non-verbal.

Lyn Marie Hulsman

"The basics of improvisation is to trust your instincts and get in there as quickly as possible. Girls will always stand in what I call the 'flamingo pose' with their hands covering their bits. The first thing I do on my courses is to shake out their hands and get them to stand properly with their legs directly firmly planted on the floor directly underneath their shoulders. You have to be present in your body to tell the truth and women are taught to dissociate from our bodies."

Someone who is entirely connected to her body and her physicality is Adrienne Truscott. She performs her show, 'Asking for it' dressed only from the waist up and ankles down. Many of my fabulously feisty and funny females take on some seriously taboo subjects such as rape and sexual violence head on. Someone who tackles another one of societies final frontiers and last taboos, and tells the truth about her own mental health issues is Fern Brady and she is very vocal about challenging the notion that it is hard to be a FSUC.

Fern Brady

"Don't go on and on about how hard it is being a female comedian because it really isn't. No one ever asked me how hard it was being a female support worker with male ex-convicts. No one ever asked how hard it was being a female secretary for a board of male directors who thought women were inferior. No one complains nearly enough about street harassment of women when they really, really should. A lot of women who say it's hard being a female comedian aren't actually funny. What I'm saying is that on a stage I have the most amount of control over a roomful of men than I have in any other job and can command the most respect, so it seems mad to complain about how hard it is. The best bit of advice I was given when I wanted to quit was to 'Think of all the time and money you've invested into your stand up. You need to see a return on your investment.' So I just tried to think of it that way."

In the same way that money is money and funny is funny, the gender of a comic shouldn't really matter, apart from the fact that our truths and life experiences are very different. What did my Interviewees feel about this?

Sara Sugarman – Hollywood Film Director

"Don't think of yourself as a female Director, think of yourself as a Director, go with your strengths, go with what you know that no one else can do as well as you. If someone tells a good story, it doesn't matter what gender they are so do an A plus story, give it your all and then some! Don't try and please anyone, work from your own gut. Be authentic."

Donna McPhail

"Never think of yourself as a female comic. You are a comic. Now they're going to think of you as a female comic but your idea is to make them forget the word woman or female or dyke…and to do the job that the boys do which is to be funny and entertain. My aim is not to be a woman in comedy, it's to be a funny person. I'm a 'stand-up' comic, who's a woman, who's a lesbian. I'm defined by my work, gender and sexuality in that order and it makes me really angry."

Rhona Cameron

"I would never see myself as a female comic. I see myself as a comic. I just think you're either funny or you're not. If you're a funny enough woman and you want to be a comedian then you will be. If you're talented and you're hungry enough, you'll do it. I mean there's nothing else to say, seriously. You know it's very easy. If a woman wants to become a comedian or a doctor or an air force pilot then she will. You have to be determined."

Some of the careers mentioned by Rhona Cameron take a very long time before you have acquired all the skills necessary to do the job well. In these days of overnight success and X Factor fame which extinguishes like a soggy Catherine wheel once the talent and pound making potential has been sucked dry, it is good to remember that to be good at anything you need to put the hours in and learn the skills and tricks of the trade.

Holly Burn aka Kirst Kay

"My only advice to aspiring female comics is it takes a long, long time so don't be in a hurry."

Michele A'Court

"I sometimes think that I started too late in this game but then I remind myself what I have to always bear in mind, is that there will always be a time for my voice to be heard."

Jane Mackay – Owner of 'The Stand Comedy Club', Edinburgh, Glasgow

"Don't be impatient. You have all the time in the world. Don't think that there isn't room for an old comic – well actually there is, because the audiences are getting older and will grow older with you. There's no reason to stop; it's something you can continue doing at any age. The number one tip I can give anyone is be

yourself, and be true to yourself. If you are funny, and you stick
at it and you turn up on time and you get on with everybody and
you don't whinge, you'll do well."

*Another Scottish woman like Jane Mackay, who has had a foot in
both comedy and politics, the only two areas I believe in society where
women are able to verbalize their life experiences in any public way,
is Rosie Kane.*

Rosie Kane – Scottish FSUC & Previous Member of the Scottish Parliament

"Beware of the misogyny as it lives in spades full in both comedy
and politics. In fact have such a strong and clear position on
sexism that bad yins fear you. There is no greater risk to bad men
than 'gallus', smart, quick thinking women."

(**Gallus**" – *Originally used to describe someone who was self-
confident and daring it is now a word of approval in Glasgow. It is
derived from 'gallows' and originally described someone who was a
rascal.*)

*I have known Jane Davidson since the mid-eighties in another life
when I was directing theatre in education in Pembrokeshire and she
was involved with the Arts Council of Wales. I have always found her
to have a very good sense of humour in the time I have spent with
her, she can be hilariously funny when not 'on duty' as it were. Since
that time she has made a huge success of her life in Welsh Politics and
is now entering another career in Sustainability. What advice would
she give to any woman wanting to make a success of her life, whether
that be in their career or life?*

Dr. Jane Davidson – Former Cabinet Minister, Welsh Assembly Government

"My advice would always be go for whatever you really want to do – don't be put off by stereotypes. I'm always reminded that men generally will apply for a job when matching less than 50% of the person specification criteria; women generally need to feel they have to match 80%. I have always operated on the principle that whatever I apply for I really want to do and always do whatever it is to the best of my ability – doing any less is not to be true to yourself."

Another politician who I found to have a healthy sense of humour and a ready laugh was Sian James who I met at a meeting organised by Dame Rosemary Butler, the Presiding Officer of the Welsh Assembly Government (who is also quite a character) when the First Female Prime Minister of Australia, Julia Gillard, who was born in Barry, South Wales, where I went to college, came to visit the Assembly. Sian's advice was:

Sian James – Labour M.P. for Swansea East 2005 – 2015 & Women's Activist

"Be confident in your own abilities. You have something to offer and no one else has exactly the same blend of experience, skills and abilities you have. Do not let anyone convince you otherwise, if they are doing you down, they are afraid of you and your talents. Rise above it and remain on YOUR path. It's your path and don't let anyone else knock you off course."

Writing the last few words of what has seemed like a gargantuan task (because this journey of mine started way back in 1996 – but what a journey!) I feel I am also entitled to give you a few 'Tips for the Top' whatever you set out to do in life. The first one is 'When you fall off the horse – get back on it straight away before the bugger runs off'. You will get knocks in life whether you are male or female, shrug 'em off and realise that it's just part of the journey and in time you will realise what the purpose was – there's usually a lesson to be learnt.

Get yourself a MENTOR, *someone who believes in you and your abilities more than you do. I was so fortunate to have Eluned Phillips as a writing mentor for over twenty years. Eluned was the only woman in Wales to have ever won two bardic crowns (the benchmark for a* GREAT *writer in Wales) and she really believed in me and all that I have done. She knew Edith Piaf and had met some incredible people in her time on earth. She was so kind to me and I would encourage you also to be genuinely kind to people that you encounter in life if you can – who knows, you may be able to help them and in time they may want to repay your kindness, if not then they may pay it forward to someone else. Give with an open hand and expect nothing in return – that way you won't get disappointed.*

Realise that whatever you want in life is going to take at least twice as long as you thought ('cos it does!) It took me seventeen years to get this book to be looked at by a publisher, and ten years to get a television series commissioned about going around the continent on a motorbike. It took me over twenty years to sort out the cause of my disabling chronic sciatica and low back problem and thirty seven years to get my 400 meters Welsh vest after having been first reserve for the Welsh Schools Athletics team at the age of seventeen.

Don't be deterred by those who reject you, they're not rejecting you as a person, they're rejecting the product you're offering. Anything in life needs to be worth the work you are prepared to put into it. Believe in yourself – you are stronger than you think and find positive people who also believe in you and your dreams. Once you make the decision to do something but feel very nervous about it, whether that is getting up on the stage or applying for a more powerful job, I find that 'Bach's Rescue Remedy' is incredible for dealing with overpowering nerves, diaphragmatic breathing is also very helpful and usually always accessible!!! I also find that running, a love I share with several of my Interviewees; Jane Duffus, Dana Alexander, Sian Parry, Lydia Nicole, is also a very powerful personal space which I use to be creative and to problem-solve.

I have always had two parallel professions, one of educating and the other of performing. Whilst starting out as a street performer in Brussels I taught English as a foreign language in schools, banks, factories and the Spanish Chamber of Commerce. After I came back to the UK I did over fifteen years as a supply teacher teaching anything that moved from the age of three to eighteen all around South Wales and this eventually led to my present 'day job' as a Leadership and Public Speaking Coach and Trainer. It's always useful to have several strings to your bow. Some of the women I spoke to, such as Ronni Ancona and Shazia Mirzah could fall back on teaching. Find something that enables you to have 'f***k off' money as Joanna Quinn called it, so that you don't have to make money from your creative passion as it will take a long time as Holly Burn so rightly says. Supply teaching, training and coaching has allowed me to continue to work as a performer, however spasmodically, in an industry fraught with unemployment and less work opportunities overall for women. Hattie Hayridge and Nuala McKeever had their secretarial work, Mandy Knight her silver service waitressing skills, Jenny Éclair and Donna McPhail also had a stint as waitresses. Joyce Greenfell, the first female stand-up was a former journalist as were Jo Jo Smith and Jane Mackay and others such as Helen Lederer, Brenda Gilhooley and Jo Caulfield could turn to their writing, Angie Le Mar has her entrepreneurial skills. You don't necessarily have to do that work, sometimes the knowledge that you are able to survive a lean period is enough to give you the impetus to move on to the performing work you genuinely want to do. Some women however were totally focussed on what they were doing and did not want to have any safety net.

One of the things I would like to re-iterate at this point if someone ever says that women are not funny, or if you doubt your capabilities as a performer, is something said by Dr. Oliver Double, who teaches stand-up comedy:

413

Dr. Oliver Double – Author of numerous Comedy books

"The women I've taught have been as likely to be gifted as the men, in terms of material, performance, persona, imagination and even the cold, hard measure of laughs-per-minute. **Some of the very best ones I've taught have been women.**"

Thanks Ollie. Now make sure that this quote becomes your mantra if you are a prospective FSUC. Some of the advice in this book is just applicable to female stand-up comics but most of the advice is great advice for any person especially women who are often less self-confident than men. My advice for young women is find something you love to do and see how you can make a business of it. Be in control! (Of your life and your working life) Don't be put down by anyone – Rise above it. Start creating your 'Golden Shell' to protect your ego and feed it regularly by doing nice things for other people who will love you for it and that love will make your shell strong and protective. Be wary of the confidence vampires, those people around you who don't want you to succeed because it makes them feel inadequate. Find birds of your own feather and fly! Keep pushing yourself to do things that scare you, that is the only way you will grow.

My favourite word is 'chutzpah', which, as I mentioned earlier, is a Yiddish word for 'blagging it', I believe that it is always better to apologise (for doing something) than to have to ask permission – give yourself permission to just get on with it, as Angie le Mar did but my biggest mantra of all is:

NEVER EVER GIVE UP!

There have been so many different perspectives and points of view from all these amazing women, most of whom say that you have to create your own work, stick with it and be true to yourself. They have kept me company these last twenty years. I feel really privileged to have met and got to know them all. I'm going to miss their presence in my office, my life and on my computer but it was time they were also allowed to fly to the four winds. Here's a little rhyme I wrote years ago that seems to help me about being authentic.

Be yourself at any cost
Any other way you're lost
Can't be no-one but you.

But by far the most popular piece of advice if you want to do stand-up comedy is to stop procrastinating, bite the bullet, grasp the nettle, get out there and go for it.

Here's another couple of lines I wrote years ago, which may be an inspiration to you. (Actually, I don't care if it's an inspiration or not, it's probably the only way this poem will ever get published, apart from in a 'Vanity' collection!)

Never ponder on tomorrow
It only brings you sorrow
Dreams disperse
So why immerse
In time you cannot borrow.

So there we are – You only have TODAY so 'JUST **GET ON WITH IT**'!!!!!

And I'll leave the final tip to someone who was without a doubt, one of the world's greatest female stand-up comics, if not the greatest, the one and only Joan Rivers, who I was so privileged to meet in a special meeting in Cardiff in 2004 and at this point I'd like to thank again the gregarious and gorgeous Gareth Griffiths, House Manager of the Saint David's Hall, Cardiff for enabling a swift entrance into the passages behind the stage to meet my life-time icon.

Joan Rivers

"Tape your work, listen good and then learn it!"

She was always a fearless and very clever cookie, and tackled some really heavy duty subjects head on, subjects such as her husband's suicide, paedophilia, mental health issues, sexuality in older people, gender dual standards, she had few taboos and was often pretty shocking and rebellious. So to finish this book – let's join with the fabulous Joan Rivers (RIP), who was a terrific comic Role Model herself for so many, for a final couple of laughs.

- *The Royal family. A bunch of dogs. Go out on the street, call their names. Queenie, Duke and Prince See what shows up.*
- *Princess Diana and the Queen are driving down the lane when their car is forced off the road by masked thieves. "Out of the car and hand over your jewels." After the thieves rob them and steal their car, Diana begins to put her earrings, necklace, and rings back on. "Wherever did you hide those," demanded the Queen. "Where do you think?" asked Diana. "Pity Margaret wasn't here," said the Queen. "We could have saved the Bentley."*
- *A friend of mine confused her Valium with her birth control pills – she had fourteen kids but she didn't give a shit!*
- *My husband killed himself. And it was my fault. We were making love and I took the bag off my head.*
- *The whole Michael Jackson thing was my fault. I told him to date only 28-year-olds. Who knew he would find 20 of them?*
- *My sex life is so bad, my G-spot has been declared a historical landmark.*
- *People say that money is not the key to happiness, but I*

always figured if you have enough money, you can have a key made.

- *I was born in 1962 and the room next to me was 1963.*
- *Want to know why women don't blink during foreplay? Not enough time.*
- *I blame myself for David Gest. It was me who told Liza Minnelli to find herself a man who wouldn't sleep with other women.*
- *My breasts are so low, now I can have a mammogram and a pedicure at the same time.*
- *I hate housework. You make the beds, you do the dishes, and six months later, you have to start all over again.*
- *I've had so much plastic surgery, when I die, they will donate my body to Tupperware.*
- *When the rabbi said, "Do you take this man," 14 guys said, "She has." My husband bought the horseback-riding story, thank God.*

I believe that FUNNY is at the forefront of the Fourth Wave of Feminism, brought about by the connectivity of the world-wide-web, but a wave is not punchy or powerful enough, the third wave hasn't brought us enough attention or radical changes in society – we need to cause a riot, shout and scream, raise our voices and

'Stand Up & Sock it to them Sisters!'

Gwenno and Jo

APPENDIX 1

HISTORICAL TIME LINE LEGISLATION & SIGNIFICANT EVENTS

Date	Event
1737	Lord Chamberlain's Licencing Act, giving him the right to veto any unapproved performance.
Beginning of 19th Century	'Assembly Rooms' – Coffee Houses and taverns, also called 'Catch and Glee Clubs'.
1830s	A definite split of the above participants – more wealthy went to 'Song and Supper Rooms' leaving taverns and the vulgar 'Catch and Glee Clubs' to the working classes.
1830s onwards	'Evans's' Covent Garden became the first of the male (only) frequented 'Song and Supper Rooms'. Patrons did a 'turn'. Women could only watch proceedings from behind a curtain on the balcony!
Also 1830s onwards	Licenced taverns sprang out of 'Bar Parlour Concerts', 'Sing Songs' and 'Harmonic meetings'. Again some men sang.
1837 – 1901	Victoria became Queen and adopted the ideal of sexual suppression, giving rise to 'double entendres'.

1843	'Theatres Act' restricting Lord Chamberlain's Licensing Act. Gave artists more freedom to develop solo acts.
1850 – 1896	The first female 'star' of music hall, Jenny Hill was born.
1852	'The Canterbury Hall' was added on to the 'Canterbury Arms', a skittle hall and pub by Charles Morton and was considered to be the first ever Music Hall. Room for 1,500. Some 'wives' allowed in.
Later in 1852	'The Alhambra' was opened in Leicester Square as direct competition.
1853 – 1887	Nelly Power. One of the very first male impersonators, loved spangles and tights.
1855 – 1902	Bessie Bonehill. Another one of the early male impersonators in Britain. Owned a 600 acre estate on Long Island, New York.
1855	Marie Lloyd makes her stage debut at the age of 15, under the stage name of Bella Delamare at the Eagle Music Hall. She changed her name to Marie Lloyd and within two years she is earning £100 a week – a fortune at that time.
1857 – 1896	Bessie Bellwood (Man Mangler) First female singer of Cockney Songs.
1860	The first female professional singer – Miss Caulfield sang at the Evans Song and Supper Club.
1860s	Jenny Hill (The Vital Spark) was perfecting her craft as a child

	performer in the Marlebone Music Hall.
1860s	Alhambra allowed working class and lower middle-class women to be present in the audience.
1860 – 1896	Jenny Hill becomes the most successful Music Hall star of her time and makes a phenomenal amount of money, buying a farm in Streatham and the Rainbow Music Hall in Southampton in 1884.
By 1868	There were 200 Music Halls around London and another 300 around the country.
1869 – 1889	'Lydia and her Imported English Blondes' shocked New York audiences with their flesh coloured tights in 'Ixion' in 'Tights Plays'. Lydia was very popular in Riga in the Baltic.
1869 – 1950	Kate Carney – Queen of the 'Coster' songs which were all about the consequences of drinking too much alcohol. The Coster singers dressed in 'pearly costumes' which became, in time, the uniform of the Pearly Kings and Queens. She performed until the age of 80.
1870 – 1922	Matilda Wood later to become 'Marie Lloyd. Queen of the Saucy Song' is born into a family of successful female performers.
1879	Jenny Hill is mentioned in a report on her performance as 'one of the only women who can make a speech'.
1880	After the death of her husband, John, Adelaide Stoll runs the Parthenon in

	Liverpool, but had to pretend that her 14 year old son Oswald was the Boss to gain credibility!
1880 – 1910	Hundreds of Music Halls were built and the Alhambra was in its heyday.
1887	A journalist in Bradford estimates that a quarter of the audience is made up of young couples.
1893	Cissie Loftus, the first female impersonator.
1894	Jenny Hill's last international tour to Johannesburg – 'so peculiar – an all-male audience'.
1895	The luscious 'London Pavilion' made Music Hall more acceptable to middle classes.
1895	Marie Lloyd was paying nightly for beds for 150 of London's destitute and desperates.
1896	'The Empire' showed the first 'Cinematograph' – a soundless 'Bioscope' of news and events at the end of a performance. It became very popular and spread to other music halls.
1877 onwards	Edison's 'Phonograph' were becoming very popular with popular artists of the time recoding themselves on wax cylinders. These two curious novelties would eventually combine to become the cinemas, which would in time close hundreds of music halls throughout Britain
End of 19ᵗʰ Century	An example of a very popular Music Hall was 'Wilton's' with a private entrance to the brothel next door.

1902 – 1987	Irene Handl, eccentric charlady and mother in so many roles and carry on films, was particularly influenced by Marie Lloyd and did not become an actress until in her forties.
1910	Joyce Grenfell, who was to become the very first FSUC, was born Joyce Phipps.
1912	One third of all men didn't have the vote and NO women had the vote.
1912	The first 'Royal Command Performance', gave the Victorian Music Hall the Royal seal of respectability. Marie Lloyd did not appear as she was considered too vulgar.
1912	The Lord Chamberlain changed the rules about food and drink consumption in the halls to bring more in line with theatres, thus starting its downfall.
1913	Suffragettes were formed to fight for better women's rights.
1914	First World War breaks out. A new form of entertainment was making its mark, Revue, a mixture of music hall and spectacular musical comedies. Revue competes with Variety which is good all round family entertainment.
1915	Women actively recruited for work in Armament factories due to shortage of men fighting on the front.
1916	Contraception Pioneer and nurse Margaret Sanger, who coined the phrase, 'Birth Control', opened the first Birth Control Clinic in the

	United States, thus changing women's lives forever by allowing them to have reproductive rights for the first time ever in history. This led to her arrest for distributing information on contraception.
1919	First female M.P. elected. Nancy Astor was also Aunt to Joyce Grenfell, being one of her Mother's sisters.
1920 – 1996	Beryl Reid was an acclaimed character actress who served her apprenticeship in Variety and started out in 1936 as an impressionist and comic with the North Regional Follies in Bridlington. Her character Marlene was the first time the Brummie accent was used to comic effect.
1921	Britain's first birth control clinic was opened by Dr. Marie Stopes.
1922	Marie Lloyd's collapses on stage and dies three days later. Her coffin is followed by 10,000 people and twelve cars of flowers and the pub pumps in Leicester Square were all draped in black to honour her.
1922	Music Hall and Gaiety (A combination of opera and comedy) were slowly dying.
1923 – 2011	Janet Brown – the great female impersonator was born. Rumour has it that she was also in Jimmy Graftons' pub when The Goons came into being but she has remained historically invisible.
1924 – 1980	Hattie Jaques was born. A trained hairdresser and war-time nurse and

	arc welder, she became Sophie Tuckshop, the greedy schoolgirl, in BBC Radio's 'It's that man again'. (ITMA) (1939 – 1949)
1925	June Whitfield was born – Roy Hudd calls her 'The Comic's Tart' because 'she has served them all' She has worked with Ted Ray, Eric Morecambe, Arthur Askey, Bob Monkhouse, Peter Sellers, Sid James, Tommy Cooper, Spike Milligan, Tony Hancock and been the 'butt' of more male comedy than any other woman.
1928	Equal Franchise Act. All women over the age of 21 have the vote.
1928 – 1948	Mabel Constandouras first finds success on the radio with 'The Bugginsses'.
Until the 1930s	BBC Radio found all their talent in Variety and Music Hall.
1930 – 2001	Joan Sims. Another superb British character actress who became the longest serving female 'Carry On' character appearing in 24 films. She made her debut on stage in a Revue at the Irving Theatre in 'Intimacy at Eight'.
1932	BBC Radio broadcast 'The Hollywood Party'. Florence Desmond created and pioneered a (much copied) style of not only impersonating characters but of getting those characters to interact with each other.
1935	Kate Carney (Coster Queen) performs at the Palladium in a Royal

	Command Performance in a 'Cavalcade of Variety'
1936	Alhambra demolished and a cinema built in its place.
1937	Barbara Ann Deeks is born and later becomes Barbara Windsor – the sixteen year old bra-flying schoolgirl in 'Carry On Camping'.
1938	The first ground-breaking radio 'situation comedy' show, 'Band Waggon' with Arthur Askey and Richard Murdoch. This led to:
(1939 – 1949)	…'It's that man again' (ITMA) which gave Hattie Jaques, a music hall star, her breakthrough which led on to fourteen episodes in the 'Carry On' films, mostly as terrifying Matrons.
1945-95	Marti Caine started her apprenticeship as a comic in the working men's clubs 'up North' in 1964. She was the first person to break the taboo about 'sanitary towels'.
1946	Mabel Constandouras (of The Bugginsses) appears in 'Caravan' a film with future smoothy D.J. Pete Murray….
1948	…and in the comedy film 'Easy Money' with a very young Petula Clark.
1948	'Listen my Children' a ten week radio series gave new opportunities to stars such as John Pertwee (Doctor Who) Patricia Hayes, Benny Hill, Harry Secombe which became in time:
1949	'Third Division-Some Vulgar

	Fractions' which introduced the talents of Peter Sellers and Michael Bentine. Out of this permutation came:
1951 – 1960	The Goons. (In Jimmy Grafton's pub ledged has it)
Early 1950s	American Margaret Sanger encouraged philanthropist Katherine McCormick to provide funding for biologist Gregory Pincus to develop the birth control pill which was eventually sold under the name 'Enovid'. This event led to radically transforming women's lives.
1954	'The Belles of Saint Trinians'. A film about rebellious girls in a single sex school, it starred many fine funny females such as Ireen Handl, Beryl Reid and Joyce Grenfell (and others). Barbara Windsor's first film role, after having started her career as a comic and singer in the West End.
1954	'Joyce Grenfell requests the Pleasure' – her first show toured the world and was based on a member of the Women's Institute.
1959	Victoria Wood personally meets Joyce Grenfell (at the age of six)
1963	Budd and Silverman opened the New York Improvisation Centre.
1963	The Abortion Bill becomes law.
1963	The pill becomes freely available on the NHS and women's liberation has truly begun!
Early Sixties	Civil Rights movements, Martin Luther King, Second Wave of

	Feminism eventually reject racist and sexist humour.
1970	The Equal Pay Act (Now that is a JOKE!!)
1970	Germaine Greer publishes 'The Female Eunuch'
1970	Barbara Windsor portrayed Marie Lloyd in a show called 'Sing a rude song' to acknowledge the fact that she had been a very important Role Model to her.
1972	Mitzi Shore opens the Los Angeles 'Original Comedy Store' on Sunset Boulevard. Since the beginning she has been very supportive of female comics.
1975	Martin Caine wins New Faces which she then later went to present which gave television opportunities to Victoria Wood, Lenny Henry and Jim Davidson.
1979	Don Ward & Peter Rosengard after visiting L.A's Comedy Store established the London 'Comedy Store' on the site of a previous strip club. It was the starting point for French & Saunders, Helen Lederer, Hattie Hayridge and countless other women.
1979	Margaret Thatcher becomes Britain's first female Prime Minister. Severe crisis in Arts funding axed numerous left wing performance groups.
1979 – 1983	I go to Belgium to be an au-pair and discover that I have been a 'Feminist' all my life at the Maison Blanche!

	(The White House) I start my professional performing career by singing Music Hall songs with the English Comedy Club then start busking on the street, singing in cafes, gigs, radio and television.
1983	Maria Kempinska starts Jongleurs.
America – Early 1980s	An explosion of 'stand-up comedy' in the States to satiate the need for new, cheap, material for the expansion of cable t.v. Stars from the New York Improvisation Centre and L.A. Comedy Store feed into this huge hungry machine. (Betsy Salkind one of my interviewees was working within this comedy revolution and said that the politics had to be stripped from the comedy so it was very bland at the time).
Britain – Early 80s	The 'Alternative' scene starts to grow in London, rejecting racist and sexist jokes of the past. Women change from object to subject and start making the comedy.
1985	The Sex Discrimination Act.
1987	Morwenna Banks & Amanda Swift publish a book called about women in comedy called 'The Joke's on us'
1985 & 1986	French & Saunders create their highly successful series called 'Girls on Top' because there were no major parts for women in the cult 'Young Ones'
1988	Royal Mail commission five stamps to commemorate five of Britain's greatest comics, Joyce Grenfell, Eric Morecambe, Tommy Cooper, Les

	Dawson and Peter Cook.
1994	All 'Prime Time' Commissioning Editors of the BBB and ITV Network are men.
1995	Jenny Éclair becomes the First Woman to win the Perrier Comedy Prize at the Edinburgh Fringe Festival.
2005	Sioned Wiliam becomes First 'Controller of Comedy ITV Network'
2005	Victoria Wood wins a Special Bafta Tribute Award for her contribution to comedy.
2005	Laura Solon becomes only the Second women to ever win the Perrier prize.
2010	The new Equality Act pulls together all previous Equality legislation.
2013	Bridget Christie becomes the third women to win what is now no longer the Perrier but the Foster prize.
2013	Adrienne Truscott wins the Foster's Panel Prize at The Edinburgh Fringe Festival.
2013	Sarah Millican becomes the highest paid female comedy star.
2014	Women still earn 19.1% less than men and have been hit far worse in the last seven year recession than men have.
2015	One in four women are a victim of domestic violence in their life-time according to Women's Aid.
2015	There's still a myth prevailing that women aren't funny and this is what I am going to destroy once and for all – Of course we are funny so just accept it!!

APPENDIX 2

WHO'S WHO 22ND NOVEMBER 2015

The following have talked to Gwenno Dafydd about female stand-up comedy
Key: FSUC – Female Stand-Up Comic.

Joan Rivers
http://en.wikipedia.org/wiki/Joan_Rivers
http://www.joan.co/
https://twitter.com/Joan_Rivers

June Whitfield
http://en.wikipedia.org/wiki/June_Whitfield
http://www.imdb.com/name/nm0925930/

Sioned Wiliam – BBC Radio 4's Commissioner for Comedy
https://en.wikipedia.org/wiki/Sioned_Wiliam
https://twitter.com/sionedwiliam

Maria Kempinska – Owner of Jongleurs Comedy Chain
http://mariakempinska.co.uk/default.htm#ad-image-0
https://twitter.com/mariakempinska

Sian James – Labour M.P. for Swansea East 2005 – 2015 & Women's Activist
https://en.wikipedia.org/wiki/Si%C3%A2n_James_(politician)
https://twitter.com/SianCJames1

Dr. Jane Davidson – Former Cabinet Minister, Welsh Assembly Government
https://en.wikipedia.org/wiki/Jane_Davidson
http://www.uwtsd.ac.uk/inspire/about-inspire/
https://twitter.com/janebryngwyn

Jeff Scott – Resident Piano Player and M.C. at Comedy Store Los Angeles

http://comedygroupie.squarespace.com/whats-up/2010/8/8/behind-the-names-jeff-scott.html

http://www.maydayproductions.biz/JEFF_SCOTT/bio.htm

https://twitter.com/jeffscott101

Dr. Oliver Double – Author of numerous Comedy books

http://www.kent.ac.uk/arts/staff-profiles/profiles/main/double.html

http://www.oliverdouble.com/

https://twitter.com/oliverdouble

William Cook – Guardian Comedy Critic and Author of books about Comedy

http://www.harpercollins.co.uk/cr-101334/william-cook

http://www.randomhouse.co.uk/authors/william-cook

(No other details available)

Logan Murray – Leading Comedy Improvisation Guru

http://en.wikipedia.org/wiki/Logan_Murray

http://loganmurray.com/

https://twitter.com/logancomedyguru

Harry Key – Australian & Bollywood Actor & Provocative Speech Trainer

http://www.harrykey.com/

https://twitter.com/harrykey

Martin Besserman – Owner of Monkey Business Comedy Club

http://www.monkeybusinesscomedyclub.co.uk/

https://thejohnfleming.wordpress.com/2013/11/08/comedy-club-owner-martin-besserman-from-sexually-frustrated-middle-aged-women-to-increasing-monkey-business/

https://twitter.com/comedymonkybiz?lang=en-gb

Luke Rhinehart (aka George Cockroft – Author of Cult Book – 'The Dice Man')

http://en.wikipedia.org/wiki/Luke_Rhinehart

http://www.lukerhinehart.net/

https://twitter.com/whimluke

Myfanwy Alexander – Writer of BBC Wales Sony Award winning comedy 'The LL Files' & member of BBC Radio 4's 'Round Britain' quiz
http://www.bbc.co.uk/programmes/p01ghn9v/p01ghlrx
https://twitter.com/lodeslan

Music Hall Photographs generously loaned by
Roy Hudd – World Expert on British Music Halls.
http://en.wikipedia.org/wiki/Roy_Hudd
http://www.royhudd.com/

Funny women in Films and Hollywood
Sara Sugarman – Hollywood Film Director
http://en.wikipedia.org/wiki/Sara_Sugarman
http://www.dailypost.co.uk/whats-on/film-news/hollywood-director-sara-sugarman-set-7892430
https://twitter.com/sarasugarman

Joanna Quinn – Oscar Nominated Cartoonist
Has also generously created a bespoke cartoon for the book
http://en.wikipedia.org/wiki/Joanna_Quinn
http://www.berylproductions.co.uk/
https://twitter.com/joannaq

British Female Comics
Jo Brand
http://en.wikipedia.org/wiki/Jo_Brand
http://www.offthekerb.co.uk/jo-brand/
https://twitter.com/jobrand_

Donna McPhail
http://en.wikipedia.org/wiki/Donna_McPhail
No other contact details available

Jenny Éclair
http://en.wikipedia.org/wiki/Jenny_Eclair
http://www.jennyeclair.com/
https://twitter.com/jennyeclair

Ronnie Ancona

http://en.wikipedia.org/wiki/Ronni_Ancona
https://twitter.com/ronniancona

Nina Wadia

http://en.wikipedia.org/wiki/Nina_Wadia
https://twitter.com/nina_wadia

Helen Lederer

http://en.wikipedia.org/wiki/Helen_Lederer
http://www.helenlederer.co.uk/
https://twitter.com/helenlederer

Brenda Gilhooly aka Gayle Tuesday

http://en.wikipedia.org/wiki/Brenda_Gilhooly
http://www.avalonuk.com/artists/view/95

Holly Burn aka Kirst Kay

http://www.hollyburn.org.uk/1.html
http://www.pbjmanagement.co.uk/artist/holly-burn
https://twitter.com/hollyburncomedy

Naomi Paxman aka Ada Campe

http://www.naomipaxton.co.uk/
https://twitter.com/NaomiPaxton
https://twitter.com/AdaCampe

Hattie Hayridge aka Holly Red Dwarf

http://en.wikipedia.org/wiki/Hattie_Hayridge
http://www.mlatalent.com/grid-portfolio/hattie-hayridge/

JoJo Smith

http://www.jojosmith.com/
http://www.chortle.co.uk/comics/j/33168/jojo_smith
https://twitter.com/missjojosmith

Lorraine Benloss

http://www.imdb.com/name/nm2261233/
https://www.facebook.com/lorraine.benloss?fref=nf
Not on Twitter

Angie Le Mar
http://en.wikipedia.org/wiki/Angie_Le_Mar
http://www.angielemar.com/
https://twitter.com/angielemar

Ava Vidal
http://en.wikipedia.org/wiki/Ava_Vidal
http://www.avavidal.co.uk/
https://twitter.com/thetwerkinggirl

Mandy Knight
http://www.thecomedyclub.co.uk/comedians/mandy-knight.html
https://twitter.com/themandyknight

Lis Carr
http://en.wikipedia.org/wiki/Liz_Car
http://www.lizcarr.co.uk/Liz_Carr/front_page.html

Susan Murray
http://www.susan-murray.co.uk/
https://twitter.com/thatsusanmurray

Shazia Mirza
http://en.wikipedia.org/wiki/Shazia_Mirza
www.shazia-mirza.com
https://twitter.com/shaziamirza1

Kate Smurthwaite
http://en.wikipedia.org/wiki/Kate_Smurthwaite
http://www.katesmurthwaite.co.uk/
https://twitter.com/cruella1

Jo Enright
https://en.wikipedia.org/wiki/Jo_Enright
http://www.joenright.com/
https://twitter.com/jo_enright

Victoria Jordy Cook
http://www.victoriacookcomedy.com/about/
https://twitter.com/jordygal

Jo Caulfield
http://en.wikipedia.org/wiki/Jo_Caulfield
http://www.jocaulfield.com/
https://twitter.com/jo_caulfield

Nina Conti
http://en.wikipedia.org/wiki/Nina_Conti
http://www.ninaconti.co.uk/
https://twitter.com/ninaconti

Fern Brady
https://en.wikipedia.org/wiki/Fern_Brady
http://www.ckproductions.co.uk/portfolio-item/fern-brady/
https://twitter.com/fernbrady

Maureen Younger
http://maureenyounger.com/
https://twitter.com/maureenyounger

Nuala McKeever
http://en.wikipedia.org/wiki/Nuala_McKeever
Not on Twitter

Rhona Cameron
http://en.wikipedia.org/wiki/Rhona_Cameron
http://www.rhonacameron.com/see.html
https://twitter.com/therhonacameron

Jojo Sutherland
http://www.jojosutherland.co.uk/
https://twitter.com/jojosutherland

Bethany Black
https://en.wikipedia.org/wiki/Bethany_Black
https://twitter.com/bethanyblack
http://www.bethanyblack.co.uk/

Jane Mackay – Owner of 'The Stand Comedy Club', Edinburgh, Glasgow.
http://www.thestand.co.uk/aboutus.aspx
Not on Twitter

Janey Godley – Prolific Scottish Blogger & Scottish FSUC
http://www.janeygodley.com/
https://twitter.com/JaneyGodley

Ashley Storrie – World's youngest FSUC and daughter of Janey Godley
http://www.janeygodley.com/AshleyBiography.html
https://twitter.com/ashleystorrie

Rosie Kane – Scottish FSUC & Previous Member of the Scottish Parliament
http://en.wikipedia.org/wiki/Rosie_Kane
Not on Twitter.

Wendy Kane
http://wendykane.blogspot.co.uk/
Not on Twitter.

Bethan Roberts
http://reganmanagement.co.uk/project/bethan-roberts/
https://twitter.com/beechuckles

Blod Jones
http://blodjones.com/stand-up.php
https://twitter.com/Blodweener

Josie Taylor
https://www.youtube.com/watch?v=kGqpDoeeoKc
Not on Twitter.

Sian Parry – Ex Comedy Club Booker. Music Agent & Manager
http://punkygalore.com/about.html
https://twitter.com/PUNKYGALORE1

Lynne Parker – Founder of 'Funny Women' UK's leading community for female comedy
http://funnywomen.com/
https://twitter.com/FunnyWomenLynne

Hazel O'Keefe – Laughing Cows Comedy Club and Women's Comedy Festival
http://www.dulcetsounds.co.uk/live/home.html
https://twitter.com/hazelokeefe

Jane Duffus – Director Bristol Based Women's Comedy Club
http://www.whatthefrockcomedy.co.uk/
https://twitter.com/WTFrock_Comedy

International Comics
America
Amy Schumer – New York
http://en.wikipedia.org/wiki/Amy_Schumer
https://twitter.com/amyschumer

Rhoda Hansome – New York
http://www.rhondahansome.com/
https://twitter.com/RhondaHansome

Lyn Marie Hulsman – New York
http://www.lynnmariehulsman.com/the-funny-stuff/
https://twitter.com/LynnMarieSays

Susie Felber – New York
http://about.me/susiefelber
https://twitter.com/susiefelber

Adrienne Truscott – New York
https://en.wikipedia.org/wiki/Adrienne_Truscott
http://www.adriennetruscott.com/asking-for-it/
https://twitter.com/mrs_truscott

Nancy Witter – New York
http://www.nancywitter.com/comedy.html
https://twitter.com/WittsTwitts

Annie Witter – New York
https://twitter.com/wittttter

Lydia Nicole – Los Angeles
http://www.lydianicole.com/lydianicole.com/Welcome_to_Lydia_
Nicoles_Site.html
https://twitter.com/CommonSenseMami

Betsy Salkind – Los Angeles
http://www.betsysalkind.com/
https://twitter.com/BetsySalkind

Cathy Ladman – Los Angeles
http://en.wikipedia.org/wiki/Cathy_Ladman
https://twitter.com/CathyLadman

Dana Goldberg – Los Angeles
http://danagoldberg.com/
https://twitter.com/DGComedy

Dyana Ortelli – Los Angeles
http://www.imdb.com/name/nm0650969/
Not on Twitter

**Rigby Jones – Los Angeles. International Singer & huge
Improvisation fan.**
http://rigbyjonesmezzo.com/
https://twitter.com/rigbyjonesmezzo

Nadia Kamil – Los Angeles based. Welsh born.
www.nadiakamil.co.uk
https://twitter.com/nadiakamil

Lynn Ruth Miller – San Fransisco (World's Oldest FSUC)
http://lynnruthmiller.net/
https://twitter.com/lynnruth

Cynthia Levin – Chicago & London
http://cynthialevin.com/
https://twitter.com/sheseemsnice

Rest of the World

Aditi Mittal – Mumbai – India
http://en.wikipedia.org/wiki/Aditi_Mittal
https://twitter.com/awryaditi

Sindhu Vee – India & UK
http://www.sindhuvee.com/
https://twitter.com/sindhuvfunny

Spring Day – Tokyo – Japan
http://springdaycomedy.com/
http://www.tokyocomedy.com/standups
https://twitter.com/springdaycomedy

Michele A'Court – New Zealand
http://www.micheleacourt.co.nz/
https://twitter.com/MicheleACourt

Julia Morris – Australia
http://en.wikipedia.org/wiki/Julia_Morris
http://juliamorris.com.au/

Kitty Flanagan – Australia
http://en.wikipedia.org/wiki/Kitty_Flanagan
http://www.kittyflanagan.com/

Tanya Lee Davis – Canada & Las Vegas
http://en.wikipedia.org/wiki/Tanyalee_Davis
http://www.tanyaleedavis.com/

Dana Alexander – Canada and World-wide
Only black female Canadian comic now working in Britain
http://www.chortle.co.uk/comics/d/33828/dana_alexander
https://twitter.com/Comediandana

Katerina Vrana – Greece & UK
http://www.katerinavrana.com/
https://twitter.com/Vranarama

Thenjiwe Tay Moseley – South Africa & UK
https://twitter.com/thenjiwecomedy

Advice and encouragement given by:

Professor Germaine Greer

http://en.wikipedia.org/wiki/Germaine_Greer

https://twitter.com/TheFemaleGreer

Kirsty Wark

https://en.wikipedia.org/wiki/Kirsty_Wark

https://twitter.com/KirstyWark

APPENDIX 3

BIBLIOGRAPHY OF BOOKS AND JOURNALS EITHER CITED OR USED AS RESEARCH FOR THIS BOOK

1.

Atkinson, Diane (Editor) 1997
Cartooning for Equality
London Penguin Books Ltd.

2.

Banks, Morwenna and Swift, Amanda (1987)
The Joke's on us
London Pandora Press (Routledge)

3.

Barr, Roseanne (1990)
Roseanne
(My life as a woman)
London Collins

4.

Barreca, Regina (Editor) (1992)
New Perspectives on Women and Comedy
(Studies in Gender and Culture, Volume 5)
Philadelphia Gordon and Breach

5.

Bilger, Audrey (1995)
Goblin Laughter : Violent Comedy
in Women's Studies
Volume 24 – 4 pp 323 – 340

6.
Bratton, J.S. (1986) Jenny Hill: Sex and Sexism in the Victorian
Music Hall out of Music Hall: Performance and Style, edited by
J.S.Bratton
Milton Keynes. Open University Press,

7.
Breakwell, Glynis M (1985)
The Quiet Rebel (Women at work in a man's world)
London Century Publishing

8.
Carr, Jimmy. & Greeves Lucy
The Naked Jape (Uncovering the hidden world of jokes)
Michael Joseph an imprint of Penguin Books

9.
Chapman, Anthony J. and Gadfield, Nicholas J. (1976)
Is sexual humour sexist? Laughing Matter
in The Journal of Communication
Volume 26 Autumn pp 141 – 153

10.
Chevalier, Albert. (1901)
Before I forget
(Being the Autobiography of a chevalier d'industrie)
Unwin

11.
Cixous, Hélène (1981)
The Laugh of the Medusa
in Marks, Elaine and de Courtivron, Isabelle (Editors) New French
Feminisms
An Anthology
Hemel Hempstead Harvester Wheatsheaf

12.
Double, Oliver (1997)
Stand-up: (On being a comedian)
Methuen Publishing

13.
Eckert, Penelope (1989)
The Whole Woman : Sex and Gender differences
in variation in Language, variation and change
Volume 1 pp 245 – 267

14.
Equity Journal
1996 March edition pp 12 – 13

15.
Fahey, Maryanne (1995)
Laughing Women in Journal of Australian Feminist Studies
Volume 21 Autumn pp 69 – 77

16.
Faith, Karlene (1993)
Unruly Women
(The Politics of confinement and resistance)
Vancouver Press Gang Publishers

17.
Faludi, Susan (1992)
Backlash
(The undeclared war against women)
London Vintage (Chatto and Windus)

18.
50/50 Campaign Report (1994)
The Women in Film and Television 50/50 Campaign
London

19.
Finch, Janet (1984)
It's great to have someone to talk to : the ethics and politics of
interviewing women in Bell, Colin and Roberts, Helen (Editors)
Social Researching. Politics, Problems, Practice
London Routledge and Kegan Paul

20.

Fine, Gary Alan (1976)

Obscene Joking Across Cultures (Laughing Matter)

in Journal of Communication

Volume 26 Autumn pp 134 – 140

21.

Fink, Edward L. and Walker, Barbara A. (1977)

Humorous Responses to Embarrassment

in Psychological Reports

Volume 40 – 2 pp 475 – 485

22.

Fisher, Lucy (1991)

Sometimes I feel like a motherless child

in Horton, Andrew S. (Editor)

Comedy, Cinema, Theory

Berkeley University of California Press

23.

Fishman, Pamela (1992[1983])

in Crawford, Mary

Just Kidding : Gender and Conversational Humour

in Barreca, Regina (Editor)

New Perspectives on Women and Comedy

(Studies in Gender and Culture Volume 5)

Philadelphia Gordon and Breach

24.

Freud, Sigmund (1990 [1927])

Humour

translated from the German under the general editorship of James Strachey

Dickson, Albert (Editor)

Sigmund Freud 14 : Art and Literature

London Penguin Books

25.

Freud, Sigmund (1991[1905])

translated from the German and edited by James Strachey
Richards, Angela (Editor)
Sigmund Freud 6 : Jokes and their relation to the unconscious
London Penguin Books

26.
Gagnier, Regina (1988)
Between women : a cross class analysis of status and anarchic humor
in Barreca, Regina (Editor)
Last Laughs – Perspectives on Women and Comedy
(Studies in Gender and Culture. Edited by Wendy Martin)
New York Gordon and Breach

27.
Goodman, Liesbeth (1992(a))
Chapter 6 – Comic Subversions
in Bonner, Frances; Goodman, Liesbeth; Allen, Richard; Janes, Linda and King, Catherine (Editors)
Imagining Women : Cultural Representations and Gender
Milton Keynes Polity Press in association with the Open University

28.
Goodman, Liesbeth (1992(b))
Chapter 6 – Comic Subversions
in Allen, Richard; Bonner, Frances; Goodman, Liesbeth and King, Catherine (Editors)
Study Guide 4. Issues in Women's Studies
Milton Keynes Open University

29.
Graham, Hilary (1983)
Do her answers fit his questions ? (Women and the survey method)
in Gamarnikow, Eva; Morgan, David; Purvis, June and Taylorson, Daphne (Editors)
The Public and The Private
London Heineman

30.
Glasstone, Victor (1975)
Victorian and Edwardian Theatres
London. Thames and Hudson Ltd.

31.
Gray, Frances (1994)
(Women in Society : A Feminist List edited by Jo Campling)
London The Macmillan Press Ltd.

32.
Green, Eileen; Hebron, Sandra and Woodward, Diana (1987)
Women, Leisure and Social Control
in Hanmer, Jalna and Maynard, Mary (Editors)
Women, Violence and Social Control
London The Macmillan Press Ltd.

33.
Groskop, Viv (2013)
'I laughed, I cried':
(How one woman took on Stand Up and (almost) ruined her life)
Orion

34.
Horowitz, Susan (1997)
Queens of Comedy: (Lucille Ball, Phyllis Diller, Carol Burnett,
Joan Rivers, and the New Generation of Funny Women) (Studies
in Humor & Gender) Routledge

35.
Jeffers, Susan (1987)
Feel the Fear and do it anyway: (How to turn your fear and
indecision into confidence and action.)
Vermillion

36.
Grotjahn, Martin (1970)
Beyond Laughter
(Humor and the Subconscious)
New York McGraw Hill Inc.

37.

Greer, Germaine (1999)
The Whole Woman
London Doubleday

38.

Hanmer, Jalna and Maynard, Mary (1987)
Women, Violence and Social Control
London The Macmillan Press Ltd.

39.

Harding, Sandra (Editor) (1987)
Feminism and Methodology:
(Social science issues)
Milton Keynes Indiana University Press and Open University Press

40.

Hoher, Dagmar. (1986)
The Composition of Music Hall Audiences 1850 –1900 out of
Popular Music in Britain;
The Business of Pleasure. Edited by Peter Bailey
Milton Keynes. Open University Press.

41.

Hyem, Jill (1987)
Entering the arena: writing for television
in Baehr, Helen and Dyer, Gillian (Editors)
Boxed in: Women and Television
London Pandora Press (Routledge and Kegan Paul Ltd.)

42.

Jespersen, Otto (1985[1922])
Language: its nature, development and origin
cited in Spender, Dale
Man Made Language
London Pandora Press (Routledge and Kegan Paul Ltd.)

43.

Keith – Spiegel, Patricia (1972)

Early conceptions of humor : Varieties and Issues
in J.H. Goldstein and P.E. McGhee (Editors)
The Psychology of Humor
London / New York Academic Press

44.
Keith – Spiegel, Patricia (1976[1969])
Preface to symposium proceedings
Social Aspects of Humour : Recent Research and Theory
Western Psychological Association Meeting, Vancouver
in Chapman, Anthony J. and Foot, Hugh C. (Editors)
Humour and Laughter
(Theory, Research and Applications)
London John Wiley and Sons

45.
La Fave, Laurence; Haddad, Jay and Maesen, William J. (1976)
Superiority, Enhanced Self Esteem, and Perceived Incongruity
Theory
in Chapman, Anthony J. and Foot, Hugh C. (Editors)
Humour and Laughter
(Theory, Research and Applications)
London John Wiley and Sons

46.
La Fave, Laurence and Mannell, Roger (1976)
Does Ethnic Humor Serve Prejudice ? Laughing Matter
in Journal of Communication
Volume 26 Summer pp 116 – 123

47.
Lakoff, Robin (1985[1975])
Language and Woman's Place
cited in
Spender, Dale
Man Made Language
London Pandora Press (Routledge and Kegan Paul Ltd.)

48.

Levine, Joan B. (1976)
The Feminine Routine : Laughing Matter
in The Journal of Communications
Volume 26 Autumn pp 173 – 175

49.

Leslie, Peter. (1978)
A Hard Act to Follow
(A Music Hall Review – Introduction by Pearl Bailey)
New York and London. Paddington Press Ltd.

50.

Lovric, Michelle. (2002)
Women's Wicked Wit
Chicago Preview Press

51.

Mander, Raymond & Mitchenson, Joe (1974)
British Music Hall
London Gentry Books

52.

Mellor, Geoff J. (1982)
They made us laugh
A compendium of comedians whose memories remain alive
Lancashire Kelsall

53.

Merril, Lisa (1988)
Feminist humor: rebellious and self affirming
in Barreca, Regina (Editor)
Last Laughs, Perspectives on Women and Comedy
New York Gordon and Breach

54.

Najimy, Kathy
in Gross, Brenda (1992)
The Parallel lives of Kathy and Mo

in Barreca, Regina (Editor)
New Perspectives on Women and Comedy
(Studies in Gender and Culture Volume 5)
Philadelphia Gordon and Breach

55.
Nelson, T.G.A. (1990)
The theory of comedy in Literature, Drama and Cinema
Oxford, New York Oxford University Press

56.
Oakley, Ann (1981)
Interviewing Women : a contradiction in terms
in Roberts, Helen (Editor)
Doing feminist research
London Routledge and Kegan Paul

57.
Parry, Lorae (1995)
Laughing Women
in Journal of Australian Feminist Studies
Volume 21 pp 69 – 77

58.
Purdie, Susan (1993)
Comedy, The Mastery of Discourse
Hemel Hempstead Harvester Wheatsheaf

59.
Radford, Jill (1987)
Policing male violence – policing women
in Hanmer, Jalna and Maynard, Mary (Editors)
Women, violence and social control
London The Macmillan Press Ltd.

60.
Rheinhart, Luke. (aka George Cockroft) (1971)
The Dice Man
William Morrow

61.

Rorison Caws, Mary Ann (1988)
Truth telling : The Self and the Fictions of Humour
in Barreca, Regina
Last Laughs – Perspectives on Women and Comedy
New York Gordon and Breach

62.

Rowe, Kathleen (1995)
The Unruly Woman
Gender and the Genres of Laughter
Austin University of Texas Press

63.

Rivers, Joan. (2009)
'Men are stupid….. and they like big boobs'.
Gallery Books

64.

Seager, Joni and Olson, Ann (1986)
Women in the World – An International Atlas
London (Photo Press) Pan Books Ltd.

65.

Short, Kayam (1992)
Sylvia Talks Back
in Barreca, Regina (Editor)
New Perspectives on Women and Comedy
Philadelphia Gordon and Breach

66.

Smith, Ronald L. (1992)
Who's Who in Comedy:
Comedians, Comics and Clowns from Vaudeville to today's stand-ups
Facts on File Inc.

67.

Took, Barry (1989)

Comedy Greats:
A celebration of comic genius past and present
Equation

68.
Thomas, Helen (1991 / 1992)
Equal Opportunities in the Mechanical Media
a report commissioned by Equity cited in
The Women in Film and Television 50/50 Campaign
Women in Film and Television U.K. Ltd.
London

69.
Wilmut, Roger (1985)
Kindly leave the Stage
The Story of Variety 1919 – 1960
London Methuen

70.
Wilmut, Roger and Rosengard, Peter (1989)
Didn't you kill my mother in law?
The story of alternative comedy in Britain from the Comedy Store
to Saturday Live
London Methuen

71.
Wilmut, Roger and Grafton, Jimmy (1998)
The Goon Show Companion:
(A History and Goonography)
Robson Books Ltd.

72.
Wilt, Judith (1980)
The laughter of Maidens, the cackle of Matriarchs – Notes on the
Collision between Comedy and Feminism
in Todd, Janet (Editor) Gender and Literary Voice
New York Holmes and Meier

Miss Hortense yn uffern   2001
Porc Pěis Bach. Cyfannyddwr Huw
                                  Thomas

With Many Thanks

As a runner I am used to short sharp sprints like a 400 metres, a more prolonged 5k plod, a reasoned and measured half and full marathon but this book has been like twenty 'ultras' rolled into one so where do I start to thank people? Well I suppose first place must go to my Dad who encouraged and enabled me to become his 'little farmer', a big tomboy and develop the ability to get stuck in, get my hands dirty and get on with things. He also taught me how to be stubborn! Next my Mother who has the most unexpected laugh you could ever imagine in a retired and very respectable Primary School Head-teacher and who has always needed, along with my brother Huw and sister Siwan to have a very strong sense of humour to cope with me and my shenanigans! My thanks go to my husband Pol for his constant support both moral, practical and financial which has enabled me never to really give up on this project. Next thanks to my little 'Giggle Box' our daughter Lowri and all the fun and laughter the three of us have had and shared throughout the years. May they outweigh the tears in years to come. There have been friends who have cheered me on from the side-lines over the years, too numerous to mention. I am very fortunate in having friends that go back throughout all my life and I am grateful for all the giggles and guffaws. There are some names I would really like to specifically mention; Richard Davies of Parthian for being on the right train at the right time and for his endless patience and fine tuning of this big huge meaty document, Maria Zygogianni and Jantine Broek (God bless the European Union and all who stay in her!) from Parthian for all their help with the marketing; Comedy experts and authors: Dr Olly Double and William Cook for their enthusiasm; Jenny Kowalczuk for helping me put together a half decent Proposal all those years ago; The Welsh Books Council for the award of an author's commission grant that enabled this book to be completed; Welsh comic Noel James who introduced me to Nina Conti and Ronni Ancona who then introduced me to Hattie Hayridge who introduced me to etc. etc; Mel Smart, my Wing Wonder Woman for all your marketing suggestions; Dr Naomi Paxton who went way over and above and actually edited my history Chapter without me asking her – it was a big help and gave me a nice confidence boost; Roy Hudd, who I approached probably 15 years ago – for his encouragement and the use of his personal Music Hall photographs; Jon Gower, Sarah Hill and Tony Bianchi for encouraging me to be a mule and dig my heels in at a very tricky point in the book's trajectory; my lovely buddy in Los Angeles and resident pianist at the Comedy Store, Jeff Scott for keeping in contact when I kept hassling him and for his suggestion of Tanyalee Davis as an interviewee; Animator Joanna Quinn for being up for the best barter I ever made – an original cartoon for the book in exchange for a step machine and for the wonderful friendship that has developed since I interviewed her; Naomi Munroe, my soggy saga sister and revved-up rain runner – what goes on run stays on run!!! One woman who has helped me more than anyone especially when I started losing faith that this book would ever happen, is my amazing Mishawaka (Chicago) based agent and transatlantic running buddy, Tracy Brennan. Thank you for being there and for believing in me and this idea. And finally I would like to thank all those people who have kindly given me their time, shared their memories and experiences and without whom this book just wouldn't have happened. Thank you from the bottom of my heart. You are a true inspiration and I have loved running this race alongside you.

… and although they are no longer with us, I would like to dedicate this book in memory of the following guys that I had such a laugh with: my Uncle Owain Bebb, my father in law and brother in law Walter and Piet van Steelant and finally my wonderfully wacky and funny brother Dafydd Williams.

Gwenno Dafydd, Cardiff 2016

About the Author

Gwenno Dafydd has been a professional broadcaster, singer and actress since 1980, when she began her performing career as a street singer in Belgium, soon after taking up a post as an au-pair in Brussels, after completing her Drama and Welsh Certificate in Education at Barry Teacher Training College.

Since that time she has worked extensively in film, television, radio, theatre in education and cabaret. She has sung extensively in Belgium and several times in the United States including once in Los Angeles and four times in New York's world famous "Don't Tell Mama" piano bar.

She has had numerous pieces of work and articles published, including a one-woman show about French chanteuse Edith Piaf, entitled *No Regrets*, and she has been touring her new show *Passionate about Piaf* extensively.

She has had children's poetry published and wrote the script and lyrics for a children's musical Christmas show for BBC Radio Cymru, called *Santa on Strike?* In addition, Gwenno Dafydd has written over 150 lyrics in both Welsh and English, with several being recorded by Welsh artists including the new Saint David's Day Anthem, which she both instigated and wrote the lyrics to.

This book came about as part of her research for a Masters degree in Womens' Studies which she began in 1994. It has been a labour of love and a long and fascinating journey.

She is married to Pol van Steelant who is a freelance project manager and who also runs Cardiff Cycle Tours and they have a daughter, Lowri, who is an artist.

Gwenno loves to sing and travel but her other passion is running. She came reserve in the 400 meters Welsh School Championships and vowed that she would never give up on her dream of getting a Welsh vest, which she did, 37 years later at the age of 54.

You've got to give it to this woman – she doesn't give up easily!!!!!

www.gwennodafydd.co.uk

Gwenno a Deri. Tanymuni.
Ail o Dachwedd 1971.
33 gini ym mart
Llanybydder